THE DICTATOR'S LEARNING CURVE

THE DICTATOR'S

LEARNING CURVE

INSIDE THE GLOBAL BATTLE
FOR DEMOCRACY

William J. Dobson

HARVILL *SECKER*
LONDON

Published by Harvill Secker 2012

10 9 8 7 6 5 4 3 2 1

First published in Great Britain in 2012 by
HARVILL SECKER
Random House
20 Vauxhall Bridge Road
London SW1V 2SA

www.randomhouse.co.uk

Addresses for companies within The Random House Group Limited can be found at: www.randomhouse.co.uk/offices.htm

The Random House Group Limited Reg. No. 954009

A CIP catalogue record for this book is available from the British Library

ISBN 9781846556906 (hardback)

The Random House Group Limited supports The Forest Stewardship Council (FSC®), the leading international forest certification organisation. Our books carrying the FSC label are printed on FSC® certified paper. FSC is the only forest certification scheme endorsed by the leading environmental organisations, including Greenpeace. Our paper procurement policy can be found at: www.randomhouse.co.uk/environment

Printed and bound in Great Britain by Clays Ltd, St Ives PLC

For Kelly, Kate, and Liam

Democracy, freedom, human rights have come to have a definite meaning to the people of the world which we must not allow any nation to so change that they are made synonymous with suppression and dictatorship.

—ELEANOR ROOSEVELT SPEAKING AT THE SORBONNE, SEPTEMBER 28, 1948

CONTENTS

INTRODUCTION

||||||||||||||||||||||||||||||||||||||||||||||||||||||||||||||||||||||||||||||||||||||||||||||||||||||||||||||||||||||||||||||||||||||||||||||||||||||||||||||||||||||||||||

Peter Ackerman sits in his spacious corner office at the end of Pennsylvania Avenue. From his perch, he literally looks down on the World Bank. The sixty-four-year-old Ackerman is the managing director of Rockport Capital Incorporated, a discreet boutique investment house, and on a crystal clear August afternoon he is walking me through a PowerPoint presentation, talking to me about "risk returns." The slides, however, have nothing to do with investments, dividends, or finance; rather, the topic is the best way to overthrow a dictator.

Twenty-five years ago, Ackerman would have seemed an unlikely person to be giving advice on how to confront the world's worst regimes. He was too busy making a killing on Wall Street, the right-hand man to the junk bond king Michael Milken. In 1988, Ackerman earned $165 million for organizing the $25 billion leveraged buyout of RJR Nabisco. When an insider-trading scandal broke, sending Milken to jail, Ackerman paid $80 million in fines and walked away with roughly $500 million.

A considerable part of that fortune is now being channeled into helping topple tyranny around the globe. In 2002, Ackerman founded the International Center on Nonviolent Conflict, which runs seminars, workshops, and training sessions on successful nonviolent strategies and tactics for overthrowing repressive regimes. Activists from Egypt, Iran, Russia, Venezuela, Zimbabwe, and dozens of other countries know Ackerman well. Some have visited these top-floor offices in Foggy Bottom. Some have attended his workshops in half a dozen different foreign capitals. Others have watched his films—most commonly, *Bringing Down a Dictator,* which tells the story of how young Serbs deposed Slobodan Milošević in October 2000. The film won a Peabody Award and has been translated into Arabic, Farsi, Mandarin, Vietnamese, and at least seven other languages. Georgians widely credited the film for helping to inspire their 2003 Rose Revolution, a peaceful democratic rebellion that removed the former Communist boss Eduard Shevardnadze. In 2006, Ackerman also got into the video game business, paying for the development of *A Force More Powerful,* a game that lets activists practice their strategies for ousting tyrants in a virtual world. He has had thousands of copies smuggled into some of the world's most repressive countries. In 2010, he released a new version of the game called *People Power.* ("The game is the most subversive thing I have ever done," he says. "I have spent millions improving it.") When I ask him why he is making the task of defeating tyrants his life's work, he looks at me and says, "I'm just in the distribution business. I'm just responding to demand, that's all." And, he could have added, business is good.

It is not easy being a dictator today. Not long ago, an autocrat, whether a nationalist strongman, revolutionary hero, or Communist apparatchik, could use blunt weapons to keep his people under his thumb. Joseph Stalin sent millions of his countrymen to the gulag. Mao Zedong launched mass revolutionary campaigns targeting intellectuals, capitalists, and any group in China he believed to be insufficiently "red." His Great Leap Forward cost more than 35 million lives in a handful of years. The regime of the Ugandan dictator Idi Amin murdered as many as 500,000 people. In three years, nearly 2 million Cambodians died in Pol Pot's killing fields. In February 1982, Hafez Assad crushed an uprising in the Syrian city of Hama. After besieging the city with attack helicopters and heavy artillery, his troops went house to house. More than 25,000 Syrians were slaughtered before the month was over.

Dictators are still capable of great crimes. But today the world's despots have more forces arrayed against them than ever before. With the end of the Cold War, many lost their chief sponsor and economic lifeline in the Soviet Union. The democracy promotion business became a cottage industry, almost overnight: an army of Western experts, activists, and election monitors now stands at the ready to shine a spotlight on human rights abuses, gross corruption, and election rigging. Twenty years ago, Beijing's leaders only needed to worry about the glare of television cameras when the tanks rolled into Tiananmen Square. As soon as the Chinese Communist Party declared martial law, it literally pulled the plug on CNN's broadcast. No longer. In 2006, an expedition of European mountain climbers filmed Chinese soldiers shooting Tibetan monks, women, and children on a nineteen-thousand-foot mountain pass high in the Himalayas. The slaughter was quickly broadcast on YouTube and led to denunciations of China's violence toward refugees by international human rights groups. In 2011, Syria banned all foreign journalists from reporting on the country's uprising against Bashar Assad's regime. No matter; each day Syrian activists posted shocking footage of the government's brutal repression, as peaceful protesters and funeral processions became targets for the regime's snipers. Today, the world's dictators can surrender any hope of keeping their worst deeds secret: if you order a violent crackdown—even on a Himalayan mountain pass—you now know it will likely be captured on an iPhone and broadcast around the world. The costs of tyranny have never been this high.

The tide began to turn against dictators long before the Internet or Twitter, and even well before the collapse of the Soviet Union. Their troubles really began in Portugal in 1974. To be precise, they began at 12:25 the morning of April 25, when a Lisbon radio station played the song "Grândola, Vila Morena," a signal to units in the Portuguese military to commence a coup. By the next day, Portugal's dictator, Marcello Caetano, had been driven into exile. According to the scholar Samuel Huntington, the political forces released on that day marked the beginning of a global democratic wave that would lead to authoritarian regimes giving way to democracy for decades to come.

After Portugal, a string of right-wing dictatorships collapsed across southern Europe. The military juntas in Latin America and authoritarians in East Asia followed. All were shocks, but the 1989 collapse of Communist governments across Eastern Europe was a seismic shift. In 1974, there had been only forty-one democracies throughout the globe. By 1991, when the Soviet Union also fell, the number of democratic governments had jumped to seventy-six.

And it proved to be only Act I of democracy's boom years. Africa soon accounted for more than a dozen new democracies. Key democratic transitions occurred in major states like Indonesia and Mexico. By 1998, the United States had set up democracy promotion programs in more than a hundred countries. Serbia's revolution added another country to the democratic column in 2000. The "color revolutions" in Georgia in 2003, Ukraine in 2004, and Kyrgyzstan in 2005 symbolized the high-water mark of freedom's advance against authoritarianism. By 2005, the number of democracies in the world had more than tripled since Portugal's young military officers first heard that song on the radio.

But then something changed. The democratic tide crested, and the world's most unsavory regimes—a mélange of dictators, strongmen, and authoritarian governments—made a comeback. Political freedom around the world declined for the next five years, according to Freedom House's annual survey. The five-year drop was the longest continuous decline in political rights and civil liberties since the watchdog organization began measuring these trends forty years ago. Military coups overturned democratic governments in Asia, while a populist brand of authoritarianism gained ground in South America. Even the fresh success stories in Georgia, Ukraine, and Kyrgyzstan appeared to unravel. In 2010, the number of democracies had dropped to its lowest point since 1995. More broadly, the percentage of countries designated "free" had remained unchanged for more than a decade, frozen at roughly 46 percent. Huntington's wave appeared to have run its course.

The problem didn't rest with democracy itself. As the Arab Spring reminded everyone in 2011, even amid a global recession, the ideals of political and economic freedom have not lost their saliency. People everywhere still aspire to be free. What changed is the *nature* of dictatorship. Today's dictators and authoritarians are far more sophisticated, savvy, and nimble than they once were. Faced with growing pressures, the smartest among them neither hardened their regimes into police states nor closed themselves off from the world; instead, they learned and adapted. For dozens of authoritarian regimes, the challenge posed by democracy's advance led to experimentation, creativity, and cunning. Modern authoritarians have successfully honed new techniques, methods, and formulas for preserving power, refashioning dictatorship for the modern age.

Today's dictators understand that in a globalized world the more brutal forms of intimidation—mass arrests, firing squads, and violent crackdowns—are best replaced with more subtle forms of coercion. Rather than forcibly arrest members of a human rights group, today's most effective despots deploy tax collectors or health inspectors to shut down dissident groups. Laws are written broadly, then used like a scalpel to target the groups the government deems a threat. (In Venezuela, one activist joked that President Hugo Chávez rules through the motto "For my friends, everything, for my enemies, the law.") Rather than shutter all media, modern-day despots make exceptions for small outlets—usually newspapers—that allow for a limited public discussion. Today's dictators pepper their speeches with references to liberty, justice, and the rule of law. Chinese Communist Party leaders regularly invoke democracy and claim to be the country's elected leaders. And modern authoritarians understand the importance of appearances. In the twentieth century, totalitarian leaders would often hold elections and claim an absurd percentage of the ballots. Soviet leaders routinely stole elections by announcing they won an improbable 99 percent of the vote. Today, the Kremlin's operatives typically stop stuffing the ballot boxes when they reach 70 percent. Modern dictators understand it is better to appear to win a contested election than to openly steal it.

We like to believe that authoritarian regimes are dinosaurs—clumsy, stupid, lumbering behemoths, reminiscent of the Soviet Union in its final days or some insecure South American banana republic. And to be sure, a small handful of retrograde, old-school dictatorships have managed to limp into the twenty-first century. They are the North Koreas, Turkmenistans, and Equatorial Guineas of the world. But they represent dictatorship's past. They make little to no effort to appear to be anything other than what they are. They have been reduced to remote outposts while other regimes have learned to evolve, change, and, in some cases, thrive. No one wants to be the next North Korea.

Totalitarianism proved to be a distinctly twentieth-century phenomenon. It was the most ambitious undemocratic gamble ever made, and it performed poorly. Arguably, only North Korea clings to the totalitarian method, enabled in large part by its development of a nuclear weapons program and the late Kim Jong Il's willingness to starve his own people. But modern dictators work in the more ambiguous spectrum that exists between democracy and authoritarianism. Most strive to win their people's support by making them content, but failing that, they are happy to keep their critics off balance through fear and selective forms of intimidation. "My father used to say that he would rather live in a dictatorship like Cuba," Alvaro Partidas, a Venezuelan activist, told me. "At least there you knew if you criticized the government, they would put you in prison. Here they rule through uncertainty."

From a distance, many of the world's leading authoritarians look almost democratic. Their constitutions will often provide for a division of powers among the executive, the legislature, and the judiciary. There may be important differences among them: some have one legislative house instead of two, some offices are appointed rather than elected, different bodies have varying degrees of oversight. But many of the institutional features of authoritarian states—at least on paper—have close analogues to some of the most boring, humdrum European democracies.

Take, for example, Russia. Even as Vladimir Putin became increasingly authoritarian, he never did violence to the Russian constitution; he worked in the seams of Russia's political system, centralizing power through channels that could at least appear to be democratic. Thus, critics could complain that the Kremlin's requirement of minimum voting thresholds to win election to the parliament—each party must capture at least 7 percent of the vote—is a cynical ploy to block opposition candidates. Indeed, it was. But Putin could point to similar requirements in the electoral systems of democratic stalwarts like Poland, Germany, and the Czech Republic. Likewise, in Venezuela, Hugo Chávez has proposed replacing the direct elections of governors with presidential appointments for regional leaders. Again, it is a transparent attempt to centralize political power and eliminate opponents. And it is also a feature of some of the world's most placid democracies, countries like the Baltic states of Estonia and Lithuania. The point is that on their own these revisions are not abuses of power.

Many of the features of a modern authoritarian regime are individually not at odds with a healthy democracy. A discrete piece of a government's mechanics can be highly ambiguous. After all, even aspects of American democracy—like the Electoral College and the Federal Reserve—are undemocratic. You must, instead, look at how a modern authoritarian political system works in practice. To do so, you must get up close.

Few know better how dictatorships have remade themselves than Ludmilla Alexeeva. The eighty-four-year-old human rights defender is one of the last Russian dissidents who can trace her resistance to official Moscow to the late 1960s, to the early days of the Soviet leader Leonid Brezhnev. Even now, frail and unable to walk far without assistance, she spearheads a movement to win Russians their right to freely assemble. On the morning I sat with her in her apartment in Moscow, the phone rang off the hook. ("Human rights defenders are in demand today," she said, laughing. "We are very popular in our country.") When she began as an activist, the risks were grave. A Soviet dissident needed to be "prepared to sacrifice himself or one day find himself in prison or in a mental clinic. Nowadays, the same person must face that he can either be made disabled or murdered." Once the regime would have arrested someone, and he would never be heard from again. Now he has an accident or appears to be the victim of a random attack.

Likewise, the Soviet citizen had few legal protections. That is not true of Russians today. "The Russian constitution guarantees the same set of freedoms and rights as any Western constitution," says Alexeeva. "But actually only one right is really observed—the right to travel abroad, to leave." The effect is that many people who might have opposed the regime simply left. Thus, while the dictatorship of the Soviet system required closed borders, the authoritarianism of Putin's Russia aims to sustain itself with open borders and passports. The world may have changed, but the savviest dictators have not been sitting still. As fast as their world may have turned upside down, as fast as the old rules may no longer apply, so too did the most skilled regimes learn and adapt.

At its root, a dictatorship's most inviolable principle is the centralization of power. It is that principle—the control of the many by the few—that makes today's authoritarian regimes increasingly anachronistic. In every venue of modern life, hierarchies are falling, institutions are flattening, and the individual is left empowered. The central tenets of dictatorship become more outmoded every day. Thus, in a world of unfettered information and open borders, authoritarian regimes are conscious, man-made projects that must be carefully built, polished, and reinforced. The task is less complicated for the pariah states that have chosen to fall into a defensive crouch and hold the world at bay. They may endure for years or decades, but it is hard to see how they are not imprisoned by the walls they build to protect themselves. More complex are the modern dictatorships that choose to interact and open themselves to the very pressures that have imperiled others. They seek to blend repression with regulation to gain the most from the global political system without jeopardizing their grip on power. There is a deliberate architecture to the modern authoritarian regime, and it requires constant repair and refurbishment. And not just because of abstract forces of modernity. Because, as dictators have become more nimble, so too have those who threaten to tear them down.

This book is the story of a global contest, a struggle with battles and skirmishes that are often hidden from view but are transpiring every day. But as much as is written about U.S. democracy promotion or UN intervention, today the struggle between democracy and dictatorship is rarely, almost never, a conflict between or among nations; it is a contest between people. The truth is that sovereign states are usually too slow to act, even when they see a regime teetering on the edge of revolution. The United States did not abandon its autocratic allies in Tunisia and Egypt in 2011 until the last possible moment and remained hesitant to push against a despised regime like Syria. Even in 1989, as the Berlin Wall came down, American diplomats worried about what the new political landscape would bring, going so far as to caution former Soviet states against declaring their independence. It is not that the United States' role does not matter. It does; indeed it can be decisive. But like it or not, it is rare that the United States' interest in democratic change—even a change that might remove a reviled strongman—is not balanced by competing interests or fears of the unknown. Seldom do the variables line up as they did in the final months of Muammar Gaddafi's Libya, where the international community managed to agree to move against a hobbled dictatorship with few friends on the verge of committing a gross humanitarian tragedy.

Authoritarian regimes are not particularly fearful of the United States. Why should they be? We are too intertwined. The United States is one of China's largest trading partners, is the biggest buyer of Venezuelan oil, sends billions in aid to the Egyptian military, and courts Russian diplomatic support on a range of crucial strategic issues. Authoritarian governments rarely fret over United Nations sanctions or interference from a foreign human rights group that can be easily expelled. Indeed, the mere threat of foreign intervention, whether from the United States, the United Nations, or a body like the International Criminal Court, can be a useful foil for stirring up nationalist passions and encouraging people to rally around the regime.

What dictators and authoritarians fear most is their own people; they know the most potent threats to their rule are homegrown. Peter Ackerman understands this as well. In fact, he doesn't believe a dictatorship is ever "ripe" to fall. In his view, there are no conditions that are more or less favorable for a nonviolent revolution. Regimes that once seemed on the brink remain in power. Dictatorships no one expected to collapse disintegrated in a matter of days. There are no clear correlations to be drawn between a regime's brutality, economic hardship, ethnic makeup, or cultural history and the probability of revolution today, tomorrow, or ten years from now. What matters is how you play the game. It is a question of skills—the skills of a regime versus the skills of its opponents. The side that engages in the best preparation and demonstrates the most unity and discipline is most likely to win out. That, better than anything else, explains why the people Ackerman invests in are the people dictators fear most.

When observers look at only one side of the coin—the dictators—they see regimes that appear all-powerful. They concentrate on a dictatorship's massive security apparatus, its divisions of riot police, soldiers, intelligence officers, informants, and paid thugs. They focus on the regime's tight grip on media, major industries, the courts, and political parties. Perhaps they see a culture of fear, grinding poverty for the majority of society, and government coffers fed by corruption and control of oil fields or other natural resources. And of course there is the brutality: any regime that has no compunction about jailing, torturing, or murdering its critics will not be easily ousted, so the thinking goes. When they consider all of these conditions, outsiders see little reason to believe anything will change soon. So when the revolution does come—whether it be in the Philippines, Poland, South Korea, Indonesia, Serbia, Tunisia, or countless other places—most experts, academics, and policy makers write it off as a fluke, a rare or unique circumstance unlikely to be repeated. "There isn't an expert who has ever predicted one of these [revolutions]," says Ackerman from across his desk. "In fact, they have been in a state of denial until the moment they've happened. Then, after the dictator falls and loses, they say, 'Well, the guy was a pussycat anyway.'"

The piece of the puzzle they are missing is an appreciation of the skills of those who seek to topple a dictator. They don't watch as activists learn how to mobilize a movement, chip away at a regime's legitimacy, or master the tools of propaganda. They don't pay attention to how democratic movements learn from each other, bringing new and innovative tactics to the fight.

Two years ago, I set out to witness this battle firsthand. The front lines in this fight are far-flung. I traveled to a range of authoritarian countries—a list that included China, Egypt, Malaysia, Russia, and Venezuela—to look up close at what innovations, techniques, or methods these regimes had employed to maintain their rule. To do so, I met with the people who served the regimes, the political advisers, ideologues, cronies, technocrats, and officials who helped to perpetuate its rule.

I also met the diverse and unexpected army of people determined to overthrow some of the world's most sophisticated dictatorships. My reporting led me to Venezuelan students, Russian environmentalists, Chinese lawyers, Egyptian bloggers, Malaysian opposition leaders, and Serbian revolutionaries. Perhaps more surprisingly, I discovered that today's activists and democratic movements are talking to each other, studying each other's work, and brainstorming ideas. A Venezuelan student leader can fly to Mexico City to have Serbian activists—who ousted their own dictator ten years earlier—teach him how to identify Hugo Chávez's weaknesses.

Across the globe, I walked the unmarked battlefields of the struggle that is being waged to determine the balance of power between dictatorships and democracies: the coffee shops where activists conspire, the forests where campaigns are hatched, the slums where anger slowly burns, the streets where youth begin to fight, the prisons where a dictator's enemies languish. This conflict has fractured in a thousand directions, with rapidly modernizing regimes squaring off against an unlikely collection of individuals and organizations who are moving up their own learning curve. In more than two hundred interviews, I listened to both sides as they laid out their strategies for survival and success.

Even as I reported, the newest chapter in this battle was being written in the Middle East. Until 2011, it had been the only region in the world that lacked a single democracy, with the exception of Israel. The average Arab leader ruled for more than sixteen years. The Middle East lagged behind the rest of the world in almost every measure of what makes a people free. But as in Portugal in 1974, the revolution began in the least likely of places, Tunisia, a country that had long been considered to have one of the sturdiest regimes in the region. On December 17, 2010, local police harassed Mohamed Bouazizi, a fruit vendor in the Tunisian city of Sidi Bouzid. Ashamed, angry, and pushed beyond what he could accept, Bouazizi took his own life in a public act of self-immolation. The world watched as the popular rebellion inspired by a single man's death spread from one country to the next. After Tunisia fell, the revolution jumped to Egypt, the political and cultural epicenter of the Middle East. Massive protests sprang up in Bahrain and Yemen, just as Libya descended into carnage and then outright civil war. The shocks were soon felt in Algeria, Jordan, Oman, Saudi Arabia, and Sudan as protests and rallies of varying size came to life. Even after the brutal forty-two-year reign of Gaddafi came to its violent end, the fires continued to burn in Syria as Assad struggled to combat a widening campaign to topple the regime his father had built. A fruit vendor takes his own life, and the Middle East is turned upside down. Is it the beginning of a new democratic wave?

The truth is it is too soon to say. It took nearly fifteen years for Samuel Huntington to confidently identify his democratic wave, and the task of building a democracy is harder than razing a dictatorship, as Egypt learned all too well. The pace of progress will be uneven.

Autocrats who clung on may soon find their grips loosening again. But regardless of how quickly deeper change comes, the first casualty of these revolutions is the idea that some corners of the world are somehow immune to democratic demands. What the Arab Spring revealed is something that young people, hardened activists, and outspoken critics of these regimes had long known: that in repressive countries around the world there is a battle being waged between the ruler and the ruled, a struggle between warring camps as the future of democracy and dictatorship hangs in the balance.

CHAPTER 1 THE CZAR

||||||||||||||||||||||||||||||||||||||||||||||||||||||||||||||||||||||||||||||||||||||||||||||||||||||||||||||||||||||||||||||||||||||||||||||

A s a KGB officer, Lieutenant Colonel Vladimir Putin had one foreign assignment. In 1985, at the age of thirty-two, Putin was stationed in Dresden, East Germany. He moved there with his wife and his one-year-old daughter, Masha; soon after they arrived, his second daughter, Katya, was born. The Putins lived in a drab apartment building. Most of their neighbors were members of the Stasi, the East German intelligence agency. But the location was convenient, putting Putin a short five-minute walk from the KGB's headquarters at 4 Angelikastrasse. As a case officer, the young Putin recruited sources, ran agents, gathered the latest scuttlebutt on East German leaders, and cabled his analysis back to Moscow. For a Soviet spy, it was fairly unremarkable stuff. What was more remarkable were the years that he lived there. Putin remained in Dresden, on the edge of the Soviet Empire, from 1985 until January 1990. He was, in other words, a witness to the collapse of a dictatorship, and of the Soviet system that followed soon thereafter.

The German Democratic Republic was a postcard of a twentieth-century totalitarian state. The Stasi had infiltrated all parts of life. It kept secret files on more than six million East Germans; in Dresden alone, the files the secret police compiled would stretch almost seven miles. According to the regime's own records, the East German government employed 97,000 people and had another 173,000 working as informants. Nearly one in every 60 citizens was somehow tied to the state's security apparatus. Even as a KGB officer, Putin was shocked at how "totally invasive" the government's surveillance was of its own citizens. He later described his time in East Germany as "a real eye-opener for me." "I thought I was going to an Eastern European country, to the center of Europe," he told a Russian interviewer. But it wasn't that. "It was a harshly totalitarian country, similar to the Soviet Union, only 30 years earlier."

As a Soviet intelligence officer working in a client state, Putin very likely saw signs of East Germany's rot before others. He likely would have read the Stasi reports—many of which were sent unfiltered to Moscow—that painted an increasingly dark picture. These reports documented the rising demands of the people and described the regime's own economic record keeping as fraudulent. He would have seen the signs of a moribund economy, as government subsidies had long outstripped state revenue. In 1989, near the end, the signs of collapse were on his doorstep. There was a run on Dresden banks. At the Dresden train station, crowds tried to fight their way onto trains bound for the West. On October 4, ten thousand East Germans gathered, and the police used truncheons and tear gas to keep them from overrunning the station to board the cars. The crowds tripled in size over the next several days.

The confusion of watching a Soviet outpost collapse around him was quickly followed by fear. The ties that bound the Stasi and the KGB were plain to anyone. The East German officers referred to their Soviet counterparts as "the friends." Indeed, the KGB station where Putin worked was across the street from the Stasi's offices. After the Berlin Wall was breached, Putin and his colleagues set about covering their tracks. "We destroyed everything—all our communications, our lists of contacts, and our agents' networks. I personally burned a huge amount of material," Putin later recalled. "We burned so much stuff that the furnace burst." On December 6, when crowds of East Germans stormed the Stasi's building, Putin worried that they would direct their anger across the street at him and his colleagues. And they almost did. As angry East Germans began to assemble, Putin went outside to address the crowd. Claiming he was no more than a translator, he told them it was a Soviet military organization and they should move on. Worried about the crowd's aggressive mood, Putin called the detachment of local Soviet military officers to protect them. And he remembers being told, "We cannot do anything without orders from Moscow. And Moscow is silent." His fear turned to alienation. "That business of 'Moscow is silent'—I got the feeling then that the country no longer existed. That it had disappeared."

It is hard to imagine that those years did not leave a mark on the psyche of the young intelligence officer. Putin saw firsthand the costs and inefficiencies of the East German police state. He watched as the country's centrally planned economy fell further behind and East German officials worked furiously to hide these failings with subsidies they could never recover. And the experience brought home the weaknesses of the Soviet system that he served as well. "Actually, I thought the whole thing was inevitable," Putin later said, referring to the fall of the Berlin Wall. "I only regretted that the Soviet Union had lost its position in Europe, although intellectually I understood that a position built on walls and dividers cannot last. But I wanted something different to rise in its place. And nothing different was proposed. That's what hurt. They just dropped everything and went away."

Putin saw Moscow's failure to recognize its weaknesses and then adapt as a catastrophe. Having been its foot soldier, left practically alone to defend its interests from an angry mob, he longed for the strong, sovereign Russian state that had once been. He felt frustration that the center had never listened to the periphery. "Didn't we warn them about what was coming? Didn't we provide them with recommendations on how to act?" recalled Putin.

Nearly ten years later to the day, that young KGB agent would become Russia's second president, unexpectedly replacing Boris Yeltsin as his health and personal popularity failed him. Putin's experience from those years may explain what he meant when, later as president, he said, "He who does not regret the break-up of the Soviet Union has no heart; he who wants to revive it in its previous form has no head."

"A Kind of Dream of the Soviet Past"

On January 1, 2000, Putin made a pledge to the Russian people. Few people he addressed that day were happy with what Russia had become. The decade that had followed the collapse of the Soviet Union had been marked by economic hardship, crisis, and unpredictability. The country's early experiment in democracy had seemingly spawned little more than feuding politicians and fractious political parties that everyone assumed (probably rightly) were on the take. Cynicism rose as Russians came to believe that they had traded the sins of communism for the false promises of a corrupt democratic system. Worse yet, they felt as though they had been duped: they had followed the democratic model set by the West and had only been repaid with suffering, as a few profited at the expense of everyone else. And as if to add insult to injury, their country had been reduced from a superpower to something far more middling.

The moment, therefore, was ripe for what Putin promised on the first day of the new century. Beyond the pledges of growth and renewal, Putin offered the thing that everyday Russians missed most: "stability, certainty, and the possibility of planning for the future—their own and that of their children—not one month at a time, but for years and decades." They were welcome words to those yearning for safety and security after a decade that left Russians feeling vulnerable and forced to fend for themselves. Putin's vision was of a strong, resilient Russia that would return to its natural place as a great power. Moscow would no longer be silent.

Although he did not spell out how this stability would be achieved, Putin's plan gradually revealed itself. If there is one defining characteristic of Putin's brand of authoritarianism, it is the centralization of power. If Russian politics had become too noisy, divisive, and tumultuous, Putin set out to tame it. Russia would become more stable and predictable because it would, in essence, be directed by one man and the small circle of people around him. It was, as Putin and others would sometimes describe it, a "power vertical." Among Russia's political and economic institutions, the Kremlin would not settle for being first among equals; everything would be subordinate to it.

Putin began with the oligarchs. These Russian tycoons, many of whom had been awarded sweetheart deals for major centers of industry like gas, minerals, and steel, had become fabulously wealthy during the years of cowboy capitalism that followed the Soviet Union's collapse. Within two months of Putin's inauguration, the Kremlin warned these billionaire businessmen that they would be either loyal or out of business. Those who challenged this advice quickly found themselves in exile or prison. None learned this lesson harder than the oil magnate Mikhail Khodorkovsky, who was arrested when SWAT teams stormed his corporate jet in 2003 and placed him under arrest. His prosecution was clearly politically motivated, and the trial was widely criticized for gross irregularities. Nevertheless, he remains in prison to this day, an object lesson for anyone who fails to heed Putin's warning.

The country's regional governors followed. In a land the size of Russia, these governors had been able to run their corners of the country as personal fiefdoms. Under Yeltsin, Kremlin edicts had been treated as suggestions, more easily ignored than enforced. This, too, would eventually come to an abrupt end. In 2005, Putin did away with the direct election of Russia's governors, opting instead to give himself the power to appoint them. In addition, their finances would now be supervised by Kremlin loyalists, whose ranks were drawn from Putin's friends in the KGB.

Perhaps most remarkable was the way in which Putin brought the media to heel. At the beginning of Putin's presidency, only one of the top three television networks was state owned. Three years later, the Kremlin controlled all three. (The oligarchs who owned two of the main television networks—ORT and NTV—were forced to sell their shares or face imprisonment. Both sold and fled the country.) Kremlin cronies also began to buy up the largest-circulation newspapers and magazines. Today the Russian government controls roughly 93 percent of all media outlets. Some print publications and radio stations are still able to operate with a measure of independence; the radio station Ekho Moskvy, for example, is one of the most critical remaining voices. But more incredible than the takeover of many Russian media companies is the degree to which the Kremlin is willing to manipulate the news—especially the news you see on TV.

Until recently, a senior Kremlin official met with the directors of the three major TV channels every Friday to plan the news coverage for the week to come. Television managers reportedly received a steady stream of phone calls throughout the week, honing how that coverage should be presented, even delving sometimes into how a particular news story should be edited. The Kremlin is not shy about giving TV executives instructions to follow. For example, after Dmitri Medvedev became president in 2008, the television networks were instructed that news broadcasts each day were to begin with coverage of him, followed by nearly equal time for Prime Minister Putin, whether or not either of them did anything newsworthy. When I was in Moscow, I would watch the evening news just to see how bizarrely balanced the coverage between the two men would be, with each of them getting roughly the same airtime. A senior television executive at one of the networks called this rule "the principle of informational parity." A journalist from *Russian Newsweek* reported on visiting one of the state-controlled radio stations. While there, he saw notes in front of the radio announcers reminding them to "say only good things about Kazakhstan" and "don't mention that Dmitri and Svetlana Medvedev arrived to the summit separately."

The Kremlin wasn't satisfied with simply taming billionaires, governors, and media heads, though; it also sought to stage-manage politics. From as far back as his Millennium Statement, Putin always stressed the need for political and social unity. He naturally sought to extend this cohesion to the realm of political parties, which had been among the most unpredictable and fractious players in post-Communist Russia. But Putin and his team did not wish to crush all opposition with a single dominant ruling party. Rather, they engineered space for a small handful of opposition parties to exist and in some instances invented the parties out of whole cloth. These parties—typically referred to as the systemic opposition—ostensibly play the role of regime critics while never pushing their criticism beyond the boundaries set by the Kremlin. In their ideological orientation, these opposition voices are intended to represent social interests—namely, nationalists, the poor, and older voters—who may feel neglected or dissatisfied with the ruling party, United Russia. But they regularly demonstrate their fealty, as in December 2007, when the heads of each so-called opposition party publicly informed Putin that they could think of no one better to lead Russia than his longtime aide Dmitri Medvedev. Putin could then tell the TV public that since the nomination of Medvedev came from different parties that represented "the most different strata of Russian society," Medvedev was clearly the choice of the people.

The degree to which Putin concentrated power in the center cannot be overstated. According to the Russian journal *Ekspert,* which is edited by a confidant of senior Kremlin advisers, the number of officials who had serious influence over national policy and politics from 2002 to 2007 dropped from two hundred to fifty. This pro-government publication admitted that this list of fifty officials reads "almost like a telephone book of the [presidential] administration." But this centralization of power should not be understood as an attempt to achieve total control of all aspects of Russian life. Rather, it is something more precise.

In talking with members of Solidarity, a liberal political movement that is not part of the systemic opposition, I found out how precise. One of its leaders, Boris Nemtsov, a former deputy prime minister and legislator, is easily one of the most outspoken critics of Putin and his regime. Nemtsov has a laid-back demeanor that is younger than his fifty-something age. Wearing weathered blue jeans, a gray zippered sweater with no shirt, and pointed black boots, he looked more like an aging rock star than an opposition leader. A Ph.D. in physics and mathematics, Nemtsov has a sharp mind, and he gets right to the point. "What's the difference between communism and Putinism?" he says. "This is very important. Putinism looks smarter, because Putinism comes just for your political rights but does not touch your personal freedom. You can travel, you can emigrate if you want, you can read the Internet. What is strictly forbidden is to use TV. Television is under control because TV is the most powerful resource for ideology and the propaganda machine. Communists blocked personal freedom plus political freedom. That's why communism looks much more stupid than Putinism."

It is hard to dispute Nemtsov's analysis. No one would say that life isn't freer in present-day Russia than it was under the Soviet Union. That is unmistakable. And it is certainly more affluent, as the oil boom that accompanied Putin's two terms as president raised the standard of living for Russians to levels never seen. When his presidency began, oil prices were considered high—at $21.50 a barrel. By the end of his second term, oil had climbed to $147.00 a barrel. It was a windfall for the government's coffers. But, as Putin had observed as a young man in East Germany, there was no need to channel this wealth into re-creating an invasive totalitarian state that tried to pry into the personal beliefs of each citizen. The costs of such control were too high and ultimately unnecessary. Putin's form of authoritarianism represents an evolution of the model, something far more scaled down but more effective. Ilya Yashin, a young leader of the Solidarity movement who says he was expelled from another party because he refused to "act like a member of the systemic opposition," put it this way: "Putin has created a kind of dream of the Soviet past. It's like the Soviet Union without the lines, deficits, and with open borders."

Even if the system that Putin has devised represents an improvement on twentieth-century attempts at dictatorship, it does not mean that it doesn't have its costs. Centralizing power in so few hands raises the likelihood of corruption, complacency, and an abuse of power—all sins that Nemtsov says Putin's administration is guilty of committing. These failings represent a danger for the regime, but not necessarily because they amount to poor governance. Rather, for Putin and his clique, the constant worry is that the costs of the strategy they have chosen undermine their main objective: manufacturing a stable political system. Expensive oil may help to shield them from many social dangers—it is always easier to purchase rather than coerce support—but their attempt to simulate so many facets of a democratic system significantly shrinks the regime's margin for error. Having eliminated so many other centers of power—the business community, governors, media, opposition political parties—the Kremlin must chart the correct course if it hopes to maintain control. It's a difficult balancing act. "They don't want to lose control over the changes like Gorbachev. It means they try to keep this control every moment," says Alexander Verkhovsky, a leading human rights defender. "If they plan, for example, to give us 3 percent freedom, maybe they will give us 4 percent but not 5. I think that is really their plan. To make the situation not so tight as when they had no connection to the society, when they had no signals to the objects of their manipulation. I don't know if it will be 3 percent or 10, but I am sure that they do not want to permit any real democratization as there was in the late '80s."

Popov's Graph

If you were casting the part of Communist apparatchik, you couldn't do much better than Sergei Popov. He's a mountain of a man, and his face betrays almost no emotion, except perhaps those that exist between mild condescension and anger when someone questions the wisdom of the political system he represents. If he looks the part, it may be because a little more than twenty years ago that is precisely who he was. In the twilight of the Soviet Union, he was the Communist Party's first deputy chairman of Moscow, holding the post from 1983 until the end. When I met him in his corner office at the Russian Duma, the country's parliament, he was still every bit the party man. The only difference was the lapel pin he wears on his dark blue suits. Right away you know you are meeting with United Russia, the party of Putin.

If the Duma is a rubber-stamp parliament—which most people will rightly tell you it is—it still requires some loyal soldiers to make sure the stamp gets applied. Not long after we sit down, Popov makes clear that "90 percent of the civil laws are created here at this table." (Translation: meet the stamp.) As chairman of the Committee of Public Unions and Religious Organizations, he rides herd on the laws governing political parties, nongovernmental organizations (NGOs), media companies, commercial organizations, and religious groups. He is, in other words, the most senior member of the Russia Duma with responsibility for that most unpredictable variable: civil society. For any authoritarian regime, managing that variable is a crucial part of its ability to remain in control.

Putin's choke hold on Russian NGOs was a late but inextricable part of his effort to centralize power. After he had moved against other pillars of the state, and in the wake of the Orange Revolution in Ukraine, an onerous 2006 law targeted civil society. The law gave the Kremlin broad powers over all NGOs. Any nonprofit organization can be inspected at any time, groups need to comply with rigorous reporting requirements, and the Ministry of Justice has utter discretion to request any documents and determine whether they comply with Russian "interests." Simple errors, like typos or the improper formatting of documents, can lead to harsh sanctions. Authorities require only the flimsiest excuse to dissolve an organization. And the more sensitive the subject that a group addresses—for example, human rights or freedom of expression—the more likely it is to be targeted for tax audits, building-code violations, or the use of pirated software. Once passed, the law did not simply exist on the books; it was vigorously enforced against selective targets, especially Kremlin critics and human rights defenders. In the first year, the Ministry of Justice led 13,381 NGO inspections. A slew of foreign human rights organizations, such as Amnesty International, Doctors Without Borders, and Human Rights Watch, were forced to temporarily close their doors. Thousands of NGOs have ceased to exist, although the exact number is unknown. The resources available to those that remain were strangled further when Putin followed this law with a 2008 decree that cut the number of international organizations allowed to give tax-free grants to Russian groups from 101 to 12. Groups that lost the ability to offer these tax-free contributions included the World Wildlife Fund, the International Red Cross, and the Global Fund to Fight AIDS, Tuberculosis, and Malaria—hardly national security threats to the Russian government. It takes five days to register a business in Russia; it takes roughly two months to register an NGO. It's also more expensive. The legal costs for starting an NGO in Russia are 40 percent more than they are for starting a private business.

Of course, Popov doesn't see the government's relationship with Russian civil society as repressive. Like almost every pro-Kremlin politician, he began by praising the stability that United Russia (in truth, Putin) had brought to Russian politics. I suggested that this stability can come at a cost for a regime; for example, strong governments with a weak civil society often fall prey to a lack of quality information, feedback from citizens about society's needs and demands. Popov shook his head. In theory, yes, it could be a problem, but the Russian government had come up with solutions. When I ask for an example, he points to the creation of public reception offices across the country. Their role is, in essence, to provide a direct line of communication for citizens to air their problems, grievances, and complaints to the central government. "In practice, here is how it looks," explains Popov. "You come into the office, and you are given a special form to fill out that includes your personal data and a brief description of your problem. This information goes in the computer right away, and immediately the machine gives you the name of who's going to be responsible for this, who's going to look at it, when the answer is supposed to come back, and how it's going to be delivered to you. And immediately this request or demand is sent to the center . . . We can judge immediately which problems are the main concern for people; we can also see how many men applied, how many women, pensioners, young people, all these categories."

Ultimately, the authorities intend to have two thousand of these offices scattered across all eighty-three regions, not just in major cities, but also down to the level of individual voting districts. In 2009, more than a million people visited these offices to file complaints, he tells me. He pauses for a couple of beats and, as if to underline the point, looks at me across the table and says, "This is to avoid stagnation."

It is a step a government might take after it has eliminated most democratic mechanisms for people to express their frustrations. With its governors (and increasingly its mayors) appointed, the vast majority of representatives from a single party, and the media controlled by the state or its cronies, the Kremlin recognizes it does need one thing in particular—accurate information on the national mood. In fact, gaining this type of information becomes an acute need as independent democratic institutions are reduced to supplicants. It's a blind spot that has led to ruin for authoritarian regimes everywhere. Centralizing power may mean one has complete control, but it also means eliminating many of the filters that help sort good ideas from bad. The Kremlin is intelligent enough to recognize that monitoring public opinion is a job worth doing, if only to keep a better gauge on discontent. In most democracies, such feedback would come from elections, legislators, and civil society; in Russia, they are using a computer.

The regime has come up with other innovations besides the digital connection Popov was touting. One is the Public Chamber. From the inside, with its white marble floors, large glass chandeliers, and red velvet sofas on either end of a spacious lobby, it almost has the majesty of a miniature national assembly or legislature. But it isn't; this body is a consultative forum made up of representatives from various parts of Russian civil society selected by the Kremlin itself. Members may be experts in media, the law, public health, or human rights; some are members of genuine NGOs. These handpicked representatives act as a sort of advisory panel, offering Russian authorities their opinions on legislation and pending policy decisions. Although most members of the Public Chamber are considered dutiful supporters of the regime, there are critics among them, and they have issued statements and reports that are critical of the government and its policies. In fact, this is precisely their job: to provide the advice, counsel, and criticism that a toothless Duma cannot. Having hollowed out one branch of government, Putin created the Public Chamber to provide a semblance of the independent ideas, expertise, and connection to wider society that a legislature typically brings—just without the power to do anything other than offer an opinion. "The Public Chamber is *allowed* to be critical," says Tanya Lokshina, the deputy director of the Moscow office of Human Rights Watch and a veteran of the struggles that NGOs face in Russia. "But what [the authorities] do not want to tolerate are those critics of the government getting to talk to people, getting support in society, getting their messages out—this is something that they're not ready to tolerate at all. That's why television is so rigidly state controlled. They want independent information, but they want to use it for their own purposes."

In fact, the need for reliable, independent information is so great the party doesn't even trust that its own members will give it the unvarnished truth. In July 2010, United Russia announced a new center for analysis that is intended to identify and focus on the country's "newly dissatisfied." Ruslan Gattarov, a thirty-three-year-old United Russia representative and head of this center, told a Russian news agency that the purpose of this organization will be to "collect information which the governors and mayors are hiding." The party has felt compelled to create its own watchdog to report to the Kremlin on the public's frustration, resentment, and discontent, things it fears are not moving up the chain of command or are even being covered up. "Speaking crudely, the regional and municipal powers frequently do everything [they can] to keep quiet about problems in order that nothing about them will leak out," Gattarov told the reporter. "And who do [members of the public] blame for [the problems]? . . . Our leader Putin and our President Medvedev." The flip side of centralizing so much in the hands of so few is that the regime cannot assume that its political opponents, a free press, or local NGOs will draw its attention to the problems that must be solved—because these critics have already been sidelined. The burden rests squarely on the Kremlin and its ability to come up with new ways to get the information it needs.

After I mention some of the evidence for the country's incredible centralization of power, I ask Popov an obvious question: Is the Kremlin in control of too much, and couldn't this be dangerous for the country's stability?

A faint smile passes across Popov's face. He reaches for a pencil and a clean sheet of paper. "Any process, as you know, has two vectors of development. Questions and problems may occur all the time. But let's see what forces are prevailing." As he says this, Popov begins to draw a graph on the piece of paper. He draws a vertical line and then bisects it with a dotted horizontal line. Where the lines meet, he marks as point zero. As he continues to talk—or it may be more accurate to say, lecture—it becomes apparent that this senior member of the Duma is actually going to graph the state of Russian democracy for me.

"I just want to say that many of the democracies are threatened with going back to totalitarianism or authoritarian regimes," Popov continues, without a hint of irony. "For Russia it is not possible. It is not possible even theoretically. Very slowly, very gradually, the influence of the civil society grows, and I can definitely tell you that the factor of public opinion is different from what it was ten years ago. Any power instinctively avoids critics and influence or pressure. Nobody likes it."

He draws two arrows, both starting from zero. One arrow rises above the dotted horizontal line, the other drops below it at the same angle. He labels the rising arrow civil society. The arrow falling below the dotted line is the government. "So, as I said, there are two vectors which influence each other. From my point of view, if we build this, then the result will be here." Popov is pointing at the dotted horizontal line. "It's the vector of democracy development."

In Popov's diagram, the country's political direction is to be arrived at by the contending forces between civil society and the government. Each acts as a pressure on the other, and the end result, he says, is a relatively healthy line of progress right down the middle.

It is a reasonable enough formulation—if we could only agree on the degree of the angles for the lines going up or down. On the graph, Popov has Russian political dominance marked at a mild 10 to 20 degrees. I suggest that many people would object to his rendering, that even much of the Russian public would say that the government is more authoritarian than he has allowed here. I point to a spot on the graph that would be roughly 60 degrees. Popov sits up in his chair and barks, "So what?"

For a moment, I'm not exactly sure how to respond.

As he stares at me, a few more seconds pass. He then repeats, "The opposition is weak, the government's voice is powerful—so what? . . . We're not talking about authoritarian or totalitarian regimes. We just say that the system is developing."

He returns to the graph and scribbles some more lines, now circling the number 30. "The government understands," he continues, ratcheting his voice down, "that you cannot go beyond 30 degrees. If you go down to 45 degrees, for instance, you can just slip off the opposition like a clock pendulum. So the government needs to control itself."

"What is the guarantee that the government will control itself?" I ask. "History shows that governments do a very poor job of controlling themselves, especially when there are fewer and fewer people who have to show that responsibility."

"Well, you can never be confident in anything!" he says indignantly. He pushes his chair away from the table, signaling that our time together has come to an end. "We have an expression here. 'Even an insurance policy doesn't guarantee you anything for 100 percent, because insurance companies always look for a way not to pay.'"

He takes the piece of paper, which by now has lines, circles, and scribbles going this way and that, and signs it with a flourish across the bottom. "There, my autograph. An original work."

Despite his attempt at near-scientific precision, it's absurd to imagine the forces of government and civil society locked in anything that comes close to a fair fight. In Russia, these are not equal and opposite forces that, having collided, arrive at some reasonable middle ground. The Russian government has literally licensed its civil society, denying permits to the groups it finds most troublesome or inconvenient.

There may be no way in which the regime has shown more creativity than in the methods it has concocted to warn, reprimand, or bar organizations from conducting work it believes poses a threat. "There are a lot of instruments of control, even the fire department," one Moscow activist told me. "Fire inspections are a very popular tool."

The European University in St. Petersburg learned this lesson in January 2008. That month, local authorities visited the school to conduct what was believed to be a routine fire safety inspection. Despite having passed previous inspections, on this visit the university was cited for fifty-two violations. The university, like many in St. Petersburg, is partially housed in historic, centuries-old buildings; it's simply impossible for some buildings to be brought up entirely to code. But the authorities were unmoved in their judgment; on February 7, the district court ordered the university to be immediately closed, even though it was in the middle of the semester. All instruction had to stop at once. The university took steps to correct twenty of the violations almost overnight and appealed the court's decision to no avail. In truth, the problem had never been whether fire ladders were available or whether the exits were clearly marked. The university's mistake occurred months earlier when it accepted a $900,000 grant from the European Union to fund research on election monitor training. The grant had drawn the ire of people like Gajimet Safaraliev, a United Russia member of the Duma, who told the local press that the funds amounted to "interference by a foreign quasi-government into Russia's 2007–2008 electoral campaigns." And this wasn't just any election season: Putin was expected to pass the presidential baton to Dmitri Medvedev on March 2. On March 21, nearly three weeks after the presidential election, the government allowed the university to reopen its doors. The university's election research was suspended, and the regime's warning was heard clearly: this was not a topic for study.

Far subtler is the way in which the regime can co-opt or manufacture a civil society of its own. Among authoritarian governments, Russia has been at the forefront of one particular innovation—the GONGO. GONGOs are, as the acronym suggests, government-operated NGOs. These organizations typically profess to be independent entities and may hide behind innocuous-sounding names that suggest that their chief mission would be human rights, legal reform, or the protection of minorities. In truth, their goal is to legitimize government policy, soak up foreign funding from genuine NGOs, and confuse the public about who is in the right, the government or its critics.

Take, for example, the Moscow Bureau for Human Rights. It is led by a member of the Public Chamber named Alexander Brod. By most accounts, Brod's organization, which claims to be focused on fighting xenophobia and racism, did not begin as a GONGO. Many would say that even today the organization does some good work, publishing material on the danger of neo-Nazi and fascist groups. But somewhere along the way the organization's statements started to shift, until it began to appear more interested in supporting the interests of the regime than anything else. As one U.S. State Department official told me, "The term 'Gongolization' was invented for Brod."

For Tanya Lokshina, the Moscow deputy director of Human Rights Watch, this became clear on the eve of a report her organization planned to release on Ingushetia, a violent corner of Russia's north Caucasus region. Lokshina's report detailed the abductions, executions, acts of torture, and forced disappearances that had occurred there. Ahead of the report's release, Brod himself traveled to Ingushetia and met with local officials there. By the time Human Rights Watch held its press conference for the report, Brod had already announced his own press event—to be held with the government's ombudsman for Ingushetia. "The only message from his press conference was clear and simple: Human Rights Watch was lying about everything," recalls Lokshina. "How do you figure out who to trust? He's been there, he's done it, he's got the T-shirt. That is a very particular, sophisticated feature of this authoritarian regime."

According to several activists I spoke with, Brod repeated this pattern a few months later when war broke out between Russia and Georgia over South Ossetia. Brod was there again—on the scene—echoing the government's most dubious claims about ethnic cleansing committed by the Georgians. I went to meet with Brod in his spacious, if spartan, office at the Public Chamber, and he of course would not characterize himself as the head of a GONGO. He spoke slowly and in a measured way that often omitted important details to give the best possible gloss to Russian politics, as it is practiced. (For example, Brod told me straight-faced that all political parties were guaranteed equal access to television airtime. When I pressed him, he qualified his statement by saying this was true of parties that were registered to participate in presidential elections. Which might be persuasive unless you knew how effectively the Kremlin had barred liberal and other unwanted parties from registering or fielding candidates.) Ultimately, Brod explained his activity with a familiar rationale, saying, "The activity of an NGO is not really possible without making good contact with government people, without meeting with them, without consultations, without expertise, without discussion, without all of this."

Of course, what gives the biggest lie to the lines and angles on Popov's graph is the number of journalists and human rights activists who have been murdered for their attempts to unearth the truth. Despite the Kremlin's continued pledge to protect activists and journalists from these threats, very few have been punished for the killings in the past decade. According to the Committee to Protect Journalists, 2010 was the first year since 1999 without a targeted murder of a Russian journalist. Since 2000, nineteen journalists have been killed. In the past year, journalists have been beaten and threatened for covering topics deemed politically sensitive. And the government's record for chasing down those who harass or murder members of the human rights community is no better. "Attacks and beatings have become almost routine," says Lokshina. "People are concerned. People are looking over their shoulder. I mean, I am."

For Lokshina, the risks that come with fighting for human rights are not abstract. "2009 was an absolute disaster; it was just the most tragic year for Russia's human rights community," she says. "So many people were killed—someone like Natasha Estemirova, who was very well-known, Stanislav Markelov, and that young girl Anastasia Baburova. That was at the very start of the year." Lokshina can count friends among the murdered. Natasha Estemirova, a leading researcher for the human rights group Memorial, was her best friend. Estemirova's reputation extended beyond Russia. She won numerous international awards for her work, including one named for the Russian journalist Anna Politkovskaya, another fallen friend who was executed as she entered her Moscow apartment building in 2006. Estemirova was considered a meticulous, crusading human rights researcher and activist, always drawn to the toughest places. In Russia, that meant war-torn Chechnya. On July 15, 2009, she was abducted outside her home in Grozny. Witnesses at the scene would later tell investigators that they saw a woman being thrown into a sedan, yelling, "I'm being kidnapped!" Later that day, she was found on the side of the road in a neighboring republic, shot dead. Shortly after Estemirova's murder, Lokshina wrote in the *Washington Post* about how she and Natasha had attended the funeral of Stanislav Markelov, a human rights lawyer, earlier in the year. "We sat at my kitchen table talking into the wee hours about Markelov and Politkovskaya and speculating about who would be next." She hardly expected it would be her friend sitting across the table from her.

Lokshina and her husband, Alexander Verkhovsky, have had numerous death threats. Like her friend Natasha, she has been doing research on Chechnya for many years. Her husband is the director of the SOVA Center for Information and Analysis, a Russian NGO that monitors hate crimes, racism, and xenophobia. Just a few days before I arrived in Moscow, a senior judge was assassinated in a contract-style killing inside the stairwell of his downtown apartment building; the judge had handed out heavy sentences to ultranationalist and neo-Nazi groups. The government is concerned about the growing levels of violence tied to such extremist groups, but critics note that its past policies which have stirred up nationalist fervor while repressing Russian civil society have helped spawn the problem. Because of these threats, Lokshina and Verkhovsky have had to change apartments to find a place with better security that is not listed in the phone book. Lokshina claims it's not just because of the sensitivity of her work at Human Rights Watch. "It's because of his work as well. Basically, we have had quite a few visits paid to us by skinheads who have a thing for him," she says, smiling. "We are quite a hazard."

Meanwhile, Natasha Estemirova's murder remains unsolved. Although there were witnesses to her abduction and her killers passed through at least two government checkpoints, the police have no leads. Indeed, the only thing that has changed since that day in July 2009 is the body count. There is no place for them on Popov's graph.

Spin Doctors

Sergei Markov is often referred to as a Kremlin mouthpiece. It is not meant in a pejorative sense; it's a fact. The fifty-two-year-old Duma deputy is a good talker, and he is frequently tasked with helping the Kremlin get its message out, especially to the foreign media. Markov is sometimes described as a former liberal who got too close to power and lost his intellectual independence in service to that power. Still, he has skills—fashioning arguments, a gift for euphemisms—that make him useful. But as a basic rule in politics, whether it's within the White House, the Kremlin, or anywhere else, the messenger is part of the message. In using Markov as its mouthpiece, the Kremlin sends an unambiguous signal: swagger.

Markov looks more like a sparring partner than a political player. With short, cropped hair, a broad nose, and a sunken, hound dog expression, he rarely smiles, even when he delivers a quip that is intended to amuse. He exudes a cocky bravado as soon as he sits down, putting his three mobile phones on the table, as if to assure me: "We will be interrupted, and yes, I will take the call." As someone who is supposed to reflect the Kremlin's thinking, he hasn't shied away from delivering rhetorical bombshells. In 2009, he unexpectedly told a crowd of Washington policy wonks that his office was behind cyber-attacks on Estonia in 2007. The attacks that summer had crippled the backbone of the Baltic state's Internet infrastructure, targeting its ministries, legislature, and financial institutions. In the aftermath, NATO committed itself to helping defend member states from such threats. Russia had always denied allegations of being behind the attacks, but Markov nonchalantly confirmed the charges, saying, "About the cyber-attack on Estonia . . . don't worry, that attack was carried out by my assistant. I won't tell you his name, because then he might not be able to get visas." Later he added, "Incidentally, such things will happen more and more." Whether his admission is accurate or not is almost beside the point. The bigger question is whether the Kremlin likes having Markov speak on its behalf despite these remarks—or because of them.

Markov and I meet at a Chinese restaurant a few blocks from the Kremlin. After we have settled in and he has ordered his noodle soup, I ask him where the lines of political competition are in Russia today. Is it between his party, United Russia, and some of the quasi-opposition parties the Kremlin created? Does the legitimate but marginalized opposition have any voice? Does competition exist only within United Russia? Markov says it's none of the above. Parties are just not part of the equation. "We have no competition inside the party. We have competition outside the party," he explains. "[But] it's really fighting for power."

In other words, it's a turf battle. The political competition, to the degree it exists, is more a battle of financial interests than ideas. It's a frank statement from a member of parliament. Sensing that it might be logical for someone who holds such an opinion to also see this as being partially responsible for the country's incredible corruption, I ask if he worries if this lack of political competition is spilling over, drowning Russia's economic performance. But Markov sees it differently. "Let me just say that corruption is not a good thing, but there are no strong connections between corruption and lack of development," Markov says. "Of course, it should be fought against, but you know there are no strong connections between the lack of development and corruption, and there are no strong connections between political competition and the lack of corruption. So why pursue political competition if both of these connections are so uncertain?"

Markov isn't simply being argumentative; he is expressing a central tenet of modern authoritarian regimes. A fundamental question is whether societies organized around more open and free political competition grow faster and provide better lives for their citizens than more stable, closed societies. The answer, which appeared to be yes in the aftermath of the Cold War, has clouded with China's precipitous rise. China and the authoritarian city-state of Singapore are the most frequently cited examples, and Markov—as if on cue—mentions them both. "Look, look at China—no political competition but great," he says, quickly adding, "Look at Singapore—no political competition but it's great."

The idea he is getting at is that strong, stable technocratic governments may not only be able to build a foundation for fast, efficient development but also have an advantage over democracies in doing so. The trouble is that authoritarian regimes have hardly proven to be surefire bets to succeed economically. In the past forty years, on average, autocracies and democracies have developed at the same rate. For every successful East Asian tiger, there are several authoritarian basket cases. Indeed, if you set East Asia aside, autocracies have had median per capita growth rates that are 50 percent lower than poor democracies.

Asian autocracies are, in many ways, the exception that proves the rule. The gulf that separates the stunning success of the Asian tiger economies from Russia's malaise is staggeringly wide. For example, when South Korea was a developing authoritarian state in the 1960s, manufactured goods made up 65 percent of its exports. By the 1970s, that figure had risen to more than 80 percent. In other words, its economy increasingly relied on producing tangible, real products that the rest of the world wants. Russian exports, on the other hand, are incredibly dependent on a single commodity—energy. In 2008, oil and gas accounted for 70 percent of Russian exports. Goods and services made up just 1.7 percent of exports, with high-tech exports at a paltry 0.3 percent. Taiwan may have been ruled by a single party until the late 1980s, but when it was surging in the 1970s, it kept state employment at a relatively lean 12.5 percent. In Russia today, the state remains bloated; the government and its state-owned enterprises employ nearly 40 percent of workers. Or consider education. In its early days, Singapore made enormous investments in schooling and saw its number of students enrolled in high school triple between 1959 and 1972. Russia is moving in the opposite direction. Under Putin, Russia's annual spending per high school student put the country behind Brazil, Mexico, and Turkey. There is virtually no ingredient in the Asian economic miracle present in Russia.

If they aren't citing Asian autocracies, Russian elites will mention another Asian powerhouse: Japan. Markov and other government officials I spoke with are enamored of the example set by Japan's Liberal Democratic Party (LDP). The appeal is obvious: The LDP ruled Japan for an uninterrupted fifty-four years. In the same period, Japan rose from the ashes of World War II to become the world's second-largest economy. Along the way, almost all political competition was little more than factional jockeying within the LDP camp, and corruption between political and business elites was commonplace. Russian elites see something to admire in the Japanese example. For them, the secret to the Asian economic miracle begins with the political leadership in countries like Japan (or China, for that matter) holding on to power. If it hadn't, if some other political force had somehow wrested control from the LDP or from Chinese Communists, then, in the Russian view, it surely would have mucked things up. But what the Russians aren't willing to admit is that they may have it reversed, that the ability of their Asian counterparts to remain in power for so long might be based on something Russian political elites have not yet proven they can manage: sustained economic progress.

Markov is smarter, however, than to rest his argument entirely on modern exemplars of the Asian miracle, whether democratic or authoritarian. He also reaches back to the example of post–World War II Italy, a country that was long ruled by a single party, had high levels of corruption, and managed to succeed. "An extremely high level of corruption. Maybe [Italy] was the most corrupt country; almost every prime minister was under the control of the Mafia," says Markov, growing more certain of his argument. "[Yet] Italy [had] great prosperity, development, and modernization. Italy was one of the leaders in postwar Europe."

It's true that political scientists haven't established an iron law between a country's level of corruption and its development. But if the devil is in the details, the details aren't good for Russia. Corruption is so great in Russia's case that it is cannibalizing the country's growth. Graft erases roughly one-third of the country's GDP every year. The World Bank estimates that nearly half of the Russian economy is linked to some form of corruption. Russia finished 143 out of 182 countries on Transparency International's Corruption Perceptions Index in 2011, below Bangladesh, Pakistan, and Syria.

I point out to Markov that just that morning I read that the number of billionaires in Russia, according to *Forbes* magazine, had nearly doubled from thirty-two to sixty-two in the past year. In the same twelve months, almost all of the country's economic metrics were in decline. The national economy contracted almost 8 percent, its worst performance since the end of the Soviet Union. According to the World Bank, industrial output declined more than 10 percent, the manufacturing sector fell 16 percent, and fixed capital investment dropped

17 percent. Didn't that underline the problem, especially given that we know how some of those billionaires earned their wealth?

Markov brushes away my question. "It's the kind of capitalism we have. Russia is a country of extremes," he says. "All societies should be [understood] by practice, by reality, and by clear logic. Just because the *New York Times* is publishing an article about this . . ." He trails off for a moment. "It is not for Kremlin people. All these newspapers who publish so many articles about the direct connection between the monopoly of United Russia and the high level of corruption, they publish hundreds of articles about Saddam Hussein's weapons of mass destruction."

His attempt to cloud the connection between his country's political system and its rampant corruption is classic Kremlin spin. But the political operative doesn't sugarcoat everything. He admits that the political body he is a member of, the Duma, is essentially a rubber stamp and has no say in how the country is run. At one point, he even jokes that the Russian parliament should be renamed "the Ministry of Lawmaking"—just another appendage of Putin's rule.

Gleb Pavlovsky agrees. "Practically, we can say that we have the democracy of zero reading," he tells me in his corner office overlooking the Moscow River. "When the law comes into the Duma for hearings and readings, almost nothing changes in the law." At the time, Pavlovsky was one of the Kremlin's top political advisers and the head of a consultancy called the Foundation for Effective Politics. He has been working as a political consultant longer than just about anyone else in Russia, and he acknowledged, before I could, that there is no shortage of rumor about the work that he has done. "There are a lot of myths around my activity and my involvement in this or that thing," he told me, adding that is why the Russian press likes to refer to him as the "gray cardinal."

Pavlovsky is short and stocky, with closely cropped hair, and he is dressed entirely in black. In the corner a television is on, replaying a speech Putin delivered earlier that day. Indeed, the then prime minister loomed large in Pavlovsky's office. Although he said he worked for Medvedev—his third Russian president after Yeltsin and Putin—a large portrait of Putin hung on the wall, and there were no photographs of anyone else. In the early 1990s, Pavlovsky worked for organizations that supported democracy promotion initiatives, including George Soros's Open Society Institute and the National Endowment for Democracy. He refers to that time as his "major political experience." "In fact," he told me, "my career has been based on the experience that I gained working in those independent democratic organizations." His critics would agree. They say, however, that he spent that time learning about Western democracy promotion efforts so that he could better understand how to subvert them and later maintain Putin's monopoly of power. In 2006, the Ukrainian Security Service banned him from traveling to Ukraine because of allegations that he had created Russian-focused NGOs that interfered with the country's presidential elections. When I asked him how he would describe his work, he remained vague about what he does but not for whom he does it. "I generate ideas for the resolution of internal problems. During the last ten years, my almost exclusive client is the presidential administration."

I asked Pavlovsky if the stability that Russia enjoys could, in fact, be a false stability, and if the system as it is devised cuts itself off from feedback, new talent, and competition. "The considerations that you just expressed are very similar to Putin's considerations of stability," he replied. "That's actually what he thinks about." The trouble is that when it comes to political competition, he said, there is really no one who can compete with Medvedev and Putin. Pavlovsky believes Medvedev and Putin understand this problem and that the next step is for there to be a "contest of ideas." This contest, he says, "is going on almost permanently in the Kremlin, in the think tanks, in different brainstorm centers." But not in the Duma? "I'm afraid there's no one to really argue with in the Duma. The problem is that in the nonsystemic opposition there are not many heads you can really debate with," says Pavlovsky. "They don't have any ideas except one: when we were ministers, everything was great."

The criticism is hardly fair. Opposition parties have to struggle to find anyone willing to give them financing because doing so can have consequences. They must learn to operate under rules that have made it progressively harder to win seats. Their attempts to hold rallies or public events are easily blocked by authorities, and they are completely barred from national television. Pavlovsky himself is credited with coming up with the idea of the Public Chamber, an institution that exists to help supplant some of the role a parliament could play. He is considered an important draftsman of the political system as it exists. For him to criticize the opposition for not having ideas is a bit like a doctor complaining he doesn't have any patients—because he already poisoned them. I tell him his criticism seems unfair since the opposition is forced to spend most of its time simply trying to exist. "You are right. We'll have to risk [great political competition]," he says. "We'll just have to make a choice in what we are going to risk and when we are going to risk it."

But there is little indication that anyone in a position of power is willing to risk much. This fact becomes abundantly clear nearly every time Russians go to the ballot box, because evidence of election rigging quickly follows. As members of the opposition and United Russia explained to me, the problem is bigger than a senior leader ordering that ballot boxes be stuffed; in some ways, the fraud and tampering that go on at election time are now ingrained into Russia's authoritarian system. Sergei Markov readily admits that the allegations of election tampering are true. But it isn't because Putin is handing out orders over who should win what percent. "You should understand the mechanism and how it works. Never does Putin say, 'Get me such and such percent.' He even says he doesn't need this. What's Putin's interest if [someone] doesn't have 50 percent but 70 percent? Fifty percent is also the majority, yeah? He doesn't care," explains Markov. "But governors and mayors absolutely think about this because it's a reflection of how popular they are. And that's why they use it."

In other words, lower-level officials engage in election fraud because they don't want to look bad. Whether they are fearful of not delivering the votes for a superior or they are concerned they won't appear as popular when compared with other officials across the country, the tactic is the same: steal the election. We think of elections within authoritarian regimes as being uncompetitive charades. But that isn't precisely right. There is competition. It is just between officials jockeying for favor, rather than between ruling party candidates and their opponents.

Perhaps one of the more suspicious recent elections was the most high-profile one: the 2008 election of President Dmitri Medvedev. In

Putin's previous presidential election, he captured 71 percent of the vote. When Medvedev, Putin's handpicked successor, stood for the vote, he walked away with precisely 70.2 percent. To many, it appeared like a textbook example of Russian election engineering. There had been a desire to make sure that Medvedev came into office with a clear mandate, but no one wanted the protégé's tally to trump the mentor's numbers. Markov essentially agrees. "Yeah, it's not totally controlled," he says, "but nobody [wants] to give Medvedev a [greater] percentage. I call it self-winding hyper-bureaucratic loyalty. It's a real problem for United Russia and for dominating parties [elsewhere]."

Igor Mintusov knows what it takes to win a Russian election. He is the fifty-two-year-old chairman of the Niccolo M Group, one of the best-known political consulting firms in Moscow. (The name refers, of course, to Niccolò Machiavelli; Mintusov's business card features a portrait of Machiavelli, peering at you from behind a globe.) Founded in 1992, the firm has run campaigns across Russia. Nor has Mintusov's work been limited to his native land: he is well traveled, having helped direct political campaigns in Bolivia, Bulgaria, Chile, Estonia, Nicaragua, South Korea, Venezuela, and even the United States. And his services don't come cheap. Lunch with Mintusov can reportedly cost a client thousands.

When we met, I asked him which campaigns he had worked on in the United States. One was a failed Democratic gubernatorial campaign in Florida against Jeb Bush. The other, he told me, was Senator Chris Dodd's 1998 Connecticut reelection campaign. Mintusov was supposed to help with media messaging, so when he arrived, he went to meet with Dodd's campaign manager. Straightaway, Mintusov asked about the media budget. So the campaign manager showed him what he had to work with. "He pointed to the budget for research, the budget for staff, the budget for getting out the vote, things like that," recalls Mintusov. "I saw the salary for the press secretary, the expenses for equipment, office space, shipping costs, Internet, and I'm looking at it and say, 'Well, it's okay. But where's the money for working with the media?'"

The campaign manager then repeated himself, reviewing the list of salaries, expenses, and whatnot. So Mintusov asked again. "I said I understand, but where is the budget for working with the media?"

Again, the campaign manager walked down the same line items. And then it dawned on Mintusov. "Suddenly I understood that he didn't understand my question at all," says Mintusov, laughing. "Then I understood how spoiled I am in Russia!" Mintusov just assumed media, like everything else, was for sale.

It's impossible that Mintusov could work in Russian election politics for so long, be regarded a success, and still have clean hands. He described Russian campaigns to me as "wars without rules," and in this lawless environment Niccolo M had profited handsomely. Nevertheless, he claims even he had his limits. "The level of fraud in the last few years has become so extremely high that it discredited elections as elections," he told me. So, at the end of 2008, Mintusov published a book detailing the rigging that had gone on in the Duma elections in 2007 and the presidential election of 2008. In an homage to his country's most famous author, he titled it *Crime Without Punishment*.

In the murky world of Russian politics, it is hard to draw a straight line between motivations and actions. It could be true that it was some violation of integrity or lost professionalism that led Mintusov to break ranks. It also may be that the political operative had a falling-out with the ruling party's kingmakers and then saw no disadvantage to publishing his book. In either case, Mintusov told me that United Russia sent a letter to its members telling them they could no longer retain the services of Niccolo M. With that, his firm was effectively barred from 80 percent of Russia's political space. Then again, if Mintusov's description is accurate, the fraud has gotten to the point where being a political consultant is almost a pointless profession. "Because what's the point of developing a message and delivering the message well, when the result will be calculated the night after the election?" he told me.

As I was leaving, I asked him if he was familiar with the recent election involving Sergei Mitrokhin. He laughed, saying, "Yes, it's an excellent example."

Sergei Mitrokhin is the leader of Yabloko, a liberal, pro-Western opposition party. In the fall of 2009, Mitrokhin stood for reelection to the Moscow City Duma. On October 11, the day of the election, the forty-six-year-old politician cast his ballot in his home district, District 192. His family also went to District 192's ballot office to cast votes for Yabloko. He had friends who did the same. Mitrokhin did not win the election. That wasn't entirely surprising. What was surprising was the margin of defeat. "The electoral district where I voted showed that there were zero votes for Yabloko," Mitrokhin told me. According to the election rolls, not a single person had voted for Mitrokhin's party—not even Mitrokhin himself.

I met with the opposition leader at his party headquarters in downtown Moscow. Mitrokhin is a bulldozer of a man, solid, stocky, with eyes set deep beneath a furrowed brow. He was elected Yabloko's leader three years ago, and judging by even recent photographs, the experience has aged him. We talked about the difficulties of trying to operate in a political system so heavily stacked against the opposition. He agreed with Markov's explanation, that the election rigging is probably the result of "bureaucratic competition." And this competition, he noted, gives rise to an even stranger consequence. In Mitrokhin's opinion, the voting in Putin's own district is probably the cleanest in Russia. The stakes are just too high for someone to be caught red-handed. "It is very dangerous for them to falsify elections there," he says. "There is always a chance that someone will detect such fraud." It would be terribly embarrassing for tampering to occur in Putin's own district, and after all his popularity is great enough that no one thinks—including Mitrokhin—that Putin needs to stack the deck to win. And in the prime minister's district, Yabloko won nearly 20 percent of the vote. Given how hostile an environment it is for opposition parties, it's not a bad showing. "These are the realities of authoritarian regimes," he says. "If we had a democracy, we would have been in the parliament. We have to fight for survival."

The absurdity of having all of the opposition's ballots disappear was another example of Markov's self-winding hyper-bureaucratic loyalty. Amusingly, for all his defense of the system as it exists, Markov did admit that there was one downside to Russia's lack of open, unfettered political competition: it was holding him back professionally. "I am personally extremely interested in political competition because I can talk on TV," says Markov, immodestly. "My personal status is lower than it could be." Even if he wouldn't admit to the potential benefits of political competition for Russian society at large, the Kremlin insider sees no contradiction in his own personal desire for it.

Medvedev's Brain

Few people dared to expect much from Dmitri Medvedev. He was the dutiful aide who had been plucked from obscurity and made a president. Like Putin, he had never held elected office before becoming president. His name was rarely mentioned as one of those most likely to succeed Putin. It was suspected by many that whoever would follow Putin would be little more than a placeholder. The Russian constitution forbade Putin to serve three consecutive terms as president, so rather than revise the constitution, Putin simply required a reliable surrogate. If he wanted to return to the presidency, he could always do so. In this way, whoever the next president would likely be, he was just another plank in Putin's democratic facade. It took less than twenty-four hours for that impression to gain credence. On December 11, 2007, the day after Russians learned that he was Putin's choice for president, Medvedev went before television cameras and appealed to Putin to serve as his prime minister. "What is Putin's main dream? To be in power up until the end, like everyone," says Boris Nemtsov, the opposition leader. "According to our constitution, we have just two terms. That is why he suggested Medvedev as his successor. It was selection, not election."

Less than three months later, on March 2, 2008, Medvedev won in an apparent landslide. That night, wearing a leather jacket and blue jeans, he celebrated his victory alongside Putin at an outdoor rock concert in Red Square. At only forty-two, he was a young, handsome, if somewhat bland protégé. The former lawyer from St. Petersburg had done very little to distinguish himself to Russian voters, making vague pronouncements about his desire to fight corruption and promote the rule of law. As one of his current advisers told me, with so little time between his debut and his election, it wasn't as if he had any vision or program for how to lead Russia. But from Putin's perspective, that may have actually been one of his greatest qualities as a temporary successor. As Medvedev told the people in Red Square that night, his victory meant "we will be able to maintain the course suggested by President Putin."

But the mere fact that the country was being led, at least formally, by a new face gave some people a reason for hope. Medvedev did not share Putin's KGB background, and he had come of age during the reforms of the 1980s. Some noted that Medvedev had likely had a hand in some of Putin's early reforms, before he turned more auto-cratic. If nothing else, his legal training suggested that he might value the role of institutions and legal protections, not just power. Arseny Roginsky, a former Soviet dissident and the co-founder of Memorial, one of Russia's most respected NGOs, told me as much when we met in Moscow. "As a rule, the skeptics are always right in Russia," he said. "And believe me, I am not a Medvedev man. But we need hope, and we need to hope for something."

Medvedev's own words fueled those hopes. A year into his presi-dency, his speeches and remarks were frequently peppered with criticism for the political system he led. He described the country's democracy as "weak." He said the economy was "primitive." He called the country's social systems at best "semi-Soviet." In a speech to the Duma, Medvedev declared, "Our state is the biggest employer, the most active publisher, the best producer, its own judge, its own party, and, in the end, its own public. Such a system is absolutely inefficient and creates only one thing—corruption." If nothing else, Medvedev sounded like a president who understood the system and its flaws.

And that was the trouble. There was nothing else; Medvedev was long on rhetoric and short on results. From the beginning, he had talked about the dangers of corruption, and it remained unchecked. He had promised that the people behind the murders of journal-ists would be brought to justice, but cases remained unsolved. He unveiled proposals to reform the police and the Interior Ministry. Rus-sians barely noticed, and according to the Levada polling center 66 percent did not believe his reforms would accomplish anything. It did not help that in early 2010 Medvedev was publicly complaining that by his count, 38 percent of his presidential orders were ignored by governors and ministers.

Medvedev could be as hapless as he sometimes appeared. After all, he might have been the president of the Russian Federation, but it wasn't as if he had many centers of support inside his government. Putin loyalists—the ministries, the Duma, United Russia, the security services—essentially flanked him on all sides. Given how much these politicians and bureaucrats had personally benefited from the system as Putin had constructed it, what interest did they have in reform? Indeed, despite his vocal criticisms, some viewed Medvedev's role as both president and chief critic as an innovation in its own right. The tandem leadership of Medvedev and Putin took on the appearance of good cop, bad cop, with a twist. "You can see the whole tactics of Medvedev-Putin as a very interesting communication approach where Medvedev is addressing minorities and Putin is addressing majorities," says Grigory Shvedov, editor of the Russian online journal *Caucasian Knot*. "Medvedev is talking specifically about the problems. It's a very wise division. They are talking to different sides of society— those who are rich and those who are poor, those who are supporting the political rule and those who are protesting them."

Nevertheless, the signs that Medvedev might actually harbor ideas at odds with Putin's "power vertical" grew with time. And if there was one laboratory working to cultivate these ideas, it was the Institute of Contemporary Development, a liberal think tank that is said to have advised Medvedev. Medvedev served as the think tank's chairman and is rumored to have backed the founding of the organization as an independent source of analysis for his administration. (Igor Yurgens, the director of the think tank, told *Newsweek* in 2009 that Medvedev had said the Kremlin didn't need "brown-nosers.") A month before I arrived in Moscow, the institute released a report that sent a jolt through the Russian political establishment. In essence, the authors called for rolling back almost every feature of Putin's power structure. Among its proposals, the report recommended restoring the direct election of governors, creating a genuine multiparty democracy, abolishing the FSB (the successor to the KGB), and ending the state control of media.

If Medvedev had an independent streak, the researchers at this think tank may have been the ones feeding it. I went to meet with Evgeny Gontmakher, the institute's deputy director and one of the report's authors. I asked Gontmakher what was the purpose of the report. "Our main goal is as a provocation," he replied. "[The idea] is democracy—not imitation democracy. The reaction of Medvedev was very good. Unofficial, but very good." The provocation, as Gontmakher explained, was directed very much at those who typically promote less pluralistic ideas. People like Gleb Pavlovsky.

By chance, I had actually raised this report with Pavlovsky when we met a few days earlier. I told Gontmakher what Pavlovsky told me: "It is a political fiction." As soon as I mentioned it to Gontmakher, he laughed. "A propagandist. He is very clever, and he is right. It is a fiction, even science fiction." But, as he explained, in the competition for Medvedev's thinking, it didn't matter. The report had scored a victory in influencing Medvedev, and it was at odds with the direction promoted by Pavlovsky, so naturally he was disparaging it. "Pavlovsky is a very dangerous person. [His ideas] are all manipulation. It's all ideas about how to control TV, how to control our civil society. But this power vertical is not science fiction."

The institute's report had put forward a number of ideas for reform. So, I asked Gontmakher, what was the one reform that would do the most good? He didn't hesitate. "The first step is to free TV. It will be an absolutely new atmosphere here. New faces. Open discussions. It will be a new beginning in our political history. That's why Putin in the beginning closed TV. And he was right, from his position," replied Gontmakher. "But to change TV takes one day. It only requires a decision from two people."

Free TV. Not a change in election laws, not greater respect for human rights, not more genuine NGOs, not even a drop in the price of oil. It was a telling suggestion from this economist and political adviser. He would begin with freedom of speech over the airwaves. Russians already enjoy unfettered access to the Internet, and it had increasingly become a venue for political satire as well as the exposure of official wrongdoing. But even as the number of Russians online grows rapidly, as much as 80 percent of the country still gets its news and information from television. In Gontmakher's view, ending the Kremlin's ability to stifle the free flow of information, ideas, and conversation on that medium would be a good place to start.

A few months earlier Medvedev had momentarily made waves for a manifesto he published that was highly critical of the regime as it existed. I was told that the Institute of Contemporary Development had been behind this initiative as well. In many ways, this article, titled "Russia Forward," had previewed many of the ideas in the report that had brought me to speak to Evgeny Gontmakher. But what stood out to me was how the president's reformist ideas were received. Although

Russian politicos parsed the president's words, Russian state television was unimpressed. That night the news focused on a visit Putin paid to factory workers south of Moscow. Medvedev's manifesto—a proposal by a country's president to effectively remake the political system—was buried at the bottom of the broadcast. Gontmakher might be right that the effect of freeing TV in an authoritarian system such as Russia's could be powerful, perhaps immediately so. But I wasn't sure if it was a decision to be made by two people—or one.

"This Is Mubarak No. 2"

From the moment Dmitri Medvedev became president, one question loomed over Russia: Would Putin return? For four years, journalists and modern Kremlinologists parsed both men's speeches, statements, and rare public disagreements for signs of Medvedev's growing independence or Putin's nostalgia for the executive suite. Putin remained coy. He told Larry King that he and Medvedev would consult each other and "come to a decision." In September 2010, when Putin was asked about his future political plans at the Valdai group, a meeting of foreign academics and Russia experts, he reminded those assembled that Franklin Roosevelt had served four terms as U.S. president. Speculation over who would step forward as United Russia's candidate was confused by the fact that both men often acted as if they wanted the job. Putin's thirteen-hundred-mile drive across Siberia in a Russian Lada (which supposedly broke down at least twice) looked like the opening gambit of a political campaign. For his part, Medvedev repeatedly said he was open to the idea of a second term. As late as the summer of 2011, he told the *Financial Times*, "Any leader who occupies a post such as president is simply obliged to want to run for [reelection]." It often seemed as if Medvedev were simply waiting for Putin to tell him if he could.

A year and a half before the decision would be announced, I asked Nemtsov, the opposition leader, who he thought would become president in 2012. "I think the chance for Medvedev is 10 percent, and for Putin it is 90 percent," he replied. When Medvedev became president in 2008, one of his early moves (with almost no public discussion) was to lengthen the presidential term of office from four to six years.

That meant that if Putin were to return, he could serve another twelve years as president. This fact seemed to concern Nemtsov most. "The worst scenario for Russia is if Putin comes back," he said. "This is terrible. It means that he will run the country for twenty-five years [in total]. This is Mubarak No. 2."

On September 24, 2011, at United Russia's party congress, the speculation came to an end. Speaking to a packed hall of eleven thousand party members, Medvedev managed a slight smile when he said, "I think it would be correct for the congress to support the candidacy of the party chairman, Vladimir Putin, to the post of president of the country." The hall instantly filled with applause as the crowd rose to its feet. In the new arrangement, the two men would simply swap roles, with Putin returning to the presidency and Medvedev going to the prime minister's office. When Putin walked to the podium to address the crowd, he paused and tapped the microphone. It appeared to be malfunctioning. Then, making light of it, he told the assembled party faithful it wasn't necessary: "Nothing can stop us. I have not lost my commander's voice." The election was six months away, but the matter appeared to be settled: Putin was back—if indeed he had ever left.

In retrospect, Medvedev's years seemed to be destined to become a historical footnote, a bridge connecting one chapter of Putin's rule to another. But what could Putin claim to be returning to do? When he first took office in 2000, he had promised Russians stability and certainty. He had promised Russian families that they would be able to plan for their children's future "not one month at a time, but for years and decades." But eleven years on, those promises rang hollow. Indeed, on the eve of the announcement of Putin's return, an independent Russian poll indicated 75 percent of Russians still did not plan more than two years ahead, and 22 percent of Russians wanted to move abroad, a threefold increase from four years earlier and the highest percentage since the collapse of the Soviet Union.

Although Putin remained more popular than any other political figure, his poll numbers had been in decline for months. Russians began to draw unflattering comparisons between Putin and the eighteen-year reign of the Soviet leader Leonid Brezhnev. (Two additional presidential terms would make Putin the longest-serving Russian ruler since Stalin.) The sentiment was probably best captured by a Photoshopped image that quickly went viral on the Internet: it was of an aged Putin wearing one of Brezhnev's old Soviet uniforms, the chest covered in military medals. Putin may have promised stability, but it increasingly felt like stagnation.

But in December 2011 the stasis that had long settled over Russian political life was unexpectedly shaken. On December 4, Russians cast ballots in the country's Duma elections. As in recent contests, the vote was rigged. In the hours after the polls closed, videos of ballot stuffing, multiple voting, and other violations were posted on YouTube and spread quickly. However, unlike past elections, the Russian people were no longer mere spectators to the fraud. Tens of thousands of citizens poured out into Moscow's streets for two massive antigovernment rallies before the month's end, the largest protests in Russia since the collapse of the Soviet Union. Like almost all of the popular uprisings against authoritarian regimes in 2011, the movement lacked a clear leadership. It was, in some sense, a "power horizontal"—perhaps the perfect antidote to Putin's carefully crafted "power vertical."

The Kremlin advisers and members of United Russia I had spoken to had stressed the regime's ability to manufacture stability and keep a close watch on public sentiment. But Putin and his team proved to have a tin ear. The gross manipulation of the Duma elections, following close on the heels of the brazen announcement that Putin intended to return to the presidency, had provoked an educated, middle-class public long considered apathetic. It is, in fact, a familiar pattern in authoritarian systems. Where the results are manufactured and the outcomes are largely predetermined, a regime's officials will overreach or commit gaffes, sometimes extremely embarrassing ones, in an attempt to prolong their power. The danger for the regime is that these mistakes, when they are revealed, serve as sparks for greater opposition or protest to the legitimacy of the government's rule. It was precisely this chain of causation—regime insecurity, a stolen election, and public outrage—that inspired the Green Movement to take to the streets in Iran in 2009 and helped stoke the fires that ultimately toppled Egypt's Hosni Mubarak in 2011.

Indeed, stealing elections has been a trigger for the end of many dictatorships. Activists will tell you the reason is simple. The public often feels removed from the struggle between an opposition and a regime, inclined to view both sides with suspicion. The contest seems ideological, separate from people's daily concerns. But when the state has stolen your vote, the battle becomes far more personal. If the discontent is real, people who would never have been expected to demonstrate or march come out because they feel as though something personal has been stolen from them. Those are the moments that can transform a small opposition of rabble rousers into a national movement for change.

Putin had no intention of ceding power easily. In short order, the Kremlin began to demonstrate the skills which had long kept genuine political change at bay. Its response was crafted to create internal rifts within the opposition. Reviled regime figures were jettisoned. The Russian oligarch Mikhail Prokhorov announced that he would challenge Putin at the upcoming presidential elections, a move many suspected was engineered by the Kremlin to persuade demonstrators that they had already achieved a partial victory. In his first televised response to the protests, Putin even said he was "pleased" to see "young, active people formulating their opinions." He tried to link his government to the new public mood, saying, "If this is the result of the Putin regime, then that's good."

Of course, the people were in the streets because of the "Putin regime"—but not because it had fostered a robust civil society. Indeed, it was quite the opposite. Putin had come to power promising Russians a return to stability. Twelve years later, it was his disregard for those same people that had sparked the country's turmoil.

CHAPTER 2   ENEMIES OF THE STATE

I wasn't safe for Pu Zhiqiang to go home. Or, to be more precise, he could go home, but once there he might not be able to leave again. Over the previous forty-eight hours, Chinese authorities had detained more than a dozen lawyers and activists. More than eighty dissidents had been put under house arrest. Two lawyers simply disappeared. Pu, a well-known free speech attorney, was among the so-called rights lawyers who might be swept up in any regime crackdown. (He had been detained a few months earlier, shortly before the Chinese scholar and dissident Liu Xiaobo received the Nobel Peace Prize.) Pu wasn't sure why he had not been targeted yet. But he had a guess: he had been away on a business trip for a week. He simply hadn't been home. When I reached him, he was still in Shanghai and planning to return to Beijing in a few days. He gave me the name of a teahouse near his apartment where we could meet. I was supposed to meet him there on a Saturday evening. Just to be safe, he would land at Beijing Capital International Airport and go directly to the teahouse. Otherwise, our meeting might never happen. As Pu told me, "Some leader will tell the secret police: 'No, Mr. Pu cannot meet [anyone] tomorrow.'"

I had arrived in China ten days after the fall of Hosni Mubarak. Journalists and television crews were still walking the streets that led to Tahrir Square, capturing first-person accounts of how the Egyptian people had risen up and forced an end to a dictator's rule. The revolution that had begun in Tunisia and then spread to Egypt was now ricocheting across the Middle East and North Africa. Each day there were new reports of popular rebellions cropping up in Yemen, Bahrain, Libya, Jordan, Iran, and elsewhere.

In China, there had been little more than a whisper. A few days earlier, an anonymous call for a Chinese Jasmine Revolution—a reference to the popular rebellion that had begun in Tunisia—had spread over social media sites and the Chinese equivalent of Twitter. It had not gone any further. The Arab world's revolutions had not inspired marches, rallies, or protests against the Chinese Communist Party. Still, despite being far removed from the epicenter of those protests, Beijing was on edge. The sheer fact that a growing wave of people thousands of miles away were rising up to challenge authoritarian regimes made the Chinese leadership nervous. In a special meeting the day after Mubarak was toppled, China's senior leaders discussed the need to tighten control of all media and online discussion of the events in the Middle East. Any mention of "jasmines" was scrubbed from Web sites, chat rooms, and discussion boards. A week later, Hu Jintao brought together top party leaders for a special "study session" in which he reminded them of the need to maintain the country's stability in the face of rising social demands.

I saw evidence of the regime's anxiety as soon as I checked into my hotel room. I turned on CNN International as I unpacked my suitcase, listening as the anchor interviewed an analyst on the rebellions that were erupting in Libya and elsewhere. As soon as the anchor asked how China's leaders might be interpreting events, my television's screen went dark. Roughly a minute later, the TV screen came back, just in time for me to see the anchor thank her guest for his analysis. The regime did not mind if CNN reported on events in the Arab world, but it did not want anyone speculating about what those events could mean for China.

It was clear what this crackdown could mean for Pu. Scores of lawyers and activists—people he considered colleagues, people he admired—had already been detained, and he fully expected he could be next. The wide scope of the arrests had surprised people inside and outside China and suggested that the regime was looking to redefine the red lines of what was permissible. In the weeks that followed, the government would round up even more people, including prominent dissidents like the artist and filmmaker Ai Weiwei. But despite the risks, Pu was determined we meet. At 9:00 p.m., he walked into the teahouse in the Fengtai District, about thirty minutes from downtown Beijing, on the city's Fourth Ring Road. He strode across the room and greeted me with a firm handshake.

Pu has a powerful presence. With a crew cut and a strong jaw, this rights lawyer is large and solidly built. His shoulders and limbs seemed to occupy his entire side of the booth. With a cigarette and a wry grin, he speaks in short declarative bursts, with more of a growl than a voice. Of course, the secret police know we are meeting, he told me straightaway. His phones are tapped, so they heard every word. And they are never very far away. In Shanghai, Pu's minders stayed in the same hotel as he did, and they flew back to Beijing on the same plane. Knowing that they had listened in on the phone call, Pu informed them of our meeting a day earlier, although he tried to allay their concerns. "I told them we set this appointment a long time ago, that it has nothing to do with the thing you care about, the jasmines," says Pu. "If you try to stop me from meeting someone, that's illegal. You can do your job, but you cannot stop me from doing what I'm doing. If you disagree, detain me, take me away."

I had never met Pu, so I was surprised to hear how brazenly he addressed the security officers who tailed him everywhere. What did they say? I asked. "They didn't say anything," Pu replied, taking a long drag on his cigarette. "I told them without asking them. I meet my friends with their permission? Bullshit."

The parking lot outside the teahouse was pitch-black. Whether they were watching us from outside, we had no way of knowing. Pu didn't think so, but he couldn't be sure. Either way, one of China's top free speech attorneys wanted to talk, and he wasn't going to be told otherwise.

The Tyrant's Tools

Today's twenty-first-century authoritarians crave the type of legitimacy that only the law can provide. For regimes that seek to mask their true nature behind a democratic facade, the law is one of the most powerful weapons they can wield. It offers the government the pretense it requires to accomplish its aims, all without stepping out of the shadows. Thus, if you seek to disband an NGO, you don't arrest its membership. You send health inspectors to temporarily close its headquarters, pending a review of a series of alleged health code violations. If you are troubled by what a radio station is broadcasting, you don't have the Ministry of Telecommunication force it off the airwaves. Rather, you send tax inspectors to audit the station's books and find financial irregularities that require the station's temporary closure. In fact, even this step may be unnecessary. The mere threat of legal sanctions or administrative review may encourage the radio station's management to engage in the very self-censorship that accomplishes the regime's ends—all without ever inflicting the punishment. Law, regulation, and procedure can be a dictator's most effective tools for strangling an opponent, precisely because these weapons appear to be benign, apolitical, and objective.

The picture is made more complicated by the regimes' dependence on law for stability and development. Most governments— whether authoritarian or not—appreciate the value of an impartial judicial system. Reliable and professionally administered courts offer a way for citizens to resolve conflicts and reduce the desire to seek redress through protests or public demonstrations. They encourage business and foreign investment, while tamping down corruption and graft. But a reliable legal system becomes problematic once it begins to threaten the regime's political monopoly. Authoritarian regimes that enlist the law to facilitate their rule open themselves up to a small but real vulnerability: if the regime can seek refuge in the law, so too can its opponents. Zhang Jingjing is sometimes referred to as the "Erin Brockovich of China." An environmental attorney, she has won some of the largest class action suits against Chinese companies and has often found herself at odds with Chinese Communist Party officials. "The Communist Party always talks about law; they want to rule the country by law," Zhang told me in her Beijing office. "I advocate for the rule of law, but it is different. My law is different from the party's law."

Across authoritarian regimes, lawyers, activists, and political organizations have proven adept at using a regime's own rules against it. In China, rights attorneys like Pu Zhiqiang have taken up the cases of the society's most defenseless and forced the regime to defend itself on exposed ground. Chinese officials may still violate the law, but the fact that they attempt to appear to be working within the confines of legal procedure offers weaknesses for others to exploit. The Russian government may regularly ignore its own legal code, but its desire to maintain close ties to European countries has opened it up to the rulings of international courts like the European Court of Human Rights. Political organizers and protesters understand that authoritarian regimes often base themselves on legal fictions. But by acting as if these legal fictions are genuine, they can stymie a regime's efforts to run roughshod over its citizenry. Even if the regime is seemingly all-powerful, its own laws—and the hypocrisy of flouting them—can constrain its ability to act, and thereby embolden others to challenge the regime. None of these lawyers or activists have any illusions about the corruption of the courts or the integrity of the political systems they seek to change. Nevertheless, they work patiently, brick by brick, to expose legal inconsistencies and deceits, creating minor victories that ripple throughout the system. Yevgenia Chirikova, one of Russia's most outspoken and effective environmental activists, explained it to me this way. In her view, whether she wins or loses, almost any result could be used to her advantage in an authoritarian system. "Sometimes the losses produce the bigger impressions on society. I would accept almost any outcome because they would be equally good for me," she told me. "We will show that our government lies."

For authoritarians seeking the legitimacy that only the law can offer, the law—even their own twisted version of it—can leave them appearing naked and utterly illegitimate. Ultimately, it may come down to no more than that.

Stubborn Blood

Pu Zhiqiang credits two fathers for making him who he is today—"the father who gave me life, and the father who raised me." When Pu was growing up in a rural village in Hebei Province, his family was of modest means but relatively well-off compared with most of their neighbors. He described his biological father as honest and of "stubborn blood." "I'm stubborn too, and I have this persistent character that even if I think things stand in the way, I will not change my attitude," Pu told me as we waited for our tea. He was raised by his uncle, who was an entrepreneur and businessman before the founding of the People's Republic in 1949. Although he had supported the revolution, Pu's uncle was persecuted by the Communists after they came to power. It was a bitter lesson he passed on to his nephew. "He would tell me, 'The Communist Party doesn't keep their promises. They don't have morals.'"

Pu and his siblings were quick studies. Of the six people in their village who made it to college, three of them came from the Pu family. Pu was particularly bright. On the college entrance examinations, he had the highest score from the county and was ranked in the top hundred for the whole province. (Nearly two million students stood for the exams nationally that year.) On those scores, Pu was accepted into Nankai University, one of China's most prestigious universities, where he studied history and classical Chinese. Once there, he attracted the interest of the Communist Youth League, which was eager to recruit promising young students. One of Pu's professors approached him and asked him if he wanted to join the Communist Party. If he did, the professor could help. "I told him, 'Give me a week to think about it.'" Seven days later Pu came back with his answer. He told his professor, "I will never join this party." He was nineteen at the time. He understood the costs of making such a decision, as well as the benefits he was forgoing by not joining. Membership in the party would potentially offer privileges, and it would certainly be good for his career. But he hadn't forgotten his uncle's lesson: the party couldn't be trusted. In Pu's opinion, even as a young history student, the Communist Party's chief skill was its ability to fabricate history. "They make people and things disappear according to their needs," he told me. He felt strongly enough to make the decision that he did. And, once he did, his "persistent character" ensured he never looked back. As he put it, "I closed my door when I was nineteen."

He may have closed a door, but he had not paid his biggest price until several years later, in 1989. As a graduate student at the China University of Political Science and Law, Pu organized his fellow classmates and led the first group of students from his university to Tiananmen Square. He participated in the hunger strike in the square, and he remained there until June 4, when Chinese soldiers opened fire on the protesters and sent the students running for their lives. In the aftermath of the massacre, Pu refused to cooperate with authorities or recant his role in the protests. In fact, far from recanting, he honored the students who died that night by returning to the square on the anniversary. In the scramble to dodge the soldiers' bullets, Pu had made a promise. "I promised myself that if I make it out alive tonight, I'll come back every year," he told me. For the past three years, he has been detained by police, who keep the square under tight security as the anniversary approaches.

But his refusal to help the party cleanse this stain on its history by recanting is what has caused him the most trouble. Pu had planned on becoming a professor, but when he graduated, no one would hire the star pupil. "If you refuse to admit things, you cannot be a teacher," he explained. "I've been paying the price over the years."

Pu struggled to find work after graduation. He drifted from one dead-end job to the next. With an elderly mother and a young family to care for, he felt the pressure of providing for others, but he didn't want a job that required him to compromise on his beliefs. "I didn't want to change my mind about what the Communist Party had done in 1989," says Pu. One of his former teachers recommended he try becoming an attorney. Pu studied the law in his spare time and passed the bar in 1995.

The law was the perfect refuge. Pu could take on commercial work that helped him provide for his family, but he eventually found a higher purpose in the law. He believed that if he took the right cases, he could challenge the very party whose methods he detested. Pu told me how he had been deeply influenced by two things he read: the Chinese dissident Hu Ping's essays on free speech and the U.S. Supreme Court decision *New York Times v. Sullivan*, a landmark case for freedom of the press. The man with the "stubborn blood," who refused the party's invitation and then refused to help cover up its crimes, would work to help others hold on to their beliefs and speak their minds. "We hoped to change the system on June 4, 1989," Pu told me. "I used to think that I could turn the sky and the ground around. [Now] I think maybe I can do one or two things that matter in my lifetime."

One of the earliest free speech cases Pu took on was the defense of *China Reform* magazine. In an article titled "Who Is Splitting the Fat?," a journalist named Liu Ping reported on how a Chinese real estate development company's business dealings had resulted in massive losses that led to workers being laid off. Liu based his reporting on official documents, as well as the corporation's own filings. Outside China, it would be a fairly unremarkable story. Nevertheless, in what is a familiar tactic, the company sued the magazine for libel, seeking more than $700,000 in damages, a sum that would have effectively shuttered the publication. After hearing Pu's defense of Liu and his reporting, the Guangzhou court ruled that journalists could not be held liable for news stories that were based on credible sources. One of Pu's first defamation cases became a milestone for Chinese free speech protections.

Pu quickly took on more. He defended newspapers, magazines, and writers whose work offended powerful party bosses. Pu had begun to make a name for himself as one of China's leading free speech attorneys. He was not always successful, indeed not usually. Sometimes the best outcome was to prevent there from being any outcome at all. For example, there was the case of Chen Guidi and Wu Chuntao. The husband-and-wife team had written a best-selling book that detailed the tyranny and abuse meted out by a local party official in Fuyang, a city in the hardscrabble eastern province of Anhui. Zhang Xide, the official exposed in Chen and Wu's book, sued the authors for defamation of character. Typically, defendants like Chen and Wu would stand no chance. When a party official is sitting in the plaintiff's chair, it is hardly a surprise that judges, who are themselves party members, rule in favor of their political masters. But Pu made that outcome next to impossible. In his cross-examinations, he aggressively attacked the prosecution's witnesses, putting the spotlight on the corrupt practices that had marked Zhang's rule. Even more effectively, Pu called a string of witnesses, most of them poor peasants, who recounted story after story of Zhang's corruption, abuse, and draconian enforcement of the one-child policy. Each witness's testimony added further evidence of the claims made in Chen and Wu's book. As Philip Pan, a *Washington Post* reporter who attended the trial, wrote, the court faced a terrible choice: "It could ignore the evidence [Pu] presented in open court about Zhang's transgressions and rule against the authors, risking a backlash that could further erode the party's legitimacy. Or it could reject Zhang's lawsuit and send a powerful message to the public about the law as a weapon against the party."

Confronted with such a dilemma, the court chose a different tack: it issued no decision at all. When Pu and I met, it had been more than six years since those legal proceedings had ended. And still there had been no verdict. For a free speech attorney in China, that counts as a win.

What struck me most as Pu talked into the night about how he worked the seams of his country's authoritarian system was the way he dealt with the people he knew best: the secret police dispatched to monitor his every move. His tactic, as much as anything, seemed to be to humanize them. They may be on opposite ends of a fundamental disagreement—whether the rule of the Chinese Communist Party is legitimate or not—but that did not erase his interest in dealing with them as people. When I raised this with him, his brawny frame rose in its seat. "I respect them, I respect them. I constantly tell them what the procedures are," Pu replied, stubbing out his fourth cigarette to emphasize the point. "If you come to my office and you want to detain me, okay, then there's a procedure to go through. You need a certificate to do that. They can't provide it, so the result is we have dinner, we drink, we talk with each other. We need to face the secret police. Why not try to change them, if you have the chance to do that?"

Has he succeeded? It's almost impossible to know. When they are pressed and Pu corners his security minders with the force of his argument, they admit they agree with some of what he says, but then they fall back on familiar excuses: We have no choice. If we weren't working for the state's security apparatus, what would we be doing? Pu tells them that they are selling themselves short, that they have options above and beyond those presented by the state. And then he leaves them something to ponder. "I tell them, 'China is going through a transformation. We're about the same age. Twenty years from now, what will you tell your children you were doing during the transformative years?'" says Pu.

Like most things, it's an argument Pu thinks he can win, if only because the other side doesn't have a persuasive case. "The people that

I meet, they have no sense of pride in what they're doing," he tells me. "The ideology and the legitimacy of the party has already disappeared. It's naked interests. The slogans, they don't work anymore. They need to buy people; they need to pay them for them to do anything." They may be threatened or coerced or they may be bribed, but either way the costs of running the regime are rising.

Near the end of our hours together, I asked Pu how he thought the revolutions stretching across North Africa and the Middle East were affecting China's leadership. "They are getting more afraid, and there are less choices for them. They have this need to maintain stability, and the regime, Hu and Wen, appears to be less confident than when they took power." The most immediate evidence of that insecurity was the lengths to which Pu and I had to go to even meet on this evening. Again, Pu drew conclusions from the faces of the regime he knew best. "They are very cautious; they're nervous, very nervous," he told me, speaking of the security detail following him around. "Many of them have accompanied me to dinner just because of these [revolutions in the Middle East]." He would tell them they are wasting their time. Pu isn't a protest organizer, and he isn't rallying people to take to the streets. If the regime has enemies, it's because it creates them, he says. "You make so many enemies, and you don't have the guts to face your enemies," he told them. "You should find ways to prove that you are different from Gaddafi." I asked him how his friends in the secret police replied. "They agreed with that," he said.

It was now well past midnight. We walked out of the teahouse, down the street, and toward Yihai Garden, the compound of apartments where Pu lives. It was already Sunday, and the second anonymous call for a Chinese "Jasmine Revolution" had gone out, asking people to assemble in nearly two dozen sites across China later that day. Neither one of us expected much would come from it, but it was significant that the online call had been made at all. For Pu, the bigger question was whether the government would restrict his movements through some form of house arrest. "A lot of things have happened to other people, and I hope I don't make trouble for myself, but I am not afraid of trouble," he told me. Pu said there was only one thing certain about tomorrow. "He will come," referring to a member of the secret police. As I got in a cab and rode away, I saw Pu walk through the gates of his apartment's compound. He nodded to the security guard on duty as he entered.

The Accidental Activist

Yevgenia Chirikova moved to Khimki for the forest. In 2000, she and her husband decided it was time to leave the urban confines of Moscow for a more natural setting. Their jobs required that they stay close to the city, but they wanted to find a more peaceful place to raise a family. They settled on Khimki, a small community about an hour northwest of Moscow. At first glance, this town of nearly 200,000 isn't particularly picturesque. Most of Khimki's residents live in drab, Soviet-era apartment buildings arranged on grids with narrow rows of sidewalks and strips of grass between them. During the height of the Cold War, Khimki was a closed city, off-limits to any foreigners and most Russians because of the strategically important work its townspeople did. Locals worked in several aerospace defense factories, churning out surface-to-air missiles and advanced engines to power Soviet intercontinental ballistic missiles. But Yevgenia and her husband moved to the suburban enclave because of one of its other vestiges: the Khimki Forest Park.

Covering an area of roughly twenty-five hundred acres, the Khimki Forest is a rarity in Russia—a publicly protected green space. The land is said to have been one of the czars' favorite spots for hunting boars. The boars—along with elk, foxes, rabbit, and many species of birds—still wander the dense oak groves, but the expanse of wild forest has dwindled to its present size after decades of development. Nevertheless, what was left had been set aside as environmentally protected lands; indeed, the Khimki woods had received the government's highest level of green zoning, ensuring that it would remain free from commercial use. (The law was so stringent that, technically, anyone found guilty of cutting down a tree in a specially designated "forest park" could be punished with prison time.) So, seeking a refuge of their own, Yevgenia and her husband bought a house at the edge of the forest. "When we lived in Moscow, it was just so polluted, and over here it was very green and peaceful and nice," says Yevgenia. "We decided it was the place to be."

In 2008, Yevgenia was at home on maternity leave with her second child. She bundled up her baby girl and five-year-old daughter and went for a walk in the woods. As she made her way under the oaks, she noticed something she had never seen before: many trees had been marked with red paint, and others had small cuts in the trunks. When she returned home, she went online to investigate. There, sitting with her husband, she found a document from the office of the region's governor, Boris Gromov, that explained why the trees behind her house had been painted red: Khimki Forest had been marked for demolition. It was to be clear-cut to make way for a new highway between Moscow and St. Petersburg. The governor's order left Yevgenia confused. She knew the land was legally protected. She thought it must be a mistake. If she just wrote a letter and informed the proper authorities, she was sure the error would be corrected. Recalling that day, she says, "I was very naive."

There hadn't been a mistake. After writing ten letters to the authorities, she received a pro forma reply from the government saying it was a normal project and it was going forward. But in truth, there was nothing normal about the construction that the local authorities had in mind. No one in the Khimki community had been informed about the project or the destruction of their forest. The only public notice of the project appeared in a small local paper, sandwiched between advertisements for fortune-telling, and failed to even mention Khimki Forest or the new highway. What was most odd, however, was the route that the highway would take. Initially, the road would follow the path that had been carved out many years earlier for the October railway line that connects Moscow to St. Petersburg. That railway follows a direct path between the cities. This proposed highway, however, would make a curious detour. After crossing the Moscow Ring Road, it veers sharply toward the northeast, directly through Khimki's forestland. Once it has passed through the seven kilometers of the forest, the road loops back to the October railway line's more direct route and continues to St. Petersburg. Yevgenia pulled out a map of the area and sketched the path of the planned highway construction for me with her finger. The proposed ten-lane highway literally takes a sudden detour to careen into these pristine lands. "In fact, this road [would] run through all the protected territories we have in this area,"

Yevgenia tells me. Nevertheless, by the time she had taken her walk in the woods and discovered the trees marked to be bulldozed, Governor Gromov and Khimki's mayor, Vladimir Strelchenko, had already approved the project.

It's impossible to know for certain why the authorities had set a path that would cut through the heart of Khimki Forest. A government as opaque as Russia's isn't in the habit of offering its citizens explanations, and the deliberations among Governor Gromov, Mayor Strelchenko, and the minister of transportation, Igor Levitin, have never been made public. Yevgenia and her neighbors can only speculate.

The most obvious explanation is money. Charting a path through environmentally protected lands—an area that has no private land—would avoid creating disputes that result in paying compensation to landowners along the highway's path. Civil engineers would not be required to build tunnels, overpasses, and ramps to navigate preexisting development. But the potential profits are probably an even greater motive. The highway's detour through Khimki Forest would bring the road extremely close to Sheremetyevo International Airport, the second largest in the country. Any road that links Moscow and St. Petersburg, enjoys close proximity to an international airport, and could have generous-sized lots with century-old oaks dotted along the way would be a developer's dream. The corruption and graft that surround Russia's construction industry are the stuff of legend. According to a Russian anticorruption group, new roads in Russia cost roughly $237 million a kilometer; in the United States, it is roughly $6 million for the same distance. Russian roads, it is safe to say, are some of the most expensive in the world. (Incidentally, the government gets very little for its money; its roadway infrastructure is ranked 111th, among the world's worst.) The government officials approving the highway project almost certainly stood to benefit personally.

There existed a clear conflict of interest for Igor Levitin, the minister of transportation. "He is the director of Sheremetyevo airport," Yevgenia explains. "So at one and the same time he is a minister and private entrepreneur." In fact, Levitin is the head of several commercial enterprises tied to the airport; among them, he was chairman of the board of directors of Aeroflot, which is based at Sheremetyevo. "I asked the bureaucrats, 'How could that be?' They said, 'Very simple. When he's in the ministry, he is the minister. When he comes to the airport, he is the minister as well, but he represents the interests of private business, too.'" Yevgenia looked at me with disbelief.

With her two baby girls in tow, Yevgenia returned to the forest. This time, she came armed with flyers to post on some of the same trees the government planned to clear. Her flyers told residents about the planned highway construction and encouraged them to come to her house for an organizational meeting. More than a hundred people showed up to the first meeting. She was surprised by the turnout. Like her, many of her neighbors wanted to help save the community's forest. Soon, with the help of fellow residents, she founded the group Defenders of Khimki Forest. She created a Web site for her movement, www.ecmo.ru; began organizing demonstrations, protests, and rallies; started a petition drive; and worked with local journalists to publicize her efforts to preserve the very thing that drew her to this community. Yevgenia didn't realize it right away, but her transformation into a grassroots environmental activist had begun. "An organization like Greenpeace is trying to rescue or save a forest in some place far away like Siberia or Sochi, but they are not involved in smaller, local problems," she says. "We had to do it ourselves."

It is safe to assume that if the Kremlin even had known who Yevgenia Chirikova was, it would have never perceived her as a threat. The petite thirty-three-year-old mother of two with blue eyes, a delicate figure, and a round, smiling face doesn't look like a troublemaker. She earned good grades studying electrical engineering at Moscow Aviation University. Later, she studied for her M.B.A. and spent several years working as a management consultant, before joining her husband in the engineering firm he founded before they married. She wasn't raised in a political family, and growing up, she had no interest in social issues. Like most Russians, she considered politics a remote activity, something to be viewed from a distance, best left to elites or other powerful interests. "I didn't know anything about elections. I never participated in anything. I was an absolutely nonpolitical person," she tells me. "My family did not cultivate in me civic feelings, the feeling that you are a citizen and you are in charge of your country and in charge of what's going on around you." A few moments later, smiling, she says, "There were no signs in my childhood that I would become a fighter."

The first time that Yevgenia and I met was at a popular Italian restaurant near Moscow's Pushkin Square. She greeted me with a smile and a firm handshake. Over three hours, her most striking feature wasn't her friendly demeanor; it was her gift for strategic thinking. Every challenge she detailed, every scenario she described, was broken down and diagnosed. Every government action was analyzed and dissected and met with a logical and well-reasoned response from her and her small band of supporters. She attributed much of her approach to her business school education, but to me it seemed more innate. "I understand that no one can withstand constant pressure," she said between sips of her cappuccino. "Even strong people like our mayor and governor cannot withstand systematic pressure. If I have a little more time, like two years, I am sure we are going to fend off Putin, too . . . if we are systematic and persistent." She would have seemed entirely methodical, if her personality wasn't so warm. Here was Napoleon, without the complex.

If she was looking for a fight, she soon found it. People who had signed up to join Yevgenia's campaign quickly became targets of harassment. The group's meetings were disrupted or banned by officials. Police officers fined activists for handing out leaflets; some supporters were detained arbitrarily. Authorities held sham public hearings that they would abruptly end as soon as citizens began to voice their complaints. Supporters began to receive threatening phone calls. "One of my colleagues, she was threatened to have her eyes gouged out," Yevgenia recalls. "The next day she stopped working with us."

The threats were real. Her close friend and one of the grassroots supporters of the effort to save Khimki Forest was Mikhail Beketov, a local journalist. A former Russian paratrooper and enormous bear of a man, Beketov established a small paper in 2006 with a circulation of roughly ten thousand called the *Khimkinskaya Pravda,* or *Khimki Truth.* When the government's plans to turn the forest into timber were revealed, Yevgenia says that Beketov was the first journalist to write about it. Week after week, Beketov criticized government officials for their backroom deals and the corruption that he believed was behind their plans. He began to receive threatening phone calls. He found his dog dead on his doorstep. After he called for the resignation of Khimki's mayor, his car was blown up in the middle of the night. But Beketov did not let up. Then, in November 2008, when he returned home from a trip to the grocery store, he was beaten and left for dead outside his house on the edge of Khimki Forest. A neighbor found him unconscious in the snow the next day. The beating was so severe he was left with permanent brain damage. He lost a leg, and three of his fingers had to be amputated. When he woke from his coma, he had no memory of how many attackers there had been. Even in his Khimki hospital bed, he remained a target; someone called the room to say he would come back to finish him. "It's a very sad story," Yevgenia says as she comes to the end. "After Beketov was attacked, the mayor thought we would close our mouths, there would be no more protests, there would be nothing in the newspapers. But it was a mistake. Beketov is paralyzed at the moment, but the whole world knows about him." She pulls out a map of the Moscow region and puts it on the table between us. "Look on this map, Khimki Forest is not even marked. It is so small, but it has become important."

Of course, there is no proof that the authorities ordered the attack on Beketov. According to the Committee to Protect Journalists, Russia was until recently the third-deadliest country in the world in which to be a journalist, behind only Iraq and the Philippines. Just as troubling, almost all the attacks or murders of journalists in Russia remain unsolved. (Between 2000 and 2010, 18 journalists were murdered with no one held accountable.) And the Khimki struggle is no exception. Yevgenia points out that the politicians Putin has charged with governing the Moscow region don't have a typical political pedigree. The governor, Gromov, led the Fortieth Army during the Soviet invasion of Afghanistan and was the last Soviet commander to leave the war-torn country. Khimki's mayor is another veteran of the Afghan campaign. In Yevgenia's view, they only understand force, and they underestimated the public relations disaster that would result from Beketov's attempted murder. "Clever politicians do not kill journalists," she says.

Far from being intimidated, Yevgenia stepped up her campaign. Her supporters issued press releases and contacted every journalist who would listen to tell the story of what happened to Mikhail Beketov. Stories appeared in papers across Russia and Europe. "We analyzed our situation, and we understood that the less people or activists use media, the less that they are known, the more danger they face. This is not a guarantee, of course," says Yevgenia. "But openness is our main weapon."

Openness—and Russian election laws. Nothing could be more public than to challenge the mayor directly. So, in the fall of 2009, Yevgenia decided that she would run against Strelchenko for mayor of Khimki. It was a bold gambit. She had no illusions about her chances of defeating United Russia's candidate for mayor. She was relatively unknown, had no money to finance a campaign, and wouldn't be permitted any media attention. Instead, as she explained, "The election campaign was a part of my forest campaign." Strategically, she had three goals. First, by merely challenging Khimki's mayor, she would gain attention for her cause. She decided to run as a single-issue candidate, so everywhere she went she talked about one thing: the preservation of Khimki's environment. Second, she had a tactical goal. The day she announced her candidacy, she filed two applications. The first was the necessary paperwork to enter the election. The second was a request to hold a local referendum on the cancellation of the highway construction project. She had calculated that if the mayor believed he would receive enough pressure on the project, from both her election campaign and the prospect of a referendum, he might scrap his support for the plan. She was right. "In three days, the mayor canceled his edict," says Yevgenia. "He was forced to cancel. If he would have stayed with his approval of this routing, he would have lost a lot of voters during the election." Several weeks later, Governor Gromov also withdrew his order approving the highway's route through the forest.

Her third goal was to use her candidacy as a test of the strength of her cause. She wanted to know just how much environmental issues weighed on voters in Russia and in Khimki in particular. Ultimately, she was only allowed to campaign for seven days. Even though she had paid the necessary fees, twice local authorities claimed she had not, barring her from campaigning. But in those seven days, the mother of two turned activist secured enough support to win 15 percent of the vote. It was a bigger foothold than she had ever expected to gain.

The fact that both the governor and the mayor had withdrawn their construction orders was only a temporary victory. On November 5, 2009, Prime Minister Putin stepped into the battle over Khimki Forest. On that day, he signed a decree saying that the environmentally protected forest could be rezoned as land for a commercial highway or construction project. The problem for Putin is that according to Russian federal law, his decree is actually illegal. The country's federal law forbids changing the use of protected forestland if alternative routes for construction are available. Of course, it would be easy enough for the Transportation Ministry to claim that there were no viable alternatives. Unfortunately for Putin, a year earlier the deputy minister of transport had officially admitted that other routes did exist. Yevgenia's group immediately launched a legal challenge to Putin's order in Russian courts and brought a suit in the European Court of Human Rights in Strasbourg, France. Again, Yevgenia has no illusions about her ability to challenge Putin in his own courts. Smiling, she says, "In life, you can have only one choice, which has been selected by Putin."

But for Putin and his political allies, Yevgenia had yet to exact her biggest price. To build this increasingly controversial highway between Moscow and St. Petersburg, the Russian government was counting on foreign financing from the European Bank for Reconstruction and Development and the European Investment Bank. In fact, roughly two-thirds of the money to build the highway was going to come from European banks. Yevgenia saw the foreign money as the Russian government's soft spot. She knew that the European public would be much less tolerant of its banks financing a construction project that promised to damage the environment. So she shifted part of her campaign to reach that foreign audience. For example, the French construction firm Vinci had signed on to the construction project. So Yevgenia and her fellow activists staged a protest in which they piled "Khimki firewood" outside the firm's office in Moscow. Yevgenia also reached out to Europe's Green parties. The Greens in the European Parliament passed a resolution warning the Continent's investors off the Khimki project. More than forty environmental organizations from Russia and abroad signed an open letter insisting that European banks and companies steer clear of Khimki. Ultimately, the resolution, media coverage, and Yevgenia's own lobbying convinced the European Bank for Reconstruction and Development and the European Investment Bank to suspend their funding. The cost to the Russian government was more than $750 million in foreign investment. It was an enormous victory for Yevgenia and her movement. "We managed to destroy their financing," she tells me proudly. "To raise money in Russia, it will take a long time, and time in this situation works for us."

It would be too much to say that Yevgenia Chirikova had Russian authorities locked in a stalemate. If Vladimir Putin ordered Khimki Forest razed, it would be done overnight. And yet, three years after Yevgenia wrote her first letter of inquiry, at a time when the Kremlin would have expected the highway project to be near completion, it hadn't begun. The country's political leaders probably believed that with a few simple steps, they would be pouring asphalt. And yet the road connecting Moscow and St. Petersburg existed only on blueprints.

Why? Like Pu in China, Yevgenia skillfully exploited the subtle vulnerabilities of the modern authoritarian regime. While the Russian government sees law as a tool to wield selectively against its opponents, she used the same system of laws to expose the regime's inconsistencies and contradictions. While the regime seeks to benefit from maintaining ties to the outside world, Yevgenia proved adept at marshaling international opinion in her favor and was able to leverage those very relationships against the regime. She succeeded in raising the costs for the regime in the places where it mattered most. For a government that had rarely encountered credible political opponents, she proved a terribly worthy adversary. What's more, by embarking on a single-issue campaign, Yevgenia denied the regime its most common means of smearing an opponent, pronouncing her a threat to the nation's security. Yevgenia was no radical, asking Khimki's voters to topple the government. She was not, in a sense, even asking them to support her. Her campaign merely asked that citizens care about their own environment. Faced with such a modest and politically benign agenda, the local authorities had little recourse other than to try to scuttle her campaign through trumped-up technicalities.

A few days after our first meeting, I traveled out to Khimki so that Yevgenia could take me on a walk through the forest she has spent the last three years fighting to preserve. It was a drizzly April afternoon, and the ground was still damp from the morning's rain. Although we were only a few minutes' walk from her home and Khimki's streets, it was surprisingly quiet once we were surrounded by the oaks. In each direction, they stood almost perfectly straight, swaying only when a cold wind blew from the north. We walked deeper into the forest. After about ten minutes, we came across a place locals call Oak Roof. It's a natural spring, and while we stood there talking about her struggle to keep the government at bay, six people came and went, filling up plastic jugs with the ice-cold water to take back to their homes. We began asking each of them if they had heard about the plans to build a highway on the very ground on which we all stood. They had, and they were angry about it. One man in his mid-thirties wearing a dark jacket and blue jeans said, "Yes, I am upset about it." And then, jokingly, "Where are the weapons?"

We laughed for a minute as each of us imagined the diminutive Yevgenia and her ragtag army of Khimki residents taking up arms against an armada of Kremlin bulldozers. As we continued our walk, I asked her what she thought the government would do next, what would be its next move? She didn't think the battle was close to finished.

Her supporters had set up forest patrols, keeping a lookout for the first sign of construction crews. "The next step is probably that they will start building, and there will be resistance," she replies, stiffening. "We are ready. We have thought through all of the various scenarios. We are sure that the construction is not going to pass in a quiet way. It is going to be very loud."

Again, she was right. Several months later, in June, one of Yevgenia's colleagues came across workers felling trees in the forest near Sheremetyevo airport. When the colleague demanded to see a work permit, the construction crews quickly packed up and left. Sensing that the workers would return, Yevgenia and more than two hundred supporters set up a camp in the forest so they could guard these woods day and night.

The attack she long expected came at 5:00 a.m. on July 23. While the environmentalists slept, nearly a hundred men wearing masks attacked their camp, tearing down banners, collapsing tents, and beating many of the activists as they emerged. "These were big guys, very aggressive," Yevgenia later told me. "They looked like skinheads. They started to chase us away and threatened to tear us to pieces, to kill us." The attack had clearly been coordinated alongside the plans for construction, because crews of workers started to cut trees just as the attack occurred. They had brought a large, Japanese-made harvester that could quickly separate trees from their roots. Yevgenia called the police, but they were slow to arrive. When they did, they refused to do anything about the skinheads. What the police did do was call for backup: specifically, the OMON, Russian special forces. (The OMON has a reputation for a rough, hard-edged brand of crowd control; its motto is "We know no mercy and do not ask for any.") When the OMON unit arrived, they arrested Yevgenia and the other protesters.

In the wake of this, and another attack on the environmentalists five days later, Yevgenia decided she had to regroup. She needed to broaden the fight, and she needed an ally who could give her effort a boost. She called Yuri Shevchuk, a famous Soviet and Russian rock star. Shevchuk had long lent his name to human rights causes, and Yevgenia thought the music icon might be sympathetic. A couple of months earlier, in a rare live television appearance of Putin with a collection of famous Russian musicians, Shevchuk had shocked the viewing audience by asking the visibly annoyed prime minister why Russia had no freedom of the press. After Yevgenia's phone call, Shevchuk came to Khimki. Yevgenia described her shock. "He had always been my idol since student times," she said, "and he came." Sitting in her kitchen, Shevchuk had a simple solution: "Let's do a concert to support you guys," recalled Yevgenia.

On August 22, in Pushkin Square, more than two thousand people attended a concert in support of the fight to save the forest, an impressive number at the time for any public rally in Russia. Police prevented a sound truck from coming to the square, but Shevchuk performed anyway. Two nights later, Bono invited Shevchuk onstage to perform during U2's first-ever concert in Moscow. Many interpreted it as support for Shevchuk and his fight against Russian authorities, and Bono later spoke out in favor of the Russian environmentalists while still in Moscow.

At that moment, the idea of the Russian government clear-cutting a forest seemed particularly poorly timed. The country had just

endured one of its worst heat waves on record, and wildfires that summer had consumed nearly two million acres of forests, farms, and villages across the country. According to a poll conducted by the Levada
Center, 73 percent of Russians were supportive of the fight to preserve
this rare green belt outside Moscow. In the face of so much public
pressure, President Dmitri Medvedev decided he should intervene. In
an unexpected move, Medvedev announced on his video blog that the
construction in Khimki would temporarily stop until the government
could "conduct further civic and expert discussions."

Publicly, Yevgenia called it a victory, but privately she suspected
it was a ploy. Again, her instincts were right. In December, the government commission that had been convened to study the highway
project announced that the construction would proceed. All that was
required was the president's signature.

But the powerful interests behind the highway did not wait for
Medvedev's pen. Yevgenia soon exposed that a real estate development company was already selling off tracts in Khimki Forest, even
without Medvedev's approval. (Yevgenia simply called the company,
posing as a potential buyer. She asked the company representative,
whose name was Oleg, if it was possible to buy a tract near Oak Roof,
where Khimki residents bottle their spring water. Oleg replied, "Yes,
that's possible." The whole exchange was posted on YouTube.)

In March 2011, members of the Defenders of Khimki Forest contacted me to describe how the pressure on Yevgenia was stepping up.
Rather than coming after her directly, they were targeting her family. That month officials raided her husband's firm. Although they
brought no charges and had no court order, they interrogated him and
several of his employees and seized company documents and paperwork. The harassment of her husband's company had begun months
earlier when authorities demanded that the firm account for all of its
transactions in the past twelve months. The justification for the order
was the outlandish claim that the electrical engineering firm was
somehow financing "extremists." Once clients and banks understood
that authorities had singled out the company, they began to back away.
The March raid hadn't been a complete surprise. A few days beforehand, someone had left a comment on the Defenders of Khimki Forest Web site, writing, "We'll raid your company in the nearest future,
prepare your papers!"

More frightening was when the government targeted Yevgenia's daughters. Representatives of the municipal department of guardianship unexpectedly "dropped by" her apartment. The officials alleged that they had received a letter from one of her neighbors claiming that Yevgenia "beats" and "starves" her daughters, Liza and Sasha. Afraid that they would attempt to take her children, Yevgenia refused to open her door. Later, the department admitted that none of her neighbors had written such a letter. It had simply been its "duty" to check on the children's well-being. I hadn't been able to speak with Yevgenia immediately after this incident, but I remembered how much she talked about her girls. I suspected that this threat had probably shaken her the most.

The day we had walked through Khimki Forest together, I had asked her if she ever feared for herself or her family.

"Many times I have asked myself, 'Yevgenia, what are you doing here in this forest?' I have everything. Why am I, a normal woman, working in this dangerous place?" she says. "I've just forbidden myself to think about it; otherwise I would go crazy. Because living in Russia and attempting to think about what can happen to you the next day, you can get yourself sick."

Earlier that week, I had met with Boris Nemtsov, one of the leaders of Solidarity, the Russian opposition group. "The main idea of Putin [is] to reduce the level of political activity of the population. This is his absolutely cynical strategy," Nemtsov told me. "He is very lucky when people say 'nothing depends on my view.' He is very much afraid of independent views. This is his main idea."

Nemtsov's statement could just as easily have applied to the Chinese Communist Party, to Hugo Chávez, or to almost any other strongman. Widespread political apathy is the grease that helps any authoritarian system hum. And in the smoothest-functioning authoritarian systems, the regimes have gone to great lengths to turn disinterest in political life into a public virtue. When that is the case, the Yevgenia Chirikovas of the world are the people whom dictators may fear most. They possess the independence and persistence to challenge the prevailing system, the dreaded antidote to the apathy that an authoritarian regime requires to succeed. It doesn't matter if the fight is over a rigged election, corrupt courts, or a serene forest. Such people are capable of emerging from the least likely places to infect others with their stubborn ideas. Looking out over the spring at Oak Roof that day, Yevgenia summed it up. "Because [Putin] didn't take into account my opinion, he is being punished."

Then we walked out of the forest.

The Three No's

Omar Afifi was proud of his police uniform. In 1981, when he was sixteen years old, he had entered the police academy, the same year that Hosni Mubarak replaced the assassinated Anwar Sadat as Egypt's president. He had been attracted to the job because of the pay and security; finding a job working for the Egyptian government was one of the few paths to a stable paycheck. What he had appreciated less was how becoming an Egyptian police officer would change his status in the community. The first time he returned to his village wearing his uniform, he was astounded by how people reacted. Old men, people who had known him since he was a boy, stood when he walked into a room. He was treated with a deference he had never known. Of course, he quickly realized it wasn't so much respect as fear. "The tailor has his tools, and so does the police officer," says Afifi. "The government wanted everyone to be scared of the police. The air of intimidation was worse than the bad acts. We defeated the people before we even made contact with them."

Despite its reputation, Afifi never believed that joining the Egyptian police necessitated that you become a monster. Far from it. He thought well of most of his fellow officers and believed that only a minority—maybe one in seven—were the cruel, abusive bullies that so many people feared. And for the most part, his first two years on the force did nothing to change his opinion. His work seemed entirely routine, very much the job that he thought he had signed up for when he first entered the academy. But that changed in his third year wearing the uniform. He had what he would later call the first of his "three no's."

A police officer had been killed. As it would be for any police force, apprehending the man who had slain their colleague was a top priority. The authorities were tipped off that the man they believed to be the killer was on the outskirts of Cairo, hiding in a cornfield. Afifi was among those dispatched to find him. Police units were stationed at points around the field. Afifi and other officers were to start on one side of the field and, walking in close formation, slowly advance through the high rows of corn until they flushed the fugitive out. Minutes later, as Afifi made his way through the field, he saw movement out of the corner of his eye. The stalks several yards ahead of him had moved. It was the suspected killer. He ran, and Afifi and his fellow officers gave chase. The stalks of corn cut his face as the distance between them slowly shrank. He estimates the suspect ran full tilt for nearly two miles. But the pursuit ended when the man stumbled, exhausted and unable to run any farther. He surrendered, cowering in the middle of a cornfield, his arms raised above his head. The alleged killer, unarmed and unable to catch his breath, was surrounded. Then the superior officer ordered Afifi to shoot him. Afifi didn't understand. "Why should I kill him when he has surrendered?" he protested. "No, I can't." The senior officer looked at Afifi in disgust. "You are too soft. Go! Get out of here!" he barked. Afifi walked alone the distance back to where they had left their squad cars. As he did, he heard a battery of shots ring out. They were enough to leave the man's body riddled with bullets. "This made me change," Afifi told me. He knew now that there were tasks he could not perform and that his refusal to do so would probably have consequences. It also changed how fellow officers viewed him. "My superiors wouldn't include me on missions that did not have a legal basis." This was his first no.

The second and third no came in 1995 in quick succession. Egypt's parliamentary elections were a week away. Afifi's career as a police officer had largely stalled, if only because senior officers didn't believe he could be trusted. In 1995, he was working as the warden of a small police jail in the center of Cairo. On that afternoon, a state security officer unexpectedly showed up at his jailhouse with nearly five hundred people in tow. They were supporters of opposition parties, and by the look of them Afifi believed many of them had been severely beaten during their arrest. The officer told Afifi he was dropping off the protesters to be detained in his jail. "Okay," Afifi replied. "Give me the arrest warrant with the order they be detained." The state security officer looked at him incredulously. "There are no papers. These are orders from on high. It's an emergency."

Afifi wasn't moved, and he stood his ground. He argued that some of the protesters looked as if they needed medical attention. If they died in one of his cells, Afifi would need the paper trail to explain why they were being housed there; otherwise he could be blamed for their deaths. The state security officer shook his head because both men knew that someone dying in an Egyptian jailhouse would hardly lead to an inquiry, let alone an uproar. "Why aren't you being more cooperative?" asked the officer, becoming more frustrated. "You must obey our order. These are the enemies of Egypt." Afifi didn't argue that point with him; he just repeated his condition. "I know," he replied. "But I need the arrest order from someone, from the judge, from you, from someone." Afifi didn't entirely understand why he wasn't backing down. He simply didn't want to be an accomplice to the abuse of these citizens. "I was acting on my conscience," he told me. "That's it. I knew nothing of human rights." And he also suspected that state security would be either too lazy or unwilling to create a paper trail. And he was right. The state security officer left to find somewhere else he could detain his prisoners. Afifi believes they were ultimately held in police barracks. That was the second time he said no.

It only took six days for him to find himself again at odds with his superiors. The night before the parliamentary elections the chief of the Cairo police, Habib el-Adly, called together a meeting of seven or eight hundred officers. (By 2011, Adly had risen to be Egypt's interior minister, becoming one of the most feared men in Mubarak's regime.) Adly warned the officers that if the opposition won the elections, they would lose their jobs, maybe even their lives. Given the stakes, he said, they would play a special role on Election Day. The officers were to show up the next day in plain clothes, leaving their IDs and guns at home. Most would be expected to distribute marked ballots at polling stations. If they were prevented from doing that for some reason, he instructed the officers to start a fight outside the polling place. Once the scuffle began, officers would make arrests while others would stuff ballot boxes inside. If for some reason even this failed to work, then the officers were to detain the men responsible for transporting the ballot boxes after voting had ended. The officers could then either stuff the boxes with previously marked ballots or await further instructions. "There was no imagination or intelligence to the plan. [Adly] didn't even understand how voting worked," Afifi told me. "His only qualification was that he had no conscience."

Afifi spoke up; he had some questions he wanted answered. Adly replied, "You again? Get out!" He added that if others had a problem following these orders, they should leave, too. About five other officers walked out of the meeting hall. That was Afifi's third and final no.

Afifi's lack of cooperation had now caught the attention of senior security officials, and there were real consequences. Not long after the election—which, unsurprisingly, the ruling party won by large margins—the order came down that Afifi would be transferred to Upper Egypt. At that time, clashes with violent Islamist groups were on the rise there, and Egyptian police officers were often targeted in attacks. Afifi feared that he would die either at the hands of militants or, more likely, as the casualty of friendly fire. He submitted a complaint and managed to gain a transfer to a firefighting unit back in Cairo.

Afifi was unhappy and unsure what to do. His career as a police officer was effectively over, and he continued to fear for his own safety. It was then, in 2000, when he was near his lowest, that he got lucky. He learned about a contest sponsored by the International Red Cross that gave Egyptian judges or police officers the opportunity to study international human rights law abroad. Four people would be awarded the scholarship. Afifi won the scholarship and first studied in Tunis. His course work left an immediate impression on him. He realized for the first time that there was an entire body of law and literature on human rights, something he had felt intuitively when he stood up to his superiors but never knew existed in such concrete terms. When the program in Tunis ended, he won another scholarship that allowed him to earn a law degree. In 2004, the former police officer returned to Cairo an attorney.

He quickly put his education to work as a criminal defense attorney. Within two years, he had developed a reputation as a skilled lawyer and advocate. But the advantage that Afifi had over other attorneys wasn't his foreign legal training; it was his knowledge of proper police procedure. He knew how the system worked in practice, and he was extremely effective at pointing out procedural violations. Few of his clients had any notion of their rights. More important, police officers, unaccustomed to having their actions scrutinized, often took an undisciplined approach to their work. Afifi was able to exploit this vulnerability to the advantage of his clients.

His work as a criminal defense attorney did not provoke the ire of the regime. What angered the regime was when he began to share his expertise with the public at large. Because of his work, Afifi was invited to be a recurring guest on *Cairo Today*, a live satellite television show. During a forty-five-minute segment, he would explain some aspect of Egyptians' legal rights in clear and simple language. In the first episode, which aired on November 13, 2007, he tackled the subject of what people's rights were if they were stopped by the police on the street. In the second episode, he discussed what people's rights were within their homes and the need for search warrants.

By the second episode, the regime had sat up to take notice. A state security official called the anchor of the television show during a commercial break. He was furious with what Afifi was telling the television audience. "Have you lost your mind?" he yelled at the anchor over the phone. "Fuck you! We are going to cut off your satellite link if you keep going!"

The third episode was supposed to discuss people's rights in a police station. But there would be no third episode. State security contacted Afifi after the second show and asked him if he wanted to do a show for them on the virtues of the police force. They would pay him $2,000 a week. (Afifi was making $800 a week for the satellite channel.) When he refused, they threatened him. "They told me that if I don't comply, a shot could just go astray. Don't be a hero," recalls Afifi. He understood that he had touched a nerve and that they were serious. He agreed he would not speak out anymore.

But he didn't say anything about writing. Based on the public reaction to his first two television appearances, Afifi had already decided that he would write a book offering the same straightforward advice on people's rights when dealing with the police. He worked on the book for several months but had difficulty finding a publisher; no one wanted to run afoul of the regime. In early 2008, he found someone who was willing to print copies in secret. On March 20, he began to distribute five thousand copies of his book, *So You Don't Get Slapped on the Back of the Neck*. (The title came from a colloquial Egyptian saying.) Afifi sent a thousand copies to journalists at both official and independent newspapers. It drew a front-page headline in a popular newsweekly. The reaction, he recalls, was almost instantaneous. He quickly received requests for ten thousand more copies. Then forty thousand more. He had put his own cell phone number in the book, so calls were coming in directly to him. "It was like the Bible," he says, laughing at his book's popularity. "I didn't expect it."

By April 7, he had received orders from bookstores for thousands more copies. He never got a chance to fill those orders. The next day, at 10:00 a.m., his cell phone rang. It was the owner of a bookstore selling his book. State security had just walked in and seized all of his copies. In short order, they had taken roughly five thousand books, the bulk of the remaining copies he had printed.

Afifi didn't have very much time to worry about printing more books. The next call on his cell phone was from a friend on the police force. He told him he was no longer safe. State security had staked out his home and his office; whatever patience the regime had had for Afifi had run out. Afifi believed his old colleague was overreacting. He knew he had been playing a dangerous game, but he hadn't actually broken any laws. Indeed, he was only explaining the law, as it was written, in a way that people could understand. He called a trusted contact at the Ministry of Interior, someone he knew would tell him how serious things had become. When he heard his friend answer, he said, "Hey, it's me." He won't forget what he heard next.

"It's the wrong number," his friend replied.

"What? What do you mean?" said Afifi.

"Sorry. You have the wrong number," he repeated as he hung up.

Afifi was terrified when the phone went dead. He had just received his final warning. His friend on the police force had been right; it was no longer safe. He believed at best he would be locked away and tortured; at worst, the authorities would just dispose of him. He knew he couldn't go home and he couldn't go anywhere near his office. He made the instantaneous decision that he had to flee. He couldn't remain in Egypt. It was as simple as that.

He turned off his cell phone and took out the battery. He would use only landlines and no credit cards. He found a way to get a message to his son: he would have to retrieve his passport and meet him in a safe location. For the next three days, Afifi lived in the street and in the back of his car. It wasn't safe for him to go anywhere state security might expect to find him. When his son brought him his passport, the only valid visa was for the United States. The other, for the European Union, had expired. He was going to the United States.

Security for Cairo International Airport is provided by police officers from Cairo central security. Fortunately for Afifi, he knew several officers from earlier in his career who now worked at the airport. He arrived at the airport late in the evening on April 11. One of his fellow police officers took his passport; he would get it stamped without going through the official system. The others got Afifi through security and told him to wait at a different gate, not the one for his flight. He waited until everyone had boarded the flight. At the last moment, he was given the signal and boarded the plane just as the door was closing. He was on the last flight to JFK. He landed in New York, a little over twelve hours later, with nothing but $50 and a gold watch.

For a dictator, the exile of his opponents might seem like a tidy solution. There would be no outcry over the murder of Omar Afifi. No funeral processions that turn into public demonstrations. No demands for justice. Afifi would be granted asylum abroad and live out his days far away. He would be safe from the regime, and the regime would be safe from him. It has the makings of a stalemate, maybe even a truce.

Few people set out to be branded enemies of the state. Pu Zhiqiang, Yevgenia Chirikova, and Omar Afifi did not intend to be at odds with their governments. They had not been born advocates and activists; they were made. Indeed, they worked within the system, as imperfect as it may be, to attempt to hold a regime accountable to its own rules. But once they were branded as opponents, once their governments marked them for their persistence, they became people no longer interested in tidy solutions. Even as Pu Zhiqiang saw his colleagues hauled away, he gave no thought to stopping his work. He would still bring his cases. In April 2011, the Kremlin sent bulldozers into Khimki Forest, and Chirikova and her supporters were repeatedly beaten and arrested. But, she had told me a year earlier, her fight was now bigger than a single forest. The regime had made her into an activist, and she would continue regardless of the outcome.

Nor was Afifi prepared to abandon his fight, even after he boarded a plane to New York. He gained political asylum in the United States, but his opposition to Mubarak's regime did not rest. He understood that his background in the Egyptian security apparatus made him unique among the regime's opponents. Even from six thousand miles away, in an apartment a short drive from Washington, D.C., he knew the regime from the inside out; specifically, he understood how the police would be deployed to stop a rebellion.

When Egypt's revolution unexpectedly erupted in January 2011, the youth in the street quickly learned they had a potent ally in the former police officer. At a command station he created in his small Falls Church apartment, Afifi advised Egyptian youth leaders on the police tactics they would face. At his desk, three oversized computer screens fed him a steady flow of information from activists in the street—as well as, he says, from old colleagues still inside the regime. With the help of Google Maps, he pinpointed routes that would give the protesters the upper hand. Via Twitter and Facebook, he stayed in contact with the revolution's foot soldiers, helping them prepare for Mubarak's inevitable crackdown. When I visited him, it was nearly impossible to speak for more than five minutes without our conversation being interrupted by a call on one of his five cell phones and a stream of messages being relayed to him over Skype. "I am not here," Afifi told me, gesturing at the northern Virginia apartment that surrounded us. "I'm in Egypt."

The regime had created an enemy it couldn't shake.

CHAPTER 3   EL COMANDANTE

The Ramo Verde military prison became smaller as we drove away. We had just left the last cordon of the prison's security—a bored, young soldier lazily holding a machine gun in one hand and opening and closing the metal gate with the other. The prison sits right above Los Teques, the capital city of the state of Miranda. Still, the jail seemed utterly desolate when you stood outside its walls, a small outcropping atop a dusty Venezuelan mountainside. It was a destination you could not have arrived at by accident. The prison appeared to be the only physical structure for miles.

But from the front seat of our rental car, we kept staring back at it. A friend and I had visited Ramo Verde on this Saturday morning to interview one of its inmates. The fact that a foreigner was visiting the facility had made the guards—all of them military police officers—uneasy. While the handful of other people who had turned up this morning were weighed down with parcels, presumably gifts for family or friends housed inside, I hadn't been permitted to bring anything within the prison's walls, not a tape recorder, not a pen and paper, nothing. Indeed, no one in the prison felt senior enough even to permit me to enter. They pulled me aside as an officer called military intelligence for instructions. Afterward, on my way out an hour later, they searched us a second time. It was then, as we exited, that one of the military police said into his cell phone, "Yes, sir. I will follow them."

His name was García; it was written in black letters across the chest pocket of his green fatigues. He was the same military officer who had questioned me before I entered the prison. He was a large, somewhat portly soldier, with a round face and serious expression. García appeared to outrank the others on duty, and he was the one who had felt it necessary to alert intelligence officials far from this outpost. The road snaked down the mountainside, swerving to the left and right as we descended. As we did, we kept looking in the rearview mirror for García. Ten minutes later, near the base of the hill, there still was no sign of him.

Besides keeping an eye out for García, I was dealing with one other complication. Once inside the prison, I had borrowed pen and paper from an inmate, so I could take notes during my interview. Knowing I would likely be frisked again on the way out, I had also found someone in the prison—someone who would not be searched going in or out—to smuggle my notes outside. The plan was to meet up with this contact once we were a safe distance from Ramo Verde. I worried we could unintentionally be leading a military police officer to our rendezvous.

The road leveled off as we approached Los Teques' traffic-clogged streets. Just as we did, I saw him: García, wearing a helmet and reflective sunglasses, was following us on a motorcycle. I only caught a glimpse of him for a second; he was traveling a safe distance behind us, at least two, maybe three, curves in the road. At the same moment, I also saw our contact with the sheaf of notes. He was driving a four-door sedan and appeared to be trying to angle his vehicle so that he could pull up alongside us, presumably to pass the papers from one car to the other. But now, with García following us, it was far too risky. We darted ahead, pulling into the city's traffic to prevent our contact from pulling alongside us. He followed, merging into the lane, three or four cars behind us. Several cars behind him, I could now see García take his position in the line of traffic.

We had to find a way to warn our contact about García. He had no idea we were being followed, and if he attempted to pass the notes to us again, there would be no way García would miss it.

Traffic was at a crawl. As we inched through Los Teques, vendors lined the road. Some of the more aggressive hawkers walked between the traffic lanes, coming directly up to car windows to try to make a sale. I motioned one man selling trinkets toward us. As I rolled down the window, he began to show me the items he had today—

small wooden figurines, strings of beads, and the like. Looking at him, I said, "Go to the car three cars behind us. Tell them, 'You are being followed.'" I then reached for my wallet and offered to buy something. The middle-aged hawker smiled and raised his hand, saying, "No, no." A purchase wasn't necessary.

He slowly strolled through the traffic, approaching several vehicles to make his pitch. Then he stopped at our contact's car and lowered his head near the window for a moment. A second later, he moved on, making his way again through the line of vehicles that stretched as far as you could see.

A quarter of a mile later, the traffic began to ease. Up ahead, there was a fork in the road. We bore to the right; our contact veered to the left. Keeping an eye on the rearview mirror, we saw García steer to the right. We would have to retrieve the notes from our contact later. It could wait.

It is roughly an hour-long drive between Caracas and Los Teques. The bulk of the distance, the portion on which you can make the best time, is the Pan-American Highway. During this stretch, Venezuelans whiz along at a fast clip, enjoying the rare chance to open up their engines before hitting the wall of Caracas's notorious traffic jams. We had no hope of trying to lose García with speed; our cheap rental car couldn't outpace his motorcycle. Then fate intervened. Just before we turned onto the Pan-American, our car hit a crater-sized pothole. The front passenger-side tire exploded.

We had no choice but to pull over to the side of the road. The tire had an enormous gash in the sidewall. Fortunately, the rental came equipped with a spare, and we set about swapping it. As we did, we looked around; García was gone. "You can never find a police officer when you need one," my friend joked.

Twenty minutes later, we were on the Pan-American, hugging the right lane and driving much slower than the rest of traffic heading back to Caracas. We hadn't driven more than a few minutes when we spotted a motorcycle several vehicles behind us, hiding behind a tractor trailer. García had never left.

No one enjoys being followed by military police. But at this point García's attempt to trail us took on a comic feel. With cars moving at seventy or seventy-five miles per hour, it is difficult to inconspicuously follow a vehicle that is barely moving half as fast. Every vehicle that García tried to hide behind quickly joined the flow of traffic and raced by us. García had to keep braking, finding another car, bus, or pickup for cover. Even worse, we stopped several times to gauge the spare tire's air pressure, which was flagging. Each time we stopped, our furtive military escort had to hide. The third time we pulled over, we got out of the car and stood over the tire inspecting it. As we did, I looked out of the corner of my eye and spotted García. He had slid off his motorcycle and hidden in a thatch of tall grass reeds. I could see his sunglasses peering out at us where he parted the grass with his hands. We jumped back in the car and headed to the highway ramp a hundred yards away. As we did, we had to laugh: we could see the surprised, slightly round García scrambling back to his bike.

García followed us all the way to Caracas. He was now a long way from his hillside prison. We didn't want to take him to where we were staying; even if the authorities could find our whereabouts, we weren't about to lead them there. So we chose a large shopping mall in the center of downtown Caracas. We could stow the car in the bottom of the mall's parking lot, several stories below ground, and García would then have no choice but to follow us on foot. Once inside the mall complex, we would have several options for transportation among the cabs and microbuses that came and went. The last time I saw García was as we descended into the mall's underground parking. He had come to a full stop a couple of traffic lights away. He seemed to be thinking about what to do next, his helmet and sunglasses reflecting the sun in our direction.

What had been the point of having García follow us back to Caracas? Perhaps it truly was an attempt by authorities to spy on us. It might not even have ended when García turned his bike back toward Los Teques. He may have only been called back to his post once someone else was in place to take over his surveillance duties, someone we wouldn't know or recognize in advance. Or, more likely, we were supposed to know we were being followed. (It would be the more charitable explanation for the Keystone Kops nature of García's pursuit.) The order to tail us had been an attempt to frighten or intimidate. Either way, the entire episode seemed consistent with almost all my interactions with the Venezuelan government. On the one hand, it was permissive enough to allow a journalist to enter one of its prisons. Most authoritarian regimes would have kept the doors locked. On the other hand, it suffered from a paranoia that compelled it to send García on a long, winding drive across the state of Miranda. It felt like the same reflex that led most members of the government I met to refer to me, without jest, as a "member of the empire." The government wanted to appear permissive and open, but that appearance was at odds with a siege mentality that saw enemies lurking everywhere.

The trigger for that paranoia may have been the person I had visited that morning: Raúl Baduel. Few people know Venezuela's president, Hugo Chávez, better than Baduel, a former general. They first met as young cadets in Venezuela's military academy in 1972. They were close in age and struck up a friendship. So close were their ties that on December 17, 1982, Chávez, Baduel, and two other young officers made a secret oath to defend Venezuelan democracy. All four men were worried about the direction in which the political class was taking the country; much of what was wrong with Venezuela—its economic decline, massive poverty, deteriorating social services—they blamed on an increasingly corrupt and venal leadership. At the time, Chávez and Baduel were on a military detachment in Maracay, west of Caracas. It was the anniversary of the death of Simón Bolívar, the great South American liberator, and the four young officers had gone for a jog. Under a very old tree, the Samán de Güere, under which Bolívar is said to have once rested, they made a promise to one another. "We paraphrased the oath that our liberator Bolívar took in front of his teacher," Baduel told me. "We swore not to give rest to our arms or rest to our souls until we saw a true democracy consolidated in our country."

This secret cell of officers was the birth of Chávez's revolutionary movement, which was originally known as the Bolivarian Revolutionary Movement-2000. (The 2000 was a reference to the year 2000, when they believed they would have ascended to high command. A year later it was changed to 200, to commemorate the 200th anniversary of Bolívar's birth.) In February 1992, Chávez's underground cell led a failed coup against the government. After two years in prison, Chávez returned to public life and began to build a populist, antigovernment political persona that would help catapult him into the presidency in 1999. The most vital test of Chávez's friendship with Baduel came in the third year of his presidency in April 2002. It was then, during a brief coup against Chávez's government, that Baduel, now a general, came to the aid of his comrade. During the coup, Chávez was temporarily ousted and exiled to Orchila Island, a dot in the Caribbean 150 miles off the Venezuelan coast. From there, Chávez fully expected he would be either killed or sent to Cuba to live out his days. Factions within the military, which had initially either acquiesced or supported Chávez's ouster, started to waver. As military opinion began to turn, Baduel sent an elite team of paratroopers in three Super Puma attack helicopters to rescue Chávez and reinstall him in the presidential palace.

Chávez eventually repaid Baduel by making him minister of defense, and in many ways this is when Baduel's troubles began. Now in Caracas, he was in close proximity to Chávez and his political advisers. Baduel told me he was bothered by what he saw; his longtime friend ruled like an autocrat and was surrounded by people who told him he could do no wrong. Baduel claimed that his criticisms quickly made him an outsider with Chávez and his circle. At the same time, Baduel was also gaining critics within the military, especially among senior officers who believed he had been too accepting of Chávez's interference in military affairs. When Chávez sought to change the military's salute to "Fatherland, socialism, or death"—something that offended the most professional officers—Baduel claims he told Chávez it was a violation of the constitution, which "clearly states that the [military] is a service to all and not personal or party interests." Chávez simply went around him, instructing individual generals to spread the slogan to soldiers directly. When they began to repeat it, "Chávez said it was coming from the hearts of the soldiers," recalled Baduel.

The breaking point came in 2007. Chávez put forward a constitutional amendment that would grant him extraordinary executive powers, including the ability to be president for life. Baduel felt compelled to resign and soon became an outspoken critic of the proposed amendment, which was defeated. The last time he spoke to Chávez was at his farewell speech as minister of defense. "Chávez came near me to say good-bye," says Baduel, sitting in his jail cell. "He told me to say hello to my family. And in an ironic tone, he put his hand on my arm and said, 'I imagine you are going to have a lot of time on your vast lands.' I looked at him and laughed. But I took it as a subtle threat." It was a threat, he believed, because Baduel had no vast lands to retire to. "I knew he was going to retaliate against me," he said. "I was certain it would happen."

In April 2009, Chávez confirmed his fears. Military intelligence officers forcibly detained Baduel, putting a gun to his head and pushing him into a waiting vehicle. In May 2010, he was sentenced to seven years and eleven months in prison on allegations of corruption. I met with him in Ramo Verde military prison two months later. Baduel told me the sentencing was pointless. "When will I leave?" Baduel asked. "Only when Chávez is out of power."

Baduel knew Chávez the cadet, the soldier, the politician, and the president. He had helped him plot against the old Venezuelan political order and had been a defender of Chávez's own government. He no doubt must have had suspicions about Chávez even before his brazen 2007 constitutional referendum. No one who rises to minister of defense could be entirely blind to the man he served. Perhaps he had simply underestimated Chávez. But now, in prison, Baduel wonders if he ever knew Chávez at all. "They say I know him well, but now I think I met an impostor. He wanted power. He was able to hide that well through the years," he told me. "He takes actions to sustain his only political project, which is to be president for life."

But Baduel did offer one parting insight into who Hugo Chávez is. He told me that everyone always makes a fuss over the fact that Chávez is a military man and that he thinks and acts like a soldier. This, however, struck the former Venezuelan general as far too vague to be instructive. "Military experience influences everything we do, and yes, he is military. But we have to be more precise," says Baduel. "His specialty is tanks and armored vehicles. That is the type of weaponry he knows. Those units, we call them the armored hurricane. The concept is to roll over your adversaries, to flatten them. That's his approach, to flatten his enemies."

Who Speaks for D and E

What would make four young military officers take a secret oath to defend Venezuelan democracy? When these officers had first met, in the 1970s, it appeared that Venezuela might catapult itself into the ranks of the world's top-performing countries. In 1970, it was the wealthiest country in South America and ranked among the twenty richest countries in the world. As many reeled from the 1970s oil crisis, Venezuela, with the largest oil deposits outside the Middle East, enjoyed a bonanza. There were so many highway and high-rise construction projects that people in Caracas started referring to their city as "Miami with mountains." When Venezuelans traveled abroad to splurge on luxury items, they were often known as the *dame dos* (give me two!). Colombians, envious of their neighbor's success, would say, "The Venezuelans fell out of trees and into Cadillacs."

But those Cadillacs soon began to sputter. The high price for a barrel of crude had masked the inefficiency, mismanagement, and corruption of the Venezuelan government. As the price of oil fell, Venezuela's economic troubles came into full view. Venezuela soon had the highest per capita debt in Latin America. Real per capita income dropped 15 percent between 1973 and 1985. The country's neediest were largely ignored: between 1980 and 1989, poverty rose 150 percent. Inflation and unemployment soared, surpassed only by the sharp rise in violent crime.

Chávez and Baduel had made their 1982 pact at the beginning of what became two "lost decades" for Venezuela. By 1998, Venezuela's per capita GDP had spiraled down by an incredible 21 percent. Two-thirds of the country's banks had collapsed. Unemployment had more than doubled since 1980. More than 50 percent of the population was poverty-stricken, and nearly 30 percent were living in extreme poverty. No one could argue with the fact that Venezuela's political parties had failed the country. So, not surprisingly, the people gave up on the parties and the politicians who led them. In one survey, on the eve of the 1998 presidential elections, 70 percent of the poor and 84 percent of the wealthy believed political parties created more problems than solutions. Sixty-three percent of the poor and 58 percent of the wealthy said they served no purpose at all. Such a climate was tailored perfectly for a candidate who could credibly claim to be a political outsider. That man was Hugo Chávez.

Chávez should be understood, first and foremost, as a consequence. Venezuela's democracy failed its people over two decades, opening the door for the candidate who could most convincingly promise to kill the old political order. That is how Chávez got his chance. But if you want to understand how he chose to capitalize on it, explains the Venezuelan businessman Alfredo Croes, then you need to understand A, B, C, D, and E. These five letters signify the five socioeconomic classes, as measured by the government, of the people of Venezuela. If you live in Chacao, have a nice three- or four-bedroom apartment, and send one of your kids to the United States for school, then you probably belong to A. Altogether, only 3 percent of the population—the country's elites—belong to A and B combined. The dwindling number of people who fall into C—Venezuela's middle class—make up 18 percent of the population. The rest are either D or E. The poor and the extremely poor make up 37 percent and 42 percent of the population, respectively. "For the first twenty years of Venezuelan democracy," says Croes, "people had a chance to advance themselves. In the second twenty years, all that was forgotten. D and E were left behind."

I met Croes in the offices of his business supply company, on the east side of Caracas. Ten years earlier, he and five other Venezuelan businessmen decided to establish a small strategic cooperative called the Grupo La Colina. All run their own businesses or have retired from successful companies, but they donate their time to the effort to bolster opposition to Chávez's government. The afternoon I walked into his office, Croes was analyzing spreadsheets and projections for the upcoming legislative elections, pinpointing the best places for the opposition parties to field candidates.

Political objectivity is in short supply in Venezuela, and many of Chávez's critics find it impossible to say anything positive about the man. Not Croes. He has a grudging respect for Chávez the political strategist. The failings of Chávez's predecessors may have created the opening, but Chávez proved himself capable of seizing the populist opportunity they handed him. And he is much more than a populist, says Croes. "In the case of Chávez, he did something brilliant. He understood better than anyone that the segment of the country known as D and E were nearly 80 percent of the country," says Croes. "For the first five years, he spoke only *to* the D and E. Then, for the next five years, he spoke *for* D and E."

It's an enormously important point. For the first half of Chávez's rule, he gained the support, trust, and fealty of the country's desperate majority. After so many years of neglect, his attention was understandably intoxicating for them. But the genius is in what Chávez did with his newfound following. With the bond forged, Chávez could then turn that support into a weapon to bludgeon those who stood in his way. At first, D and E were his audience; then they became his recruits. "They feel themselves represented in Chávez," says Croes. "Some Chavistas are now more Chavista than Chávez."

Chávez's primary political strategy is, in essence, leading Venezuela against itself. Having won the support of a segment of the population, he actively champions them against the rest. Although he came to power through democratic means, his main idea is not democratic; instead, he proposes revolution. In a democracy, differences are expected. Chávez begins with a single answer, and those who question, criticize, or oppose him are "traitors," "criminals," "oligarchs," "mafia," and "lackeys of the United States." Although he originally promised to break the political parties in order to return power to the people, Chávez has centralized nearly all power in his own hands. Today, he controls every branch of government, the armed forces, the central bank, the state-owned oil company, most radio and television channels, and any segment of the private sector he chooses to expropriate. Authoritarian leaders typically rationalize their rule by pointing to foreign enemies and threats; Chávez gives equal time to looking for enemies within Venezuela. In many ways, his approach is the inverse of Russia's Vladimir Putin. Where Putin manages a carefully choreographed process intended to maintain order and stability, Chávez courts chaos and promotes division. His rhetoric, policies, and actions have made Venezuela more polarized than at any time in its history, injecting an almost Manichaean political struggle into all aspects of everyday life. "This is not Cuba. This is not the Soviet Union . . . for now," says Teodoro Petkoff, a prominent Chávez critic and the editor of the opposition paper *Tal Cual*. "This is a much more sophisticated regime than the past regimes of repression. But why can it be sophisticated? Because he has had deep and vast popular support. And that is a very important difference with some other regimes of this kind."

Venezuela is not the totalitarian state of the Soviet Union. It is not nearly as repressive as Fidel Castro's Cuba. There have been no massive human rights abuses. Dissidents do not face the firing squad, and enemies of the state are not "disappeared" in the night. Despite his brash and outlandish speeches, Chávez's rule is far subtler than such heavy-handed regimes. Instead, he effectively took the remnants of the imperfect democracy that elected him and twisted them into tools to perpetuate his power. If Chávez were just a populist, he would be reminiscent of many other Latin American leaders before him. But he married his populist origins to an autocratic scheme that concentrates power and reduces democracy to nothing more than the ballots people cast on Election Day. It is the use of a system to destroy a system, a democracy to destroy democracy. As Virginia Rivero, a political organizer, asked me plaintively, "What happens to a society when a democratically elected president rules in an antidemocratic way?" Venezuelans have been living the answer to that question for more than a decade.

"On This Dying Constitution"

In 1998, ahead of the upcoming presidential election, Maruja Tarre invited Hugo Chávez and the other presidential candidates to Simón Bolívar University to speak to the students on oil policy. Tarre, a former diplomat and longtime professor at the university, had invited Chávez to come speak to her classes several times since he had been released from prison for leading the failed military coup. The Simón Bolívar event was the only time that all the candidates spoke at a single venue during the 1998 presidential campaign. The university's auditorium holds eleven hundred people; it was full, standing room only, with more people lined up outside. Tarre remembers it as an awkward, somewhat unpleasant occasion. "I was very embarrassed because people booed him in an awful, awful way," recalled Tarre. "I tried to calm the students, but it was impossible."

Standing at the podium, in front of the students and university community, candidate Chávez was clearly incensed at how the students had received him. It was then that Tarre heard something that took her aback. Speaking away from the microphone, Chávez muttered, "You are booing me, but I will be in power and you will accommodate me." Tarre was stunned. As uncomfortable as the event had become, she expected Chávez to just brush it off, to make some joke to minimize the impact of the students' rudeness. After all, they were just university students. Instead, Chávez's words gave her a chill. "I was the only one who heard him. It was not on the microphone," she remembers. "That for me was a shock."

Few people knew precisely what to expect from Chávez after he won the December presidential elections. For all of the criticism he heaped on the political order as it existed, his campaign had been short on specifics of what he would do once in power. He did not begin by introducing new economic policies to shore up the faltering economy. He did not start by addressing poverty, crime, or education. Instead, he began by calling for a new constitution. (During his swearing in, Chávez had unexpectedly inserted the words "on this dying constitution" as he recited the oath of office.) Buoyed by his high approval ratings at the beginning of his term, Chávez succeeded in forming a new assembly to rewrite the constitution within the space of a few months. In a tactic that would soon become familiar, his supporters carefully drew up electoral rules that allowed Chávez to control 93 percent of the seats in this new body with only 53 percent of the votes. His solid command of the assembly delivered Chávez what he sought: a vast expansion of presidential powers.

Under the new constitution, the presidential term of office grew from five to six years, with the possibility of a second term. Chávez took full control of all promotions within the armed forces. The Senate was dissolved, leaving the legislature with a single chamber. Public financing for political parties was outlawed. Chávez also took advantage of this moment to stack the leadership of the National Electoral Council with loyalists. He apparently understood early that controlling the institution that organizes elections, administers voter registration, draws up the electoral maps, decides on the electoral rules, distributes the voting machines, and sets the date for elections would be crucial to consolidating power behind a democratic facade. Other offices—for example, the courts, attorney general, and the comptroller general— were soon under his sway as well. In less than two years, Chávez had full command over the government and unprecedented power for a Venezuelan president. This early period was emblematic of what was to come: the skilled manipulation of democratic processes to amass unchecked executive power. Far from expanding public participation in democracy, Chávez was proving how malleable a concept democracy could be.

The linchpin of Chávez's authoritarianism has, somewhat para-doxically, always been elections. For most people, elections are the very essence of democracy. People are less likely to privilege constitutional protections, separation of powers, or other less tangible democratic rights over the ballot box. "If the majority of people think democracy is voting," says Luis Vicente León, one of Venezuela's leading pollsters, "then they must think we are living in the best democracy in the world because we have never voted so much." Indeed, many Venezuelans I spoke with could not tell me how many elections there have been since Chávez came to power. (Incredibly, if you include elections and national referendums, Venezuelans were called to the polls thirteen times in Chávez's first eleven years.)

Elections are an important weapon in Chávez's autocratic arse-nal because, if properly conducted, they satisfy many of the prereq-uisites for furthering his rule. For starters, it is through elections and referendums that Chávez eliminated almost all checks and balances, creating an unaccountable government with extraordinary executive control. Further, no matter when you visit Venezuela, it is almost always election season. For a president looking to polarize the country into competing camps, it behooves him to create a permanent cam-paign environment. Such moments are an opportunity to transfer windfalls of cash and benefits to supporters, both inside and outside the government. Loyalists are rewarded, and enemies are punished in a feverish, ideologically driven movement that distracts people from many of the basic problems that plague them. And, of course, elec-tions allow Chávez to renew his legitimacy, even as he radicalizes his agenda. "Elections are not a threat for Chávez, they are a necessity," says Eugenio Martínez, a reporter who covers the election beat for *El Universal*. "It is hard to accuse someone of being a dictator after so many elections."

Many people would assume that any authoritarian ruler who held so many elections must simply be holding one sham contest after another. But that is not the case. Most people, including members of the opposition, believe that the election results reflect the will of the people. Of course, there are irregularities. But they are not the type of massive voter fraud or ballot stuffing you might expect. Chávez's man-agement of elections is far more nuanced than outright rigging, and indeed it doesn't even occur on the day when people turn up to vote. "Election Day is not a problem," a former member of the National Electoral Council told me. "All the damage—the use of money, goods, excess power, communications—happens beforehand."

Elections in Venezuela are free, but they are far from fair, she explained. She was one of the many technocrats at the electoral council fired by Chávez. She claims she saw the institution quickly become subservient to the office of the president. While many highly competent professionals continue to work there—some of whom are sympathetic to the opposition—they report to department heads who are all loyal to Chávez. They, in turn, report to the institution's five directors, four of whom are avowed Chavistas, even though they are supposed to be without party affiliations. "The National Electoral Council has no independence left," she explained. "Before it was very transparent. It was very open." Now it is the technical brain of a well-oiled machine designed to tilt the playing field in Chávez's favor long before Election Day.

Once the country's electoral monitoring body became politicized, there was no independent arbiter to prevent electoral abuses committed by a government that was already under the control of one man. While the new constitution had banned public financing for political parties, the prohibition was only applied against the opposition. Government ministries openly flouted the ban, pouring millions of dollars into pro-Chávez banners, leaflets, and billboards, as well as sending state employees to canvass for the president. Although the evidence is on every street corner, the National Electoral Council doesn't say a word. According to Electoral Eye, an election watchdog group, as much as 30 percent of Chávez's February 2009 campaign to eliminate all term limits—opening the way for him to be president for life—was paid for by government ministries and public institutions.

For years millions of Venezuelans had effectively been disenfranchised by the poverty that plagued Venezuela. No one could object to an effort to ensure that these people be incorporated into society by giving them the same voter ID cards that had been provided to other citizens. However, in an effort to inflate the voter rolls, the National Electoral Council dispensed with the requirements that verified the identity of the cardholder. Mobile units were dispatched to the poorest neighborhoods, handing out voter IDs to anyone who asked for one. In 2003, eleven million people were registered voters. There was a bump of nearly three million voter registrations by the end of 2004, which meant the authorities were handing out roughly thirty-seven hundred voter IDs each day. By 2009, the total number stood at nearly eighteen million. According to *El Universal*'s Eugenio Martínez, 40 percent of registered voters do not even have an address listed. Election experts naturally feared that such a massive influx of unverifiable voters would open the system to phantom voters, multiple voting, and other types of hard-to-detect fraud. "Before, the system handed out secure voter IDs," the former National Electoral Council staffer told me. "Now they will give you an ID in the street. They have given voter IDs to people who are not even Venezuelan."

Some of the tools that Chávez has employed are dirty tricks familiar in any democracy. For example, Chávez's electoral engineers have been fond of gerrymandering, not unlike what was once practiced in America's Deep South to prevent African American candidates from being elected to predominantly white legislatures. Ahead of the last legislative elections, the government announced it would redraw the district lines. Everyone expected the redistricting would be an exercise in gerrymandering, and indeed it was: the number of representatives coming from urban areas, where the opposition usually fared best, was diluted in favor of rural areas that favored Chavista candidates. (For example, in Amazonas, a rural state considered a Chávez stronghold, it took only 42,000 votes to get a member of parliament. Meanwhile, in Zulia, a state where the opposition had performed well, it required 708,000 votes to earn one representative.) However, the National Electoral Council went further than just gerrymandering the districts: once it drew them up, it then withheld the information from opposition candidates. When I first visited Venezuela, although it was only ten months until the election, opposition candidates still did not know the districts from which they could run. It is hard to know in which neighborhoods to campaign if you cannot find your district on a map. However, no one, including the former member of the electoral council, doubted that Chavista candidates knew where the lines had been drawn. After a steady stream of complaints, the government published the new electoral districts, roughly eight months before Election Day.

Perhaps the most sophisticated way that Chávez has been able to maintain his majorities in parliament is by contorting the election rules to ensure favorable results. Venezuela's system of voting is a so-called mixed electoral system; each voter is allowed to cast ballots for an individual candidate as well as for a party. Most officeholders are elected as individual candidates from single-member districts, as in the United States. But 40 percent of the seats are allocated based on the principle of proportional representation. The idea behind the mixed electoral system is to prevent any single party from dominating an election. In theory, the second-largest party—which would presumably be an opposition party—should be safeguarded by having a fair percentage of its candidates selected from the party lists.

Chávez's advisers, however, found a loophole. They have gamed the system by having candidates loyal to Chávez run under the banner of political organizations that are legally distinct from Chávez's main party. Thus, Chávez is able to capture seats won by individual candidates as well as the seats that are allocated based on the party lists. Martínez showed me how it was theoretically possible for Chávez's party to win only 51 percent of the vote but walk away with 80 percent of the seats.

The results are astounding. In the September 2010 legislative election, Chávez's party and the opposition captured roughly the same percentage of the popular vote. Still, with nearly the same vote count, the opposition won only 39 percent of the seats in the National Assembly, while Chávez's party earned 59 percent. In the state of Carabobo, the opposition won 54 percent of the popular vote. Yet, with only 46 percent of the electorate, Chávez's candidates won seven of ten seats. The same occurred in the Caracas Capital District: Chávez's party lost the popular vote but won seven of ten seats. One simple revision in the election laws had the net effect of swinging eleven seats from the opposition to Chávez's allies. "If you count only the fact that there are elections and votes, Venezuela is a democracy," says the former electoral council staffer. "If you look beyond that, deeper than that, it is not."

Not that Chávez is content to leave his political dominance to his ability to finesse the vote. When his attempt to end presidential term limits was narrowly defeated in 2007, he simply brought the proposal back in another reshaped referendum in February 2009. Many of the executive powers he sought in his failed 2007 referendum were later achieved through presidential decrees and legislation produced by his rubber-stamp congress. Chávez has enacted more decrees than any president in Venezuelan history—169 decrees in his first ten years. Venezuela's first eight presidents only enacted 172 decrees in nearly forty years.

The net effect of Chávez's manipulations, end runs, and power grabs has been to make Venezuela a unique paradox: with each election, the country loses more of its democracy.

"Fear Does Not Leave Fingerprints"

Robert Serra can't sit still. He gets up from his desk and sits back down. A few minutes later, he is up again, now pacing. Back at his desk, he can't figure out what to do with his hands. When he is speaking, he uses them to slice through the air and punctuate his points. He speaks quickly, the words tumbling out, so his hands have a lot of work to do. The blown-up photographs that decorate his campaign headquarters show him in motion. In each, Serra, with his signature spiked hair rising a good inch above his head, is outside, addressing crowds, leading marches, shaking hands. In his office, when he isn't speaking, he seems less sure. He stops to listen, is even quiet, but you can see the tremor building underneath, as if the twenty-three-year-old politician were a volcano about to erupt. He isn't angry, and he isn't nervous; he is simply impatient to do what he does best: fill the air with words. After ten minutes, his nickname seems appropriate; some people call him mini-Chávez.

Serra made a name for himself as one of Chávez's most aggressive and outspoken student leaders. Now, two months before the legislative elections, he is running as a candidate for Chávez's ruling party, seeking to represent the gritty neighborhood of January 23rd. (The name January 23rd is a reference to January 23, 1958, the day that the Venezuelan dictator Marcos Pérez Jiménez was ousted.) His office is on the sixth floor of a high-rise in north Caracas, across the street from the National Pantheon, which houses the remains of Simón Bolívar under its main altar. The Pantheon is the site of many of Chávez's presidential addresses. Just a few days before I visited Serra, Chávez had shocked Venezuelans, even some Chavistas, by exhuming Bolívar's body live on television, shortly after midnight. Chávez had the body raised for "forensic tests"; he believes that Bolívar, rather than dying from tuberculosis, was assassinated by Colombian oligarchs. During his speech, Chávez asked Jesus Christ to bring Bolívar back from the dead and later claimed to have spoken with the liberator's bones. (It is rumored that he often leaves an extra chair in cabinet meetings for Bolívar.) Chávez live tweeted the entire macabre event.

Speaking with a Chavista, especially one as devout and ideological as Serra, can be a somewhat surreal experience. When I asked him about the country's deteriorating economy—the only South American economy in decline, with mounting inflation—he looked perplexed, replying that every year salaries had risen. Of course, he ignored the fact that those raises had been devoured by that same inflation, or that price controls had led to a shortage of basic goods like sugar and milk. When I pressed him on the country's economy, he explained that the hike in prices for simple grocery items was the result of hoarding by the wealthy. Even the shortage of water was the result of hoarding. He did not, however, see any connection between the food shortages and the shipping containers, owned and operated by the government, that had recently been discovered to hold more than 100,000 tons of rotting food. Over the course of two hours, Serra confronted facts with a stream of bizarre claims, denials, and deflections.

Near the end of our meeting, I asked him if he thought his legislative campaign may have been made any more difficult by Chávez's sagging approval numbers. Naturally, Serra denied that Chávez's popularity had declined at all, despite multiple polls and recent elections that suggested the opposite. Referring to the upcoming legislative election, Serra said, "I believe we will have very good results. The peace of our country rests on what happens."

The comment stopped me.

"Peace? Why peace?" I asked.

"Chávez is the principal guarantee of peace in Venezuela," he replied. "He is the barrier to all of those Venezuelans who are not going to take power through force because they see themselves represented in Chávez. The day Chávez is not there something will happen. Those millions of people will go to the streets and take power by any means necessary."

Here I thought we were discussing an upcoming election. Serra was now raising the specter of civil war. Without Chávez, he implied, there would be blood in the streets. Never mind that we were discussing a legislative contest and President Chávez was therefore not on the ballot. It would be an extraordinary thing for a politician to say, if it wasn't something that Chávez, and other Chavistas, repeated all the time. It was almost reflexive for Serra to imply that Venezuela's social contract would collapse if the correct result was not reached. It is emblematic of the loaded, high-stakes rhetoric frequently employed to both inflame public opinion and frighten people on either side of the political divide. The threat, even implied, does not ring hollow to Venezuelans after Chávez has spent years creating people's militias, the so-called Bolivarian Circles, to defend the revolution. (In their oath, members of the Bolivarian Circles pledge to sacrifice their lives to defend the revolution.) Beyond encouraging voters to revolt, Chávez has even suggested he would overturn an election that did not go his way, saying, "If the oligarchy is allowed to return to power, I might end up letting the . . . tanks out to defend the revolutionary government and the people."

For more than a decade, Chávez and his allies have perfected the subtle use of fear and intimidation to achieve their aims. It is a way of shaping voter behavior without the outright violation of people's rights. Of course, Serra wouldn't have described his words as intimidating. He was simply stating the facts, suggesting that now that Venezuela was so polarized, it was his and other Chavistas' job to help contain and calm the people. It was like saying that if a lion is poked and prodded, his handler is more necessary than ever—true, even if he is the one who upset the beast. The political message is not aimed at Chavistas or members of the opposition. Both of those camps know how they will vote come Election Day; no words will easily sway them. The target is the bloc of undecided voters—the so-called *ni-nis* (neither-nors)—who make up more than 40 percent of the electorate. Fear can be a very effective weapon for the sizable bloc who reside between the poles of Venezuelan politics.

One of the most notorious examples of voter intimidation came in the form of something called the Tascón List. The opposition had managed, after repeated attempts, to force a recall referendum on Chávez's presidency in August 2004. Several months before the referendum, Chávez requested that the National Electoral Council release the names of the three million people who voted in favor of holding the referendum to his campaign manager, Luis Tascón. Chávez's stated rationale was that he believed many of the signatures were forgeries, and he planned to expose them as such. Once he had the election data, Tascón posted the names on his Web site. Anyone could refer to the Tascón List to see who had been in favor of holding a referendum on Chávez's rule.

Of course, the publication of the names had another purpose: political persecution. The health minister, Roger Capella, said that any doctors or nurses who had signed the recall referendum would be fired for what amounted to an "act of terrorism." Alí Rodríguez, the head of PDVSA, the state oil company, said he expected that workers who had signed the referendum would be dismissed. In one instance, more than eighty state employees from a government banking agency were fired because they supported the referendum. Jesús Caldera, the agency's president, said it had conducted the purge to make way for civil servants who "adhered to the government project." Rampant reports surfaced of people being denied jobs, promotions, and basic government services because their names appeared on the list.

A year later, Chávez's supporters developed an even more comprehensive tool called the Maisanta. A reference to a nineteenth-century rebel commander, the Maisanta was a digital database that pulled together detailed information on all of Venezuela's registered voters. The Maisanta included a person's name; address; voter identification number; and whether he or she had voted for the referendum, abstained in earlier elections, or received support from the government's social programs. All of this information, for more than twelve million Venezuelan voters, was stored on a single compact disc. Worse, it had been copied and distributed across the country.

In fact, you don't even need to look for the Maisanta; the Maisanta will find you. In the summer of 2010, I was waiting on the front steps of a government building in downtown Caracas where members of the National Assembly keep offices. I had an appointment with a Chavista congressman later that day. While I waited, people came up to me to try to sell me pirated DVDs. At least at first that is what I assumed they were. When I looked more closely, I realized they weren't the

Hollywood knockoffs you find on street corners in New York, Paris, or Beijing; they were copies of the Maisanta. For about $1.50, I had voter information on millions of Venezuelans.

The cost has been much greater for the people on the disc. In one case documented by Human Rights Watch, a ninety-eight-year-old woman was denied medical prescriptions she had been receiving for years; when her family inquired, they were told it was because she had signed the referendum. One person I met told me a similar story. Her fiancé required immediate medical attention and went to the emergency room of a government-run hospital. The hospital representative was in the process of admitting him, until she ran his voter identification card through the computer. He was told he would have to go someplace else. Statistical analysis supports the anecdotal evidence. Several academics compared the list of people who signed the referendum with data from household surveys and found that Chávez's opponents saw a 5 percent drop in income and a 1.5 percent drop in employment after the voter rolls were made public. In a society ruled by patronage politics, being identified as an enemy of the state can have serious consequences. Once the information was released, it did not even require the government to use the data against its opponents. Venezuelans used the list against fellow citizens to decide everything from who is hired or fired to who gets a passport or is audited by the tax authorities. If Chávez knows who his friends are, then it is best if you don't do business with his enemies.

María Corina Machado knows firsthand the price of opposing Chávez. She is the co-founder of an election watchdog group called Súmate. During the 2004 recall referendum, her organization played a lead role in encouraging people to participate in the vote. Her work did not go unnoticed. The government brought charges against Machado and three other members of Súmate for conspiring to "destroy the nation's republican form of government." In particular, the government latched onto the fact that Súmate had received a grant from the National Endowment for Democracy, a Washington-based organization, for $53,400. The money had been used to conduct workshops to educate citizens on the referendum. Ultimately, the government could not prove how educating Venezuelans about their government's own constitutional process threatened to destabilize the regime. But it did not stop Chávez from launching a full-scale media war to try to destroy the NGO's credibility; Machado and other members of Súmate were regularly attacked on TV and in the press as traitors and lackeys of U.S. imperialism. "They choose people in every sector, in the media, in the private sector, in the unions and some political parties, to intimidate, hurt, or persecute," Machado told me. "That has a direct effect on the rest of the people."

Seven years after founding Súmate, Machado stepped up her opposition to the regime: she decided to become one of the only independent female political candidates to run for the National Assembly. On a warm evening in July 2010, I went to see her on the campaign trail. It was just about dusk, and the street was starting to fill up with people. It is hard for opposition candidates to find public spaces to hold their events, so on this evening the meeting is in the middle of a quiet street behind a neighborhood development in Bonita. The banners say, "Somos Mayoría" (We Are the Majority). The people turning up tonight are old and young, professionals and pensioners—and nearly all of them are women. It is not entirely surprising that so many women would come out to see María Corina Machado speak. Magalli Meda, Machado's campaign manager, tells me that women, especially mothers, have been key to the campaign. "Our communication strategy has always been to talk about families," says Meda, an expert on branding and a mother of two. "The thing is, every time you talk about family here, you empower women. And they bring their family along."

Mothers had, in effect, become ambassadors of the campaign, mobilizing their entire families to come out to vote. And the results were obvious, not just on this evening, but in Machado's level of support. In order for candidates to run for office, they must first collect a required number of signatures. It took most candidates several weeks to collect these names. "It took them two to three weeks," says Meda. "It took us one day to get four times the minimum number of signatures."

Although it is her first election, Machado's time at Súmate made her a veteran of the election wars, well schooled in the ways in which an authoritarian wins at the ballot box. She rattles off demographic data on states around the country. She recalls the percentages for seemingly every election of the past decade. She knows the election laws backward and forward. When I ask her why the government has been so successful, she settles on one word: fear. "Fear does not leave fingerprints," she tells me. "I think it has been Chávez's biggest and best-used instrument from day one."

She makes her case by pointing to one of the figures she thinks matters most: 49 percent of Venezuelans do not believe the vote is secret. "Remember," she tells me, "there are about 5.6 million people, according to official data, that depend on money given to them by the government, either from pensions or jobs. And then somebody comes and knocks on your door and asks how you feel about crime? Horrible. Corruption? Terrible. President Chávez? Oh, I love him. The conclusion is that Chávez is a charismatic leader that has an emotional connection. And of course he does. But I believe it is also fear." If you believe the vote may not be secret, that your political preferences could be used against you—hardly far-fetched after the creation of the Tascón List and the Maisanta—you might think twice before answering the third question. "You do not have the incentive to risk voting against [Chávez], because either nothing is going to happen or you will be punished," says Machado. "The whole idea of making people that dissent believe that anything they say or do will hurt them . . . is strategic."

Sometimes, of course, the regime is hardly subtle in the ways it tries to intimidate. A decade after she had invited Chávez to discuss oil policy at Simón Bolívar University, Maruja Tarre, the former diplomat and professor, had become a sharp critic of the president. She regularly gave interviews or wrote articles criticizing his statements and policies. Much of her commentary came via Twitter, where she would give real-time reaction to Chávez's public addresses. In September 2009, she wasn't watching Chávez speak; she was on the phone, talking to her daughter, who lived in Washington, D.C. On that evening, they were discussing a recent spate of anti-Chávez demonstrations that had been held abroad. They compared them to some of the international protests that had been held in solidarity with the Green Movement in Iran, which was still struggling to take to the streets after it had erupted a couple of months earlier. It was a conversation between a mother and a daughter.

Two nights later, it was on the six o'clock news. Tarre and her daughter, Isabel, were shocked to see their private conversation broadcast on national television. The news anchor offered his TV audience no explanation of how he had acquired the recording; it was simply understood that Tarre's phone had been bugged. Once it aired, Alberto Nolia, the host of the show *The Devil's Papers,* proceeded to deconstruct the conversation to help viewers understand what they had just heard. He said that Tarre's daughter had just admitted to being the organizer of "anti-Venezuelan" demonstrations in foreign countries, although the protests were against Chávez's government, not Venezuela, and she hadn't organized anything. Nolia then went on to say, in an aggrieved voice, "What type of mother calls her daughter abroad to talk about politics?"

If people missed it, then they might have caught the conversation a few hours later when it was rebroadcast on a late-night political talk show called *The Razor.* The host, Mario Silva, an ardent Chávez supporter, regularly attacks members of the opposition in the strongest possible language. Projecting a thuggish persona, Silva uses his show to threaten or humiliate people, often promoting anti-Semitic conspiracy theories. After re-airing the conversation, he argued that Tarre had just admitted the Venezuelan opposition had failed. He made fun of her daughter, saying she must have lived abroad for a long time judging by her "Spanglish." He then read from their Twitter accounts. "They record everything we say," Tarre told me. "They say I am in the 'hands of the empire.' I don't know what it means to be in the hands of the empire. I do know it was meant to scare us."

"We Have Good News, and We Have Bad News"

The National Institute of Female Orientation sits high on a hilltop. The name is a euphemism for the overcrowded, dilapidated structure that serves as Venezuela's only women's prison. (Like the military prison that holds Raúl Baduel, it is in Los Teques.) Wednesday mornings are visiting day, and more than two hundred people have lined up early. It takes about forty-five minutes to reach the front of the line, register, be stamped on your forearm, searched, and then cleared to enter. A pack of stray dogs, however, simply wander in and out, sauntering by the security guards and into the prison complex. One small brown-and-tan shepherd mix, not more than six months old, sits in the shade, watching as people inch closer to the front gate. Occasionally, he gets up to sniff at the bags of food people have brought—the prison sometimes runs out during the week—hoping for a handout. When I pass through security and walk onto the prison grounds, the same puppy is already there, on the inside, looking for another spot to avoid the midday sun.

The prison is disorientating at first. Many guards don't wear uniforms. It's hard to distinguish who is an inmate and who works there. Some guards wear the correct prison-issued pants, others are in street clothes. But it may not make any difference. As soon as I am inside, a prisoner in a tank top and shorts asks me, "Who do you want to see? I'll take you." I had come to see Judge María Afiuni.

Eight months earlier, Judge Afiuni had been presiding over a hearing in her courtroom, at the Thirty-First Control Court in Caracas. The case involved a man named Eligio Cedeño. The government contended Cedeño, a Venezuelan businessman, was corrupt, guilty of evading currency controls. But the hearing on December 10, 2009, wasn't about the merits of the case. At issue was whether the government had the right to continue to hold Cedeño in custody. The Venezuelan government had kept the businessman in pretrial detention for three years, although the country's laws permit someone to be held for only two years. Judge Afiuni had grown aggravated when the prosecutor's office had failed to send an attorney to two prior hearings. Basing her decision on Venezuelan law and guidance from a panel of United Nations legal experts, Afiuni ordered Cedeño's conditional release on bail. He would have to surrender his passport and report to the court every fifteen days, but he could not be held in indefinite detention. Cedeño, who believed himself to be a political prisoner—he had previously helped finance opposition politicians—immediately fled the country. But even before he did, Judge Afiuni found herself in handcuffs. "The intelligence officers, the same ones that brought Cedeño into the hearing, were the ones that arrested me—fifteen minutes after I made my judgment," says Afiuni, sitting on a green plastic stool outside her jail cell.

When I visited her, she was being held in a wing of the prison with additional security, separate from the general population. The prison was built to hold 250 inmates, but today it holds 682. Afiuni shares a tiny cell with two other women; there is only one bunk bed, so someone must sleep on the floor. Light comes in from the grid of twelve small windows at one end of the cell, most without any panes of glass. The paint on the walls seems relatively fresh. (The last inmate in this cell burned herself alive, Afiuni tells me, so they had to repaint.) Suicides, violence, and deaths are common here. Only a couple of weeks earlier an inmate down the hall hanged herself.

Afiuni never goes beyond the narrow hallway that leads to her cell. It's a necessary precaution since she is responsible for sending at least twenty-four criminals to the same prison that now holds her. For the first four months, there was no lock on her cell door. "When I first got here, they would come near my cell and yell, 'I am going to cut your eyes out. I'm going to cut you to pieces, bitch,'" she tells me, smoking Belmonts. Several inmates had to be transferred to another prison. They had been discovered waiting outside her cell's window with cans of kerosene. Even now, sequestered from everyone but the twenty other women on this wing, she receives death threats outside her door. How do prisoners from the general population get past the guards and locked door at the end of the hallway? "That's a good question," she says, smiling.

Attorney General Luisa Ortega Díaz charged Afiuni with corruption, abuse of power, and facilitating the evasion of justice. The very handcuffs that had been on Cedeño were soon slapped on the judge. "All of my court was detained for twelve hours—three assistants, two bailiffs, my bodyguards, and intern—nine people in total," says Afiuni. The next evening, Chávez took to the radio and television airwaves to denounce Afiuni. He accused her of being guilty of crimes "more serious than an assassination." He railed that in earlier times she would have been executed by a firing squad. "That judge must pay, with all the force of the law, for what she did, along with any judge who thinks about doing something similar," exhorted Chávez. As he spoke, the television cameras panned over to the attorney general, who sat there dutifully listening. If Afiuni were guilty of the charges, Venezuelan law would allow a maximum of seven years' imprisonment. Chávez found that unsatisfactory: "I call for thirty years in prison in the name of the dignity of the country."

Afiuni did not watch Chávez's remarks on television. The intelligence police had already confined her to a jail cell. But she remembers how she found out about Chávez's tirade. "A senior intelligence official came in and said, 'We have good news, and we have bad news. The good news is that we have found nothing against you. The bad news is that Chávez just condemned you to prison for thirty years on national television.'"

Apparently, Chávez's words were enough. Eight months later, the government had still failed to substantiate any of its claims. The attorney general explained that Afiuni was guilty of "spiritual pollution." Judge Leidys Azuaje—who, Afiuni told me, was a magistrate the government had relied on in the past to handle political cases—presided over the case. At her first preliminary hearing, the government's prosecutors admitted that they had found no evidence to support the charges. Despite the fact that evidence of a "benefit" is an essential element for a charge of corruption, Judge Azuaje saw nothing amiss. "The prosecutor said there is no evidence. There is no money, no contact [between me and Cedeño]," recalls Afiuni. "And the judge said, 'Well, you are going to trial.'"

Chávez had long since stripped the Venezuelan judiciary of its independence. In 2004, the National Assembly passed a law that allowed him to pack the Supreme Court with loyalists. The law also made it easy to purge any justices whose "public attitude . . . undermines the majesty or prestige of the Supreme Court." This new pro-Chávez high court then fired hundreds of judges across the judiciary, replacing them with more politically acceptable choices. If there was any question whom the members of the Supreme Court served, they answered it at the beginning of the 2006 judicial session. At that opening ceremony, several judges began chanting, "¡Uh, ah, Chávez no se va!" (Uh, ah, Chávez is not leaving!).

I asked Afiuni if she had ever felt political pressure on a case. "Never. Never," she replied. She had generally handled routine criminal cases. "It would be naive to say that I didn't know what goes on in the judicial system. There is executive pressure in all the branches. But I was not going to resign or give up my post because other people were being pressured. I had been a judge for nine years, and I had not had to deal with that."

Nor did she think of herself as a hero or have any regrets. "This man had been detained for three years. I did what I was constitution-ally bound to do," she tells me. She expected there might be some reprisals for her decision or that she might be relieved of her duties. "But I never thought it could get to this," says Afiuni. "I never thought that my freedom or life would be at stake. What happened to me sent a clear message to all the other judges. Even Chávez said this is an example, she has to be made an example of."

When you exit the prison, the security guards sign you out. The form includes a space for your name, the name of the inmate you are visiting, and the crime that person has committed. Up and down the rolls, the crimes are listed. Drug smuggling. Theft. Murder. Next to Afiuni's name the space for her crime was left blank. It was as if even the guards didn't know what to say.

As she marked time in prison, Afiuni was diagnosed with cancer. In February 2011, after months of her pleading, the attorney general agreed to let her continue her pretrial detention under house arrest. Eligio Cedeño, the Venezuelan businessman, was granted political asylum in the United States. Judge Afiuni is still waiting for her day in court.

Hello, President

After twelve years of Chavismo, the mask is slipping. Despite the largest oil boom in Venezuelan history and despite large infusions of cash funneled into social programs, the signs of decay, deterioration, and disorder are abundant. First there is crime: everyone's chief worry is for his or her own safety. Under Chávez, homicides have reached epidemic proportions. Caracas is the most dangerous capital in the world, and one of the most violent cities. On the average weekend, more people will die in Caracas than in Baghdad and Kabul combined. In 2009, there were 19,133 murders in Venezuela, according to the Venezuelan Observatory of Violence. (The Venezuelan government stopped publishing the number of murders several years ago after it began to skyrocket.) The number of violent deaths in Venezuela has outpaced the body count of Mexico's drug war. And for the slain, there is little hope of justice: 91 percent of murders go unprosecuted.

Everyone I met knew someone who had been robbed, kidnapped,

or worse. One afternoon I attended a lunch thrown by a number of academics and former diplomats. The host arrived late, his face pale and his hands trembling: he had just been robbed—inside a bank. When you point out the level of crime to Chávez's own supporters, some will admit it is a worry. They then quickly point out that it was a problem in 1998, before Chávez became president. That is true. But the number of murders each year is now triple what it was when Chávez became president.

The second major concern is the economy. More and more, Venezuela finds itself alone among South American countries, as its economic prospects plunge. Despite being the continent's only oil-rich economy, it is also the only country in South America that saw its economy shrink in 2010. Its levels of inflation have exceeded even Africa's most mismanaged economies. Foreign investment disappeared after a wave of nationalizations ordered by Chávez. In 2010, Venezuela was the only South American country with a negative balance sheet for foreign investment. In the same year, Transparency International listed Venezuela as the continent's most corrupt country, ranking it 164 out of 178 states, alongside the likes of Laos and Angola. Corruption, graft, and a failure to invest in its basic infrastructure have led to power outages, rolling blackouts, and water shortages. Even the country's cash cow, PDVSA, the state-owned oil company, is suffering: it reported falling profits in 2010, even as the price of oil rose.

One of the most basic ways Venezuela's economic crisis reaches the general public is in the shortages of staple foods like meat, milk, and sugar. But how could a member of OPEC have a shortage of groceries? A local butcher, who asked that I not use his name, said sometimes it made more sense for butchers not to sell anything. Once or twice a month, he explained, the government sends inspectors to check his prices. He told me that the inspectors wanted him to sell meat at 17 bolivares a kilo. The problem is that he could usually only buy a kilo of meat for 19 to 21 bolivares. If the inspectors found his prices were above 17 bolivares, they would fine him 11,000 bolivares each time. "The problem is the price [controls]," he explained from behind his counter. "Since the price is regulated, you can't sell. Sometimes you buy with a little fear. I have three fines to pay right now."

It is not complex economics; the government's insistence on price controls during a period of massive inflation had predictably led to shortages. The butcher pointed to another butcher's shop down the street that had just closed. He didn't see the point in staying in business. I looked at the prices he had listed that day, and I noticed they were above 17 bolivares. "It's a risk we are running," he admitted. But he added that there was one upside to Chávez's economic policies. "When people are scared, they sometimes buy a lot," the butcher said, laughing. "Even a rumor can make people buy."

The fact that so many ingredients of everyday life are in a state of disrepair, if not utter ruin, presents a conundrum: How is it possible for Chávez to maintain public support when so much is going so wrong? Of course, his electoral strategies have been part of the equation. So too have the government's enormous handouts to its supporters and to those who have been living hand to mouth for years. Chávez's gross centralization of power has also left his government less reliant on swings in public opinion. But one of his most innovative tools is one available any hour of any day. As president of Venezuela, Chávez is CEO of a media empire unlike any other, and its main product is Chávez himself.

Chávez is everywhere. Turn on the television, change the radio station, walk to the newsstand, surf the Internet, and you will find him. Perhaps the most effective and utterly unique weapon he wields is the *cadena*. It is, in essence, a national presidential address. According to Venezuelan law, during a *cadena* all radio and television channels must broadcast the president's words. Typically, presidents resorted to using a *cadena* during an emergency or special event. Chávez uses it constantly. Specifically, in his first eleven years, he delivered nearly two thousand *cadenas*, which amounts to one every two days. He will use any occasion to call for a *cadena*, denouncing his enemies, extolling his work, or discussing whatever is on his mind. And once he starts talking, no one other than Chávez knows when he will stop. If you add up the length of all of his *cadenas*, they would amount to fifty-four full days. Chávez can effectively throttle all radio and television broadcasts and then saturate the airwaves with whatever message he chooses. "The *cadenas* are a huge form of control," says Andrés Cañizález, a professor and leading expert on Venezuelan media. "Chávez is able to control at any moment the content and the time that the *cadena* goes on the air nationally. It is basically a nonexistent tool in any other country."

The centerpiece of Chávez's media universe is his unscripted Sunday afternoon television show, *Aló, Presidente (Hello, President)*. Here, each week, Chávez sings, dances, rants, raves, shouts, jokes, questions, reports, prays, and—sometimes—calls Fidel Castro on the telephone. The show has no precise running time, although it averages a little less than five hours. It is a rambling program that resembles a telethon with a heavy dose of politics—a cross between Jerry Lewis and Glenn Beck but with an emphasis on "the socialism of the twenty-first century." (For the show's tenth anniversary, he aired a four-day special episode.) Chávez will often use the show to visit government projects, lambaste his opponents, or denounce the United States. As he downs one cup of coffee after another, he unveils new policies and makes bold announcements. Famously, during one episode, he ordered the head of the military to send ten tank battalions to the Venezuelan-Colombian border. Special guests have included Danny Glover, Diego Maradona, and, of course, Fidel.

Although the showman never acts like a head of state, one of the program's more important elements is the picture it gives of Chávez governing. Amid his monologues and impromptu tirades, Chávez will quiz his ministers—whose attendance is mandatory—often berating them for their failings. The Comandante has even been known to fire a minister live on television. The whole lot of them sit among the audience, wearing socialist red, their heads tilted down, praying that they are not called out on a whim. Chávez dressing down a hapless minister for the pleasure of the viewing audience on national television is what passes for accountability in Venezuela today. It is also a vital part of the image making that keeps him blameless for the country's mounting troubles. The message is clear: if the incompetent ministers and bureaucrats would only do what Chávez told them to do, everything would be fine.

If Chávez's antics are unrehearsed, his creation of a media state is anything but spontaneous. It began in the wake of the April 2002 coup. When Chávez came to power, the Venezuelan government operated one state television channel and two radio stations, and Chávez had done surprisingly little to change that in the early years of his presidency. After the coup, Chávez saw the crucial role the media played in shaping events and, in his view, encouraging his ouster. He referred to the four private television channels as the Four Horsemen of the Apocalypse. "[Chávez's government] saw how weak they were after April 11, 2002," says Cañizález, referring to the short-lived coup. "They realized they were a communication minority, so they developed a strategy to create a strong media infrastructure."

In 2004, the National Assembly provided the government with the legal framework to control the media. The government was given broad discretionary powers to punish slander and disrespect of public officials. Defamation of the president can lead to thirty months in prison, and the government has the right to impose hefty fines on any media company for "offending" public authorities. Two of the major television channels—Venevisión and Televen—soon changed their editorial stance to fall in line with the government's wishes. Politically objectionable shows were canceled, and the channels' focus shifted to entertainment. In one telling example, a popular political talk show was replaced with a program on astrology and tarot readings. A third channel, RCTV, was closed, and the fourth, Globovisión, remains in a bitter struggle with the government, always under the threat of sanctions. (In October 2011, for example, Globovisión was fined $2 million for reporting on deadly prison riots a few months earlier.) Meanwhile, Chávez has poured millions into creating his own pro-government media conglomerate. Today, there are six government television channels, two national radio stations, three thousand community radio stations, three print media companies, and a growing presence on the Internet. "These channels are clearly a propaganda machine of the state," Cañizález told me. "It is sort of what you would think of the official state TV of Cuba."

Perhaps the regime's most sophisticated tool has simply been uncertainty. In August 2009, Chávez shuttered 34 radio stations for alleged "administrative infractions." At the same time, the government announced that it was investigating 240 other stations for similar violations. However, it never specified which stations were under its microscope, nor did it intend to notify them. With the threat of closure already made real, the government knew the stations would do its censorship for it. In such an environment, any story that comes too close to the edge is either watered down or killed. "Their strategy is to keep them on their heels," says Cañizález. "This is a way that media critical of the government can exist, but always under threat and at a high cost. Because the government doesn't give a clear set of rules, it puts independent media in a constant state of uncertainty."

If Chávez's media war began with television and radio, his sights now appear to be set on the Internet. (He has largely ignored print media. The majority of Venezuelans watch or listen to their news, and he knows that a significant percentage of those who regularly read newspapers would never support him anyway.) Several years ago Chávez nationalized CANTV, the only central provider of the Internet in Venezuela. In late 2009, he appointed a former head of the intelligence police to the company's board of directors. And in December 2010, the National Assembly passed laws forbidding any Internet provider to post content that causes "anxiety or unrest among the public order."

What you will not hear from Chávez's many media outlets is the number of people who died in Caracas over the weekend. You will not see a report on the government's failure to build the housing that it promised ahead of the last election. You will not learn that some stores are running low on basic goods or that inflation is rising. I was in Venezuela in July 2010, shortly after the story of state-owned shipping containers carrying more than 100,000 tons of spoiled food broke. The scandal dominated newspaper headlines but was utterly ignored by Chávez's networks. All Chávez spoke of was his growing war of words with neighboring Colombia. With his media empire in place, he can simply ignore the stories he doesn't like or change the conversation. When I brought up the subject of crime with Robert Serra, the loyal Chavista, he admitted it was a problem, then proceeded to blame the media for sowing conflict. That argument might have worked ten years ago. But it is far less plausible today. That is the problem for authoritarian leaders everywhere. Eventually, you run out of scapegoats.

Democratic Antibodies

Teodoro Petkoff is not easy to interrupt, especially when the topic is Hugo Chávez. In the space of a few minutes, the editor of *Tal Cual*, a respected opposition newspaper, refers to Chávez as a "fascist," a "banana tyrant," and, in perhaps the strongest language, "a very good disciple of Hitler and Goebbels." Like many Venezuelans, he claims that he always knew Chávez's intentions. The difference is, when it comes from Petkoff, you are inclined to give him the benefit of the doubt. The editor with the signature bushy mustache has been a fixture of Venezuelan politics for decades. Born in 1932 to immigrant parents—his father was Bulgarian, his mother a Pole—he has been an economist, author, leftist guerrilla, presidential candidate, minister, and political prisoner. He was even a prison escapee. (In 1967, he and several other leftist guerrillas tunneled their way out of the San Carlos military prison.) And today, from his editor's perch, the cantankerous Petkoff is one of Chávez's most outspoken critics.

Time, however, has not made him cynical. In fact, it is his faith in Venezuelan history that makes him believe there is a limit to what Chávez's authoritarian project can accomplish. "This is not a totalitarian society," bellows Petkoff. "The Venezuelan society has what I call democratic antibodies. We have lived not only a half century of democracy, but there is a tradition, a history before us that makes it very difficult to impose on us a totalitarian society. Is this an authoritarian government? Of course. Is this an undemocratic government? Of course. There is not an inch of separation of powers. There are no checks and balances. Chávez has encroached on all political powers, all of them—parliament, justice, attorney general, comptroller, ombudsman, and the National Electoral Council. Is this a militaristic society? That's true. And the society has a propensity for totalitarianism. There is a *propensity*." He draws out the syllables slowly for emphasis. "And the country, so far, is containing that propensity."

The key in his mind is that the one thing that made Chávez different from most autocrats—massive popular support—is withering. "Sixty percent of our population believed in him. People love him," he says from across his crowded desk. "But this is changing. Today it is not 60 percent. It is less than 50 percent. There is a slow but persistent and, in my opinion, irreversible tendency of decline in his popular support."

I ask him, "When do you think Chávez is most dangerous?"

"Right now, because he is losing popular support," replies Petkoff.

Just as the words come out of his mouth, his eyes look up, beyond me, to a television in his assistant's office. I turn to see what has distracted him. It's a live news broadcast on Globovisión that has interrupted programming. Emilio Graterón, the opposition mayor of Chacao, is holding an impromptu press conference outside in the street, only a few blocks away from Petkoff's office. An animated Graterón is describing how a local piece of municipal property, designated to house a new community center, has been "invaded" by Chavistas. Locals surround the mayor, shouting their support. Holding the city government's legal title to the property, Graterón explains that Chavistas showed up and seized the land. No title, no authority, no process. They just took it in the name of the revolution. Moments later, national guard units begin to arrive. They spray tear gas over the mayor and his supporters, who quickly disperse. It is as if, hearing Petkoff's last statement, Chávez conjured up a demonstration of his muscular power at work—live on TV.

Picking up on his train of thought, Petkoff says, "Will he try to make a massive fraud? Will he be much more repressive than oppressive? I don't know. I think he is at the threshold of what to do. Will he cross that threshold of repression?" He lets the question hang in the air, without answering.

Still, Petkoff is optimistic. He believes deeply in the "democratic antibodies" of the Venezuelan people and has faith that whatever distance separates Venezuela from Cuba or other more repressive regimes will remain. Despite the difficulties of the past decade, he sees signs of new political life. "We have lived a historical tragedy. All the old leadership of this country went to the showers. They disappeared from the political scene. All the big, old parties are dead," says Petkoff. "Now this country is reconstructing its system of political parties. It's creating a new leadership . . . Until a year ago, people were asking, 'What opposition leaders?' Today, you find the names—the mayor of Chacao, the mayor of Caracas, the governor of Miranda, the governor of Zulia . . . Of course, they are young, but after eleven years of Chavismo they are veterans."

It is not simply that the opposition is rebuilding; the problems Chávez faces are also growing more entrenched. Alfredo Croes, the businessman turned opposition strategist, made this point when we met. Croes is good at crunching numbers. Almost a year before the National Assembly elections, with his desk covered with spreadsheets, he told me he thought that the opposition would win sixty-six to sixty-eight seats. He proved remarkably accurate: Chávez's opponents picked up sixty-seven seats. But he wasn't basing his calculations only on the appeal of the opposition in key districts. He also understood that the demographics of Chávez's support are shifting. When Chávez started, he could credibly claim to represent nearly all of Venezuela's poor. But more than a decade on that was no longer true. In 2008, growing blocs of urban poor began voting for the opposition. Election maps started to show an increasing urban-rural divide, with voters in the countryside making up the bulwark of Chávez's support. The fact that someone is poor is no longer a reliable indicator that he or she is pro-Chávez. "The rejection of Chávez will grow on the hills," Croes told me, pointing out his office window to one of the many slums that ring the city of Caracas. "They will not vote for the opposition; they will [vote to] punish him."

I looked out the window in the direction Croes was pointing. Along a steep slope, I could see thousands of small, makeshift structures, built one on top of the next like some precarious pyramid. "What you see over there, on that hill, is where the D and E people live." Croes was pointing at Petare, one of the largest slums in South America. "They have never had regular water. And they have never had a reliable power supply. What kills them is inflation," he says, his expression turning grim. "They need to climb a thousand steps to get home. They must cross circles of danger—gangs, narco-dealers, murderers. To carry food up those steps, they have to buy food in small quantities. The cost goes up to carry it up. They can't catch up. Inflation kills them."

In late 2009, Venezuela's inflation had risen to nearly 30 percent. A few weeks before I met Croes, the International Monetary Fund said that it expected Venezuela's inflation to continue to climb, surpassing even Zimbabwe and the war-torn Democratic Republic of the Congo. A few months later, according to several estimates, Venezuela had the highest inflation in the world. And many economists expect it will remain there for years to come. For Croes, it's Chávez's inability to tame this economic variable that will push a growing percentage of the Venezuelan poor into the arms of the opposition. "Inflation will be there in 2012," says Croes. "The distance between D and E and Chávez is now economics. It isn't easy to solve, because you have no infrastructure to get food prices down."

The question may be how much the factors that should matter—crime, decaying infrastructure, the price of food—will determine Chávez's political future. Each day he proves that the durability of his regime has only a passing relationship with the success of his own governance. Has the architecture of his authoritarian state advanced to such a point that he will be able to continue to ride roughshod over any opponent? Now that the country's democratic facade is paper-thin, if the moment comes, will he become more repressive? Or will the formula that has taken him this far continue to succeed? "Chávez is weaker, but he is not weak," says the pollster Luis Vicente León. "Chávez is like a tenor—he is getting older, but he knows how to sing. And he knows how to sing the important song."

In late June 2011, Venezuela learned that Chávez was weaker in another sense as well: he had cancer. For months, Chávez ferried back and forth to Cuba for chemotherapy treatments as rumors of his health and speculation of the political fallout his prognosis would have for the regime swirled around Caracas. In October, he declared himself cancer-free, but his true condition remained a state secret. Whatever the case, there was no question that he had long been gearing up for the fight—and intended to see it through to the 2012 presidential election.

After the opposition made gains in the National Assembly in September 2010, Chávez effectively hollowed out the institution from the inside. In late December, during the waning days of the session, he directed the National Assembly to grant him the power to rule the country by decree for the next eighteen months. (Chávez supposedly asked to have the power for twelve months, but the delegates insisted he take eighteen.) The new congress now only meets four days a month. Speeches from the well must not exceed fifteen minutes. True to form, the former tank commander would rather destroy the institution than share it.

Chávez also knew he needs to be able to foot the bill. In April 2011, using his new decree powers, he unilaterally revised the tax on oil revenues to fill his campaign war chest. With the price of Venezuelan oil hovering around $108 a barrel, he declared that 95 percent of the amount above $100 a barrel will now flow to Fonden, an opaque off-budget fund that operates at Chávez's personal discretion. If the price of oil remains relatively stable, this surplus tax would conservatively generate more than $10 billion in new revenue by the end of 2011. (Near the end of the year, Venezuela's finance minister claimed there was roughly $32 billion sitting in Fonden.) In effect, Chávez decreed himself a war chest of billions, months ahead of a presidential election season.

But perhaps the surest sign that he is steeling himself for a fight came in one of the last-minute laws passed by his pliant National Assembly. In the final hours, Chávez's regime passed a law that forbids representatives to switch political parties. This law had nothing to do with the opposition; this time the sharp point of the spear was pointed squarely at Chávez's own party. Chávez knows the battle may get ugly, and he does not plan to suffer defections. The message was clear: Once with Chávez, always with Chávez. No exceptions.

The late political scientist Samuel Huntington once observed that what decides if a democracy survives is not the size of the problems it faces or even its ability to solve those problems. What matters is the way in which a democracy's leaders respond to their *inability* to solve the problems that confront their country. By the late 1990s, Venezuela's political leaders had effectively stuck their heads in the sand. When they looked up again, Hugo Chávez was their president, and their democracy, however poor and ill functioning, was at the beginning of a slow descent into the authoritarianism that rules it today.

CHAPTER 4 THE OPPOSITION

Sunday mornings in Caracas are one of the few times the city stands still. The traffic jams are gone. The honking car horns fall silent. People are at home with their families or preparing to attend Sunday Mass. A couple of hours outside the city, however, it is anything but quiet. We had traveled in a pickup truck for two hours into the countryside of the state of Miranda, our destination the small town of Cupira in a poor farming area called Pedro Gual. While Chávez's approval ratings had begun to slump in Caracas and other urban areas, the countryside is still largely a Chavista stronghold, and Cupira is just like countless other small agricultural towns. Its mayor is a staunch Chavista. Pro-Chávez signs and billboards dot the roadway, some claiming credit for one public project or another, others simply proclaiming their love for a leader. Cupira is also emblematic of how Chávez's political opponents are beginning to take the fight to him. On this Sunday, Henrique Capriles, the governor of the state of Miranda, is doing precisely the sort of work that he and other leaders of the opposition hope will turn the tide against Hugo Chávez.

As soon as we get out of the pickup, we can hear the ruckus. The noise is coming from the Chaguaramal Primary School. Nearly all of the school's three hundred children, ranging from kindergarten to sixth grade, plus parents, teachers, and a very proud school principal, have gathered to celebrate the inauguration of their newly renovated school. They are waiting for Governor Capriles to arrive. It's hot outside as the sun takes its position directly overhead and even hotter under the school's bright new roof. But the students aren't sitting still. Wearing their school uniforms and sporting brand-new book bags emblazoned with "State of Miranda," they are singing, dancing, and jumping up and down. Enormous stereo speakers in the corners of the room are blaring reggaeton, Shakira, and fast-paced Venezuelan dance beats. As the girls spin in their pleated skirts and the boys belt out Latin pop hits at the top of their lungs, the place looks more like a dance party than a pep rally for a renovated school.

We hear a helicopter pass overhead. For a moment, the students pause and their eyes go wide as it dawns on them that it must be the governor. A few minutes later, Capriles jogs through the school's entrance and the students erupt with screams. The thirty-seven-year-old leader of Miranda is wearing a blue baseball cap, oxford shirt, and sweatpants. You can see the sweat on his face and shirt, as if he has run all the way from his office to the school's front steps. In fact, you might mistake him for the school's gym teacher rather than the governor of Venezuela's most politically important state and, by many people's reckoning, the man most likely to challenge Chávez for the presidency.

Slowly, Capriles makes his way through the crowd to the podium in front. He begins by pointing to homemade banners hoisted up by parents in the back of the room and reading them aloud. One sign reads, "Our Schools Are Falling Down"; another says, "Governor, Our Children Need New Schools, Too." The children of these parents aren't attending the newly renovated school in Pedro Gual. The parents have traveled from other parts of Miranda to bring their concerns directly to the governor. Capriles asks them to tell him about the condition of their schools.

His manner of speaking is as informal as his clothes. He says his goal is to help every single school in the state of Miranda. In the next twelve months, his team is aiming to repair 166 schools and build 14 new schools, followed by 40 more in the next four years. More than 150,000 new book bags have been handed out. He asks one of the schoolboys in the crowd to come up front and show him his book bag. Capriles reaches in and pulls out several books. "Arithmetic. Science . . . but no politics," he says as he looks at each of the books, and

the crowd laughs. Capriles's joke is also his message: he won't practice President Chávez's divisive brand of politics; his is an inclusive
style that is unconcerned with whom you have supported in the past.
"I don't care what political party you are from," he says. To make his
point, he tells a story about a day laborer he met recently. Recounting
their conversation, Capriles says, "The man told me, 'I love Chávez,
but I love you, too.' I said, 'That's okay. Sometimes a man falls in love
with two or three women or a woman falls in love with two or three
men. It's all right—it's part of life.'" As if on cue, an older woman
in the back can't resist any longer. She pushes her way through the
raucous crowd, comes up to the podium, and says she must kiss him.
Beaming, Capriles is happy to oblige.

A few minutes after the rally has come to an end, the governor
and I meet in the school's new air-conditioned computer lab. Capriles
is bathed in sweat and still radiating the energy from the crowd outside. He is downing bottles of water, and one of his advisers reminds
him how much time he has before the next event. As we sit down to
talk, I comment on how grueling a schedule he seems to keep. "It's
not going to be a fair fight, but you have to fight. The challenge is
to fight and keep fighting," he says. Then, pausing, he takes another
swig of water, smiles, and says, "Whoever gets tired loses."

Few jobs are harder than being a member of the political opposition in an authoritarian country. Your rallies and marches are banned
or disrupted. You are forbidden to raise money at home or abroad.
You have virtually no opportunity to communicate your message on
national television. The only time you appear in national media is
when you are being vilified or accused of corruption. Your party leaders live under constant surveillance. The voting rules are consistently
revised to stack the odds against you. The courts refuse to hear your
complaints. The regime creates clone opposition parties that crowd
you out come election time. Your most popular candidates are either
forbidden to run for office or occupied fighting trumped-up charges
in courtrooms, keeping them off the campaign trail. Supporters are
intimidated and, in the worst cases, silenced.

Vocal, independent, rabble-rousing opposition leaders are public
enemy No. 1 for an authoritarian regime. They are the small group of
people who are willing to confront a regime head-on, speaking out

against abuses, denouncing illegitimate policies, and, when permitted, challenging the strongman at the polls. Often, they do all of this at great personal expense and sacrifice. Opposition leaders I have met from Caracas to Cairo, from Moscow to Kuala Lumpur, have told me stories that invariably involve similar plot points, similar twists and turns, as the regime they challenge ratchets up the pressure. They have been imprisoned. They have been harassed, beaten, and denied their livelihoods. Their names and reputations have been destroyed, their families torn apart. And despite the hardships these leaders endure, the regimes work hard to deny them even the symbolic value of their suffering. Rather, they aim to distance and divide these would-be democratic leaders from the people they hope to mobilize. "They are extremely sophisticated in what they do, and I'm not only talking about the Russian regime," says Vladimir Milov, a leader in the Russian opposition, referring to modern authoritarians. "They stay away from too much pressure on the general public. They prefer a very focused repression against a few people who are active in proclaiming opposition feeling. They alienate the active opposition from the general public, saying, 'Look, these are not repressions against you, but instead these are guys who are against you, foreign spies financed by the CIA, a fifth column if you will.'"

It isn't easy fighting a dictator. But while it may seem unfair to criticize anyone who would take on such a burden, it is true that some political opposition leaders are less effective than others. Some refuse to innovate, sticking stubbornly to the same strategies and making the same mistakes that marginalized them in the first place. Like any political party, they can be distracted by petty power struggles and outsized egos. Some are merely reactive, criticizing but never proposing new ideas or political alternatives to distinguish their vision from that of the ruling party. Indeed, for regimes that wish to hide behind a democratic facade, some semblance of a democratic opposition is necessary, even desirable. Opposition parties can, in the worst cases, become outgrowths of the regime itself, providing cover for the government's true dominance. Co-opted opposition leaders are a vital piece of the architecture of authoritarianism. Thus, the sheer fact that the leader of an opposition party declares himself to be in a pitted struggle against a regime isn't reason enough to applaud his efforts. They too can become another piece of the state's authoritarian machine, in sharp contrast to those who are engaged in a genuine fight.

Drowning the State

Often when Venezuelans talk about Henrique Capriles, they call him a fortunate man. Sometimes they are referring to his good looks or the fact that he comes from a prominent and wealthy family. Sometimes they are referring to his political stardom. His career has been a series of firsts. In 1998, at twenty-six, he was elected to the parliament, the youngest person ever to be elected to the body. He was soon catapulted to Speaker of the National Assembly, again the youngest in the country's history. But not long after he met Chávez, Capriles's luck ran out. "My first experience meeting him was as Speaker of the House," Capriles recalled to me. "I had the opportunity to meet Chávez and interact with him. I thought, 'This is the guy who is going to transform Venezuela.'" The transformation that followed—for his country and himself—wasn't what he expected.

In 2004, while serving as the mayor of Baruta, a relatively affluent municipality in Caracas, Capriles was arrested for inciting an attack on the Cuban embassy during the 2002 coup against Chávez. In fact, Capriles had been invited to the embassy, which sat in his district, to try to dissuade rioters from looting the Cuban ambassador's residence. In the aftermath, the Cuban ambassador, Germán Sánchez Otero, even thanked Capriles for personally coming to his aid. Nevertheless, Capriles was imprisoned for two years on the trumped-up charges. To delay a final verdict, the government transferred his case from one judge to the next, as each recused himself. Ultimately, it was passed among more than forty judges before he received a final verdict. In 2008, after four years and two sets of trials, he was declared innocent. During this time, he had inadvertently achieved another first: while he sat in prison, much of the time in solitary confinement, he was among Chávez's first political prisoners.

With the charges against him dropped, Capriles came back with a vengeance. In 2008, his victory in the race for governor of Miranda was one of the biggest for the opposition camp. Miranda is Venezuela's second-most-populous state, with more than three million people, and arguably the most important politically. Perhaps an even greater sting for Chavistas was that the man Capriles defeated, Diosdado Cabello, was a key Chávez ally, often referred to as the "super minister." Underlining how bracing a loss it was for Chávez, Capriles says that "it's like defeating Raúl Castro."

Of course, if you beat Chávez's right-hand man, there are consequences. Capriles was met with an overnight assault on his ability to govern the state. Chávez immediately began to strip Capriles's young government of its resources. With the help of an aide sitting behind him, Capriles begins to tick off the costs of his winning the last election. Chávez closed 19 of his hospitals and 250 emergency and primary care centers and seized highways, airports, and state government land. More than $200 million was lifted from his budget, and seven thousand state workers became federal government employees. Capriles puts his hand to his throat and says, "He is slowly trying to drown the state."

The rally that brought us to Chaguaramal Primary School is a small part of Capriles's plan for fending Chávez off. One of the governor's aides gave me a tour of the school before Capriles arrived. It was pretty much as one would expect. Classrooms with chalkboards, bulletin boards, and desks. But when we opened the door to what I assumed would be another classroom, it wasn't. Behind the door was something completely unexpected: a dentist's chair and examination room. As the aide explained, because the central government had closed so many health facilities in retribution for Capriles's election victory, they were taking the opportunity of renovating the school to provide the community with additional services. The thinking was that it would be much harder for the government to close a health facility that was embedded in a remodeled school, something the community had clearly embraced as its own and would not give up. "[Chávez] is taking away competencies and resources, but he can't take away contact with the people," says Capriles.

For all his passion, Capriles has no illusions about what he is up against. "In Miranda, we are in the Barlovento region. It has the biggest population of African descent in Venezuela. The violence is at the point that 136 people are killed by guns per 100,000 a year—four times the crime rate in Latin America. A hundred and forty thousand children in Miranda are still not going to school. I have to build new schools. It is not going to be enough. It means working seven days a week."

But in his mind, the one antidote to Chávez and the political barriers he has constructed across the country is building a direct line to the people, very much the connection he was forging on this Sunday in the countryside. It was losing this connection, becoming alienated from the vast majority of Venezuelans, that was the democratic opposition's original sin. "In the past, the opposition dedicated all of its efforts to certain spaces but didn't put effort in the rural areas. When you have a woman and you don't like her, but she is the only one you have—it is the same. In some areas, Chavistas only have Chávez. There is no competition. We are changing that reality," says Capriles. "If poor people hadn't voted for me, I wouldn't be governor. Seventy percent of my state is poor."

His aides are looking at their watches, and the governor must move on to his next meeting. I ask him how he would describe Venezuela after ten years of Chávez's rule. He tells me there is a phrase he recently heard that he thinks perfectly sums it up. He heard it from, of all people, a member of the Chinese Communist Party. "I was invited to China, at the official invitation of the Chinese Communist Party," Capriles explains. "A Chinese official asked me, 'What is happening to Chávez? He is a good friend, but what is he doing?'" Capriles told the Chinese official that if he, a friend to Chávez, didn't know, why should he? "Then the Chinese official gave me his opinion," says Capriles. "'Venezuela is a country that grows but does not make progress.'"

"Crazy with Power"

Beijing is more than nine thousand miles from Caracas. But one morning in Petare, one of the larger slums that ring the hillsides of Venezuela's capital, the Chinese Communist Party official's observation strikes me as spot-on. Petare is a crowded and notoriously dangerous corner of Caracas. Yovanny, a middle-aged man and father of two who has invited me into his makeshift home, calls his neighborhood a place that has been good for little more than "robberies, stripping cars, and rape." Nevertheless, Yovanny is proud of the house he has built there for his wife and two daughters, and rightfully so— he has had to fight for every inch of it. The structure is built from pieces of corrugated scrap metal, wood, and brick and held together by wire and a little joint compound. It rests, like the homes of all his neighbors, somewhat precariously on the edge of a steep incline. On this morning, a light breeze is coming off the mountains. We sit on a small open-air patio behind his house, underneath an avocado tree that has grown out of the hillside. Butterflies fly overhead, land for a few seconds near our glasses of orange soda, and then retreat to the tree. For a moment, you almost forget that you are in one of Caracas's most dangerous neighborhoods.

Yovanny is a pragmatic, no-nonsense voter. He respects the Colombians who live up and down his street—almost all of his neighbors are Colombian immigrants—because they are hard workers. He cast his lot with Chávez not because of promises of a revolution but because of promises of results. Today he considers himself a former Chavista. The accomplishments are just not there. "I like how he started," he tells me, referring to Chávez. "He came from nothing. But then he got to power. Twice he has been elected president, and because of that he thinks he owns the world." I asked Yovanny what he thinks explains Chávez's failure to deliver. "Simón Bolívar and Castro have made him crazy," he says. "Why doesn't he worry about what really goes on in this country? He talks a lot, but he doesn't do much."

What matters to Yovanny is the price of food and the cost of building material. In the corner of his concrete patio, he has stacked a small pile of bricks, a few metal pipes, and a bag of cement. He has his eye on putting a rooftop over this patio so that he can make a separate bedroom for his daughters. He buys a little material here and there, whenever he can afford it. But it isn't easy. "Almost every day there is an increase in prices," he says. "Construction material is in the clouds."

As Chávez's ideological campaigns alienated him, what came to matter more for this resident of Petare is his local representatives. I ask him if he is happy with the new mayor. Yovanny says he is. He has been in the neighborhood, and he has gotten many of the streets paved. "Here there have been many mayors and governors, but [the new one] has done a good job," he says. The previous mayor was José Vicente Rangel, a staunch Chavista and son of a former vice president. Referring to Rangel, Yovanny says, "He came once with fifty police escorts before the election and once after. We didn't even know if he was alive or dead."

The new mayor is Carlos Ocariz. The thirty-nine-year-old opposition leader oversees the mayoralty of Sucre, one of the largest barrios in Latin America. (Yovanny's home in Petare is just one part of a much larger slum.) Roughly two million people call Sucre home, and 80 percent of them are poverty-stricken. Like Capriles, Ocariz won his post in a surprise victory for the opposition in the 2008 regional elections. Ocariz had spent years doing community work in Sucre, so the people there knew him long before he announced his candidacy. Nevertheless, it was a bruising campaign. "There were forty days of campaigning. Out of the forty days, Chávez came to Sucre fifteen times and delivered thirteen national *cadenas* from here," Ocariz tells me as we sit in his office. Chávez had been determined to keep Sucre as a political stronghold, he explained. "All of the power structure was Chavista. All the local officials were Chavistas. They were giving away washing machines, mattresses, and refrigerators."

It wasn't enough. On Election Day, Ocariz won 55.6 percent of the vote over his Chavista opponent's 43.8 percent. But Chávez didn't take long to respond. "The day after the election, the government took away sixteen garbage trucks, which was 60 percent of garbage collection," says Ocariz. Also, the pipelines that carry water up Sucre's steep hillsides mysteriously had less water pressure. Many people in the poorest sections saw their taps reduced to a drip, if they had any water at all. According to Ocariz, "It's a mixture of negligence and political revenge."

But Ocariz knows his constituents aren't interested in excuses or, as he says, "the problems of politicians." Like Yovanny, they want results, and whether the central government is hamstringing him or not, Ocariz must deliver. One thing he has going for him is the incredible mismanagement of the previous mayor. When he saw the books, Ocariz was stunned at how inefficient his predecessor's team had been. In his first year in office, Ocariz reduced administrative expenses from 51 percent to 38 percent of the budget. Doing so helped him increase the police force by 20 percent, as well as double their salaries. In turn, Sucre's homicide rate dropped 25 percent. When water stopped flowing from the faucets, Ocariz created a program called My Water that drives trucks filled with water to the most impoverished areas of the community. He also invested in revamping the entire pumping system.

One of his more innovative educational initiatives is called Study and Progress. The program offers small cash stipends to mothers of fourth, fifth, and sixth graders who attend public schools in Sucre. In order to receive the stipend, the student must attend at least 85 percent of his or her classes. In the first month, roughly 75 percent of those eligible signed up for the program, but one-third did not receive the stipend because of their children's absences. It was a better start than most expected, and the program's mix of incentives quickly took hold. By the fourth month, the number of mothers not receiving stipends dropped to 12 percent. "In order to govern within an authoritarian system, you have to be a lot more creative," Ocariz tells me. "Many opposition leaders haven't realized that the problem isn't Chávez. The problem is the problems of the people. If you efficiently address those problems, that is how you take support away from Chávez."

Many of the younger leaders in Venezuelan opposition parties view Chávez as a problem they inherited. He is, in part, a product of the mistakes made by an earlier political generation, especially those leaders who failed to adjust once Chávez came to power. Ocariz takes a dim view of the opposition's leadership from these years and puts a fair share of the blame on their shoulders. "There were many errors. One of the main ones being the opposition wanted to take a shortcut to power, instead of understanding that we needed to construct a new majority or a new political proposal. They wanted to get to power through a shortcut, be it through a coup, the oil boycott, or something else," he says.

But the more shortcuts the opposition leaders attempted, the more they compounded the problem, reinforcing Chávez's message that they were elite, moneyed interests disconnected from everyday Venezuelans. These mistakes and miscalculations led to "the worst possible mistake" in Ocariz's view—boycotting the political process altogether. In 2005, opposition leaders abstained from competing in congressional elections in protest. Chávez was more than happy to run his candidates and take full control of the National Assembly. All 167 of the body's representatives were Chavistas. Now Chávez was truly in a position to run the table. "When we retreated from the congressional elections," says Ocariz, "Chávez was able to take control of the rest of the institutions and branches of government. So in the end, he didn't take control. We gave it to him." Ocariz closes his eyes and shakes his head, as if even now he can't fully understand the strategy the opposition pursued. "The opposition always asks ourselves, 'What will Chávez do when he runs out of money and popularity?'" he continues. "Instead of asking what Chávez is going to do, we need to ask what we are going to do."

It's a good point, and one shared by many younger opposition leaders. In my meetings with more than a dozen members of the opposition, there is surprising consensus about the broad outlines of what is necessary to be successful in the upcoming campaigns against Chávez and his political machine. Like Capriles, they must be connected to the people. Like Ocariz, they must offer true political alternatives to Chávez, solving problems and not simply complaining about how they are treated in a system that almost everyone agrees is unfair. And they must be unified. Even with the gains made in the 2008 elections, the opposition lost seventy-six elections around the country because it failed to throw its support behind a single candidate. One senses that most leaders, especially the younger rising stars, understand what is necessary to put forward a credible challenge. The question is whether they will act on it.

Of course, it isn't fair to say that it is entirely up to them. The rules will be rigged against them. They won't have the opportunity to broadcast their message on national television. Chávez will pour hundreds of millions of the state's oil revenue into supporting himself and his own people in races. The head of the Venezuelan military has even intimated that the armed services might not defend an election if the result was anything other than a victory for Chávez. Ocariz is right that the opposition needs to ask itself what it can do to make itself the most viable opponent to a regime that has amassed extraordinary powers. But I am still interested in Ocariz's first question, "What do you think Chávez will do?"

"I don't know," Ocariz replies, warily.

"Is that scary?" I ask.

"Yes," he says, pausing for a moment. "Right now he is crazy with power."

López v. the State of Venezuela

Carlos Ocariz had been reluctant to talk about Chávez and his government's dirty tricks. In our conversation, he wanted to focus on the innovations and solutions he and his team had implemented in Sucre. He didn't want to seem like a mayor under siege. It is, in part, his desire to change the narrative about the Venezuelan opposition. He believes it is important to showcase more than the complaints and injustices of governing in Chávez's authoritarian system. The other reason he didn't want to complain, perhaps, is that he knows he is lucky. As difficult as it may be for Henrique Capriles and Carlos Ocariz to govern, they are more fortunate than those who are barred from trying.

In early 2008, Chávez unveiled a new instrument against the opposition: the political ban. That February, only ten months before candidates would be competing in elections, Comptroller General Clodovaldo Russián presented a list of four hundred public officials who he declared were immediately banned from running for public office. His declaration was not accompanied by a court order. There had been no legal proceeding that arrived at this result. Those who appeared on Russián's list were told they had no avenue for appeal. With the stroke of a pen, the comptroller general had simply eliminated them from Venezuelan political life. Not surprisingly, of the names on Russián's list, 80 percent were members of the opposition.

One of the candidates banned from holding office was Leopoldo López. It is obvious why Chávez would want to keep López's political star from rising: the young, handsome Harvard-educated López had been immensely successful as the two-term mayor of Chacao, one of Caracas's wealthier districts. While Chávez hails Simón Bolívar as South America's liberator and has dubbed his political project a "Bolivarian revolution," López is from the famed hero's bloodline. (He is a direct descendant of Bolívar's sister; Bolívar himself had no children.)

When he was reelected in 2004, he won with a whopping 81 percent of the vote. During his time in office, his approval ratings were regularly above 70 percent. In 2008, López had set his sights on becoming the next mayor of Caracas. He was a virtual shoo-in for the job. López was leading the field of candidates with 65 percent of the vote when the comptroller general issued his edict. López believes that his campaign would have widened that margin by Election Day, and he thinks the regime knew it, too. "If we had won with 70 percent," López told me in his offices, "it would have been a message."

But Hugo Chávez struck first. In an effort to tilt the playing field, his regime was willing to use the flimsiest rationale to eliminate the candidates it believed it couldn't otherwise defeat. The alleged justification for the political disqualifications was corruption. Yet those being banned had not been found guilty of committing any crime, and the allegations were often absurd. William Méndez, the former mayor of San Cristóbal, made the government's list for allegedly accepting invoices without tax numbers printed on them. The law requiring tax numbers had been passed in 2003. But Méndez had accepted the invoices in 2001. He was therefore supposedly guilty of breaking a law that did not even exist. But Chávez gave his full support to the tactic and saw the initial list of disqualifications as only the beginning. "I want to express my support as chief of state, and the support of my administration, and the support of the people for these honorable compatriots who represent our state institutions and a special vote of confidence for Clodovaldo Russián," Chávez told a crowd of supporters shortly after the announcement. "Because now we are really fighting corruption."

Although López was no stranger to Chávez's tactics, the political ban left him stunned. His campaign—and perhaps his political career—had been snuffed out before it could truly begin. No Venezuelan president had wielded such a weapon against his opponents before. "In order to disqualify someone, there needs to be criteria. There needs to be a definitive sentence by a criminal court. There was no court. I didn't even go to trial," he told me. "It was an administrative decision. Our case presents a clear tool the government is using to not let strong candidates stand for office. It is similar to what is happening in Iran, Belarus, and Russia."

He did not expect any part of the Venezuelan government to overturn the comptroller's decree, but he tried nonetheless. He took his case to the Venezuelan Supreme Court. The court has never decided a case against President Chávez. Still, López addressed the constitutional chamber of the court, saying, "You have the historic responsibility of becoming either the constitution's executioner or the constitution's defender. You are responsible for either burying the constitution or fully supporting the rule of law, with justice for all Venezuelans, so they can decide." The court opted for a burial.

If López couldn't get justice inside Venezuela, he decided to look for it outside his country. He brought his case to the Inter-American Human Rights Court, an international tribunal that convenes in Costa Rica. The court agreed to hear arguments between López and the Venezuelan government, the first time it expanded its mandate to include the protection of political rights. Clodovaldo Russián and others intimated that Chávez's government would ignore a judgment from the international court, but López saw it as his only way to find an impartial hearing and hoped it would build political pressure on the regime. "This will have an impact not only in Venezuela but in the region," he told me. "This mechanism of disqualifying elected officials will become a way of winning elections permanently." López could sense my skepticism that Chávez would ever honor a decision handed down by an international tribunal. "Rationally, I can't tell you we can overcome this government. Funding, media control, abuse of power, the military—it's all on their side," López said. "But politics is about hope." In the meantime, political bannings have become one of the government's favorite tools. More than eight hundred candidates have been erased from political life since 2007.

As for the race for mayor of Caracas, it ended in an ironic twist. After López was forced to drop out, opposition voters threw their support behind Antonio Ledezma, a veteran member of the opposition and outspoken regime critic. Ledezma triumphed in the November elections. But Caracas's new mayor also soon felt the full brunt of Chávez's vengeance. His office's funding was slashed to less than 20 percent of its previous budget. The mayoral post was stripped of almost all of its authority. Those powers were then transferred to a new position, "head of government" for the Caracas Capital District, which Chávez created five months after Ledezma's election. And, in the most surprising turn, armed Chávez supporters seized city hall and other municipal office buildings and refused to relinquish them. Offices were ransacked, equipment and city vehicles destroyed or stolen. When I went to meet Ledezma more than a year after his election, he still had not been able to move into the mayor's office. We had to meet in a private office building in downtown Caracas where he had set up a temporary work space. "Chávez is like a boxer who beats an opponent without mercy," Ledezma told me. "He has done that to the political parties. This is when the neo-dictatorship movie begins."

Ledezma tried to put the best spin on events, explaining some of the projects and goals he was trying to implement. But he was clearly making the best of an untenable situation. He has had to travel abroad to raise money for the city's coffers. A few months before we met, he had embarked on a hunger strike to get the attention of the Organization of American States. He and his team have had to put as much energy into defending their right to exist as governing. As one of Ledezma's top advisers, Milos Alcalay, told me, "Chávez wins when he wins, and he wins when he loses. If he doesn't win, he just takes it."

But for López, there may be a different ending. In September 2011, the Inter-American Human Rights Court sided with the young Venezuelan politician, ordering Chávez's government to lift the ban on López running for office. In response, Chávez denounced the international court as "worthless." Precisely how the machinery of the Venezuelan state would respond was less clear. The Supreme Court at first issued an opinion that seemed to reject the international court's decision. The head of the Venezuelan court explained the ruling by saying that López could run but not take office if elected. The National Electoral Council followed the court's decision by clearing López to compete. Was the government allowing López to run to sow division in the opposition camp? Were the contradictory rulings an attempt to throw López and his supporters off balance? Had the government been intentionally ambiguous to leave open the possibility of banning López later? No one could be sure. But López had no doubt about his next move: he vowed to compete in the opposition's presidential primaries. When he announced his candidacy, López immediately joined a field that included the opposition front-runner, Henrique Capriles.

The young opposition leaders were willing to fight for the right to fight Chávez.

"We Are Used to Being Defeated"

My appointment was January 18, 2006, 9:00 a.m. sharp—five years before Egypt's revolution. The world hadn't yet become familiar with Tahrir Square. But on that morning, only a short walk from Tahrir, I was waiting in the second-floor lobby of the leftist Al-Tagammu Party headquarters, one of Egypt's oldest opposition parties. Cairo is not an early morning city. At that hour, there are only two groups of people in the lobby: bodyguards and a growing throng of party faithful who have come to have a favor granted or a grievance heard. Like others, I am waiting to see Rifaat El-Said. He arrives and moves quickly through the typically shabby Cairo lobby, another once-beautiful building suffering from a mixture of age and neglect. Said doesn't acknowledge anyone, and he ushers me into his office with a wave of his hand. Slight, wiry, and impatient, Said has a tendency to respond to questions with long-winded, dogmatic lectures you would expect from an aging Marxist.

Before the revolution, few people had good things to say about the Egyptian political opposition, even those in the opposition. It is undeniably true that they suffered at the hands of the state. These parties were harassed, intimidated, marginalized, and repressed by Hosni Mubarak's regime. But even their suffering somehow failed to catch much of a spark. For many, the opposition parties seemed more like beaten dogs than martyrs. They had been trained, over time, to play a part and to accept their role. More energy seemed to be spent bickering among themselves than ever mounting a challenge to the regime. For the most part, they fought over the scraps that Mubarak left them—a handful of parliamentary seats here and there—and then would retreat to their corner to either gloat or grieve.

Rifaat El-Said is a quintessential example of the older generation of Egyptian opposition leaders. The morning we met in his office, it had been a little over a month since his party had been handed a resounding defeat in the parliamentary elections. Out of the fifty-nine candidates put forward by the Tagammu Party, only two had won seats. Even by the low standards of the Egyptian opposition, this result was dismal. The losses had been so great that Khaled Mohieddin, the party's founder, a former member of the Free Officers' coup of 1952, failed to hold his seat. I expected the party leader to be at least somewhat moved by the outcome, whether angry or chastened. Said was utterly detached. "I am not disappointed," he told me from across his desk. "If I accumulate such feelings, I should not continue. We are used to being defeated."

That, it seemed to me, was precisely the problem. Even if the opposition political parties were attempting to play a rigged game—and Egyptian elections were clearly rigged—there was no desire or urgency to shift tactics, change strategy, or even think differently about the problem. Most of the opposition had long slipped into a comfortable convalescence. When I pressed him on how his party might approach its work differently after such a stinging defeat, he offered no ideas, telling me, "It takes time. It takes time." For most of the hour we spent together, he railed against the rival opposition party, the Muslim Brotherhood, not against Mubarak. Indeed, he told me that the bodyguards I had passed on my way into his office were a security detail provided by the government. He saw no irony in this fact. People had speculated that he had been co-opted by the regime when he gained a seat in the Shura Council, the upper house of the parliament that was little more than a government echo chamber, populated by notables and regime favorites. Now here he was, telling me that he was entrusting the government he supposedly opposed with his personal security? As I was preparing to leave, he offered, as a final thought, "We know how to suffer." There was no arguing with that.

The danger of someone like Said is not that he was simply missing an opportunity to properly lead a party or apply pressure on the government. He could also be an effective weapon of the regime. Several years later, while in Cairo, I met with someone who was very close to Said. His parents had been good friends with the party leader. At different times, when he was a young boy and his mother and father had been imprisoned by the regime, Said would look after him. "Rifaat Said is like a father to me," he said. So he was disgusted when he saw the Tagammu Party leader go on television and denounce young people who had first begun in 2008 to use Facebook to organize protests—the same youth who would eventually lead the revolution to oust Mubarak. In television interviews, Said told the country that such youth had essentially lost their minds and were not to be taken seriously. "I think [Said] is like Mubarak in a lot of ways, not just him, but that generation of politicians," he told me. "They all think they know, and they're the only ones that know." In his opinion, the regime had simply called up Said and other reliable senior opposition leaders and told them to speak out against the youth. It was the price to be paid for the political courtesies and privileges the regime showed them.

Dreaming of Prison

When I walked into a different party headquarters on March 16, 2011, everyone was smiling. It had been a little over a month since the Egyptian people had risen up and ousted Hosni Mubarak, but the feeling of euphoria hadn't subsided. I was visiting the offices of El Ghad, the opposition party led by Ayman Nour. Party workers came and went, often greeting each other with hugs. Down the hallway, a conference room overflowed with senior leaders and members discussing recent events and the strategy for the days ahead. Nour had made headlines within days of Mubarak's departure, suggesting that the relationship between Egypt and Israel should be reevaluated now that Egypt was free from its dictator. Although it might have made many in Washington uncomfortable to hear such speculation, it was shrewd and not wholly unexpected politics for a figure like Nour. The lawyer and former parliamentarian was one of the best-known figures from the Egyptian opposition. Nevertheless, after thirty years of Mubarak, the secular opposition parties like El Ghad did not have a large following, and Nour could be expected to engage in some political posturing. In a few days, he would announce his candidacy for president, in what everyone hoped would be Egypt's first free elections. However, unlike anyone else who intended to compete in this campaign, Nour was planning to run for president for the second time.

What was immediately striking was how different the mood was from the mood during my visit a year earlier. At that time, the debate about the country's political future had long since fallen into a tired and predictable rhythm, with the leading speculation being that Mubarak would be followed by either his son Gamal or a member of the military, most likely Omar Suleiman, Egypt's intelligence chief. I went to visit Ayman Nour at his home in Zamalek, a tony north Nile neighborhood that was home to expats and Egyptian elites. Before I met with him, several people had warned me that Nour was no longer his voluble self. His battles with the regime had taken their toll.

For most of the previous five years, Nour hadn't actually lived at that address; he had spent most of his days and nights in Cairo's infamous Tora Prison. In January 2005, Nour was imprisoned for allegedly forging signatures on petitions he had filed to create his political party. The charges were widely derided as politically motivated. Thanks to pressure from the United States and Europe, Egyptian authorities released Nour, permitting him to compete in the September 2005 presidential election. More than 600,000 Egyptians had voted for Nour. The government may have been rattled by the size of Nour's support. Even if it wasn't, it wanted to send a message. Several months after the election, he was convicted on the forgery charges and sentenced to five years in prison. He remained in Tora Prison until February 18, 2009, when his sentence was unexpectedly lifted. The government released Nour ostensibly on medical grounds, but most observers believe the opposition leader's freedom was restored as a gesture of goodwill to the newly elected Obama administration. For Nour, his surprise release just underscored how every aspect of his arrest, conviction, and imprisonment had been orchestrated by executive fiat, not legal procedure. When I arrived at his door in March 2010, prisoner number 1387 had been free for just over a year.

Nour's apartment resembled a French salon and occupied the entire eighth floor of his building. Each room was furnished with chandeliers, elaborate floor-length drapes, oversized oriental vases, and ornate sofas and chairs. Almost every surface was covered with porcelain collectibles, glass trinkets, or various objets d'art. Despite its gracious size, it was actually somewhat amazing how many things had been sandwiched into his apartment, which in places seemed more like an antiques shop than someone's home. In the main living room, above the sofa hung a large oil painting of Nour himself. It was a much younger man, perhaps from his early days as the country's youngest parliamentarian. The scene was Nour in a courtyard of the parliament building, cajoling some of his fellow legislators who represented a who's who of Egyptian politics. Although I arrived on time for our Sunday evening appointment, his staff said he was asleep, and they were clearly debating whether or not they should disturb him.

Thirty minutes later, Nour came out to greet me. With his shirt comfortably unbuttoned around the neck, in blue jeans and a blue blazer, he walked, almost glided, slowly across the room. His manner was sedate, and he talked softly—so softly that I had to move my tape recorder closer to capture what he was saying. Sitting in his living room, Nour didn't seem like a broken man, just wounded. The pain his jailers caused him seemed to be intertwined with his own disappointment in the help he thought he would receive, especially from the United States. Early in our conversation, he mentioned the false hopes raised by Bush administration officials. "I went back to prison after the presidential race, although weeks before going back to prison, I met Condoleezza Rice for the first time at a meeting she had with several people here in Cairo. And she told me to rest at ease. And I was very peaceful—in jail," Nour said dryly.

"Every [time] Condoleezza came to Egypt while I was in jail, the minute it ends, the minute her visit ends, a disaster would happen in prison," he continued. "In May 2007, one hour after Condoleezza Rice left Egypt, they broke into my cell and assaulted me physically. I still have sixteen scars that remain from that day, which was the seventeenth of May 2007." At the end of her second visit, the government denied his request for a medical release from prison. On November 6, 2008, on the eve of Secretary Rice's last official visit to Egypt, Nour's party headquarters were burned to the ground while his wife, children, and supporters were attending a meeting inside. Everyone escaped, but the message was clear: the United States cannot protect you. "Thank God this was Condoleezza's final visit," Nour said, laughing.

Life had not been easy for Nour since he left prison. Shortly after he was released, the government issued a decree barring him from practicing law. His name was crossed off the bar association's membership rolls. Nour had a contract to teach at a university, but he believed the security service had that contract canceled, too. The same was true for an offer he had with a local television station. His father had passed away while he was in prison, so in an effort to raise funds, he decided to sell his father's house. To complete the sale, he needed to have the real estate contract notarized. "I walked in and the employee at the notary office told me she was very happy to meet me, that she had belly danced in the back when she heard I was released," Nour recounts, smiling. "When I gave her my ID to process the papers, she said, 'I'm really sorry. We have instructions from the security service not to process any of your papers unless you get us a paper that says you have been released from prison.' So I told her, 'Well, I'm here. I didn't jump over the fence.' She said, 'No, but we need paperwork.'"

The notary instructed him to go to the prosecutor's office to get the necessary form. "I went to the public prosecutor, they told me, 'No, we don't have such a thing. Are you crazy? Go to the Ministry of Interior.' I went to the Ministry of Interior, and they said, 'No, this isn't our domain, go back to the public prosecutor.'" He went back, and they said the same thing all over again. "They have prevented me from selling anything that I inherited from my father," says Nour, with a look of resignation.

Mubarak's government had used nearly the full palette of tools an authoritarian regime can employ to smother an opponent. Nour had been imprisoned, beaten, and terrorized. But the regime did not rely only on its jailers and dungeons. As Nour learned, a notary public—even an empathetic, belly-dancing notary public—could become an effective tool of state repression.

Nour's story of being stymied at every turn was similar to others I had heard. Saad Eddin Ibrahim, one of Egypt's most prominent dissidents, had been living in self-imposed exile in the United States for three years when I met him. When we talked in Washington, D.C., he described how the regime used intimidation, prison, character assassination, and scandal to try to cow those who challenged it. And if all else fails, it targets your livelihood, as it was now doing to Nour and Ibrahim. "They are draining my resources filing cases against me," Ibrahim told me, speaking of his own ongoing battle with the state. "At one time, there were twenty-eight cases filed against me by different people from different places around the country." The latest spurious charge had been brought just three days earlier. "They filed a suit [against me] for inciting ElBaradei to run and therefore destabilizing Egypt. I don't know the guy [who filed it], but for the next year or two it will be like a sword hanging over me."

It was close to 9:00 p.m., and despite the hour more people had arrived to have a few minutes with Nour. Before walking out, I asked him if he ever felt as if he was more effective, at least as a symbol, when he was in prison. "Even my right to return to prison, I failed to achieve," Nour replied.

"What do you mean?" I asked.

"When I came out and found there was absolutely nothing I could do, that I was prevented from everything, I asked to go back and serve the rest of my sentence," he explained. Nour also admitted that he wanted to deny Mubarak the pleasure of scoring points with the Obama administration, even if it meant being back in his old cell.

"Would you still like to go back?" I asked.

"To be honest with you, I was late for this interview because I napped, I dozed off. I was dreaming of going back to prison. This was my last dream."

Nour had paid dearly for his opposition, more than many political leaders. He is one of the few men who have dared to run against a dictator. And by vocally challenging Mubarak in the 2005 election, he had drawn the direct fire of the regime. His scars were physical, financial, and emotional. During his time in prison, his marriage had fallen apart, one subject he refused to discuss. My memory of him that evening is a somewhat sad one, a man who was still willing to speak out but could barely fill his lungs to breathe. In 2010, Nour looked more like a cautionary tale than a rousing call of inspiration.

A year later, in 2011, all of this was forgotten. Nour had not played a lead role in the revolution. Indeed, some of the youth leaders who sparked the protests and first mobilized Egyptians to come to Tahrir were disenchanted former members of the El Ghad Party. They, like many Egyptian young people, had turned away from mainstream opposition parties they viewed as bureaucratic, ineffective, and ultimately irrelevant. But Nour had taken genuine risks and paid real costs. And even though the youth had been instrumental in bringing down the regime, the country's future might hinge, in part, on committed democrats like Nour stepping forward to help shape it.

But the festive mood I found at El Ghad's party headquarters may have been premature. In October 2011, an Egyptian court upheld Nour's forgery conviction under the Mubarak regime, effectively barring the opposition leader from running for president. The fact that Nour was being prevented from running for office fed the impression that Egypt's political revolution was far from complete. Shortly after the ruling, Nour told a group of reporters, "We ousted a military ruler to go to a military council." In his view, the opponent may have changed, but the fight remained the same.

From Cairo to Penang

I could hear Anwar Ibrahim before I could see him. The leader of Malaysia's democratic opposition was inside a modest mosque that sits almost directly under a highway overpass in the coastal city of Penang. A dry-erase board read, "Ustaz Ibrahim," indicating that he was the speaker after the evening prayer. As I approached the mosque's front entrance, I could hear the slow, even tempo of Anwar's voice coming over the loudspeaker perched on the corner of the mosque's roof. By my watch, he only had a few more minutes to speak. I had been told to meet him at this spot. I sat down on a bench outside that gave me an angle to watch him as he finished addressing the hundred or so men sitting Indian-style in front of him. He had a calm presence, and his body language and appearance were very much those of a teacher. And just as I was about to ask one of his handlers what his message had been this evening, I heard him mention the names "Mubarak," "Suzanne," "Gamal." Egypt's former first family. Like much of the world, he was talking about the revolutions that were ripping through North Africa and the Middle East. His message was that it was a coalition—a coalition of people across faiths, social strata, and groups—that brought down a corrupt dictator and his family. It's a message tailor-made for Malaysia.

It was a Saturday night, so if you wanted to see Anwar Ibrahim, you had to go out to the provinces. Although his home is in Kuala Lumpur, he spends nearly all of his weekends in other cities or the countryside meeting with party leaders and speaking at public events. Anwar represents the people of Penang in parliament. The city sits on the northwest corner of Malaysia, along the Strait of Malacca. I had flown there to spend an evening with him traveling from one venue to the next. As he exited the mosque, he motioned me toward his car, and we both jumped into the back of a black Mercedes. I ask what his schedule is for tonight. "I have three more events," he tells me. "Then I will drive back to Kuala Lumpur. I'll stop to meet with a bunch of party leaders between here and there. I should be home by 4:00 or 5:00 a.m." Then he apologizes. The next event is a lavish Chinese banquet. It's in honor of Lim Kit Siang, one of the leaders of the opposition, on his seventieth birthday. Anwar needs to swap the simple white shirt he wore to the mosque for a light blue silk one more appropriate for the next venue. "I'm sorry," he says, as he changes his shirt and combs his hair. "There is just no time."

And there isn't. Seven minutes later, the car pulls up in front of one of Penang's finest hotels. An entourage of party leaders, personal assistants, bodyguards, and press are waiting, and camera bulbs go off as the car doors open. As we get out, Anwar says to me, "Keep walking. We have to move fast." We walk briskly, shaking hands but never pausing as we are ushered into the hotel's banquet hall. I stay with the bodyguards as Anwar takes his place at the head table. There are more than eight hundred guests in attendance, and the crowd couldn't be more different from the Malay mosque-goers we just left. This is Penang's well-heeled elite, many of them lawyers, doctors, businessmen, and nearly all Chinese. We haven't been there ten minutes before Anwar is invited to the podium to speak. (The banquet planners had been warned he couldn't stay long.) Anwar is now the gracious guest and party leader, who with a mix of storytelling and self-deprecating humor pays homage to Lim's leadership. It's a quick speech, in keeping with the occasion, but Anwar earns laughs and applause as he tells stories about how Lim is one of the opposition leaders the regime fears most.

And we are off. The next event is in a run-down community center in Kedah, about a twenty-minute car ride north. Most of the three or four hundred people there are lower-middle-class Indians. (Indians make up roughly 7 percent of the population, with Malays and Chinese contributing around 65 percent and 25 percent, respectively.) They have been waiting for two hours, but they don't appear the least bit bothered. As his bodyguards carve a path through the throng of people, the crowd starts chanting, "Reformasi! Reformasi!" It is hot and gritty in the open-air hall, and the stump speech is similar to his mosque sermon, but the delivery has changed. He is now raising his voice, underscoring his points with a fist. He is almost aggressive as he leans into the podium and barks at the injustices of the ruling party and its corruption. Again, he hits the right chord, and the chants of "Reformasi!" can still be heard as our car pulls away.

The final stop is back in Penang. There are cars parked and lined up on the side of the road long before we pull over to get out. The feeling outside is more like a rock concert. The estimate is that as many as ten thousand people have turned up on this grassy lawn to hear Anwar speak, but it is impossible to tell. The only time you can see the rows of faces is for the few seconds when camera flashes go off. Otherwise, it is nearly pitch-black. (Anwar tells me later that this is intentional. More people show up for opposition events if they are held in the dark, safe from the prying eyes of the regime.) Anwar speaks for an hour, but he keeps the mood light. At one point, he welcomes the *mukhabarat*, or secret police, that have come out tonight. He gets laughs when he says, "Even Nour is here," pointing to a plainclothes officer he recognizes. If it is like a rock concert, then Anwar is the star. The size of the crowd only appears to swell over the course of the hour.

It's past midnight. He still has several hours of meetings and a drive back to the capital ahead of him as I go to my hotel. But I am struck by what I have seen over the past five hours. Each time he emerged from the car, he emerged as a slightly different version of the opposition leader he needs to be. Four different events, four different men, and just one Anwar. The religious teacher, the eloquent party leader, the fiery campaigner, and the star who commands a crowd. It's no wonder he leads the country's opposition, a coalition of parties that includes his multiethnic People's Justice Party, the Democratic Action Party, which is liberal and primarily Chinese, and the conservative Pan-Malaysian Islamic Party. Stitching together this coalition requires someone who can move seamlessly from one constituency to the next. And that raises a troubling question: How indispensable should one man be to Malaysia's democratic hopes? When I mention this to Anwar, he laughs it off and thanks me for the "ego boosting."

But the people around him know he plays an indispensable role. And so too does the regime.

"He Thought He Could Break Me"

The first time I met Anwar Ibrahim he was grinning from ear to ear. It was April 2008, and a few weeks earlier the opposition had celebrated a stunning upset against the ruling party, the United Malays National Organization (UMNO). For the first time since independence in 1957, the opposition had won more than a third of the seats in parliament, ending the government's supermajority that allowed it to change the constitution at will. The opposition also captured five of thirteen state governments. Two of these victories came in Penang and Selangor, two of the richest states. Anwar won his seat in Penang in a landslide. For six years, until 2004, the Malaysian government had kept Anwar locked in solitary confinement on trumped-up charges of corruption and sodomy. Now the former political prisoner was leading the charge against those who had imprisoned him. UMNO's grip appeared to be slipping.

Although the ruling party's reign has endured for more than five decades, one figure looms above all others: Mahathir Mohamad. A physician turned politician, Dr. M., as he was sometimes called, ruled Malaysia from 1981 until his retirement in 2003. Abroad, the Malaysian strongman is probably best remembered for his racist and anti-Semitic slurs against the financier George Soros and a supposed worldwide Jewish conspiracy. At home, his twenty-two years in power are remembered for their tremendous economic success—and a dictatorial style that steamrolled any critic or institution that stood in his way.

A standard joke during those years was that the acronym UMNO actually stood for "Under Mahathir No Opposition." Even as Malaysia climbed the ranks of Asia's wealthiest countries—aptly symbolized by the building of Kuala Lumpur's Petronas Towers, temporarily the world's tallest—Mahathir never softened. He ran roughshod over the press, the parliament, the courts, his party, even Malaysia's monarchy. When he came to power, the country's monarchy had a royal veto. Mahathir eliminated it. After the Supreme Court challenged UMNO's

legal status, he had half the justices sacked. One of his most effective tools was the draconian Internal Security Act. It permitted him to
arrest his critics without charges and detain them indefinitely. Mahathir used the power liberally, and the courts looked the other way.

Indeed, not even retirement could quiet a political infighter like
Mahathir. After he began to disagree with the policies of his handpicked successor, Abdullah Badawi—namely, his decisions to end
some of Dr. M.'s state-led megaprojects and to set Anwar free—he
spearheaded the effort to have Abdullah pushed out as prime minister. On his blog, Mahathir would frequently rail against Abdullah and
lament having not chosen his protégé Najib Razak for the top post.
He alleged that Abdullah's administration was racked with corruption
and nepotism, a shameless charge for a man who had presided over a
vast patronage system for two decades. In 2008, Mahathir raised the
political pressure by resigning from UMNO in protest against Abdullah's leadership. The following year, in the wake of the ruling party's
election losses to the Anwar-led opposition, the old autocrat got his
wish, and Najib—whom some Malaysians describe as Mahathir's
lapdog—became Malaysia's new leader.

On that April afternoon in 2008, Anwar believed he might have
UMNO on the ropes. I met him at his party headquarters, and he told
me that disgruntled members of the ruling party were contacting him,
pledging to switch sides and join the opposition. Anwar was openly
planning on toppling this parliamentary autocracy. "It is the ruling
party that is worried about people defecting now. We have the numbers," he told me. He expected that within the next four to five months
he would have the votes he needed to bring Malaysia its first change
in government. And he was already envisioning what would follow.
"We are shifting from a semi-authoritarian system to a democratic
experience," he said. "The media will be free. We will ensure judicial
independence. And an independent agency to combat corruption will
be created."

No one expected the government would use the same trick twice.
But in late June, the regime brought allegations of "sexual assault"
against Anwar, again accusing him of sodomizing one of his aides.
It was a repeat of the case that brought him to court and ultimately
prison in 1998. At the time, he had been the deputy prime minis-

ter to Mahathir. Most people believe that Anwar's true sin had been to call for a campaign against nepotism and cronyism in the government. Such a campaign would have swept up people close to Mahathir, including members of his own family. Now, in 2008, the charges seemed almost like a reflex action. The regime was clearly nervous, and it needed to sideline Anwar. The sodomy accusation was intended to embarrass him, especially with more conservative Malay voters. But the fact that the country had lived through this farce once before made the repeat charges even less credible in the public's eyes. Against the background of his coalition's sweeping victory in March, the political motivation for the case was even clearer. As one prominent Malaysian businessman later told me, "Only one Malaysian has ever been charged with the crime of sodomy. And now that one man has been charged twice."

Apparently, even the regime doubted that a smear campaign could prevent Anwar from accomplishing his goal. So it turned to another traditional tool: bribery. In a somewhat bizarre move, the ruling party flew fifty of its legislators to Taiwan for a weeklong trip. The rationale for the hastily arranged junket was purportedly to study Taiwanese farming techniques. "We are going to Taiwan to study about agriculture," Bung Mokhtar Radin, a member of parliament, told a local reporter. In fact, the purpose appears to have been to find the price of loyalty. What would it take to persuade members to remain with the ruling party and not defect to Anwar's coalition? "I knew the moment they took the flight it was gone," Anwar told me, referring to his chances to gain the necessary votes to unseat the ruling party. "They would be in discussions, transactions, whatever. Many were appointed deputy ministers and chairmen of this and that. Some still kept their word [to defect], but then we didn't have the numbers." The junket may have been a cheap tactic, but it worked. Anwar had underestimated the regime, and it had proven, once again, that corruption is one of the most durable currencies.

The morning after Anwar's speeches and rally in Penang, I flew back to Kuala Lumpur to meet with him one last time at his home. The Egyptian people's recent ouster of Hosni Mubarak had taken an important place in his stump speech, and I wanted to ask how the Arab Spring might affect events in Malaysia. For Anwar, Egypt was a turning point. The revolution in Tunisia, while important, felt remote. It could be written off as an outlier. But not Egypt. "Here, among the Malays, I would say that every family would have either a direct or indirect association with an imam trained in Egypt or family members who have been there, or are studying there," says Anwar. Some thirteen thousand Malaysians are estimated to be studying abroad in Egypt. Some were surely moved by the events they witnessed in January and February 2011 as Egypt's young people took to the streets. The revolution in Cairo had been significant enough in Kuala Lumpur that the prime minister felt compelled to make a statement, a surprisingly defensive one. "[The prime minister] came out with a very strong statement that [Malaysia] was not Egypt, don't ever assume that what happened in Egypt would happen here," recalled Anwar. "We are a democracy, blah, blah, blah . . . So I retorted by saying that's exactly what Mubarak said after the events in Tunisia—Egypt is not Tunisia." His implication was clear: we don't need to be exact replicas to be inspired to pursue the same path.

Of course, Anwar admits that Malaysia is not Egypt. For starters, Malaysia is a far more successful economic engine than Egypt ever was. While it may not have performed as well as some Asian economies, it nevertheless lifted itself out of the stultifying poverty and misery that are still common in the Middle East. Furthermore, even as passionate a critic as Anwar does not believe a revolution is necessary to bring change to Malaysia. He and his coalition parties believe that change can come from the ballot box, if the elections are free and fair. They expect that the regime will play any number of dirty tricks, including rigging and vote fraud, but that if they defend their votes sufficiently, power may pass peacefully from UMNO to the opposition. Still, Anwar maintains that the wealth, development, and limited political space are merely the sheen that makes the system's authoritarianism more palatable, not less insidious. "Now it's not like Egypt. You have to wait until eight hundred people are shot, and then you consider it the same thing," he says, referring to the protesters who were gunned down in Tahrir Square. "The system is the same, but the facade is different. We don't go and detain opposition leaders without trial; we use the courts. We go through the motions!"

And the motions, as Anwar explained, could still be effective.

Even if the regime had failed to tarnish his image with its second sodomy trial, he believed it did accomplish its main purpose: to keep him occupied. The trial, then approaching its third year, required that Anwar report to the court every day, five days a week, and that he remain there until roughly 4:00 or 5:00 p.m. The government's judge warned Anwar that any absences would not be tolerated and would likely lead to his imprisonment. And that was why Anwar's schedule in the evenings and on weekends was so grueling; it was the only time that the regime afforded him to lead the opposition. "I can't slow down, because that's what they want," he says. "They will say that my mind is occupied by the case. So, immediately after five, I drive or fly to these other places." On an average weekend, he would speak at ten public events or rallies. Indeed, having failed to sap the sixty-four-year-old's energy, the regime found itself in a dilemma. If it was bold enough to convict Anwar, there could be enough outrage to provoke a large number of Malaysians. And if it found him innocent, the regime would appear weak and foolish, having wasted years and countless funds trying the case. Many people believed it would look for a technicality that allowed it to end the case while still saving face. "It's a Catch-22," says Anwar. "They put me in jail, it enrages a crowd and brings the attention of the international community. If they don't, they have a problem."

Still, the prospect of returning to prison was surely a frightening thought, and a possibility he was forced to ponder. He knew that Najib was capable of ordering it. Indeed, many believe that even now Najib does Mahathir's bidding. Reflecting on this old enmity, Anwar said, "Mahathir probably underestimated me. He always believed people crack under torture or under detention. He used to tell me that what he dreaded most was to be detained without knowing when he'd be released. So that's what he did to me. He thought he could break me." But ironically, it is his memory of those six years in solitary confinement that fuels his indefatigable pace today. "Your passion for democracy and freedom becomes far stronger," says Anwar. "Because when you are there in solitary confinement, you realize the meaning of freedom and the fact that millions of people, in worse conditions, demand basic freedoms."

We talked about his time in prison for a while. He told me about what he read—Shakespeare, Chinese philosophy, the classics—and how he passed the time. Near the end, I asked him what he thought he learned in prison. He replied, simply, "Patience."

He didn't mean it in jest; he was sincere. It may be the most important quality for those who take on the mantle of opposition leader in a repressive political system, more important than daring, guts, or guile. In challenging a dictator, they are setting themselves up for a long fight. They are guaranteeing themselves setback after setback. Patience shouldn't be equated with acceptance or subservience. Anwar has none of Rifaat Said's comfort with past defeats. Rather, he has patience in the fight, a vigorous fight that for most leaders will not end quickly. This isn't a short race. As Henrique Capriles said, whoever gets tired loses.

CHAPTER 5 THE YOUTH

U p ahead, a checkpoint stretched across the darkened road. It's okay, he thought, sometimes there are police checkpoints. There was nothing remarkable about finding one here, even at this hour. He eased his foot onto the brake, shifted to a lower gear, and began to slow down. Just as the Fiat 128 rolled to a stop, he saw the microbus out of the corner of his eye. Driving the wrong way down the city street, the bus hurtled itself toward him. It was too late. He could do nothing but brace for the impact as the microbus rammed the side of his car. In that instant, he knew they were coming for him. This was how the police arrested him almost two years earlier.

He decided to run. Throwing the Fiat into reverse, he spun the steering wheel as hard as he could and slammed the gas pedal. His car crippled by the bus, he sped in the opposite direction and quickly made it to the main bridge.

Damn. Another checkpoint.

Rather than cross the bridge, he swerved and took the first exit. Another checkpoint waited for him at the end of the ramp. In the distance, around the corner, he could see the police roadblock set to capture him if he chose a different route. The dragnet must have come from a tip to the police that he was in the area. They had moved fast. He was trapped with nowhere left to run. With his car idling as he waited for what would happen next, he saw the microbus reappear in his rearview mirror. This time it stopped short of his car—the car he'd borrowed from his father. They knew they had him. The side door of the microbus slid open, and the police officers came tumbling out carrying truncheons. He managed to send a text message just before they pulled him from the Fiat's front seat. The next moment, the blindfold tightened around his eyes.

It was the evening of February 16, 2010, and Mohamed ElBaradei, the former head of the International Atomic Energy Agency and Nobel Peace Prize winner, was due to return to Egypt three days later. ElBaradei had in recent months spoken publicly about the possibility of returning to his native country to challenge Mubarak in the upcoming presidential elections. Ahead of ElBaradei's arrival, the driver and some of his friends had decided to welcome him with signs of support. For young activists, this support usually took the form of graffiti spray-painted on Cairo's buildings and walls. On this evening, he had tagged Lebanon Square, which sits at the mouth of the highway. Thousands of cars pass the square every day. It's also close to the home of the minister of interior, and the activists had heard that police officers get punished every time the minister sees anti-Mubarak graffiti there. On that night, his stencils traced out the messages "Baradei is coming" and "Mubarak is over." And although no one probably noticed, the logo that his stencils left on Lebanon Square was a near-perfect replica of one used by a Serbian youth group that had overthrown the dictator Slobodan Milošević ten years earlier.

It might have been easy to dismiss this young man as a disaffected twentysomething or a simple troublemaker, and in fact many people did. But the Egyptian authorities were not that vigilant about keeping Cairo's public squares pristine, nor were they in the habit of setting elaborate dragnets to catch graffiti artists. Scores of police officers had been dispatched to apprehend this young man with stencils and a can of spray paint because, although he was only twenty-nine years old, he was a veteran of the campaigns against Hosni Mubarak. Indeed, he was the leader of a pro-democracy youth movement that helped spark Egypt's revolution less than a year later.

His name is Ahmed Maher, and that night in February wasn't his first time in an Egyptian police station. He had been interrogated many times by the police, and two years earlier—when he had first seen the police use a microbus as a battering ram—he had been tortured. By comparison, his detention on that night was relatively relaxed. He was charged, as he had been before, with starting an illegal organization to overthrow the government. His police interrogator was surprisingly inept; the officer kept repeating absurd things like "the president is a good man. Gamal is a good man," as if by simple repetition it would convince Ahmed that it was true. Fortunately, he had sent his text message seconds before they threw him, blindfolded and handcuffed, into the back of the microbus. His network alerted, protesters quickly converged on the police station and prosecutor's office. Ahmed was released after two days.

In authoritarian countries around the world, the first years of the twenty-first century witnessed a rising number of youth movements challenging some of the most well-entrenched regimes and strongmen. In Serbia, it was the youth-led Otpor (Resistance) that helped topple Milošević in 2000. Inspired by their example, the Georgian youth group Kmara (Enough) brought people into the streets to successfully call for political change in 2003. A year later, Pora (It's Time) mobilized thousands of young people in the wake of Ukraine's fraudulent election. In 2007, with opposition political parties in disarray, the Venezuelan student movement led the charge against Hugo Chávez's authoritarian power grab. In fact, the Venezuelan students had higher approval ratings than any other political force in the country, including the Catholic Church. In Iran, there would have been no Green Movement without the countless youth who protested the regime's stolen presidential election in June 2009. And it was the dramatic force of millions of young people pouring out into the streets in early 2011 that shook North Africa and the Middle East, upending regimes and rewriting the region's history forever.

Of course, youth activists, like any activists targeting a repressive regime, frequently fail to achieve their goals. Groups from Azerbaijan to Zimbabwe have risen up and been brutally suppressed. But across authoritarian countries, two constants almost always hold. The most outspoken, creative, and effective activists are often drawn from society's younger members. And a significant percentage of them choose to go to battle against the ruling regime as political independents, eschewing the parties, factions, or organizations that have long been a part of their country's political tug-of-war. In conversations with youth activists in country after country, a common thread emerges: far from seeing their age and inexperience as sources of weakness, they believe these qualities bring them a status as new, uncontaminated political outsiders that is potent against regimes that are unwilling to relinquish power. "Our power is that we are not a political party," Ahmed Maher told me. "We do what we want anytime we want. We don't have a headquarters that we fear is going to be closed. There is no ceiling to our opposition. We decide what we should do and we do it. The opposition parties always have calculations."

Activists everywhere agree with Maher. The political environment in modern authoritarian regimes is typically highly artificial. In Russia, with the exception of the Communist Party, the so-called opposition parties represented in the Duma are creatures of the state, literally created by the Kremlin. No one disputes that the opposition parties in Venezuela, which governed the country for decades, are responsible for the incredible mismanagement that led to Chávez's rise. But despite their incompetence, it has taken more than ten years for the Venezuelan opposition to jettison many of these old political players in favor of new faces. In Egypt, the secular opposition parties routinely proved to be more concerned about squabbling among themselves than producing a credible challenge to Mubarak. Not surprisingly, youth in such circumstances view the traditional political actors as compromised, either from negotiating too closely with the regime or through the sheer accumulation of failures. They shun the recruitment efforts of not just the ruling party but the traditional opposition parties as well. They remain outside a political mainstream they view as poisoned or polarized, often defying the established rules of political contest. And because they do so, and because as movements they make no claim of wanting power for themselves, the regime often considers them one of the greatest threats to its continued rule. "It allows us to effectively move past the politics," says Douglas Barrios, one of the leaders of the Venezuelan student movement in 2007. "We're not here as part of the opposition, we're not here as part of the government, we're not here as part of the past. We're just a couple thousand young kids demanding something better."

In the face of dismal alternatives, Ahmed Maher, Douglas Barrios, and countless other young people joining movements across the globe have become new, unexpected threats to modern authoritarians.

How Do You Fight Mike Tyson?

Hugo Chávez couldn't lose. In late 2006, Venezuela's charismatic president was at the peak of his power. That December, he was reelected in a landslide victory, trouncing the opposition party candidate, Manuel Rosales, by a margin of 26 percent. A year earlier he had secured complete control of the National Assembly when the same political opposition boycotted the parliamentary election. His coffers were overflowing. Oil prices were already at more than $60 a barrel—up more than three and a half times from what they were when he came to power—and showed no signs of slowing down. The opposition's election defeat was just the most recent drubbing in a string of losses going back to 1998. On election night, when Chávez walked onto the balcony of the presidential palace and looked out over Venezuela, there was virtually no opponent left to conquer. If he was going to have a fight, Chávez was going to have to look for enemies. Which might explain why his next target was a TV station.

Radio Caracas Televisión, or, as it was best known, RCTV, had been broadcasting for fifty-three years. It was the oldest television station in Venezuela, and the channel occupied first place in the ratings, with 40 percent of the viewing public. Although almost all of its programming was entertainment shows—it was home to some of Venezuela's most beloved Latin soap operas—the editorial line in its news coverage took a clearly critical view of Chávez and his policies. So, a few weeks after winning his new term in office, Chávez, dressed in military fatigues, announced that he would not be renewing the government concession that allowed RCTV to operate. Come May 28, 2007, when its contract would lapse, RCTV would go off the air. Most Venezuelans, even the president's own supporters, were stunned by the move. RCTV was an institution, the TV channel everyone had grown up watching. Polls showed that 65 to 80 percent of the public was against its closure. Chávez, however, was undaunted.

Douglas Barrios was a fourth-year student of economics at Metropolitan University at the time. He was twenty years old, so, like most of his classmates, he was part of the first generation of young Venezuelans to come of age under Chávez. Barrios was in sixth grade when Chávez was first elected, so he didn't really remember what it was like to have anyone other than Hugo Chávez as president. But he does remember sitting at home on the night of May 27, 2007, as a "powerful moment." In the months leading up to that day, Barrios and many of his friends in school had watched in disbelief as no one came forward to organize opposition to the president's decree. "When I try to explain it to people, I say it's like they shut down NBC, ABC, and CBS at the same time," says Barrios. And that night, precisely at midnight, RCTV went dark. The final image people saw was of the station's journalists, news anchors, actors, and employees singing the national anthem, many of them crying, as they waved good-bye. "You were sitting in front of your TV, probably the lights were off, and you saw this TV station go to static," recalls Barrios. "It just represented how choice can go away, how your options can go away, how something that's very, very established can just go to static."

Geraldine Alvarez, a student at the Andrés Bello Catholic University, remembers that night the same way. She was a fourth-year student, studying advertising and journalism. Growing up, she had never been particularly interested in politics. But the day before the RCTV closure, her classmates had elected her to the University Council. She had always assumed becoming active in student government would mean organizing academic debates or taking up campus issues. She certainly didn't see it as a pathway into the wider political arena. That all changed on May 28. "It was the first time I felt the government was coming into my house and telling me not to do something," says Alvarez. "That was the reason why so many people felt so shocked. The next day we closed the university."

At first, the reaction was spontaneous. Venezuelan student leaders from that time all say there was no carefully choreographed plan. They hadn't thought much beyond the next few hours. Certainly no one thought their actions were about to give birth to a movement. But a small group of students from the five major universities across Caracas had decided that May 28, 2007, couldn't be just another day. On that morning these students, numbering in the hundreds, got up early and stood out in front of their various universities to protest what everyone had seen happen on television the night before. They were angry. "We just said tomorrow can't be a normal day," says Barrios. "Because if we allow this to be normal, if we allow ourselves to accept this as normal, then we will be losing a bit of ourselves."

As it happens, Caracas's five major universities occupy strategic positions around the city. Four of them are located at the entrances to Caracas; the fifth is smack in the middle of the city. So if even a relatively small number of people were to blockade the roads in front of these universities, it would shut down the city. And that is precisely what these students did.

Not surprisingly, the student protesters were quickly met with resistance. The government dispatched police and national guard units to break up the blockades. Students at the Metropolitan University were hit with tear gas and rubber bullets. They had no choice but to retreat back into their university. When they tried to return to the street, they were beaten back again. Rather than accept the stalemate, student leaders decided to regroup. They would leave their schools and start to amass at Plaza Brión. The plaza was in a safer part of town, it had a metro stop, and the authorities weren't expecting them at that location. And that was when something truly surprising happened: their numbers began to grow.

When other students, friends, and family heard about the clashes in front of the universities, many decided to go out to show their solidarity. Whereas in the morning there had been only hundreds of students spread out over five universities, there were soon more than two thousand people in Plaza Brión. That number continued to climb until, by most estimates, there were nearly ten thousand people assembled there by the afternoon. Eventually, they filled the plaza and began to spill out onto surrounding streets. Again, the regime dispatched the police and the national guard to disperse the crowds. But the rally had hit a chord that kept it from being contained to a single time or place. The next day protests erupted again. But instead of just those in Caracas, students at other universities in other major cities began to stage their own blockades and demonstrations. "We weren't people with a plan," says Yon Goicoechea, a law student and student leader from Andrés Bello Catholic University, who soon became the most recognizable face of the Venezuelan student movement. "But we understood that we needed to do something the next day. We had to guide that spontaneous expression. We couldn't imagine the dimensions of the protest."

For the next month, student protests against the closing of RCTV took place every day around the country. Even though the demonstrations had clearly caught a spark and spread quickly, they had, in truth, almost no chance of changing anything. Chávez had already forced RCTV off the airwaves and replaced it with a government-owned channel. If the goal had been to save RCTV, then it was already lost. But that had not been the goal. Rather, the protests in May and June 2007 announced the presence of the student movement as a force in Venezuelan political life going forward. "We did not achieve a concrete objective," admits Goicoechea. "But when you are in a dictatorship, the act of giving hope and defeating fear is a very important objective in itself."

The students did not feel entirely alone in their new political role. In many ways, they saw themselves as heirs to President Rómulo Betancourt, the first democratic president of modern Venezuela. Betancourt had been a member of the student movement in 1928 that fought against the repressive dictatorship of Juan Vicente Gómez. The students then had been the only ones willing to stand up to Gómez. For thirty years, they were imprisoned, persecuted, and in exile because of their fight for democracy. In 1959, Betancourt was elected president. In 2007, Venezuela's students saw themselves joining this tradition. Even if they hadn't achieved some clear objective, Goicoechea told me that he thought these early summer protests were the most important period of the student movement because they established a link to previous defenders of Venezuelan democracy. "During our history, in every dictatorship, the students have taken to the streets," he says. "The relevance of the youth movement after decades of non-activity was very important to mobilize the opposition. We were saying that the opposition isn't just the political parties, but the people who want to live in a democracy in Venezuela." If no one else was going to stand up to Chávez, then the students would.

They didn't have to wait long for another opening. On August 15, Chávez proposed a constitutional referendum that would grant him new and significant powers as president. It was an incredibly bold proposal containing sixty-nine separate constitutional amendments. One revision permitted him to declare states of emergency during which he could censor all media outlets. One empowered him to draw up new administrative regions governed by his own handpicked vice presidents. Another made it more difficult to collect signatures to recall the president—a tactic the opposition had attempted in 2004. Perhaps most controversially, one amendment abolished presidential term limits, opening the way for Chávez to be president for life. And, in an effort to help generate public support for the referendum, it was chock-full of populist proposals such as a six-hour workday and social security benefits for everyone from street vendors to stay-at-home moms. Chávez was not seeking to merely revise the constitution; he sought to fundamentally change the relationship between state and society. His proposed reforms ran over forty-four single-spaced pages.

This time the students had a clear objective: defeat the referendum. But there was probably no one in Venezuela—including among the students—who would have been willing to wager that they could succeed. The magnitude of Chávez's electoral victory eight months earlier made him look invincible. He had the full weight of the state's apparatus behind him, which seemed to get larger by the day as he nationalized one industrial giant after another. Although there was very little critical media left, what remained had been largely tamed by the example Chávez had made of RCTV. The opposition political parties were so demoralized by their bruising defeats it appeared they might sit out this round.

In fact, it wasn't even clear on Venezuelan campuses that students were interested in defending their democratic rights. After Chávez announced his referendum, Barrios remembers they called for a student assembly at his university; eight people showed up. He said student leaders realized that despite the success they had mobilizing students only a couple of months earlier over RCTV, they had to start all over again. "That was a real challenge for us, to jump-start something that had been spontaneous," says Barrios.

The movement's leaders spent nearly a month getting their classmates motivated for the fight. The first step was pure education. They needed to make the students understand what was at stake and force them to take notice. Some of the referendum's provisions would allow the government to seize private property. So student organizers would seize the school cafeterias, marking them off with yellow tape and signs saying they were now government property. They filled the universities' gardens with faux tombstones; on each tombstone, they wrote a political right that would soon expire. As people joined, they were made to feel a part of the movement. Everyone had a job to do and felt ownership in the effort, even those among the rank and file. Student leaders became pragmatic about how they branded the movement. They made T-shirts. They created their own version of the Live Strong wrist bracelets. "It needed to be cool for you to be in the student movement," says Barrios. "And if that's what you need to do in order to drive thousands of people into the streets, that's what you need to do."

The students' sharpest insight was in how they chose to present themselves to the public. One of Chávez's most potent rhetorical weapons against the opposition parties had been to conjure up the past. Venezuelans remember that the democratic governments of recent decades were mired in corruption, incompetence, and poor management. As long as Chávez could link the parties to those days—which wasn't difficult when many of them had served in those governments—he could win. But the students understood that they didn't carry this political baggage. After all, many of them had been no more than ten or twelve years old when Chávez was first elected.

The slogan for the opposition parties had been "Chávez, get out now!" To the students, that had been a mistake. They had no interest in furthering the polarizing war of words that Chávez had begun. For starters, the goal was to defeat the referendum, not unseat Chávez. The president had demonstrated his popularity, so the students realized that demonizing him would likely be a losing strategy with voters they needed to sway. "We weren't against Chávez," says Goicoechea. "We didn't start this to take out Chávez. The first important thing that distinguished us was our message. It wasn't radicalizing people against Chávez. It was inclusive. We started our campaign focused on positive values." Indeed, they felt so strongly about it that they took pains to avoid even mentioning the president. "I worked on the communications side," recalls Alvarez, "and we would never say 'Chávez' at all. We would speak about the government. We would always speak about values."

And like youth movements elsewhere, the clearest advantage that the students brought was their age and political independence. "People started supporting us because we were too young to be politi-

cians and we were too young to be asking for something in return,"
says Alvarez. "We were not fighting to get elected to something." Such
seemingly pure motives put the regime on the defensive. Chávez
reverted to his polarizing rhetoric, referring to the students as "rich
kids," "sons of the empire," and "fascists." But these attempts to tie
the students to the wealthy or the United States largely fell flat with
the public. By the fall, it became clear that the student movement had
achieved something no one else ever had: Chávez was responding to
his opponent's political message rather than the other way around.

Of course, Chávez brought more than his political rhetoric to this
fight. Like all authoritarian leaders, he had the power to suppress the
students through force and intimidation. Here the students liked to
say that the approach they took to fighting Chávez was like trying
to fight Mike Tyson. "If you're going to fight Mike Tyson, you're not
going to box against him, because, even though he is crazy, he's going
to kill you," says Barrios, laughing at the thought. "But if you can challenge him to a game of chess, you might have a chance to defeat Mike
Tyson. We're not going to fight [Chávez's military or police], because
they have guns and weapons; they'd kill us. But if we can take them
away from their game and put them in our game, a game that we control, then we can defeat them. Yes, it's possible that Mike Tyson will
get angry after you beat him in chess and hit you. But if he does that,
you're going to have the support of the population. If Mike Tyson hits
you in a boxing match, everybody says you deserve it. After all, you
went into a boxing ring with Mike Tyson."

How do you keep Chávez and his regime on their heels? The
answer was creative, original, and unexpected forms of protest. It was
well and good to have marches and demonstrations in the streets. But
the students resisted falling into a pattern of going out, marching, and
getting repressed day after day. Instead, in October and November,
Venezuelans witnessed an incredible array of new and creative protests led by the students. Like many of the actions they had first taken
on their campuses, their demonstrations were often aimed at educat-
ing the public about what Chávez's constitutional referendum would
mean for Venezuelan life. Sometimes when they blocked roads, they
would let people pass only if they could name one article of the constitution Chávez wanted to change. They made and distributed cartoons

that explained the issues in clear and simple language. Instead of a protest with a thousand people, they would dispatch teams of ten people to a hundred subway stations. There they might distribute newspapers they had created with headlines from the future. Each headline revealed the consequences that had befallen Venezuelans because of the government's unlimited powers.

Humor proved a potent weapon. "Venezuela is very famous for having Miss Universe. We really care about Miss Venezuela," Alvarez told me. So the students made a picture of Miss Venezuela from the future, and it was an old lady who refused to give up her crown. "Everyone wants a new girl every year," says Alvarez, laughing. "But what if the actual Miss Venezuela wanted to keep her crown for fifteen years?"

In a move familiar to authoritarian regimes, Chávez and his supporters began to claim that the students were agents of the CIA. So a group of students started a demonstration outside a government bank. Once there, they shouted that they were CIA spies and that they had come to pick up their checks. "We started protesting outside the bank, saying the government is delaying our payment from the CIA," recalls Alvarez. "We made people understand how silly our government can be, not by confronting them, but by making fun of them. And we were able to do it because we were students."

As the date for the referendum approached, students say that the security forces became more aggressive. Students and their families started receiving death threats. Students were being beaten up at rallies by thugs while the police stood nearby. And individual student leaders began to come under incredible amounts of pressure. None more so than Yon Goicoechea.

In 2007, while Goicoechea was helping to lead the student movement, his own family was in crisis. Earlier that year his father had gone on trial for murder. His father and his family claimed the killing was in self-defense. Regardless of the circumstances, having Goicoechea's father in prison and on trial gave the regime leverage. One day the Venezuelan vice president, Jorge Rodríguez, had his bodyguards pick up Goicoechea as he walked down the street. Rodríguez wanted to make a deal. "The vice president of the republic said that he would get my father out of jail if I stopped the protests. I didn't accept that, and my father is still in jail. We have consequences. We sacrifice things. It wasn't easy."

I asked Goicoechea to explain. "Did the vice president want you to quit the student movement or undermine it?"

"If the vice president had told me if I quit, my father would be out of jail, I would have quit," replied Goicoechea, with no hesitation. "What I couldn't do was to stop something that was bigger than me and that I was responsible for. I have consequences and I pay daily." After Goicoechea refused the vice president's offer, the charges against his father were changed in order to raise his possible prison sentence. Instead of six years, his father was sentenced to twenty years. After a few moments, Goicoechea says quietly, "They intimidate and they play hard."

Ultimately, whether the constitutional referendum succeeded would be a question of numbers. In the closing days of their campaign, the students believed they needed to show their fellow Venezuelans that they had enough support to win. They decided they wanted to have their closing rally on Bolívar Avenue, in the heart of Caracas. The avenue isn't necessarily the largest public space in the country, but it is historically associated with large, important political rallies. It was also commonly said that President Chávez was the only person who could fill Bolívar Avenue. That made it highly appealing to the students. But the Ministry of Interior, which needed to approve their request to hold the rally there, understood the avenue's symbolic value, too. It repeatedly denied the students' request, telling them they could have any place besides Bolívar Avenue. The students replied by saying they would accept any day and time the ministry chose, as long as it was that avenue. The Ministry of Interior then gave the students Thursday, November 29, at 2:30 p.m., three days before the December 2 referendum vote. "They gave us a horrible day for protest"—many of their possible supporters would have to leave work and fight the midday traffic jams to make it—"but we put all our resources—physical, capital, human—into filling up Bolívar Avenue, and we managed to do so," recalls Barrios. By most estimates, more than 150,000 Venezuelans were there that day. And the next day, Chávez held his own rally, and he too filled the avenue. "The difference is, he is the president, we are university students," says Barrios. "A lot of people left thinking,

'These kids are serious. I mean, we actually have a shot at winning this.'"

Six Bulletproof Vests

On Sunday, December 2, Venezuelans came out to vote on the referendum. Neither side knew if it had the votes to win. The bluffing began almost right away.

Yon Goicoechea got a phone call from a Chavista student leader at noon. He said he needed to meet with Goicoechea and it was important. "We got together in a public place, and there was a very high functionary of the secret police there," recalls Goicoechea. "And the high functionary of the secret police told me that they had the information that they had won. He offered all the resources that I need—whatever that means—to avoid bloodshed in Venezuela. Of course, the way to avoid it was to not go to the streets." After using his father's fate to threaten Goicoechea, the regime was now resorting to bribery. Goicoechea simply needed to convince his fellow student leaders not to protest the outcome of the election.

Goicoechea knew that the regime didn't actually know if it had won or not. It was only midday, and people were still voting. But he could just as easily bluff. So he told the officer of the secret police that they had information that the students had won. "If we win, we will go to the streets and defend it," Goicoechea replied. "And if you want to avoid bloodshed, that is your responsibility because you are the national security."

The students had no illusions about what it would take to triumph on December 2, 2007. Goicoechea told me that there are two things you must have if you want to win an election in Venezuela. "You have to win, and you have to have the army. If one of those elements fails, you lose. Because the army won't defend you if you lose, and if you win, and the army does not defend you, you also lose."

It wasn't that the military needed to support your goals or your political project. Rather, it needed to see the costs of overturning an election as too great to pursue. "One thing is understanding how the military works, especially in countries like Venezuela," says Barrios. "If there is a degree of institutionalism still alive in the military, they would take the decision that requires less use of force. So we wanted to create a credible threat, saying that if you don't recognize the official result, you're going to have to use an incredible amount of force."

Throughout the day information coming into their headquarters was largely positive, but the students had no idea if they were winning. Even at its best, they believed any lead they might have remained within the margin of error. Nevertheless, they did nothing but project confidence. Around 7:00 p.m., Goicoechea, smiling from ear to ear, gave a press conference congratulating students and supporters for their work and saying that all that was left to do was defend the vote. The clear subtext was that they had won, and it was just a matter of being announced. His bravado was pure theater. He had no idea if they were ahead or not.

By midnight, the National Electoral Council still had not reported a result. Among the student leaders, nerves were fraying. Goicoechea spoke to contacts in the military who said the generals had told Chávez he must accept the result, but the students increasingly imagined that the regime intended to steal the election. At roughly 1:00 a.m., Vice President Rodríguez called and spoke to Leopoldo López, a young leader of the political opposition, who had been supportive of the students' campaign and was there with the movement's leaders. According to Barrios, the vice president implied that the regime intended to change the election results and that the students had best not do anything about it in the interests of their own personal security. "And I remember Leopoldo answered him by saying that if you change the results of the election, you will find thousands of people in the streets, and you will find me and the university students at the head of those protests," says Barrios. The election had come down to a high-stakes game of chicken.

Even today, the students won't say entirely what they had planned for that night and the next day. It had been Barrios's responsibility to plan the student movement's counterresponse in the event that the regime tried to steal the election. And at a few minutes past one o'clock in the morning, with the government still silent on the referendum's result, the moment they hoped would never come had arrived: the student movement had to go out and defend its votes. "It was a scenario we had prepared for," recalls Barrios. "I remember we all started leaving the room. We only had six bulletproof vests, so we gave them to the most recognizable of our leaders that were going to be out there protesting. And I remember there were not enough for me."

As Barrios was about to leave, he stopped for a moment to call his parents. His mother picked up the phone.

"How are you doing, honey?" she said.

"Mom, shit got complicated," he replied.

"What happened? Did we lose the election?"

"No, we won, but they might want to take it away." And then Barrios remembers that his mom said the "cutest thing ever."

"Don't worry, honey, these things happen sometimes. We'll get them next time."

"No," Barrios told his mom. "We're not going to get them next time. I mean, we won the election, and we are going to push through."

"What does that mean? When are you coming home?" his mom asked.

"I don't think I'm coming home today, Mom."

"So that means you are coming home tomorrow? When?"

"I don't think I am coming home at all, Mom," he replied. His mother dropped the phone and started crying. His father picked it up, and Douglas told him what he had told his mother. His father demanded that he tell him where he was. He heard his father repeating, "Where are you? Where are you?" as he said good-bye and hung up. Barrios then took the battery out of his cell phone. He put it in one pocket and the phone in another as he headed outside. He climbed onto a motorcycle, heading for the next location, where they would activate their plan. Just as he started to pull out, someone yelled, "Douglas, Douglas, wait, wait! They're going to announce the results."

Barrios jumped off the bike and ran back inside.

They had won. At 1:20 a.m., the vice president conceded the election. It would be several hours before Chávez would face his own supporters. To this day, the final vote tally from December 2, 2007, has never been released. And although it is impossible to say, it might never have happened if Chávez hadn't closed down RCTV.

A Show of Force

It looked like a party: young men and women dancing to rock music and belting out songs. Wearing orange hats, scarves, armbands, and ribbons, tens of thousands of Ukrainians, many of them young people, lived in the streets of Kiev for nearly three weeks. They had flooded Independence Square and other corners of the capital to protest a stolen election and stand up for their candidate. As the November temperatures fell, they bundled up, had a little more to drink, and joined together in chanting, "Together, we are many! We cannot be defeated!" Before the end of the year, this outburst of "people power" had overturned a fraudulent election and returned Ukrainians to the voting booth, where they democratically elected the country's leading opposition candidate.

The colorfully named Orange Revolution was hailed as a peaceful democratic uprising. And it was. But the youth activists who had played a role in organizing the street protests in Kiev that winter had not worked from an entirely blank slate. The Ukrainian youth movement, known as Pora, had benefited from consultations and advice from Serbia's Otpor, the youth who had helped bring down Milošević in 2000. They had also had conversations and shared ideas with Kmara, the young leaders who helped propel the Rose Revolution in Georgia in 2003. And if you looked closely at the sea of orange in Kiev's "tent city" that November, you would have seen that others had come to learn from the Ukrainian experience. Young Kazakhs had come to see the protests firsthand. Belarusian activists mingled in the crowd and even hoisted their national flag in support of their new Ukrainian friends. Young people from across former Soviet republics were there to see what it meant to make a "color revolution."

The Kremlin did not need to wait until it saw Russian youth in the streets of Moscow or St. Petersburg to learn its lesson. Having witnessed the role that opposition youth groups played in Serbia, Georgia, and especially in Ukraine during the Orange Revolution, the Kremlin decided to manufacture a youth movement of its own. The result is Nashi. The group, which struck a militant nationalistic tone from the beginning, is today one of the key instruments for intimidating and harassing opposition leaders, civil society activists, and Kremlin critics. On the day I arrived in Moscow in April 2010, Nashi (which literally means "Ours") was celebrating its fifth anniversary. The celebration's keynote speaker was none other than Putin's right-hand man, Vladislav Surkov, then the Kremlin's leading ideologist who is believed to be behind Nashi's creation. Surkov stirred a raucous crowd of Nashi delegates, roughly two thousand twentysomethings. "We see what's happening in Kyrgyzstan—that means we are needed and have to be at our posts," Surkov told the crowd at a high-end Moscow conference hall, referring to the near civil war that had recently broken out on Russia's border. "Those who chose for themselves the political fight will never be able to relax again." His remarks were followed by Vasily Yakemenko, Nashi's leader and official founder. "The Nashi movement is the movement of those who feel outraged and mad by what they see around them," Yakemenko told the assembled. "Our movement knows no authority except the authority of the policies of Medvedev and Putin."

One Kremlin official who regularly meets with Nashi leaders described the origins of the organization as something akin to a preemptive strike. "After the Orange Revolution, all the opposition here started to talk about taking control of the streets and making an Orange Revolution here. We understood very well that an Orange Revolution would be awful, it would destroy the country." So the government set out to recruit young people, mostly between the ages of seventeen and twenty-five, from the country's provincial universities and vocational schools. "For some of them, so-called patriotism came more naturally," he explained. "They can be organized and say Americans want to destroy our country, Americans want to make revolution, so let's go to protect our country."

And they made their presence felt almost immediately. On May 12, 2005, more than fifty thousand Nashi members occupied the streets of Moscow in a massive show of support for President Vladimir Putin and his regime. Although most Russian activists at the time thought the government's fears of a homegrown revolution were exaggerated, any talk of an Orange Revolution stopped. The message to anyone who may have been inspired by the events in Ukraine was simple: You think you will own the streets? *We* own the streets.

Five years on, the Kremlin continues to nurture the youth movement it founded. The group is one of the largest recipients of govern-ment aid allocated for Russian civil society organizations. In 2008, Nashi was awarded more than $500,000, or roughly 1 percent of the government's budget for NGO grants. It receives an even greater share of its funding from private businesses that are prodded by the government to be generous with its pet project. A large portion of this money goes to support the pro-Kremlin youth movement's summer camp on the banks of Lake Seliger, about five hours northeast of Mos-cow. Members enjoy the same activities young people might enjoy at any sleepaway camp. The daily schedule is filled with opportuni-ties for kayaking, swimming, rafting, and long bicycle rides. But these summer sessions also serve as an ideological boot camp. The Nashi youth attend political lectures praising Putin's leadership, and they are taught that members of the political opposition and the human rights community represent threats to the motherland. In 2007, the organizers made headlines for a part of the camp called "the red-light district." There campers could view the faces of opposition leaders like Garry Kasparov and the former prime minister Mikhail Kasyanov superimposed on posters of scantily clad women stuffing money into their underwear. (They were called "political prostitutes.") During the 2010 summer retreat, the camp put together an exhibit that included photographic montages of the impaled heads of some of the country's leading political activists, including the eighty-four-year-old former Soviet dissident Ludmilla Alexeeva and the political opposition's Boris Nemtsov. Despite these displays, Nashi's funding has never come into question; it has only grown.

For many people, Nashi is no less than a modern incarnation of the Soviet Union's Komsomol, the former youth wing of the Commu-nist Party. The ideological emphasis, demands of strict loyalty, even the colors and symbols, are reminiscent. And the Kremlin has enticed many to join by holding out membership as a way to get ahead. "Have you heard of Komsomol? Nashi is approximately the same," says Ilya Yashin, a member of the Solidarity opposition movement. "You have to be loyal. If you want to have a career, you have to put on a T-shirt with a Putin image on the chest and then march all together along the Lenin Prospect. If you don't, then you are marginal."

I met Yashin and another member of the Solidarity movement in a bohemian restaurant in downtown Moscow, a short walk from the Kremlin. When I asked him about Nashi, Yashin's colleague started to laugh, saying, "He's an expert." That's because Yashin, who is only twenty-eight years old, is a frequent target for the Kremlin youth group. He was an early critic of Nashi's activities, and the group's members have responded to his criticism by harassing him, vandalizing his car, and coming out to jeer during his speeches before supporters. They have also tried to smear him online. A few weeks before we met, a video clip appeared on the Nashi Web site supposedly showing Yashin paying a police officer a bribe to avoid receiving a traffic ticket. Yashin is adamant the video was doctored and he hasn't bribed anyone. A few days after we met, another video surfaced showing several prominent opposition figures having sex with the same woman. It was later learned that the woman, named Katya, had seduced these and other opposition figures and taken them back to the same apartment, where they were unknowingly filmed. Although he didn't have sex with the woman, Yashin quickly came forward and admitted he too had been seduced by Katya and led back to her apartment. When he got there, she offered him cocaine. Realizing that it was a honey trap set by the regime (and incidentally, right from the old Soviet espionage playbook), Yashin left immediately. He claims Nashi organized the whole operation against him and others, and he filed a complaint with the state prosecutor's office for invasion of privacy and distribution of pornography.

There is admittedly something farcical about operatives from a Kremlin youth league trying to make sex tapes to discredit opposition leaders. But there is another side of Nashi and similar pro-government youth groups that makes people far more nervous. From the beginning, Nashi had a clear paramilitary purpose. Members who want to advance in the organization are required to participate in boot camps, pass a military assault course, and spend time on the shooting range. They run drills on how to defend against an Orange Revolution. A similar youth group, tied to United Russia, known as the Young Guard, even practiced attacking a "tent city" like the one that sprang up in Kiev during the Orange Revolution. In the exercise, these young shock troops broke up the makeshift village with baseball bats.

The only trouble was, there was no Orange Revolution to squelch. Having created an organization of roughly 120,000 angry youth, the

Russian government didn't seem to know what to do with them. The regime trained, motivated, and politicized this muscular movement and then risked leaving it without a purpose, without a mission to fulfill. When such a force is created and then left to its own devices, a tragedy like the one that occurred in the early morning of Saturday, November 6, 2010, should hardly come as a surprise.

On that morning, the thirty-year-old journalist Oleg Kashin returned to his apartment after a late dinner party. When he arrived home, two men brutally attacked him with steel rods. He was left a bloody heap in the street. They fractured his skull, broke both halves of his jaw, and crushed one leg. He was rushed to a Moscow hospital and left in a medically induced coma for days. As has happened to other Russian journalists who have been assaulted, his attackers broke his fingers, tearing several fingers from their joints. One finger had to be amputated. Although no one knows who perpetrated the attack, the focus of Kashin's reporting is well-known: pro-Kremlin youth groups. In August, the Young Guard had published Kashin's photograph on its Web site. Across the image were the words "Will be punished."

"Putin Kills Kenny"

Of course, the Kremlin's strategy for engaging its youth cannot be all force. As useful as battalions of young loyal militants might be, it is equally important for the broad swath of Russian youth to be either supportive of the regime or, at the very least, not interested enough in politics to raise a dissenting voice. Here Putin—both in his image and in his rhetoric—had long been successful. After experiencing the country's declining fortunes in the 1990s, young Russians took immense pride in Putin's effort to restore international respect to their country. Polling data consistently showed that Russian youth are some of the most supportive backers of Putin's hard-edged, tough-talking nationalistic style. While they may have no memory of life in the Soviet Union, they craved for their country the recognition and great-power status that the Communist state enjoyed. Indeed, one poll conducted in 2007 indicated that 63 percent of young Russians believe that the "collapse of the Soviet Union was the greatest geopolitical catastrophe of the 20th century."

A comparison between Ukrainian and Russian youth was telling.

In Ukraine, people younger than thirty were three times more likely to join the Orange Revolution than any other age-group. Meanwhile, in Russia, a large majority of young people accepted Putin's explanation of the revolution in Ukraine as a Western conspiracy directed at weakening the motherland. The same 2007 poll indicated that 89 percent of young people did not want an Orange Revolution in Russia. Rather than political change, they wanted a Russia that is strong, stable, and powerful on the world stage. The none-too-subtle images of a macho Putin riding a three-wheeled Harley-Davidson, hunting big game while shirtless, or wearing his judo black belt as he throws some unfortunate sparring partner to the floor are the embodiment of what many young Russians want their country to be. Putin was, in a word, cool. "You really have to admit that Putin and his rhetoric is very popular in Russia," says Dmitri Makarov, a twenty-eight-year-old Russian human rights activist. "You simply cannot deny that, especially among my generation, which is more conservative, more nationalistic, more Stalinist than the generation before it."

Likewise, it is equally important that the regime do nothing to inadvertently motivate or radicalize an otherwise apathetic generation more interested in rubles than revolution. "If you would directly ask, 'Do you need human rights in Russia?' most [young] people would answer no," says Ivan Ninenko, the deputy director of Transparency International's Moscow office. "People don't trust the human rights movement; most of them wouldn't even understand what you are asking them." But Ninenko, who is twenty-seven years old and has been active in political protests, believes that it isn't because young Russians aren't capable of mobilizing. Rather, he gives the government credit for never pointlessly making enemies with the country's younger citizens. "If tomorrow the government decides for some stupid reason to forbid free Internet access," says Ninenko, "you would have lots of young people in the streets, because for them this is a basic value."

A rare instance when authorities took a misstep that stirred the passions of Russian youth came in September 2008. Early that month, a prosecutor's office in Moscow filed a complaint against a television station called 2x2. The complaint against the station, which is akin to the Cartoon Network, came under the broad charge of engaging in "extremist activity." Prosecutors, acting on behalf of a religious group, had been offended by an episode of *South Park* called "Mr. Hankey's Christmas Classics." Besides the usual ensemble of Kenny, Cartman, Kyle, and Stan, this episode featured special appearances from Satan, Adolf Hitler, and Mr. Hankey, a piece of human feces who sings and performs at the children's Christmas show. The authorities claimed that the episode could inflame "ethnic conflict and inter-religious hatred." They also cited a number of other cartoons carried by 2x2, including *The Simpsons* and *Family Guy,* for containing material detrimental to children. Duma representatives suggested that 2x2's broadcast license should be revoked and handed over to a government-run station that would highlight patriotic values.

The authorities had gone too far. Young people in Moscow and St. Petersburg began to stage rallies and protests in defense of 2x2. They held a free rock concert to publicize the issue and started a petition drive to keep the station on the air. "Those young people who never go to demonstrations went to the streets. They were the most creative demonstrations you have ever seen in Moscow," recalls Ninenko, laughing. "They carried signs like, 'Putin Kills Kenny.' They were protecting freedom of speech, but they wouldn't say it that way. They would say they were protecting Kenny and Cartman. So, on the one hand, they would not stand up for human rights, but on the other hand they are ready to stand up for the right of freedom of speech."

The government quickly realized its mistake. Within days, the campaign against 2x2 was dropped, and the station's broadcasting license was renewed. The station did, however, make a concession. It agreed not to re-air "Mr. Hankey's Christmas Classics." It was a small price to pay to let Kenny live.

But young people are nothing if not fickle. When tens of thousands of Russians rallied in Moscow in the wake of rigged parliamentary elections in December 2011, Russian youth were among those chanting "Russia without Putin!" They too had been offended by Putin's brazen methods. Some observers believed the Kremlin would manufacture a new party to attempt to absorb these discontented middle-class youth. Any response from the regime could be backed by Nashi, which might finally be called upon to fulfill its purpose. Either way, going forward the battle for Russia's young people would be about far more than cartoons.

"When the Moment Comes"

Mostafa el-Naggar, a thirty-year-old dentist, laughs when he tells me about his most recent arrest. It had happened two months earlier in January 2010; it was the first time he had ever been detained for being a blogger. Previously, he had only been arrested for his membership in the Muslim Brotherhood, which was officially banned. As we sat in a coffee shop off Tahrir Square, he told me he fully expected that he would be arrested again soon. Naggar had even made arrangements with a colleague to take care of his dental practice. Friends had already constructed solidarity banners demanding his release. He didn't know if it would be because he was volunteering for Mohamed ElBaradei's campaign, because of his blogging, because of his membership in the Brotherhood, or some combination of all three. But he could tell Mubarak's regime was nervous. "It's these street movements that scare them," he said.

Naggar, a husband and father of two, with a kind face and gentle demeanor, remained lighthearted, even as he talked about terrifying things. He smiled as he discussed being targeted and harassed by the police. He joked when he talked about receiving threatening phone calls from state security. I thought it might come from growing up in a family with a history of activism. Gamal Abdel Nasser imprisoned his grandfather for ten years for being a member of the Brotherhood; his uncle served seven years, also under Nasser, for being a Marxist. I asked him why he was so affable, even in the face of possible jail time, and he told me he had no choice. "I have to be optimistic, there is no alternative. The only alternative is despair," says Naggar. "We laugh from bitterness."

But there was also something else. He was convinced that something was about to change. People are in a constant state of crisis, he told me. They are growing tired of their fear. "I have researched all the causes of social movements and revolutions. I have looked at the reasons behind them, and I find them [here]. Check, check, check, check," says Naggar, raising his hand as if he were marking the ingredients for revolution off a list. "Some people say we are a very patient people. But the new generations don't have this patience. People are really suffocated. The last five years have been particularly suffocating. I don't think Egypt is going to wait much longer. There has to be a change."

Ten months and ten days after Naggar said these words in a tiny café in Tahrir Square, Egypt's revolution began, with its youth leading the way. Indeed, after decades of political and economic stasis, much of North Africa and the Middle East erupted in a matter of weeks, led in almost every instance by a young generation that had lost its patience. In retrospect, the region had all the makings of a tinderbox. Sixty percent of the population was under the age of thirty, the highest percentage in the world. In the past twenty years, the youth population in the Middle East had boomed, with a 50 percent increase in Tunisia and Libya, a 65 percent increase in Egypt, and a 125 percent increase in Yemen. They were not only young; they were often jobless. Youth unemployment was 23 percent across the region, twice the global average. Ironically, rates of unemployment soared even higher for the millions who had college degrees. The region's corrupt and stunted economies were better at producing jobs for illiterates than for engineers. In Egypt, college graduates were ten times more likely to be unemployed than those with only a few years of grade school. As they spent their days looking for jobs that either were not there or paid too little, their anger, humiliation, and resentment burned. Many had put their lives on hold, waiting for a decade or more, to scrounge together enough money to move out of their parents' home, get an apartment, and start a family. One young man I met in Cairo named Khalid told me he simply couldn't afford to marry. "I have fallen in love, but I haven't asked for her hand in marriage," he said. "You can't even save 10,000 pounds." He, like 60 percent of Egyptians, had lived his entire life under Mubarak. "Everyone you think is apathetic knows more about politics than you or me," says Khalid. "They have seen the abuses with their own eyes. They walk down the street and don't feel like a human being. We have reached the edge of what we can accept."

But someone had to go first. No one would have predicted that it would be a twenty-six-year-old Tunisian fruit vendor. On December 17, 2010, the humiliation, insults, and desperate daily struggle became too much for Mohamed Bouazizi. On that morning, as he pulled his cart to the market in the town of Sidi Bouzid, a female police officer stopped him. When she began to take baskets of the young man's apples for herself—police officers frequently harassed vendors and merchants with impunity—Bouazizi objected. His mother and siblings depended on the money he made selling fruits from his cart. The policewoman struck him with her baton and then slapped him in the face. Two other officers pushed him to the ground and took his scale. Bouazizi was left, a crumpled heap on the ground, pleading with his tormentors. People who were there said that he wept, repeatedly crying out, "Why are you doing this to me?" Later that day, Bouazizi stood in front of city hall. In a final, hopeless act, he doused himself in paint thinner and lit a match. He died in the burn unit eighteen days later. Tunisia's dictatorship did not last much longer.

Tunisia was supposed to be one of the most stable of dictatorships, a modern authoritarian duchy on the banks of the Mediterranean. President Zine el-Abidine Ben Ali had kept Tunisian society in a stranglehold for more than two decades. Among Middle Eastern dictatorships, it was one of the most repressive, with tight control of the media, heavy surveillance of human rights defenders, and imprisonment of regime critics. The government had refused to legally recognize any independent human rights organizations for more than a decade. (Egyptian activists often told me how lucky they felt not to live in a country as repressive as Tunisia.) Although thoroughly corrupt, the tiny country of ten million prospered relative to its neighbors. Literacy rates are at nearly 80 percent. It has the highest percentage of Internet users of any Arab country. But when word of Bouazizi's desperate act began to spread on Facebook, Tunisia's modernity—in particular, its young, educated, and wired population—accelerated the regime's demise.

The regime's effort to quell a rising tide of protests with its own crackdown only fueled public anger, as more of the country's educated youth took to the streets. Al Jazeera quickly picked up the footage of Tunisian demonstrators and beamed it across the Arab world. Each crackdown led to more first-person accounts and video footage of Tunisian police firing on citizens, alienating the general public from the regime and adding to the protesters' ranks. Ben Ali's henchmen were always one step behind, unable to predict where the next protest or riot would take place.

Even as the number of young Tunisians in the streets swelled and their protests drew closer to the capital, few believed the regime would fall. By the second week of January, a nervous Ben Ali addressed the nation, promising to hand over power at the end of his term. But after twenty-three years of rule, the dictator's promises no longer had meaning. Sensing that he might become the next Nicolae Ceaușescu—the Romanian tyrant who was summarily executed with the collapse of communism—Ben Ali fled the country with his family. For the first time, a modern Arab dictator had been deposed by his people. Across the region, talk of a "Tunisia scenario" infecting other Middle Eastern autocracies became rampant.

Revolutions are never entirely organic. They require leaders, people at the vanguard to plot, push, and prod others to take risks they had always sought to avoid. Egypt's revolution had many authors; one is Ahmed Maher. He had been politically active for about five years. His activism actually grew inside him from, of all things, thinking about roads and concrete. "It started when I was at university as a student of [civil] engineering," he told me when we met at an outdoor café in Cairo in March 2010. As anyone who has driven through Cairo's twisted traffic patterns and congested roads can attest, it is hard to imagine that the city ever employed civil engineers. And this was the root of Maher's epiphany. "There are rules to building roads and building tunnels and building bridges. We studied these rules, but it's not implemented, and there is chaos. We have studied all this, we understand it, but it is not applied," he continued. "I realized that the system itself is corrupt. The local council and the municipality and everyone in that chain is corrupt. I found the problem is systemic."

He quickly got a new education in street protests. After a short stint, he became disenchanted with the internal politics and bureaucracy of Ayman Nour's El Ghad Party. He left to join the youth wing of Kefaya (Enough), a loose collection of anti-Mubarak political activists. There he organized protests, leaflet drops, and street theater with a decidedly political message. One of the group's favorite tactics was what it called "sudden demonstrations." Teams of five or six young people would target a popular neighborhood. A scout would first make sure the area was clear. Then two girls, one on the left and one on the right of the street, would hand out political leaflets. Two boys who trailed behind the girls provided security, and a supervisor who oversaw the whole operation, in turn, followed them. Each action would be planned to last no more than twenty minutes—the usual amount of time it took state security to react. At the first sign of trouble, the girls would drop the leaflets and run, the boys would make a scene, and the supervisor would distract the security officers by shouting like a normal passerby on the street. "It was an optimistic time, a hopeful time," says Maher. "There was pressure on Egypt to democratize. That gave us freedom of movement on the street."

It didn't last. In late 2005, eighty-eight candidates from the Muslim Brotherhood won seats in the Egyptian Parliament. A little over a month later, Hamas triumphed in Palestinian elections. Maher agrees with the conventional wisdom that the triumph of Islamists at the polls, paired with the United States' failure to make progress in its wars in Afghanistan and Iraq, led the Bush administration to tone down its democracy promotion in the Middle East. The Bush administration needed stable allies in the region, even if they were autocrats. Given this latitude, Mubarak's regime struck back against those who had been pressing for greater political reforms. "They cracked down on a sit-in we had in front of the Judges Club. We were arrested and imprisoned for two months. That was a major crackdown, and a lot of people were afraid to take to the streets again," recalls Maher. But that didn't mean a complete end to activism for everyone. "So blogging exploded," Maher continued. "That was the thing to do. Instead of the streets, we took to the computer screens."

The spring of 2008 was a moment of great discontent in Egypt. The most common complaint was economic: food prices had soared while people's wages remained flat. The price of basic staples like bread and cooking oil had more than doubled. In April 2008, the UN World Food Programme reported that average household expenses in Egypt had jumped 50 percent from the beginning of the year. With anger mounting over stagnant wages, Egypt had quickly become a hotbed of labor activism. Although labor demonstrations were officially illegal, the Egyptian government witnessed a sharp rise in workers voicing their demands through sit-ins, work stoppages, and strikes. In 2002 and 2003, there were fewer than a hundred labor protests in Egypt. Between 2004 and 2008, there were nearly two thousand. The actions did not come from one corner of the country or a single group of workers; they were widespread. Textile workers, taxicab drivers, doctors and nurses, garbage collectors, and university professors all threatened to strike. Even the government's own tax collectors went on strike in hope of better wages.

If the labor activity had an epicenter, it was the gritty northern industrial town of El Mahalla El Kubra. It is the home of the Misr Spinning and Weaving Company, the largest textile factory in Egypt and, with roughly twenty-seven thousand workers, one of the largest in the Middle East. The factory workers there had been engaged in on-again, off-again negotiations over their wages and working conditions since 2006. When the workers claimed that the state-owned company had once again reneged on its promises, they announced they would go on strike on April 6, 2008.

With very little activity in Egyptian streets, bloggers had turned their attention to the growing wave of labor unrest around the country, publicizing worker strikes and government crackdowns. Maher had some contact with the leaders of the El Mahalla El Kubra strike, but not much. He, like most activists living in Cairo or Alexandria, had failed to establish deep ties with labor leaders in other parts of the country. It had been difficult to convince labor organizers that their economic demands—better pay, safe working conditions, workers' rights—could best be solved through political demands. Nevertheless, Maher sensed an opportunity. In discussions with fellow youth activists, he wanted to find a way that people without connections to the Misr Spinning and Weaving Company could still support the workers in their fight. "We brainstormed and came up with the idea of a general strike," says Maher. "The slogan was 'Stay at home.' Don't go to the university, don't go to work, don't go out. Stay at home."

These activists didn't have a blueprint. Even after years of demonstrations, protests, and street actions, they were feeling their way. They took risks and tried to learn from them, attempting to locate the regime's pressure points as they went. And there was a lot to learn: organizing protests, defending themselves, marketing their message, connecting with local populations, maintaining morale, and trying to outwit the state's security apparatus. "As a youth movement, we are pretty much working on trial and error," Maher admitted. "We are studying nonviolent movements, following their lead, and trying to adapt it to Egyptian circumstances. But what we are working on mainly is trying to link social issues with politics."

The 2008 call for a general strike would be one of their first great lessons. After they came up with the idea, the next step wasn't organizing a march, handing out flyers, or staging a sit-in. Maher turned to Facebook. He and a friend, Esraa Rashid, set up a group on Facebook—dubbed the April 6 Strike group—in support of the workers. People who logged on and became members could post ideas to the group's wall on how people could show their solidarity. To their surprise, the April 6 Strike group's membership exploded overnight. By the first day, it had more than a thousand members. Every time they refreshed the page, the number jumped. Within a few days, they were surpassing twenty thousand, then thirty thousand members. Maher and Rashid had to work in shifts to administer the group's page, approving or deleting an avalanche of messages posted to its wall. A couple of days before the workers' strike, the Facebook group exceeded seventy-six thousand members.

In part, Maher credits the response to the power of the idea. For a public that had reason to fear reprisals, a general strike was appealing. People were not being asked to storm the barricades or stare down riot police. They didn't need to take great personal risk; they simply needed to stay within the confines of their homes. Yet if enough people joined, the regime would feel its effects as the country came to a standstill. The online group not only presented an opportunity for people across Egypt to demonstrate their support for the textile workers but also sent a powerful signal of the wider discontent and brewing anger among the population at large.

But Maher and his fellow activists don't believe Facebook was the most effective tool for publicizing the strike. For that, they give credit to the Egyptian regime itself. Soon after the government became aware of the support building for a strike, it started issuing stern warnings against participating in the protest. "The [regime's] security had fallen into the trap of putting warnings, very heavy and authoritarian-like warnings, on television, radio, and on the news bar every half hour or so," says the youth activist Ahmed Salah, laughing as he recalls it. Impersonating a deep, stern voice, he continued, "A statement from the Ministry of Interior: Anyone not showing up to work, anyone participating in this, anyone doing that, will be punished in accordance with the laws and regulations. No disorder is allowed!"

The regime had been caught flat-footed. The growing support for the workers in El Mahalla El Kubra, triggered in part by Maher's call for a strike over Facebook, had led the government to make a miscalculation. In 2008, April 6 fell on a Sunday, which is the first day of the workweek in Egypt. But people say it felt like a Friday, the day of rest in the predominantly Muslim country. The streets in Cairo and Alexandria were noticeably quiet. The little bit of traffic in the city centers moved briskly. Police and riot squads were the only crowds you found in the typically bustling public squares and markets as the security forces congregated outside. For all the stereotyping of the Egyptian people as docile and apathetic, a significant number of them apparently did not want the Ministry of Interior ordering them to go to work. "[The regime] was a great help in spreading the word, because no matter what we have, our means of communication with the people are limited," says Salah. "Television is absolutely the widest possible way to get the word out, and this was very successful on April 6."

The streets, however, were not quiet in El Mahalla El Kubra. The strike at the textile factory was supposed to begin at 7:00 a.m., when the night shift ended. Plainclothes security officers had entered the factory overnight and squashed any effort to organize. Outside, angry crowds formed. Tensions turned violent, with residents throwing stones and setting tires ablaze as police fired tear gas and rubber bullets. The rioters tore down a billboard of President Mubarak, and public buildings were torched. At least two people were killed, and more than 150 were injured in the clashes. Around Egypt, state security arrested hundreds of people accused of organizing the national day of protest. Sensing the danger, Maher went into hiding.

Having broken the strike through force, the regime then sought to smooth over tensions with handouts. Two days after the violence, Prime Minister Ahmed Nazif, with a group of cabinet officials in tow, visited the workers at the textile factory. Nazif told the workers they would receive a bonus equal to thirty days' pay. Several weeks later, President Mubarak made an even grander gesture. In a speech on the eve of May Day, he announced a major salary increase for government workers, along with expanded efforts to provide subsidized bread, cooking oil, and other basic foods. "We had talked about a 15 percent raise," Mubarak said, "but decided on 30 percent. The government will have to find the resources."

Meanwhile, Maher and his colleagues, hoping to capitalize on their recent success, called for a second strike timed for President Mubarak's eightieth birthday on May 4. This time, however, the regime issued no public response or dire warnings. Ahmed Salah went out on May 4 and asked people if they knew there was a strike that day. "Strike? What strike? Nobody knew about it," he says. It was a flop. The regime had quickly learned its lesson.

It also knew that Ahmed Maher had been the ringleader behind the online campaign. So it waited. Maher remained in hiding for a month. "I used to have my phone off all the time. I would only access Facebook from Internet cafés and only stay half an hour," he recalls. On May 7, when he thought things had calmed down, he resurfaced. He was immediately arrested and taken to dreaded Lazoghly, which is what Egyptians called the imposing state security intelligence head-quarters that sat in Lazoghly Square. Once he was in custody, his interrogators stripped him and beat him. They threatened to sodom-ize him with a stick. Maher says the beating and abuse continued for the next twelve hours. After delivering heavy blows to his back and neck, his tormentors would apply lotion to try to keep the bruising and swelling down, and then they would beat him again. The purpose was simple: they wanted Maher's Facebook password. He refused. Outside, demonstrations and protests calling for Maher's release had already begun. When the security officers realized they weren't get-ting anywhere and the pressure for his release was building, they tried to negotiate with him. "They were like, 'Okay, how about you set up an NGO? Or, how about you become the youngest leader of a legal opposition party? We're not bad people. We are nationalists, too. You can work with us,'" recalls Maher.

The regime wished to draw Maher into the artificial world of Egyp-tian politics. He and his movement would become the newest mem-bers of a co-opted opposition that coordinates its activities within the strict limits set by the government. Maher had no intention of agree-ing to the security officers' proposal, but he wanted to be released. "I said I'd think about their offer. I was released, and the first thing I did was expose them. I talked to everyone," he recalls. "One officer called me and said, 'Is that what we agreed on?' Then they stopped calling me. And we started the movement from there."

The next two years represented a time of tremendous learning for Maher and the members of the April 6 movement, and they looked far beyond the streets of Cairo to draw their lessons. Maher told me about studying examples of nonviolent struggles from Poland, Chile, and Serbia and reading portions of the book *From Dictatorship to Democracy*. Its author, Gene Sharp, was a former Harvard researcher and the leading thinker on the strategy of nonviolent conflict. His book has been translated into dozens of languages and read by democratic movements around the world. "We were following the wrong theory," Maher told me. "We thought we would take to the streets and start to demonstrate. People are very angry, so they will join us and suddenly we would be a million people and we would topple the regime. That was wrong."

Other members of the movement traveled abroad to learn more. I first met Ahmed Salah in Boston in June 2009 when he attended a five-day course organized by the International Center on Nonviolent Conflict. The center, funded by the American multimillionaire Peter Ackerman, brought together more than thirty activists from different countries to study the strategy and tactics of nonviolent struggle. Each day the participants gathered in a classroom for lectures and discussions. But Salah told me that his most important insights came from the opportunity to compare notes with other activists. Specifically, he zeroed in on the advice he received from two of the leaders of the Serbian student movement that helped topple Milošević. Early attempts to organize against the government, particularly by the youth wing of Kefaya, had been infiltrated by the regime's informants. Salah learned that their movement's efforts had been too open, indeed, too democratic. "I had always been extremely supportive of democracy, and I would say we have to be the biggest example of democracy," says Salah. But the Serbs explained that was mistaken. "They gave me the answer regarding how they managed to fight sabotage and infiltration attempts. There is no democracy in the leadership of a resistance movement. A resistance movement is not a club," he says. "You cannot leave it open to elections and debate, because this makes it prone to all sorts of interference."

The model for a successful democratic movement wasn't a democracy; it was a military operation. One of Gene Sharp's central observations was that democratic movements, even if nonviolent, needed to be as strategic and disciplined as any military unit might be. It was a lesson successfully put in practice by the Serbs in their own movement, Otpor. In their idealism, it was something Egyptian activists had misunderstood. Salah returned to Cairo with new ideas for the group's organization. "From our experience and in Youth for Change, we had meetings every month, and they were constantly infiltrated by security," says Maher. "Ahmed Salah was with me in Youth for Change, and we learned our lessons in April 6. When Ahmed Salah went to Boston, he understood, 'Yes, you can't run it democratically.' We are in a fight, and we are in a fight with this regime. We are more like a military organization."

In that same month, Mohamed Adel, a member of the April 6 movement, traveled to Belgrade to attend a different workshop. Among all the youth movements they had studied, Adel told me, they had taken a particular liking to the Serbian example. The April 6 movement's logo—the outline of a clenched fist—was a copy of the Serbian group's own stencil. Even some of the slogans they spray-painted on the streets of Cairo—for example, "Mubarak is over"—were borrowed from Otpor. (In Serbia in 2000, they had passed out stickers that read, "Milošević Is Finished.") The workshop was organized by the Centre for Applied NonViolent Action and Strategies, or CANVAS, a group founded by leaders of the Serbian youth movement. Its purpose was to help train other activists how to lead a nonviolent campaign to topple their dictators. When I met Adel in Cairo, I asked him what he had learned in Belgrade. "We learned the difference between a protest movement and a resistance movement," Adel told me. "The critical thing is how to take advantage of the regime's mistakes."

Maher had said that they were working under the "wrong theory." It was wrong because, although the revolution might look spontaneous, it would take much more than a march to bring change. The challenge for the April 6 movement—or any group of activists working in a repressive environment—is to maintain the momentum for the change it is trying to achieve. It is not easy, Maher admitted to me. The small success they achieved on that day in April 2008 had been the unexpected result of pairing a technological tool (Facebook) with a tactic of nonviolent resistance (a general strike). Not surprisingly, the April 6 movement struggled to find the next creative combination that would cause the government to stumble.

A little more than a month after Mubarak was ousted from power, I sat with Mohamed Adel in a street café in Cairo. It was shortly before 11:00 p.m., and he looked exhausted. The pace of events had barely slowed since the eighteen days of revolution that had forced Mubarak to flee. Adel, who was now serving as the April 6 movement's information officer, said the group was in constant talks with the Egyptian military, the political parties, and other activists and youth groups. After decades of no political change, each week now felt like a year. I asked Adel why they had succeeded when they did. The poverty, the repression, the abuses, the lack of genuine rights—it had all been true for years. What had made this moment different from others?

Adel saw many factors. He pointed first to the case of Khaled Said, a young man who had been brutally murdered by two police officers outside an Internet café seven months earlier. The campaign surrounding his death—especially the Facebook page "We Are All Khaled Said"—had served as an enormous wake-up call, galvanizing public opinion and, in the days before the revolution, helping to spread the message to come out to demonstrate. But he then admitted that there had been many "Khaled Saids" over the years, that many people had known someone who had been abused, tortured, or worse while in the hands of the police. He then pointed to the November 2010 parliamentary elections, which had been a farce. Of course, it was hardly the first election to be rigged by Mubarak's cronies. And then he settled on another factor: Tunisia. "After the Tunisian revolution, we said that we must start," says Adel. "Because Tunisia allowed public opinion to finally be convinced that protests can actually achieve something."

Tunisia provided the moment, and Egypt's youth, especially a core of veteran, battle-scarred activists, seized it. The example of Tunisians rising up against Ben Ali changed the conditions in which the country's youth activists operated. This time, when they went into the poor neighborhoods of Cairo to rally support, people came outside their homes, joining their neighbors as their numbers swelled. The collective fear that had kept everyday Egyptians from raising their voices had begun to melt. If Tunisians could rid themselves of a tyrant, why couldn't they do the same? Instead of protests of hundreds, their numbers quickly rose to the thousands, and then the tens of thousands, as Egyptians made their way to Tahrir Square. Everyone looked for a way to lend a hand. "Whatever small things that people could do to help, they would do," recalls Adel. "When they started firing tear gas at us, the women knew that the thing that would help us the most was vinegar. So they started throwing bottles of vinegar to us from their balconies."

But it was more than a thousand small acts of courage. Years of learning, years of trial and error, went into decisions that now had the opportunity to make a difference. In the past, protests were usually held in the center of Cairo, in front of government buildings or the Journalists Syndicate. On January 25, 2011, the demonstrations followed a different path. Activists targeted more than a dozen locations around the city, zeroing in on many poor neighborhoods and calling on residents there to come out and join the protest. "The idea was to try to create many hot spots where protests could start," recalls Salah. Besides beginning the demonstrations where people lived, this strategy had one other important advantage: it would compel the regime's security forces to disperse to many locations, rather than amassing at one central point. Small teams of activists had targeted specific streets in specific neighborhoods where they would begin. "Their job was to try to go up and down the back streets, shouting and getting people to join," says Salah. "Once they built a sufficient mass, they'd move to a bigger street and so on. Until they had a huge mass, and then they would go to the central areas we were targeting."

Kamel Arafa, a twenty-five-year-old member of the April 6 movement, belonged to one of the advance teams sent to rally people. He spent days scouting Arab League Street, in the upper-middle-class neighborhood of Mohandessin. Arafa knew the neighborhood well, it was where he lived, but his preparation had a particular focus. He spent days monitoring the area for the central security trucks the regime used to shuttle its antiriot police. As January 25 approached, he wanted to know what routes they took and where their trucks parked. Arafa planned to begin along the neighborhood's tightest back alleys, streets that were too narrow for security trucks to navigate. He also marked routes that would provide protesters with a quick exit, if they were forced to beat a hasty retreat. When the day arrived, Arafa was amazed at how quickly their crowds grew. He gives credit to the tactics. The preparation was essential. But, like others, he believed it was more than just solid planning. The timing was also crucial. "The Tunisian revolution gave faith to people that things can change," says Arafa.

One can only imagine the shock inside Egypt's Interior Ministry as the regime's riot police were overwhelmed by crowds in the street. But the interior minister, Habib el-Adly, may have recognized the fingerprints of one of his former adversaries in the plans that sent his units struggling to regain their balance. Omar Afifi—the same Egyptian police officer who had been forced to flee the country several years earlier and had clashed with Adly as far back as 1995, when Adly served as Cairo's chief of police—had been one of the architects of the strategy the youth deployed against the police. It was Afifi who had recommended beginning in the city's smallest lanes and byways. He also drew on his knowledge of police tactics to help put together an instruction manual on how the protesters could be effective against Egyptian security forces. The twenty-six-page document was chock-full of practical advice. It instructed demonstrators to wear hooded jackets, scarves, or goggles to protect themselves from tear gas. It offered diagrams on how to fashion household items like cardboard or plastic bottles into body armor. It demonstrated how garbage can lids could be shields against police batons. It advised protesters to shout positive slogans—like "Long live Egypt"—and befriend security officers at every turn. "We distributed [the manual] and lots of other people distributed it, too," says Adel. "I gave it to protesters, and it helped because people needed that. It told you how to protect yourself from rubber bullets."

After Tahrir Square was occupied, others stepped forward. Many volunteered to provide food or medical supplies or dispose of garbage. As the days wore on, the division of labor in the square became more organized. At first, people just yelled if they needed a doctor. Soon, people with medical training were wearing stickers that indicated they were doctors. Members of the Muslim Brotherhood, long familiar with the trials of leading a banned movement, helped set up a perimeter to keep the regime's troublemakers at bay. Some of their tips were as practical as showing demonstrators how to dig up sidewalk tiles to unloose the rocks they needed to defend themselves from thugs. Months after the revolution, stretches of Tahrir Square were no more than sand where the pavement tiles had been lifted. "There was a time when all we were hoping for was to have a protest in Talaat Harb Square. Maybe no more than five hundred people would have been our dream," says Kamel Arafa. "When you stand in Tahrir, and you are surrounded by a million people—there was no greater feeling."

* * *

In that first meeting with Ahmed Maher, he was quiet, precise in his answers, and utterly serious. Over nearly three hours, he never smiled; he never laughed. He sat, leaning forward in his chair, his shoulders hunched, his hands in his lap. Occasionally, he would look at the tables of the people sitting closest to us or turn to glance at the doorway to the restaurant. He did not strike me as nervous, just hyperaware of his environment, like an animal alert for his natural predator, his muscles taut and ready to spring. The last thing he said to me was this: "It's cutting the relationship between the regime and its tools that is difficult. Cutting the channels between the army and the state is of course difficult. Almost impossible. But we hope with enough numbers and enough will for change that when the moment comes, they will step aside or join us, like what happened in Serbia."

That moment came. On Friday, February 11, 2011, after eighteen days of protests and countless Egyptians taking to the street, the army chose to abandon Mubarak.

I saw Ahmed Maher once more, after the revolution. I had not planned on seeing him. I simply walked around a corner and there he was, sitting outside a café. It was nearly midnight in Cairo, and he was surrounded by a dozen or more friends. They had pulled up several small tables to be closer. A group of young friends together late on a Friday night, laughing and shouting over each other as they told stories. Nothing could be more natural. If I hadn't recognized his face, I wouldn't have looked twice.

CHAPTER 6 THE PHARAOH

amira Ibrahim, a sales manager at a cosmetics company in Upper Egypt, traveled for eight hours to get to Tahrir Square. The protests had already started. Although only twenty-five years old, she had been attending demonstrations and marches since she was a girl. Once she arrived in Cairo, she didn't leave. For days, she camped out among the crowds. She was there when President Hosni Mubarak stepped down on February 11 and for the raucous celebration that followed. But even after Mubarak was gone and most people had returned home, Samira stayed. She was among a group of roughly one thousand demonstrators who believed they must camp out in the square as a reminder to Egypt's generals, who had now assumed control of the country, of the promises that remained unfulfilled. The revolution, in her mind, was incomplete. So, on the afternoon of March 9, nearly a month after Mubarak fled Cairo, Samira was still there.

The violence began a little after three o'clock. A large group of thugs gathered near the roundabout in Tahrir. They were shouting at the demonstrators, peaceful protesters like Samira, yelling, "The people want the square cleared! Evict them from the square!" These thugs, many of whom carried wooden sticks and metal pipes, began to circle the roundabout. When they came close to the entrance of the metro station, they started throwing stones and pavers from the street at the protesters. They charged the demonstrators' encampment in the middle of the square, tearing down tents and beating up those who stood in their way. "We started sending SOS messages over Facebook, trying to get others to come and help us," recalls Ahmed Amer, a twenty-four-year-old activist who was in the square at the time. "Our numbers started to grow, and [the newcomers] were helping to defend our tents. [The thugs] attacked us using blades, and we defended ourselves with stones."

When the demonstrators first saw military units arrive, they thought they were coming to their defense. After all, the Egyptian military had been their liberators during the revolution. Army officers had kept watch over the square, and when the hour finally came, the military had sided with the people, not Mubarak. It was when the soldiers entered the square that Samira realized something was wrong. The soldiers were not arresting the thugs; they were arresting the demonstrators and looking on as the armed attackers chased people out of the square.

Samira, however, couldn't get away. A soldier grabbed her, ripped the head scarf from her head, and threw her to the ground. The soldiers beat and kicked her. And then she, and nearly two hundred other demonstrators, were dragged to the Egyptian Museum on the north side of the square to be tortured. For many who risked everything to oust a dictator and set Egypt on a democratic course, Wednesday, March 9, was a turning point: the moment when it became unambiguously clear that the Egyptian military was not the guardian of the revolution they hoped it would be.

Once inside the museum complex, Samira was handcuffed to a wall with electrical cables. For nearly seven hours—almost every five minutes, she told me—a soldier sent jolts of electricity coursing through her body with a cattle prod. The soldiers would splash water on her and others to make the shocks more painful. The electrical jolts were applied to her legs, shoulders, and stomach. The tormentors kept repeating, "You think you are better than Hosni Mubarak? Say you love Mubarak!" She pleaded with the soldier to stop. Echoing what the demonstrators had first chanted in Tahrir Square during the revolution, she said, "You are my brothers. The army and the people are one hand." The soldier scoffed at her and replied, "No, the military is above the nation. And you deserve this."

At roughly 11:00 p.m., Samira and sixteen other women were

taken to the prosecutor's office. There, military officers claimed the female demonstrators had been found with knives and the ingredients for Molotov cocktails; in fact, the soldiers had planted all of the evidence. The women were then moved to one of the main military prisons. Samira was held there for the next three days. Over those days, the abuse, insults, and intimidation continued. The soldiers spit on her. All of her belongings were stolen. (When she complained, an officer told her, "Don't say a word or I will kill you and no one will ask for you.") Her meals consisted of kerosene-soaked bread.

But the most humiliating moment came when they first brought her into the prison. She and the other women were stripped and forcibly examined to determine whether they were virgins. The officers told Samira that any woman found not to be a virgin would have prostitution added to her charges. They led her into a room; it wasn't a medical office, and she didn't believe the officer was a doctor. Just before she was about to suffer this indignity, she froze. Behind the man waiting for her, she saw a photograph hanging on the wall. It was a portrait of Hosni Mubarak. She asked the soldier, "Why do you keep that up there?"

"Because we like him."

Revolution or Succession

Egyptians love their military. It is the protector of Egypt, the defender of the nation. From an early age, schoolchildren learn of the military's heroism and sacrifice during the 1973 war against Israel. The regimes under presidents Gamal Nasser, Anwar Sadat, and Hosni Mubarak—all former generals—lionized the armed forces for their patriotism and the role they played in ending the Egyptian monarchy in 1952. Whereas the country's civilian institutions were allowed to deteriorate into corrupt and unresponsive islands of dysfunction, the Egyptian military maintained a measure of professionalism. The average Egyptian has far more faith in the military than in the country's bloated bureaucracy or reviled police. When high prices led to riots over bread shortages in 2008, it was the military that answered the call, handing out bread from its bakeries. I saw it for myself in 2006. In that year, Egypt was the choice to host the Africa Cup of Nations, the continent's premier soccer championship. But as the date for the tournament neared, it became obvious that the construction companies the government had contracted with to build and refurbish soccer stadiums would not meet the deadline. Again, the military stepped in, sending its cranes and construction crews to finish the job in the nick of time. It wasn't unheard of, even during the final years of Mubarak's reign, for opposition politicians to call openly for military rule. The message was clear: the Egyptian military was the only institution that worked.

It was in keeping with this belief that the Egyptian military became one of the heroes of the 2011 revolution. In the early days, as tanks rolled into Tahrir Square and military units staked out positions with concrete barriers and razor wire, young Egyptian officers were welcomed and embraced. The now-famous cries from the demonstrators—"The army and the people are one hand!"—echoed through Cairo. Even if the military's top brass had not yet decided whom it would support, it was not hard for the people to accept the rank-and-file soldiers as brothers in arms. And when the hour finally came, the country's generals understood that the dictator they served had become too great a burden to shoulder. They abandoned their commander and quietly took control of the government on February 10, 2011. The next day, at roughly 6:00 p.m., a solemn-looking Omar Suleiman shared the news with the people. Suleiman, the former head of military intelligence who had become Mubarak's first vice president only thirteen days earlier, announced that Mubarak had "decided to waive the office of the president of the republic and instructed the Supreme Council of the Armed Forces to run the affairs of the country." The military, according to popular feeling, had chosen to stand with the people.

The events of March 9 were one of the first in a growing string of incidents that would tarnish the military's image. With the military's star shining so bright, though, it took a lot for mainstream Egyptians to question the integrity and intentions of their men in uniform. "People worship the army. They will side with the army even when the army commits abuses," one human rights activist told me. "People are refusing to believe the torture stories. They go on Facebook and there are video testimonies of torture victims showing torture marks on their backs, and the comments are still saying, 'Not true!' "

At first, no one accused the Supreme Council of the Armed Forces of staging a coup. Field Marshal Mohamed Hussein Tantawi and the other eighteen generals on the council had been widely expected to rule for a short period, bridging the gap between Mubarak's fall and new elections that were supposed to set Egypt in a genuinely democratic direction. With those elections, the Egyptian military would return to its barracks. The only trouble with this scenario was that the Egyptian military had not been confined to its barracks for decades.

Strictly speaking, Mubarak's Egypt could not be labeled a military dictatorship as neatly as, say, Burma's military junta once could. Egypt had a president, held elections, tolerated weak opposition parties, and had branches of government and many other democratic trappings. Moreover, political power rested in Mubarak's hands. But a military dictatorship comes closer to the truth than most possible descriptions. By contrast, the militaries in China, Iran, Russia, and Venezuela are tremendously influential, but they are not peerless institutions the way the military is in Egypt. The military's reach into the Egyptian government went far deeper than Mubarak the former general. Most of the country's governors were former generals. It was not uncommon for Mubarak's senior advisers and cabinet officials to have a military pedigree. And, as the most influential institution within the regime, the armed forces had been allowed to expand their interests far beyond the defense of the nation. Indeed, the empire that today's Egyptian military is most concerned with is its own business empire. The military bottles water, builds roads, sells olive oil, operates mines, makes jeeps, and runs a successful chain of hotels and resorts. In daily life in Egypt, it is easy to come into contact with a business with military ties. Control of so many enterprises gives the military attractive perks and privileges to dole out to senior officers. The question therefore arises, why would an institution that has benefited so much from the system as it exists seek to change it?

Within weeks of Mubarak's ouster, many Egyptians had a creeping sense that the military's definition of a democratic revolution was very different from their own. The military did not move to bring civilians into its decision making. Instead, activists believed the military's so-called dialogue sessions were vacuous and all too similar to the divide-and-rule tactics of the former regime. It refused to end the emergency law—a central demand of the demonstrators—which gave it broad latitude to make arrests without evidence, hold citizens without charges, and forbid strikes and public demonstrations. These laws had been in place for all thirty years of Mubarak's rule and were one of the worst symbols of his repression. Indeed, far from relaxing some of Mubarak's most repressive tools, the military put some of its own—like trying civilians in military courts—to greater use. Rather than attempt to raze the state security apparatus that had oppressed people for decades, the generals simply renamed it. It was with these examples in mind that Hayam Ahmed, a middle-aged schoolteacher and protester in Tahrir, told me, "We have found the regime is still out there. And they are part of the army."

Nevertheless, 2011 could not be a return to 1952 in one important respect. Although the final push may have come from the military, Mubarak had not been ousted by a small cabal of generals, as King Farouk had. This was a popular rebellion. The Egyptian people, defying the myth of their own apathy, had risen up to demand an end to Mubarak's regime. And having witnessed their own collective power, they would not hesitate to return to Tahrir Square, the place that had become the locus of political change. Demonstrators continued to win concessions from the Supreme Council of the Armed Forces for months after it seized control. Few doubted that the Egyptian military wanted to go back behind the curtain or that Tantawi wanted to remain the face of the regime. The spotlight was blinding and unfamiliar territory for the generals. But as the months wore on, it became increasingly difficult to argue that they did not seek a version of the old status quo, albeit refurbished. Authoritarianism, as Egyptians were learning, was far more durable than the fate of a single dictator.

Not Business as Usual

The joke went like this. The day before the presidential election, the prime minister went to see Hosni Mubarak. He told the president, "Although I am sure you won't need it, just in case, you should probably prepare a farewell address to the Egyptian people."

Mubarak replies, "Why? Where are they going?"

It was a popular joke in 2010 as Hosni Mubarak prepared to enter his third decade as president of Egypt. (I heard three different people deliver the same punch line in just one week.) At the time, Egyptians were engaged in rampant speculation that their president might finally be departing the scene. Mubarak hadn't suggested he might be stepping down; rather, he was lying in bed at Heidelberg University Hospital in Germany, recovering from an emergency surgery. At the time, the only thing Egyptians thought could rid them of their dictator was his own mortality.

Even for a civilization once ruled by pharaohs, thirty years in power was a considerable feat. Mubarak was the third-longest ruler in Egypt's six-thousand-year history. By 2011, he had succeeded in serving as president longer than the republic's previous three presidents combined. Over the years, he had watched as the heads of state of his most important foreign ally, the United States, came and went; Barack Obama was the fifth American president to welcome him to the White House.

Mubarak, an unremarkable, colorless vice president and former air force commander, came to power after the assassination of President Anwar Sadat at the hands of Islamic militants. Mubarak is said to have urged Sadat not to attend the military parade where Sadat met his end. Sadat, who supposedly had refused to wear a bulletproof vest because it ruined the lines on his Prussian-style uniform, was left crumpled in the reviewing stand, his body riddled with bullets. Incredibly, Mubarak, who was standing next to him on October 6, 1981, as the assassins opened fire, was left virtually unscathed. Eight days later, he was sworn in as Egypt's fourth president since the country's independence.

Hosni Mubarak was not an inspiring figure. He had no gift for oratory. Even his friends admitted that he had not accomplished any great victories, political or military, in the decades since becoming president. When Cairo was hit by a massive earthquake in 1992 that killed hundreds and injured thousands, it was the Muslim Brotherhood, the powerful Islamist opposition group, and not his government that first came to people's aid with food, water, and blankets. Aside from some economic growth in the last handful of years, Egypt did not fare well under Mubarak. Roughly 44 percent of Egyptians still live on no more than $2 a day. Fewer than half the homes are connected to public sewer systems. Roughly 30 percent of the adult population is illiterate. In the UN Development Programme's 2010 *Human Development Report,* Egypt ranked 101 out of 169 countries, well behind Kazakhstan, Turkmenistan, and war-torn Sri Lanka.

Of course, as is true of other Middle Eastern autocrats, the longevity of Mubarak's rule was in part based on fear. The Ministry of Interior, which oversaw the regime's domestic security apparatus, employed more than 1.5 million people and had a budget of more than a billion dollars. But Mubarak's formula relied on more than the regime's jackboot. His primary political tool was to prey on people's fears of what would happen if he weren't there. He and his ruling party, the National Democratic Party (NDP), constantly reminded Egyptians that but for the wisdom of their president, the country would have long since been engulfed in the flames of the Middle East's violence or fallen victim to a rising tide of Islamic fundamentalism. He based his legitimacy on an alternative history, on events that hadn't happened but that he insisted could. Mubarak's chief political argument was a scary unknown that he skillfully conjured for audiences with the conviction of certainty. The message was center stage at the ruling party's annual conferences. For example, in 2009, moments before Mubarak rose to the podium to make an address, the delegates were directed to watch a short video. There, on the big screen, party members were treated to a montage of violence across the Middle East—bombings, machine-gun fire, the chaos of war-torn neighborhoods and streets—and a familiar takeaway: without Mubarak, these images would be of Egyptian neighborhoods and streets.

Still, as one decade gives way to the next, it becomes harder to rely on the same methods and message—however effective they may have been—to maintain support for a regime. Any regime, even a dictatorship, must find ways to renew its legitimacy in the eyes of its citizens. Vladimir Putin swapped the office of the president for the prime minister's chambers, if only temporarily, to maintain a democratic facade. When times are tough, Hugo Chávez rails against "the empire" to the north. China, of course, has its blazing economic growth. And as the world changed, so did the pressures on Egypt's modern-day pharaoh. At least that is how one senior member of the ruling party explained it to me: "Mubarak recognized that it isn't business as usual. And he cannot continue acting or ruling in the same way."

The words came from Ali Eddin Hilal, the ruling party's media secretary and spokesman. Hilal had served Mubarak's government for many years. He received arguably his most important post in 2001, when Mubarak appointed him—along with his own son Gamal Mubarak—to the executive committee of the General Secretariat, the small body that oversees the day-to-day affairs of the ruling party. A political scientist by training, Hilal earned a Ph.D. at McGill University in Montreal in the 1970s, did stints as a visiting professor at UCLA and Princeton, and had long held a position at Cairo University. Although he was old enough to be a member of the regime's old guard, Hilal was polished and sharp and had a silver tongue, qualities that had kept him in favor with the younger, pro-business generation associated with Gamal. Indeed, several people I spoke with referred to Hilal as "Gamal's coach"—one of those charged with helping to groom the son to one day replace the father. We met less than ten months before the regime's demise in the offices of his son's law firm, which were as sleek and stylish as any Manhattan architectural firm.

I was surprised when Hilal said that Mubarak had recognized the necessity of changing the way he ruled. It is rare for a spokesman to a strongman to link any change in behavior to forces beyond the regime's control. Typically, you could expect so much bland blather on making "judicious choices in the best interests of the people," talk specifically intended to obscure the genuine reasons for directions taken or reversed.

The obvious question was, why, after being president for so long, had Mubarak decided it was no longer business as usual? What had changed?

"Because you recognize that democratization is expanding," Hilal explained. "You recognize that you have to democratize further."

"A further factor," he continued, "could be the changing global milieu. Remember these are the years you have satellites, you have Al Jazeera, you have the Internet. You start thinking, 'Well, things can't continue as before. I no longer have an ability to have a monopoly over information.' You start recognizing the importance of transparency. Not necessarily because you are an open man, but to keep your capability. Just for practical, pragmatic reasons, you have to."

The previous ten years had been tumultuous for the regime.

Political protests, sparked by Israel's bombing of the West Bank and the U.S. war in Iraq, broke out in Cairo's streets and quickly boomeranged into demonstrations against the Egyptian government. These marches, as well as a rising number of labor strikes, were broadcast on cable news networks such as Al Jazeera. Word was spread further by bloggers, who often uploaded damning footage of violent government crackdowns. For a time, criticism from foreign governments, particularly the United States and the European Union, rose. Granted even a small space to operate, opposition newspapers became highly critical of Mubarak. In response to these and other pressures, Hilal explained, the regime had to find new ways to maintain its grip. It had to adapt. "The ruling elite over time has been intelligent enough to see the writing on the wall," said Hilal, referring to the pressures to liberalize. "Once you see the writing on the wall, you initiate the process. On one side you see the slogans of your opponents, and instead of becoming a target of a change, you become a partner, in fact, a leader of the change."

In other words, the regime attempted to remain in control of its own destiny, in part, by co-opting those trends that threatened to unhinge it. Hilal hastened to point out that it is important to understand that everything was still engineered. "It's reform initiated, engineered, and regulated by the ruling elite and in particular the president," he said. Mubarak wasn't about to let events unfold organically; he sought to get out ahead of these forces and shape them.

At least that was the theory.

Egypt is not blessed with large oil deposits. Unlike Russia or Venezuela, the regime cannot funnel massive windfalls from selling oil or natural gas into buying public support. Nor has the Egyptian government created anything close to an economic miracle along the banks of the Nile. Unlike China, no one wants to follow the "Egypt model" for lifting people out of poverty, modernizing infrastructure, or creating sustained economic growth. But, as Hilal explained, under mounting pressures Mubarak's regime was attempting to perfect another survival strategy for modern dictators: the art of conceding political space in order to maintain it.

In the final years of Mubarak's regime, if you kept your eyes closed and listened only to the public pronouncements of Egyptian officials, you would have believed the country's political system was under constant renovation. Policies and practices were being "reformed," "altered," "revised," "modernized," "enhanced," and "developed." But all the supposed tinkering and talk of flux belied the fact that nothing changed. In fact, the regime's real expertise was in redrawing the red lines of what freedoms were permissible—and which ones were not. Like a safety valve, the regime tried to let pressure out of the system without compromising its fundamental control. The challenge for the government was creating the appearance of greater freedom without inadvertently granting any freedom that created a meaningful threat to its dominion.

Take, for example, a basic element of the freedom of speech, the right to publicly criticize the president. During the 1980s and 1990s, no one in Egypt would take to the street and denounce Mubarak. It was understood that anyone doing so risked being hauled off to prison. In fact, the informal prohibition was so great that Egyptians would only refer to the "presidential institution" or "the presidency"—something that didn't actually exist in the constitution—as code for Mubarak. Speaking out against the president was a red line not to be crossed.

But it was eventually abandoned. In recent years, when protests struck downtown Cairo, it wasn't rare to hear people shout, "Down with Mubarak!" Beginning with the demonstrations over Israel's military siege of Jenin and other West Bank cities in 2002, students and activists began to direct their anger at their own government, and some say that is when shouts against their longtime leader could first be heard. On December 12, 2004, Kefaya, the loose-knit opposition movement Ahmed Maher later joined, organized the first purely anti-Mubarak demonstration.

From 2005 on, it wasn't uncommon to hear full-throated criticism of the president or the corruption of his wife and sons. At some point, the regime calculated that the costs of upholding the prohibition were greater than the benefits. In the end, so the thinking went, how much would it matter if a few hundred people yelled "Mubarak must go!" until they were hoarse? Indeed, it suited Egyptian officials just fine to be able to point to the fact that people could curse their president in a public square as evidence that the society was becoming freer. "So the red lines are not the red lines that existed before," the human rights activist Gasser Abdel-Razek told me in early 2010. "Again, not to say that Mubarak will not wake up one day and say, 'That bastard belongs in prison.' And that bastard will be imprisoned very quickly. But they have learned."

The most obvious evidence of this shift in tactics was the way the regime spoke. Not long before, Mubarak's government greeted any criticism with denials and insults. If a human rights group issued a report on the widespread use of torture in Egyptian police stations, the government would categorically deny the charges as baseless and untrue. "In 2000, if there was a UN event and Egyptian NGOs were there to present a report, [Egyptian] diplomats would either completely avoid contact with these NGOs or just accuse them of treason and working to implement foreign agendas," says Hossam Bahgat, the founder of the Egyptian Initiative for Personal Rights.

But that was not the experience that the thirty-year-old Bahgat would have several years later. His organization is an internationally respected NGO in Cairo that defends civil rights and liberties; its work made it one of the most outspoken critics of the regime. In 2010, Bahgat traveled to Geneva for the UN Human Rights Council's annual review of member states' human rights record. He was there to highlight the ongoing, systemic abuses that occur in Egypt. While in Geneva, he was invited to dinner at the Egyptian ambassador's residence and was surprised to hear promises that they would work together on the follow-up to the human rights review. Rhetorically, the modern Egyptian regime had learned that it gained more by conceding some of its failings than by castigating every critic as a liar and a traitor. "If you speak now to people in the Ministry of Foreign Affairs about human rights violations, they will say, 'Yes, yes, we have many serious problems and these are challenges, we are working on changing them, we are on the path of reform. We are perhaps not going fast enough, we should go faster,'" Bahgat said in early 2010. "Of course, implicit in this statement is that there is resistance from the old guard in the regime, or that perhaps if we have a younger president who is Western educated and reform-minded, maybe . . ." A younger president, like Gamal Mubarak.

———

The Bespoke Pharaoh

It is impossible to separate the regime's botched effort to refashion its dictatorship for the modern age from the political rise of Gamal Mubarak, the president's son. In 2000, Gamal quit his investment-banking job in London to return to Cairo to take a leadership role in the ruling party. When he talked to the press, the suave forty-six-year-old presidential scion spoke about bringing new blood into the ruling party, reinvigorating its policies to better serve Egyptians. His talking points were sprinkled with words like "reform," "process," and "consensus"—odd hallmarks for a man who hoped to inherit the presidency from an aging dictator.

From the day he returned to Egypt, Gamal's political activities were viewed as laying the groundwork for his succession, steps toward developing the credentials to make him a palatable choice to rule. Gamal almost immediately had an important portfolio within the party. His father appointed him to the General Secretariat's executive committee, making him a voice in the ruling party's day-to-day affairs. He also became the chairman of the newly created Policies Committee, which one NDP official described to me as "the brain of the party." The Policies Committee was one of the chief vehicles for Gamal to bring a younger generation of officials into the government. Whereas members of the old guard may have cut their teeth under Sadat and were well schooled in patronage politics, the people around Gamal looked more like consultants from McKinsey than bosses of Tammany Hall. Like Gamal, they were young, Western educated, and spoke fluent English. In their thirties or forties, they might hold a Ph.D. or an M.B.A. from an East Coast university. Some had spent time on Wall Street and knew a thing or two about attracting foreign investment dollars. Those on the Policies Committee were charged with helping to develop ideas, programs, and policies that went beyond the static and moribund socialist positions that had gathered dust for so long.

On the economic front, these technocrats were credited with making some progress. Egypt's economy grew at more than 7.2 percent a year from 2005 to 2008, although it was clear that these gains did not reach most Egyptians. The World Bank named Egypt the region's top economic reformer three years in a row. Foreign investment jumped to nearly $7 billion in 2009, more than three times what it had been five years earlier, and the country weathered the global financial crisis better than most people expected. But Gamal's political project—attempting to modernize the ruling party—went nowhere. It never became a party of ideas, a party with a vision beyond the continuation of its own power. Indeed, in the end, it was more a massive patronage machine than a party at all.

One person who would not accept that description, however, was Mohamed Kamal. He was one of Gamal's key political advisers and a member of the Policies Committee trying to help revitalize the ruling party. The forty-something political scientist earned his Ph.D. at the Johns Hopkins School of Advanced International Studies and was as comfortable in downtown Washington as he was in Cairo. A student of American politics and political campaigning, Kamal could easily shift from a conversation about the U.S. Electoral College to one about the intricacies of Egyptian politics. He even once worked on Capitol Hill for a congressman from Ohio. When I first met him in Cairo in 2006, I asked him what papers he liked to read, expecting him to tell me the local media he favored. "The same as you, I suspect," he replied. "I like to start my mornings with the *Washington Post* and the *New York Times*. Then I like to see if the think tanks on Massachusetts Avenue are producing anything new." It was a clever jab; the Washington, D.C., think tank I worked for at the time was on Massachusetts Avenue.

When we last spoke, only months before the end of the regime he served, he tried unconvincingly to argue that the ruling party was more dynamic and capable than it appeared. "The NDP can reinvent itself," he told me. "It has the people and the ideas." In fact, there was no evidence this was true. But he was right that one concession the regime had made was perhaps "the most significant political development of the last seven years"—namely, the decision to hold the 2005 presidential election. In that year, for the first time, President Mubarak went on the campaign trail and asked Egyptians for their vote. (For his first twenty-four years, voters had simply been presented with a yes-or-no referendum.) One of the Middle East's oldest dictators was out on the stump, shaking hands and working rope lines. And Kamal, who headed up Mubarak's communications team, set up a campaign war room worthy of James Carville. Young staffers picked apart demographic data on voters block by block. Advance teams monitored turnout at thousands of polling places. Expensive, well-produced campaign ads presented the elder Mubarak as the reform candidate. Kamal told me his inspiration was American presidential races, in particular Bill Clinton's 1992 White House run.

All of which meant that for the first time, Mubarak also had a presidential opponent. Ayman Nour, a lawyer and former legislator, was Mubarak's main election adversary, and he took advantage of his time on the campaign hustings to pound away at the regime's corruption and abuse of the emergency law. No one expected Nour to beat Mubarak in the polls; what votes the president's slick campaign could not capture could still be gained through rigging and stuffed ballot boxes. But Nour's presidential run was more significant than whatever votes it could collect. In allowing even a sham contest, the regime had made another vital concession in its bid to remain in power. The regime could never again choose its leader without a credible claim that he had been popularly elected. Another red line had been redrawn.

Ali Eddin Hilal had told me that Mubarak understood he could no longer practice business as usual. Mubarak's strategy was to create a facade of political liberalization so he could try to ensure that the regime never fell victim to the real thing. If all freedoms and reforms were created by the state, then the state could at least try to keep liberalization on its own terms. Mubarak might loosen the noose around the country's neck and then tighten the rope, only to loosen it again later. But it was never in question who held the rope.

The strategy was not without costs. When people taste a freedom, it becomes much harder to deny it to them later. With the elimination of each red line, the regime curbed its latitude and room for maneuver. There is some academic debate whether a false political opening like Egypt's can at some point become less a survival strategy and more a permanent condition, a limbo between autocracy and genuine democracy. It's an unsettled question. But for what it is worth, members of Mubarak's regime doubted whether they could, as one ruling party official told me, "play the game forever." When I put the question to Hilal, he was blunt. "Can you continue that indefinitely?" he replied. "The answer is no, of course not."

His response reminded me of Alexis de Tocqueville's admonition that "the most dangerous moment for a corrupt regime is when it attempts to reform itself." The specific dangers for Mubarak's regime revealed themselves quickly. The end of the prohibition on criticizing the president led to more protests and anti-Mubarak political activity than the country had ever seen. The government would occasionally ratchet up its repression, but of the scores of political activists I met, all considered the years 2005 to 2010 to be the most formative for honing their skills as regime opponents. Likewise, after the 2005 presidential election, the regime continued to throw barriers up to anyone who contemplated challenging its hold on power. (It quickly made an example of Ayman Nour, locking him up on politically motivated charges for four years.) Still, it was now possible that someone unanticipated could be a candidate for the country's highest office. For a regime that detests surprises, there was now a hint, if only a hint, of unpredictability. Certainly, in 2005, no one would have anticipated that four years later people would be wondering out loud whether the former head of the International Atomic Energy Agency and Nobel Peace Prize winner, Mohamed ElBaradei, was interested in being the next president of Egypt. Mohamed Kamal in 2010 had spoken dismissively to me of "the ElBaradei phenomenon." While many of ElBaradei's own supporters privately doubted his grit as a politician, the mere injection of a new name into the conversation ignited the enthusiasm of politically minded Egyptians and opened up another front against the regime.

And perhaps nothing caused more resentment and galvanized more opposition than the effort to burnish Gamal's credentials to be Egypt's next president. Despite Mubarak's firm command of the country, it was never assured that the presidency would pass from father to son. The possibility, which became more real each year, ran afoul of the country's political traditions. As authoritarian as the regime may have been, it was not a family dynasty. The suggestion that no one besides Mubarak's offspring was fit to rule Egypt violated what narrow compact still existed between the regime and its people.

And the anger did not rest in the hearts of the people alone. The Egyptian military was deeply resentful of the class of new elites—people with close ties to Gamal and his brother, Alaa—who quickly turned their connections into vast fortunes. Clearly, they had reason to fear that if Gamal became president, his evident push to privatize industries would continue to favor those closest to him—and not the military's own commercial empire. Despite how sophisticated Gamal may have looked in his Savile Row suits, there was one suit he had never worn: a military uniform. The Egyptian armed forces had been the proving ground for each of the country's presidents. With no military experience on Gamal's résumé, it remained an open question whether Egypt's generals would ever agree to him succeeding his father or whether they would insist on one of their own taking the helm.

We will never know. When the people rose up on January 25, 2011, they denied Mubarak the chance of ever foisting his son on Egypt. A question that had dominated Egyptian politics for nearly a decade would remain unanswered. But one thing was hardly a surprise: as soon as Hosni Mubarak was gone, the military seized the assets of Gamal's closest friends.

"Egyptians Feel Free"

Every dictatorship has faces, apart from the dictator himself, that come to personify the corruption, privilege, and power of the highest echelons. In Egypt, on the eve of the revolution, that face belonged to Ahmed Ezz. The billionaire tycoon and chairman of EzzSteel was roundly considered to be the most influential of the "young guard" of ruling party leaders who had risen largely due to their close personal connections to Gamal Mubarak. In 2010, if you asked everyday Egyptians who had benefited the most from his association with the president's son, the answer was almost always the same: "Ezz." In his case, it was widely believed that he had turned a middling family business into one of the Middle East's largest steel companies on the back of his close friendship with Gamal. Ezz's holdings were estimated to be roughly $2 billion, the bulk of it earned since he had become a member of parliament in 2000. But even if his wealth stemmed from corrupt sweetheart deals, Ezz was far more than just a beneficiary of crony capitalism. He was a sophisticated political player charged with giving an old dictatorship a new look. "We needed a plan," one ruling party official told me. "Ezz was the man with the plan."

Put simply, Ezz's job was to win elections. Several years ahead of the 2010 parliamentary elections, the NDP tapped Ezz to oversee the party's organizational strategy for winning seats. Of course, the ruling party had never failed to win a majority of seats in the parliament. (Since 1976, the president's party had won a supermajority in nine consecutive elections.) The trouble was, as a ruling party, it was highly unorganized in how it arrived at that majority. The weakness of the party's brand was evident in how its candidates chose to compete for seats. Most ran as independents, relying on personal or family connections to curry favor with local voters. Afterward, they would simply pledge their loyalty to the NDP, because being a member of the ruling party was the only way to access the government's patronage. In fact, a majority of the NDP's 311 parliamentarians won their seats as independents only to rejoin the party later. Ezz's task was to instill more discipline and professionalism in the party. Several officials told me that Ezz had studied the methods of Tony Blair's New Labour Party in Britain and intended to adopt them in Egypt. In April 2010, Ezz described his role to my friend the former *Washington Post* reporter Janine Zacharia. "What I do is more organizational," he explained, "how to prepare for getting out the voters, how to screen candidates, how to help sort out how the party leadership chooses candidates, and how to prepare the organization to fight elections."

Like many things Ezz said, it sounded good when he said it. But for all the talk of voter outreach, modern campaign messaging, and professional organizing, the November 2010 parliamentary elections were nothing more than a rigged game. In retrospect, it was abundantly clear why the regime had steadfastly refused to allow any foreign monitors at the polling stations. As the party's organizational secretary, Ezz presided over one of the most fraudulent elections in recent memory. The NDP captured more than 90 percent of the total seats. The Muslim Brotherhood, which had won eighty-eight seats in the last election in 2005, improbably lost all eighty-eight of its races. The regime's theft of the election was so brazen it was daring even by the standards of Egypt's oppressive political climate.

In the lead-up to the vote, Ezz was fond of saying how much freer Egypt was than just five years ago. If things were so bad, why did Egyptians seem so unconcerned? Their top issues, according to

Ezz, were jobs, inexpensive food, and clean water—not wider political concerns that ran to the heart of the regime's legitimacy to rule. "Why are people not rebelling? Why are they not coming out in millions when political freedoms are being discussed by the opposition?" asked Ezz. "Why? Because Egyptians feel free. The freedom that they want is there. The freedom of expression, the freedom to join parties, the freedom to bring Ahmed Ezz, who people perceive to be someone with some influence, and grill him and send him to hell if need be . . . Egyptians feel free."

It is impossible to know precisely why the party would turn to such heavy-handed fraud. Perhaps the party that Ezz helped lead was too weak to rein in its own members. But the party's brazen behavior was almost certainly the product of one simple truth: the regime had come to believe its own lies. That is one of the best explanations for why, after having opened political life to permit more criticism and opposition in the media, the regime felt so comfortable stealing an election from voters. It had such contempt for the people that it believed it could still rig elections without any cost or consequence. The government had gone to great lengths to create the architecture of a modern authoritarian regime. It had the tools—opposition parties to soak up public resentment, elections to reward and punish loyalists, a parliament to give voice to public concerns—but in the end it chose not to use them. These trappings of democracy became even less than the facade they were supposed to be. Facades are meant to cover up something unattractive, but they only work if people act as if they are real. After the election, some members of the opposition planned to establish a "shadow parliament" that would be more representative than the actual one. President Mubarak responded dismissively, saying, "Let them entertain themselves."

Even members of the regime weren't bothering to act as if the facades were genuine anymore. A good example was the National Council for Human Rights. Mubarak's government established the council in 2003, and it was broadly charged with ensuring "the observance of human rights" in Egypt. Given the regime's systemic use of torture, most activists were understandably skeptical of a government-run body with such a mission. It appeared to be the definition of window dressing. And in large measure it was. A diplomat at the Egyptian embassy in Washington sniggered when he recounted how they had played on the former UN secretary-general Boutros Boutros-Ghali's vanity to get him to lend his name as president of the council.

The council, however, did count some serious and genuine human rights advocates among its twenty-five members. (I interviewed several members of the council, and they generally agreed that eight to ten of their colleagues were truly committed to human rights work; the rest were a hodgepodge of opportunists and regime loyalists.) One of the respected members of the body was the man who ostensibly led it, its vice president, Ahmed Kamal Aboul Magd. An accomplished constitutional lawyer and scholar, Aboul Magd was, in Egypt, one of those rarest of men: someone whose integrity and commitment to human rights were unimpeachable, and yet who was respected by the regime as well. Aboul Magd had served as a minister to Anwar Sadat and has the cautious, deliberative nature of a seasoned jurist. However, in February 2010, he was unexpectedly sacked from his position on the National Council for Human Rights.

A month after he had been fired, I visited him in his home in Giza, a short distance from the Pyramids. Aboul Magd explained that when he had returned from a business trip to Kuwait, there was a letter waiting for him. It was a personal letter from President Mubarak. It thanked him for his service but indicated that it had come to an end. I wanted to know why he had been pushed from his post. "Why did they decide to get rid of me?" Aboul Magd replied. "People say they are planning things that I would be the wrong person to handle. So let's avoid this situation by letting him go free before he would try to do something." Even more surprising than Aboul Magd's dismissal were some of the names the regime suggested to replace him. Its first choice was a former police officer and official at the Interior Ministry—the government body most responsible for the country's horrible record of human rights abuses. That suggestion was quickly shouted down. Nevertheless, Aboul Magd was troubled by the list of names the government had drawn up. "They are not good choices," he said. "I cannot put them on a list of proponents of human rights. They send the wrong message."

But Aboul Magd was troubled by more than the government stacking a toothless council with reliable friends of the regime. He believed Mubarak and his confidants had fallen deaf to the country they lived in. He could not point to a single specific thing, but he had an unease about the moment the country was about to enter. "I hear silence," Aboul Magd told me. "And it makes me worried because it is not genuine silence."

The regime was too cocksure and confident, Aboul Magd meant. It believed its autocracy would always be safe for the autocrat, and that is a dangerous moment in the life of any authoritarian regime. In Egypt's case, the course it chose was particularly volatile. Life had not improved for most Egyptians. Basic political repression remained a fact of life. And yet, in an effort to release some tensions from the system, the regime opened up small spaces for public criticism and limited types of activism. Then, even as the government began to tolerate more freedom of speech, it continued to steal elections, harshly round up protesters, and, in perhaps its most unwise move, lay the groundwork for a dynastic succession. The regime became uninterested in following the cues or signals from the public, perceiving those concerns as irrelevant to its grip on power. Wael Nawara, a senior adviser to the opposition leader Ayman Nour, told me a month after the revolution that in the five years before Mubarak's fall, the regime and its people had effectively been put on a collision course. "These two curves had to collide. I remember writing on my blog after the November elections that the regime had boarded a train heading to the terminal and there were no stops between here and the terminal. It couldn't get off even if it wanted to," Nawara said in his office. "I think the final blow was to have the brochure: how to start a revolution, how to oust a dictator. That was Tunisia."

Perhaps Ezz had a premonition. Near the end of his April 2010 interview, he bragged for several minutes about how active the Egyptian street had become, with demonstrations at Cairo University and elsewhere at least every other month. He painted a picture of an Egypt bubbling with political life and opinions, and he rejected the idea that the regime had used the emergency law to stifle its opponents. Then he paused and said, "I will tell you quite frankly, however, I would be uncomfortable if I saw a demonstration in Tahrir Square."

Nine months later the people occupied the square. On January 29, on the fifth day of protests, Ezz resigned from the ruling party. A few days later his bank accounts were frozen, and he was banned from traveling abroad. Mubarak, who certainly knew how deeply Ezz was reviled, was quick to offer him as a sacrifice to the demonstrators, one of the first in a string of desperate concessions the regime made in its final days. On February 17, the week after Mubarak himself had been forced from power, Ezz was arrested by order of the Supreme Council of the Armed Forces. In September 2011, an Egyptian criminal court sentenced him to ten years in prison on charges of corruption. Now he was the one without his freedom.

The Last Red Line

The people had been warned. No protests—not even peaceful protests—would be tolerated. They were ordered to clear the square. Those who remained, the regime told onlookers, were "agitators" and "foreign agents" working to destroy Egypt. Tensions were running high, so it was no surprise when the first volley of tear-gas cartridges landed in the crowds. People, some in uniform, others in plain clothes, charged the demonstrators. Goons sent by the Ministry of Interior were wielding knives and chains. Others had truncheons as they descended on any protesters who had become separated from the larger groups. They beat them until they were unconscious. Rubber bullets pierced through the throng of people; snipers appeared to have taken positions in the buildings surrounding Tahrir Square. Live ammunition could be heard. One activist in the center of the chaos posted an urgent plea on Facebook. "I breathe tear gaz!" he wrote. "Help us against the military!"

It wasn't January 2011; it was late June. And the security forces that attacked the demonstrators in and around Tahrir Square that night did not do so at the behest of Hosni Mubarak. The ousted dictator had long since been confined to a hospital in Sharm el-Sheikh awaiting trial. They acted on the orders of the Supreme Council of the Armed Forces.

Nor was it an isolated event. After the March 9 attack on Tahrir that netted Samira Ibrahim, confrontations between the military and protesters became more common. By the summer, they had become almost a weekly occurrence. In the months since Mubarak's fall, the

military council's actions increasingly appeared to belie their promises to steer Egypt toward a democratic future. Although the generals had pledged to end the emergency law, it remained in place.
Rather than dissolve the dreaded State Security Investigations Service,
they renamed it the National Security Agency and placed a former
Mubarak appointee in charge of the Ministry of Interior. The Egyptian
military showed no interest in partnering with a civilian-led transition; indeed, it kept control of the smallest details. Far from encouraging cooperation with activists, the military council began issuing
communiqués falsely charging that the April 6 movement—the very
youth leaders who had played a role in mobilizing the uprising—had
received military training in Serbia. Egypt's generals forbid foreign
observers to monitor the upcoming elections and accused domestic
NGOs that expressed a similar interest in the polls of engaging in
treasonous behavior. Taken together, the military's actions suggested
that the Supreme Council of the Armed Forces was not interested in
seizing a democratic opening for Egypt as much as it was circling the
wagons to protect what remained of the old regime, particularly its
own fiefdoms. What concessions the military offered the protesters
were not intended to raze Mubarak's authoritarianism as much as
rebrand it. "I don't believe in the credibility of the military council
anymore," Kamel Arafa, a twenty-five-year-old activist, told me. "It is a
huge monster and it has fingers that are still playing."

No one knows how powerful the Egyptian military is. In fact, no
one knows much about the Egyptian military at all. It is estimated
that it numbers between 300,000 and 400,000 strong; the precise
figure isn't published. Nor are the names of its general officer corps.
The secrecy surrounding the Egyptian military extends to almost all
aspects of its affairs. It has received nearly $40 billion from the United
States in the last thirty years, but no one knows how big a slice it takes
from the country's national budget. Even Egypt's own parliament
didn't know how it all adds up. The military refuses to open its books.

Under Mubarak, although other centers of the government grew
powerful—namely, the Interior Ministry's domestic security apparatus and the new business elites associated with Gamal—the military
remained the government's backbone. And, befitting its place as the
country's most powerful institution, criticism of the military and its

interests always represented the regime's last, uncompromised red line. If the parliament could not know its budget, the people were entitled to know—or say—even less. "The one thing we cannot discuss is the army," Hossam Bahgat, the NGO activist, told me in early 2010. "That's the one red line that people pay a heavy price for comments." He then asked, "You heard about the twenty-year-old blogger?"

The twenty-year-old blogger was Ahmed Mustafa. An engineering student from Upper Egypt, Mustafa was arrested in February 2010 because of a blog post he had written more than a year earlier. In the post, Mustafa had criticized the nepotism he claimed was practiced at the country's military academies. Specifically, he had reported that a student had been forced to quit one of the academies in order to give his spot to a prospective student with better connections. I never met anyone who was familiar with Mustafa's blog or had read his post before his arrest. I suspect the military had taken more than a year to arrest him because it wasn't aware of his blog, either.

Nevertheless, the authorities weren't concerned with whether Mustafa had a following or not. He was arrested and brought before a military court on charges of "defaming" the armed forces. The charges were ultimately dropped after the ensuing international outcry for clemency, but the regime had made its point: don't cross the military.

It was a prohibition that extended beyond young bloggers. The regime made this amply clear in 2006 with the swift arrest, conviction, and sentencing of the parliamentarian Talaat Sadat. Sadat was the nephew of the former president Anwar Sadat. On October 4, 2006, Sadat gave a television interview in which he claimed that his uncle's assassination had never been thoroughly investigated and that it was clear that factions within the Egyptian military had been behind the plot. The very next day, the fifty-two-year-old Sadat was stripped of his parliamentary immunity from prosecution. Six days later, his trial began before a military court. Before the month was out, he had been convicted of defaming the armed forces and sentenced to one year in prison with hard labor. A year later a chastened Sadat was released from prison and permitted to return to his seat in parliament. "It happened because this is a red line and people are not allowed to even joke or half-seriously speculate about it," says Bahgat. "Just don't mention the army."

Even after Mubarak was gone, it wasn't a prohibition the military intended to lift. Egyptian reporters I spoke with in Cairo told me about the pressure they had come under not to report on the military's torture of protesters or use of virginity tests. If the stories were ever written, editors typically spiked them. The Supreme Council of the Armed Forces sent letters to media outlets warning them to review any coverage of the military before airing it. One famous Egyptian television host was sacked in July 2011 after interviewing a retired air force general on her morning show. Her mistake was to have asked the general if he had any evidence to back up claims he had made about two potential presidential candidates supporting a U.S. political agenda in Egypt. In the military's Egypt, asking a general to substantiate an allegation was a firing offense.

The military's utter intolerance of criticism was dramatically revealed in the case of another young blogger. Maikel Nabil was highly critical of the military. He had led a campaign against military conscription and denounced the military for conducting virginity tests. On his blog he wrote, "The revolution has so far managed to get rid of the dictator but not the dictatorship." For this, the twenty-five-year-old was arrested at his home in late March on charges of "insulting the military" and "spreading false information." A military court then sentenced him to three years in prison.

Military courts quickly became the Egyptian military's most systematic tool for denying thousands of citizens any civil or political rights. Within a month of the military's seizing power, its tribunals began trying civilians, sometimes hundreds in a single day. According to human rights organizations, demonstrators, activists, and even simple bystanders were swept up in a broad campaign of military arrests. People caught in this indiscriminate dragnet were taken to the military prosecution's office and then to a military court, where they would be sentenced and transferred to prison. (Ironically, many of these people were charged with being *baltagiya,* or thugs, even though it was already clear that the military, much like the previous regime, was still hiring plainclothes thugs for its most heavy-handed attempts to clear Tahrir Square.) It could take no more than five hours for a person to receive a sentence of five years. These defendants had no legal representation, no access to case files, and no examination of evidence. By summer, human rights activists estimated that military courts had sentenced roughly ten thousand Egyptians—more than had been tried in thirty years under Mubarak.

What troubled activists was how difficult it was to combat the military's abuses. If the Interior Ministry of the old regime seemed like a black box, the military was even more opaque. "In the old system, with all its violence and horrors, we knew how it functioned. We could save people if we knew at the right time," says Gasser Abdel-Razek, a well-known human rights activist. "Now lawyers cannot even approach the military prosecution office. People are sentenced at 10:00 p.m. in a military trial without a lawyer to five years in prison. It's worse than our worst nightmare under Mubarak. At least when he used military courts, people were represented!"

What was the military's endgame in 2011? Most believed Tantawi did not harbor a desire to take Mubarak's place as Egypt's next president. Indeed, with political activists so attuned to the military council's every move, it would be difficult for an Egyptian general to remove his uniform, don a suit and tie, and declare himself a presidential candidate. The gesture would be transparent and unacceptable to Egyptian liberals and religious conservatives alike. Indeed, there are very few full-fledged military juntas left in the world, and most activists believed Egypt's generals had no interest in adding another one. Rather, the generals had a more modest goal: to preserve the previous system, particularly their primacy in it.

The foundation of that system had been laid in 1952, when Gamal Nasser and the Free Officers ousted King Farouk. They did more than remove a king; they also swept away the limited parliamentary system and whatever political pluralism then existed. In its place, they established a strong presidential-style republic, which they have filled with their own men ever since. So it was no surprise that Egypt's generals moved quickly to maintain the presidential system as soon as Mubarak had departed. The constitutional amendments they proposed in late March—and won in a landslide vote—did little to reduce the immense powers of the presidency and seemed to end any conversation that the legislative branch might be strengthened at the expense of the executive. (If Egypt's generals are familiar with the experience of the former Soviet states, they know that every former

Communist country that opted for a strong presidential system has lapsed into autocracy.) Indeed, Egypt's generals went far enough to suggest the adoption of a "declaration of basic principles" to guide the drafting of a future constitution; it is widely believed that the purpose of such principles will be to shield the military's interests from scrutiny. In October, the government's military-appointed cabinet put forward a proposal that would elevate it above parliamentary supervision and give the military a veto over any legislation involving its affairs. The proposal also named the military the guardian of "constitutional legitimacy"—a vague phrasing that was widely interpreted as a way to enshrine its position as the final arbiter in Egyptian politics. Having enjoyed a nearly sacrosanct position for sixty years, Egypt's generals have no intention of diminishing that role in any future political arrangement. "They understand the game now," says Sherif Mickawi, a former air force officer turned political activist. "When a big storm comes, you need to lean with it. When the storm leaves, you can stand up again. They don't mean to lose what they achieved in 1952."

Officers for the Revolution

First Lieutenant Sherif Osman had a comfortable life in Mubarak's Egypt. Born into an upper-middle-class family, he had received an excellent education, graduated from the Egyptian Military Academy, and had a career to look forward to as an air force communications officer. His fluent English made him a valuable asset to senior officers on the Cairo West Air Force Base, where he served. His mother, who worked for the military as a doctor, had retired with the rank of a one-star general. In fact, several members of his family had served in the military. Although he was far from wealthy, Osman moved in fairly privileged circles, and in a place where knowing people can make life much easier, he had very good connections. "I had a really magnificent network of people," he told me. "Even down to my favorite nightspot, the Cairo Jazz Club. I knew the owner." He lived in Maadi, one of Cairo's nicer neighborhoods, which is also home to many of the city's expats. "There were chicks around from the multinational community in Cairo," says Osman. "I didn't miss a Western life. There is a softball league in Maadi. I was living a Westernized life."

Osman, however, was anything but content. In retrospect, the military had not been the best career path for him. By his own admission, he had a tendency to speak out of turn and a rebellious streak that did not sit well with senior officers. He says he realized early that he probably would not rise above colonel, the point at which the military thins the corps of officers destined for senior posts. But what troubled him ran far deeper than a few misspent years as a junior military officer. Osman's time in the military opened his eyes to the country, and more specifically the institution he served. As he rose from first lieutenant to captain and had more contact with senior officers, he saw and heard more of the military's corruption. Any illusion he had that there was distance between the military and the country's corrosive politics came to an end. "Between the rank of captain and major, you are realizing what you are a part of—a dictatorship, you're part of the regime," says Osman. "Egypt is a military-run country for the past sixty years. It's a military dictatorship with a civilian skin."

One of his first realizations of this came in 2002. Osman didn't have anything to do late one afternoon, so he went to visit a friend who was a major. He knew his friend would be working late, so he thought he would just stop by to say hello. When he walked into his office, the major, who worked in operations, was on the phone with a senior commander. They were discussing a colored map that was laid out across the desk. From overhearing his friend's side of the conversation, he could tell the senior commander was telling him to make revisions to the map, adding different locations and markers. Curious, Osman looked at the map for himself. It was labeled "Strategic Points Defensive Plan," and it covered all of Cairo. Key passages and landmarks around the city—bridges, highways, government buildings, presidential palaces, hotel districts—were marked in different colors. It was the air force's plan for the defense of Cairo.

His friend hung up the phone. "This is the dumbest thing I have ever seen," said Osman, after he had a chance to study the map. "I really don't think the Israelis are going to walk their army into Cairo. That'd be a suicide mission. I mean, they may bomb it, but they aren't going to occupy it."

"Who said anything about Israel?" asked his friend.

"What do you mean?" replied Osman.

"What do you think?" his friend responded.

Osman stared blankly at the map for a few seconds. And then he looked up at his friend. "Do you mean this is a defense of Cairo—from Egyptians? Is this a defense against revolution?"

His friend stared back at him and scoffed at his naïveté, as if to say, "Of course that's what it is." Osman says he felt incredibly young at that moment. "I had wider eyes from that point," he told me.

And that made it impossible to miss the graft, corruption, and self-dealing all around him. While Osman served as a group commander for Squadron 660, a mobile communications unit, his soldiers came to him and told him about a one-star general who had a side business selling engines and spare parts from military vehicles on the open market. The place where these vehicle engines would be lifted and then resold backed up on the lot where Osman and his unit were housed. When Osman raised it with senior officers, he was told that his rank was "too light" to discuss such things. "I reported that first-star general, and I got nothing but bullshit back," says Osman. He was soon transferred to Cairo West Air Force Base.

Cairo West, as they call it, is an operational hub for the U.S. military in the Middle East. Mubarak served as its base commander in the 1960s. Today, the U.S. and Egyptian militaries conduct Operation Bright Star, their major multinational joint training exercises, from Cairo West every two years. Osman looked forward to the transfer because he saw time on Cairo West as a chance to meet American military officers and use his English. But his perception of his own military's senior officers grew more cynical. As he saw it, generals ran a variety of schemes that allowed them to skim a little off the top of what would otherwise be legitimate enterprises. An early example at Cairo West was the sand-mining business. Outside companies had contracts to mine for sand on the base's grounds. When the trucks would arrive, one of the officers working for the base commander would shake down the mining company's representatives for a bribe. Osman asked one of the members of the commander's staff about it. "He was like, 'Yeah, but you know, if the base commander wants some money, we've got to bring him some money.'" Osman says that basic principle was applied to a wide range of "Cairo West base businesses." Everyone senior is entitled to a taste. "A chunk goes to the base commander. Another chunk goes to the air force commander. And a big-ger chunk goes to Tantawi. It's like that," says Osman. "It's a mafia."

Osman says that most of the corruption he saw with his own eyes was small-scale graft, money for padding wallets rather than filling overseas bank accounts. But with time, he began to hear from other officers a few grades higher—majors and lieutenant colonels—which generals were the biggest rainmakers. Osman says one of the most notorious is General Hassan al-Ruwaini, the Cairo commander and member of the Supreme Council of the Armed Forces. Ruwaini, who was the chief of northern command, is rumored to have had a very lucrative real estate portfolio. Officers say that he was charged with developing properties running along the Mediterranean coast-line from Alexandria toward the Libyan border. In the past fifteen years, stretches of this coastline have been turned into villas, gated communities, and attractive seaside villages. Afterward, Ruwaini was transferred to central command in Cairo, where he continued to flip properties for the military. "The regime does not like so many faces. I'm not going to hire another dirty scandalous general and test him in this area," says Osman. "No, I already know that person, I'm 100 percent sure that he's corrupt, and he'll run the business successfully. I'm going to move him from place A to place B to run the same busi-ness again."

It wasn't an easy choice, but Osman decided he needed to make a move, too. He believed his proficiency in English might be his ticket out of the Egyptian military. A handful of Egyptian officers are peri-odically selected to come to the United States for six months to receive advanced language training. Afterward, they become English instruc-tors for the Egyptian Air Force. Osman scored high enough on the exam and was selected for the training. But he had a different plan. While doing the course work in 2005 at Lackland Air Force Base in San Antonio, Texas, he was also experimenting with the idea of liv-ing in the United States—permanently. He wanted to figure out for himself if he could make it on his own there. He decided he could. So, on the last day of his training, when he was supposed to travel back to Egypt, Osman didn't show up. He defected from the Egyptian military.

Six years later, in January 2011, Osman had settled into a fairly typical American life. He was married, had a steady job working as a translator, and still called San Antonio home. During those eighteen days in January and February, Osman was glued to his television set, watching as the regime began to teeter. Once Mubarak fell, he was desperate to hear from friends in Cairo, especially his military buddies. He spent hours on the phone, talking to his friends who were still officers. They told him things were different; there had never been a better time to be in the Egyptian military. They had been given raises, and people were looking to the military to lead the way. "I had so many phone calls with officers in Egypt. They said, 'They are taking care of us. People are giving us respect wherever we go. We are the heroes.'"

For a couple of weeks, Osman wondered if things really were different. If the generals intended to set Egypt on a new path, it could mean an entirely new relationship between the military and the government. It ran against his instincts, but he wanted to believe it was true, because, if it was, it might also mean he could return to Egypt. "I had the impression—that I doubted in my head and heart—that Tantawi and his council would have a once-in-a-lifetime chance to have their names written in gold in Egyptian history. They had the chance to be the founders of the modern country," recalls Osman. "It was like seeing another Fourth of July—happening in Egypt."

Those hopes were dashed for him on February 25. On that day, with thousands of protesters in Tahrir Square, the military and plainclothes thugs attacked demonstrators. The military later apologized for this first serious clash between its soldiers and the people. But Osman had seen all he needed to see. "I saw the pictures of the military police having thugs with sticks in their trucks in Tahrir Square," says Osman. "At that moment, I was 110 percent sure that Tantawi is the same person. He was and he will always be Mubarak's toy."

So, on March 1, Osman did what may now seem like a familiar impulse for anyone seeking to challenge authority in Egypt: he set up a Facebook group. After consulting with many active Egyptian military officers, he created the page "Officers for the Revolution." He wasn't surprised that most of the officers he spoke with were resistant to helping at first. The cost for being caught up with something critical of the military would be severe. "Most of them would say, 'Well, what you are saying is right—Tantawi is corrupted—but this is not the appropriate time,'" says Osman. But as soon as he had five officers agree to join, he started the page.

He had a clear purpose from the start. "This is the first wake-up call to the people not to trust the military council," says Osman. "The page is working, on the one hand, to enlighten the people that the military council is something that you should be fearing, not hugging, and on the other hand, it is looking for the brave officers who support this idea." Osman attacked the notion that the Egyptian military was somehow sacrosanct and above reproach, with a self-described tone on the page that was "mean, insulting, and sarcastic." But for those he hoped to reach and persuade—politically active Egyptians with little knowledge of the opaque military that ruled the country—he offered real information about the military's methods, based on his own service and the tips and leaks he got from officers on the inside.

To be most effective, he needed numbers—not just readers and people willing to join the page, but also officers willing to be his eyes and ears. But Osman said he was never worried about that; he was certain the military would help him on both counts. "The more Tantawi screws up the country, the more I'll get people on the page," says Osman.

He was right. At first, the arrival of "Officers for the Revolution" was met with denunciations. People wrote that the people behind the page must be "traitors" and "betrayers." But on March 9, when the military police raided Tahrir Square and dragged demonstrators to the Egyptian Museum to be tortured, the response was different. "From March 9, the story started to change," Osman told me. "The numbers were increasing." And not just the number of people who were joining the group. Osman says that more and more officers began to come forward, offering to support the page by sharing information on the military's tactics and thinking. Within a few months of Osman's starting the group, nearly twenty-five thousand people had joined. Osman estimated that the number of officers actively supporting the group had grown from the original five to a couple of hundred.

Osman knew he had hit a nerve when he heard from an old friend from Maadi. When the page had only reached four thousand people, he was contacted out of the blue by a "close, close friend" on Skype.

"Hey, there is an offer," his friend said.

"An offer for what?" asked Osman.

"An offer to shut down the page."

Osman was thrilled; this meant the page had actually gotten to the generals. His friend wasn't nearly as enthused.

"Dude, it's no joke. The guy from intelligence called me and said to talk to Sherif and see what he wants and we are willing to get Tantawi to accept what he wants."

"Wow! They are bargaining on my three years," said Osman. When he had defected from the military, the regime had sentenced him in absentia to three years in prison.

"Pretty much," replied his friend.

"I'm not going to shut down the page," said Osman.

"Close the page yourself because they're going to shut it down in a couple of days," his friend responded.

"You're telling me that the Egyptian government is so powerful that they can shut down a Facebook page that was made in San Antonio, Texas, just because it says something they don't like?"

"Yeah, they said so."

"If they were able to close the page, they wouldn't have offered me shit," replied Osman. "They just want to shut my mouth before it gets really loud."

And so each day Osman and his growing army of officers conduct their war against Egypt's most powerful generals. "Information, information, information," says Osman. "I tell people if you really want to help the revolution, it's the information that will always put us ahead of the SCAF," or Supreme Council of the Armed Forces.

The last time I spoke with Osman, he had just exposed a cabinet appointment the military was attempting to make without revealing the person's true background. "Today they announced they are going to choose new cabinet members in the Egyptian government. One of the names was the former chief of command of the air force, the No. 2. And they announced him as Mr. So-and-So," Osman told me, laughing. "I was like, 'Hells no.' This is a former general who was selected by Mubarak to be the deputy of the air force. But they don't say General So-and-So, because people would say, 'Ah, another general!' If somebody is a general, he dies a general. He is not a mister."

Efforts like Osman's Facebook page were precisely the types of forces that made the Egyptian military want to slide back into the shadows, passing the formal responsibilities to rule to someone else. For an institution that prized its privacy, there was little to be had with people like Osman criticizing its every move. Then again, the generals had chosen to formally replace Mubarak, even if only temporarily.

It should hardly have surprised them that the same tools that once targeted the dictator would now be used against them.

The Pharaoh's Legacy

For many years, Egyptians talked about the "revolution." When they did, they were not talking about the future, about some hopeful, far-off day when they would be able to cast off decades of dictatorship. They were talking about their past, recalling the Free Officers' movement of 1952, when a group of officers led by Gamal Nasser forced the abdication of King Farouk. In the popular imagination, revolutions invoke something grand. Whether peaceful or bloody, they usher in a new age in a country's political life, a break from the past. In the eighteenth and nineteenth centuries, monarchs sometimes became— quite literally—casualties to more progressive ideas. The peaceful revolutions of more recent times—say, for example, Indonesia in 1998 and Serbia in 2000—opened the way for civilian leadership, multiparty democracy, and the gradual dismantling of the corrupt institutions that preceded them. But one element is generally true: if the revolution is to lead to genuine change, the people must participate in it.

That wasn't the case in Egypt in 1952. In the end, the people did not slaughter their royals or even put their king on trial. Instead, the military threw him a going-away party, complete with a twenty-one-gun salute. At dusk on July 26, three days after the officers had seized control, King Farouk simply boarded his yacht and sailed to the Italian coast, spending the rest of his days in Capri. Egyptians called it a revolution, but it was the world's most genteel military coup. More important, the Egyptian people played no part in it.

In this respect, it could not have been more different from 2011. The people did not wait to see if Gamal Mubarak would be more just or generous than his father. They did not wait for the military to rise up against a thoroughly corrupt regime, as it did in 1952. They, instead, spoke for themselves and became their own independent force for change, amassing in the square, defending their ground, and shattering whatever illusion of legitimacy Mubarak still retained. And, however dramatic those first eighteen days were, the impact of this popular rebellion was far greater than the first spasms of courage that brought people out to the streets. Indeed, because the rebellion was a homegrown popular movement fed, nurtured, and protected by the people themselves, they felt an intrinsic ownership of it.

In 2011, the political life of Egypt woke from a long slumber. I saw it for myself a month after Mubarak was deposed, on the eve of the vote for the military's constitutional amendments. Although the debate over the amendments was intense in the lead-up to the vote, in some ways the differing opinions were less important than the vote itself. For the first time, millions of Egyptians would be lining up to cast ballots they could honestly believe would be counted. The night before the referendum I walked by outdoor cafés in downtown Cairo. The only topic of conversation seemed to be the next day's vote. Friends were debating this and that clause of the amendments. Family members were trying to persuade each other to vote either yes or no. Just before midnight, the streets leading to Tahrir Square filled with people holding up posters and placards doing last-minute canvassing. In one of its more absurd directives, the military had issued an order two days earlier forbidding the media to print or discuss anything about the constitutional referendum that might sway opinion. But the Egyptian people did not need to rely on journalists to debate their political future. As one activist told me, "These days everyone is a constitutional expert."

Today, Egypt exists somewhere between dictatorship and democracy. As difficult as it is to imagine the country going back to the authoritarianism of Mubarak, it is by no means certain what Egypt will become. Because of the dominant role the military will continue to play, skepticism about the country's democratic prospects is certainly warranted. Egypt may move closer to the rough outline of a democracy—cleaner elections, more boisterous opposition parties, even an occasional rotation of leaders—while retaining much of its illiberal substance. Forty years ago, before the beginning of the democratic wave that began in 1972, the line that separated democracies and dictatorships was clearer. At that time, only a handful of authoritarian states masked themselves behind a democratic facade. Today, several dozen states—many that were once thought to be on the road to democracy—have become only a few shades less dark than their authoritarian past. Asia, Africa, and central Asia are littered with governments that are more democratic in form than function. The imitation of democracy isn't a mere possibility for these regimes; it is the reality.

Fortunately, many Egyptians do not need to be told this. They have a healthy skepticism left over from years of lies. It is worth remembering that it wasn't always obvious that Hosni Mubarak would become one of the Middle East's longest-serving dictators. In the beginning, he cut a very different figure from his predecessor, Anwar Sadat. He appeared set on reversing many of Sadat's strictest policies. A month before he was assassinated, Sadat had locked up more than fifteen hundred political prisoners, many of them important elites who had been guilty of nothing more than disagreeing with him. Academics, journalists, lawyers, politicians, and bureaucrats were among those thrown into Tora Prison. When Mubarak became president, he began releasing them almost immediately. The early Mubarak claimed that "democracy is the best guarantee of our future" and he had "no wish to monopolize decision making." Opposition political parties were allowed to reopen their doors and once again publish their newspapers. The number of NGOs and civil society groups grew. Mubarak changed the election rules that had been devised under Sadat in a way that initially proved more generous to opposition parties. Members of the opposition were invited to travel with the president when he went abroad. Mubarak even suggested early on that no one should be president for more than two terms.

But for all his talk of moving forward with "democracy in doses," clues soon emerged of a different agenda. Mubarak did not appoint a vice president. Each of his predecessors had eventually been replaced by his No. 2. Despite this tradition, or perhaps because of it, Mubarak never designated his own successor—only naming Omar Suleiman vice president in his final days, as the crowds in Tahrir Square grew in size. The emergency law he invoked after Sadat's assassination was not relaxed a single day in thirty years. The only instrument of the government that saw its power and influence steadily increase was the office of the president. "The creation of the dictatorship we have," Gasser Abdel-Razek, the human rights activist, told me, "started the day he took office and people decided not to push him."

In retrospect, it was a crucial mistake. Mubarak was weak and politically inexperienced. Sadat had tapped him as vice president precisely because he showed none of the ambition or spark of being the nation's next leader. In the aftermath of an assassination and with a government in crisis, Mubarak needed to buy himself time. And Egypt's public figures, including the political elites who were released from jail cells across Cairo in the fall of 1981, accepted the small, incremental reforms Mubarak offered in exchange. They gave Mubarak the time he needed to master the game of playing the opposition parties off each other and playing to people's fears of radical Islam. A year before Mubarak was finally pushed from power, Abdel-Razek told me, "We're paying the price today for the fact that those people that came out repeated a common mistake of giving him the benefit of the doubt. They gave him the chance to develop his own tactics and techniques to continue running the country for thirty years."

In July 2011, a delegation of Egyptian generals from the Supreme Council of the Armed Forces visited Washington, D.C. In a private meeting with leading Egypt experts, they delivered a familiar message. "Please trust that we are not an extension of the last regime. We are fully committed to human rights and the right of the Egyptian people to live in dignity," Major General Said el-Assar told the assembled. "Please trust me in this."

The Egyptian people are not novices. They know they are now the biggest check on history repeating itself. And they can be forgiven their skepticism; they know, better than anyone, that giving the remnants of an authoritarian regime time is never in the best interest of those who seek to establish a genuine democracy. Their vigilance in the months and years ahead will ultimately determine whether 2011 was truly the year of revolution.

CHAPTER 7 THE PROFESSIONALS

The workshop takes place at a run-down seaside hotel five minutes from the airport. Outside, vacationers relax on plastic lounge chairs lining the beach. Faux-thatch umbrellas shield them from the summer sun as they drink dark bottles of beer and stare out at the Mediterranean. The beach is close enough to the airport to be on the flight path for incoming planes. Every twenty minutes children yell and wave their hands toward the sky as another jet makes its approach. Besides a few palm trees, the landscape is dreary. A string of fish restaurants and tired hotels, generously described as two stars, dot a sunbaked road that hugs the water's edge, leading to the city center. Many of the lots are abandoned or unkempt. The salmon-colored building next door advertises "Beachside Apartments," but the only residents appear to be feral cats and the hundreds of pigeons that roost on the balconies with closed doors. The island boasts posh resorts and fine beaches. But they are not here. This stretch is a vacationland for locals and a handful of European budget travelers. It gets no mention in Fodor's.

We meet on the hotel's second floor. Twenty people—thirteen men and seven women—make their way into a conference room and take their seats around tables that have been arranged in a horseshoe. They are from their mid-twenties to their early forties in age, although they all dress like students. A lecturer addresses the group, occasionally pointing to the PowerPoint presentation projected on the wall behind him.

The hotel has designated its second floor for meetings and events, and with the help of partitions and dividers it can host a couple of functions at the same time. On this particular afternoon, a local weight-loss group akin to Weight Watchers is in the room next door. We must pass through their meeting, nodding to a group of thirty or forty heavyset older women, to attend our workshop.

Every few minutes, we hear shouts and clapping as one of the participants reports how much weight she has lost since their last get-together. At one point, it gets loud enough that the lecturer in our room has to repeat himself, raising his voice over the din outside. "If your movement grows too rapidly, it's very dangerous. You won't have the necessary structures in place. You won't have the discipline. You risk a Libya," he says, referring to Colonel Muammar Gaddafi's massacre of demonstrators several months earlier. The slide behind him lists the "pillars of support" for an authoritarian regime.

Faintly, a woman is heard saying, "Nine kilos!" The words are met by a round of applause.

In this shabby hotel, in a nondescript corner of a Mediterranean island, twenty activists had come to attend a clandestine meeting on revolution: specifically, how to start one. Their instructors in this week-long course were two former members of the Serbian youth group Otpor, which ousted the dictator Slobodan Milošević in 2000. Today, they work as trainers for an organization called the Centre for Applied NonViolent Action and Strategies, otherwise known as CANVAS. The Belgrade-based organization, staffed with veterans from nonviolent democratic struggles in Serbia, Georgia, Lebanon, the Philippines, and South Africa, is one of the leading groups training democratic political movements around the world. In the past nine years, this outfit has advised movements in more than fifty countries. The list reads like a global field manual for the battle between dictators and democrats: Belarus, Bolivia, Burma, Egypt, Georgia, Guatemala, Iran, the Maldives, Tibet, Venezuela, Vietnam, West Sahara, and Zimbabwe. The trainers running this seminar are two of CANVAS's most experienced instructors; they have run more than seventy workshops between them, in dozens of countries.

The workshop's twenty students are all members of a democratic movement from a country in the Middle East. (In order to attend this

weeklong seminar, I had to agree to ground rules to preserve the security of those involved. Namely, I could not reveal the location of the
meeting, the country the activists call home, or the identity of any of
the participants.) They came with many questions: How could they
build support for their cause? How could they counter a regime that
was becoming more draconian? What protest actions might shake
people from their apathy? They wanted to be more effective as an
organization, to make the leap from a protest group to a resistance
movement. But after eighteen months, they had hit a wall. They feared
that they had become reactive, predictable. "We always feel in a state
of emergency. It blocks our thinking," says one of the activists. "We
continue doing what we already know how to do."

For the group's leadership, the workshop is more than a lesson
in tactics and methods; it's a crossroads. The movement, which can
reliably call out several hundred people to the streets, grew faster than
anyone anticipated. Much of this growth came from activists who
engaged in direct actions and then joined forces to make common
cause. But the leadership, a core of five or six people, want to take
the movement in a more professional, calculated, and strategic direction. The trouble is they know that some of the group's lieutenants,
a second-tier leadership of say twenty to thirty people, are split on
their objectives. Some fully share their more professionalized goals.
Others, they fear, almost enjoy protesting for protesting's sake. These
members would be quick to call a more pragmatic campaign a sellout
of the movement's purest revolutionary goals. The group's top leaders are prepared for this division or disagreement to come out into
the open, and they almost seek it. Although it may thin their ranks
temporarily, they suspect they will require a greater unity of purpose if
they are to be successful and become a more sophisticated and potent
political force. So they have come to CANVAS, in part, to provoke this
discussion, win over some of their colleagues, and perhaps leave some
realizing they are on the fringe. "We are not thinking through what
we gain from our actions. We need to agree on clear objectives," one
of the leaders told me. "If that means we are fewer, at least for a little
while, then so be it."

The CANVAS trainers have seen this dynamic within a movement countless times. They are happy if the seminar proves to be a

provocation for the group, if it gives them "the critical distance to view their own struggle," as one of the trainers explains to me. What they will not do is draft them a plan or blueprint to oust a dictator. They follow two simple and strict rules: they will only work with groups with no history of violence, and they refuse to tell them what to do. "I don't want that responsibility," says one of the Serbian trainers. "I wasn't born and raised there, so I can't decide for them."

What they will do is teach them how to think strategically. They will offer them tips. They will point out common mistakes and pitfalls that have tripped up others. They will draw on their own experience to discuss real-life examples of how to shift the loyalties of the police, how to diminish a dictator's authority, and how to ultimately make a regime turn against itself. "We are not here with a bagful of magic tricks to say do this, this, and this," one of the Serbs says at the beginning of the workshop. "It's a struggle using nonviolent methods. It's like a form of warfare, only you won't be using guns."

Students of Revolution

When people rise up against a dictator, the world watches. And one audience has a particularly keen interest in how uprisings are resolved: other dictators. On Christmas Day 1989, the Romanian people summarily executed President Nicolae Ceauşescu and his wife hours after the brutal Communist regime crumbled. Zaire's strongman, President Mobutu Sese Seko, is said to have been horrified when he saw the image of his Romanian friend's corpse on CNN. At the same time, in distant Beijing, the Chinese leadership beefed up security around the capital, lest anyone there draw inspiration from the events in Bucharest. In 2005, after a wave of democratic movements toppled regimes in Georgia, Ukraine, and Kyrgyzstan, Vladimir Putin and Hu Jintao are said to have huddled on the sidelines of a summit to discuss the danger of "color revolutions." And for nearly twenty years without a hitch, Arab interior ministers—the men charged with repressing domestic dissent—met annually to compare notes.

The causes and fallout of the Arab Spring, without question, have become the newest preoccupation for authoritarian regimes. The Chinese Communist Party moved quickly to ban mention of key words like "Mubarak," "Ben Ali," and "jasmine"—a reference to Tunisia's Jasmine Revolution—from the Internet. This censorship was followed by a wide-scale crackdown against dissidents, regime critics, and human rights defenders that many believe was a preemptive measure to prevent political unrest there. It is reasonable to assume that the quick fall of Tunisia's Zine el-Abidine Ben Ali and Egypt's Hosni Mubarak frightened other Arab autocrats, making the bloody crackdowns against regime opponents in Libya, Yemen, and Syria more likely. Some of the region's dictators were not content to wait for trouble to appear within their borders. Saudi Arabia sent its own troops to help quash the rebellion in Bahrain and later gifted Egypt's military council with $4 billion to help make its work easier.

Dictators, however, are not the only ones who draw lessons and assistance from the struggles of others. In the twenty-first century, democratic movements are increasingly becoming careful students of what makes a revolution a success or a failure. In Venezuela, groups have closely studied how the opposition succeeded in ousting Chile's Augusto Pinochet. In Egypt, a year before removing Mubarak, activists had already begun to borrow tactics from Iran's Green Movement. In almost every country I visited, people challenging an authoritarian regime were deeply familiar with Lech Walesa's Solidarity movement in Poland from the 1980s.

In a globalized world, some learning occurs simply because information is so readily available. Take, for example, Girifna, a nonviolent democratic movement in Sudan that seeks to end the repressive rule of Omar al-Bashir. It has a Facebook page. Its name—which translates to "We are fed up"—is similar to that of groups in Georgia, Ukraine, and Egypt, which also chose names that literally said "enough." Much like the organizations active in the "color revolutions," Girifna chose a color to help brand its movement. (It's orange.)

Recently, the Sudanese movement produced a parody of a soap commercial in which a young man uses a bar of soap labeled "Girifna" to clean a T-shirt with Bashir's face on it. As the young man washes the shirt by hand, a voice-over says, "If you are disgusted, don't worry, there is Girifna soap bar. It's not going to be easy after twenty years with no political change. You will have to scrub and scrub . . . squeeze and squeeze . . . but you will like the result." With that, the young man lifts the T-shirt from the bowl, and Bashir's face is no more. It's just a sparkling white T-shirt.

What is striking isn't simply the ad's content; it's that it is a direct knockoff of a parody produced in Serbia ten years earlier. In it, a Serbian housewife throws a T-shirt with Milošević's face on it into a washing machine, producing the same result. ("For ten years, I have been trying to remove this stain," she says, referring to Milošević. "Believe me, I have tried everything.") I asked a member of Otpor, which was behind the creation of the original commercial, if the group had helped Girifna make its mock advertisement. "We had no idea," he told me. The Sudanese group had found it online and created their own version.

The hunger for this type of information is too great for the Internet and YouTube to satisfy. Groups do not simply wish to copy the look and feel of successful democratic movements; they want to understand the strategy and tactics that underpinned those efforts. So, in response, a network of organizations and highly trained individuals has sprung up to help those who have launched their own struggles against dictators and authoritarian regimes. Indeed, this is precisely how Srdja Popovic, one of the leaders of Serbia's Otpor movement, explains the decision to found CANVAS.

In 2003, he was in Cape Town meeting with Zimbabweans who had sought his help in their campaign against Robert Mugabe. When he met them, Popovic was amazed by the extent to which they were already familiar with Otpor's experience. They called themselves Zwakana (Enough Is Enough) and had incorporated Otpor's slogans into their movement. Earlier, a group in Belarus had reached out to Slobodan Djinovic, one of Otpor's leaders and a co-founder of CANVAS. This was followed by requests from activists in Georgia and Ukraine. But the trip to South Africa was the epiphany for Popovic. "For me, it was an eye-opener," he says. "My God! I mean, if the people in rural Zimbabwe are inspired by what we have done in Belgrade, there is something bigger we don't see. The market [for these ideas] was coming to us. And the interesting thing is the market keeps coming to us."

When we see tens of thousands of people on the streets in a foreign capital demanding greater freedoms or an end to a repressive regime, it is tempting to accept the narrative that we are witnessing a spontaneous act. That there was simply a hidden, unexpected spark that led people to pour out into the squares and demand rights that had been denied for too long. That, in fact, is seldom the case. Revolutions, if they are to be successful, require planning, preparation, and an intelligent grasp of how to anticipate and outwit a repressive regime that thinks of little beyond preserving its own power. When the tide turns, events may indeed move fast. But there is usually a movement or organization that put months or years of dangerous (often tedious) work into making that day possible. The work that CANVAS and others do defies one of the central myths of revolution. "There is no such thing as a spontaneous revolution. Spontaneity will only get you killed," says Popovic. "The more you plan, the bigger your chance for success."

And if there is a single animating idea behind the type of revolution that these groups teach, it is this: strategic nonviolence. It is not because these movements are made up of pacifists; they are not. Rather, peaceful democratic movements are most often motivated by pragmatism. Activists see the logic, and they like the odds. According to a recent study, between 1900 and 2006 more than 50 percent of nonviolent movements succeeded, compared with roughly 25 percent of violent insurgencies. When activists look squarely at the choice of toppling dictators with bullets or ballots, they see a greater chance for success by nonviolent means. They understand that a dictatorship's greatest monopoly is the use of force. So, rather than confront the regime on the ground that favors it, they shift the battlefield to arenas where their size, strength, and wit can serve them best. There are no guarantees for those who take up the fight. But if they look around, they will find people willing to give them—and their revolution—a helping hand.

The Colonel and the Professor

Colonel Robert Helvey didn't have anything to do. It was 1987, and he was closing in on nearly thirty years in the U.S. Army. The service had rewarded him by sending him to Harvard University to spend a year there as an army senior fellow. It was a sabbatical year, a time for study and self-improvement. Helvey wasn't unaccustomed to a university setting. He had spent time as an instructor at the Naval War College and had served as the dean of the U.S. Army Defense Intelligence School. But the pace of life on the Harvard campus was unfamiliar. It was leisurely compared with what he knew. So on this day, like many others, he walked across Harvard Yard looking for something to do—an event, a lecture, a speaker's series—something.

He found it, posted on a door. "Program on Nonviolent Sanctions— 2 PM," the flyer read. Helvey wasn't exactly sure what "nonviolent sanctions" meant, but he had a hunch. Pacifists and peaceniks. "I had never had experience with [the program], but I knew I didn't like them because of my Vietnam experience," says Helvey. "They were just rude as hell, sons of bitches with long hair and rings in their nose, all that shit."

Helvey, a gruff, straightforward native of West Virginia, had first served as a military adviser in Vietnam in the early 1960s. He returned again with the First Cavalry Division in 1967 and saw the thick of the fighting. His leadership and courage while serving as captain in Company A of the Second Battalion, Twelfth Cavalry are credited with saving hundreds of his fellow soldiers. One of the officers who served alongside him described him as a "natural." For the valor he showed in combat, he was awarded the Distinguished Service Cross, the country's second-highest military decoration. (His citation describes his bravery while outnumbered and outgunned by North Vietnamese soldiers. Under heavy fire, he led his men through an "enemy trench line, fighting off the North Vietnamese at ranges as close as three feet." Even after he was shot in the leg, he refused medical treatment until his soldiers were safe.) He didn't have much time for people who criticized a military they didn't understand, but he was curious. So he decided to attend the talk. "I figured this would be an opportunity to confirm my prejudices," he told me.

It was a chance encounter that changed everything for this professional soldier. He remembers taking a seat in the seminar room. "And this little guy gets up and says almost in a whisper, 'Hello, my name is Gene Sharp, and I'm here to talk about nonviolent sanctions. It's all about power, either denying it to others or seizing it. That's what it's all about.'

"And that got me. Because that's what I do for a living," Helvey remembers. "When the government wants something done, they will turn to the military and we'll get it for them or we'll protect it from somebody else trying to get it."

Afterward, Helvey went up to introduce himself to Sharp, and they soon got together for lunch at the Harvard Faculty Club. "That started a long friendship," says Helvey. "I was fascinated listening to him talk, and I think he was interested in learning about my experiences."

It was also the beginning of Helvey's education in the strategy of nonviolent conflict. Gene Sharp, a little-known academic, had given most of his life to studying how people could "deny" power to or "seize" it from dictatorships through nonviolent campaigns. He had written works on the strategic genius of Mahatma Gandhi, examining how he had used civil resistance against British colonial rule. His most pioneering contribution, *The Politics of Nonviolent Action,* a three-volume work that ran nearly a thousand pages, offered a comprehensive examination of nonviolent strategy. Other books followed. Helvey threw himself into studying Sharp's work—all of it. "I didn't have much else to do, so I read just about everything Gene had written," says Helvey. As he did, he and Sharp would meet for lunch, often at the faculty club, for what amounted to his own private tutorial on nonviolent strategy.

One of the reasons for Helvey's intense interest in dictatorships was his last posting, the one he had filled just before turning up on Harvard's campus. Helvey had spent two years in Burma as the U.S. military's defense attaché. It made a strong impression on him. "People, when I went to talk to them, would sometimes cover their mouth so that if somebody was watching them, they couldn't read their lips. Sometimes people would just turn their backs. They wanted to avoid having to answer to someone why they were talking to this American clown," recalls Helvey. "I thought this is terrifying. Everybody seemed to be aware that somebody is watching them. The government had this omnipresence of surveillance." Helvey developed an intellectual curiosity in how the Burmese junta was able to command people through fear. "What is it that causes people to obey a regime that is treating them so badly, that is so corrupt? That's where Gene's work— why do people obey?—really comes in."

Colonel Helvey retired from the U.S Army in 1992. Months later, he was back in Burma. He had given a presentation on nonviolent strategy in Washington, D.C., and members of the Karen National Union, a pro-democracy Burmese opposition group, had attended his talk. They invited Helvey to return to Burma to give his presentation to General Bo Mya, the legendary leader of the Burmese resistance. After having spent years studying and absorbing Sharp's ideas, Helvey was eager to put them to work in the field. When he heard the presentation, General Bo Mya was persuaded and asked Helvey to set up a pilot program training opposition officials in quick, three-day courses.

Once he had the program up and running, Helvey invited Sharp to come to Burma to evaluate the training sessions. For Sharp, this was a new experience; he was curious to see his own ideas applied. So he flew to Bangkok, where Helvey had someone waiting for him. From there, they traveled by truck to Mae Sot, a Thai-Burma border town. In Mae Sot, they slipped into Burma and made their way to the Moei River. Sharp boarded a cigarette boat sent by the opposition that would secretly transport him to Manerplaw, then the strategic base of the Karen National Union. "I was in Manerplaw and the radio came on," recalls Helvey. "We just got a report. There is a boat headed in this direction. It's got a white man and a big suitcase."

Helvey went down to the river. A boat came around the bend with Sharp on board. It docked, and the professor came ashore. Helvey smiled. "Dr. Sharp, I presume."

He fondly remembers those days in the Burmese jungle, and he thinks it meant a lot to Sharp, too. The training program impressed him. Moreover, Sharp was amazed to find members of the Burmese resistance who could quote his work verbatim. One person in particular, a university professor and member of the opposition, had anxiously looked forward to meeting Sharp. "I think Gene found nirvana," says Helvey. "Here in this little jungle outpost he meets a guy who has read his book and could ask him specific questions. It was the most beautiful thing. These two professors walking down this shady path for hours talking. Gene made a big hit over there. And of course, that's when he started writing *From Dictatorship to Democracy*."

Sharp had spent years studying the totalitarian systems of the twentieth century. He had written tomes on how nonviolent strategy could exploit a dictatorship's weaknesses. But the work that people know best is a slim, seventy-nine-page essay that he began writing in the Southeast Asian jungle. The Burmese had made clear that as valuable as Sharp's insights were, they needed something that distilled his wisdom in a concise volume, something they could share and disseminate easily. *From Dictatorship to Democracy* became that work. It has been published in more than twenty-five languages and freely downloaded from the Internet hundreds of thousands of times. In it, Sharp is straightforward and unsentimental. His essay never examines or targets a specific regime, but rather offers a generic analysis on how to unseat any dictator. Call it Machiavelli for the people.

Early in the essay, Sharp makes two simple but central observations. First, violence almost always favors dictators. "Whatever the merits of the violent option . . . one point is clear," he writes. "By placing confidence in violent means, one has chosen the very type of struggle with which the oppressors nearly always have superiority." Second, the people have tremendous power of their own. "Dictators require the assistance of the people they rule," writes Sharp. In other words, a ruler cannot rule if the people do not obey. Any rulers, even dictators, govern through the consent of the people. When enough people withdraw their consent, a dictator can no longer remain. He then goes on to identify the sources of power for dictatorships, the common vulnerabilities of these regimes, and the way in which nonviolent strategy can exploit these weaknesses to strip a government of its legitimacy, raising the probability of its demise. Despite a broad and reaching analysis, the essay is sometimes startling in its specificity. Sharp, for example, identifies seventeen common weaknesses of dictatorships. (They include a routinized system unable to adapt, a fear among subordinates of reporting information that may displease the regime's leadership, an erosion of the ideology, and an increasingly inept bureaucracy.) Many people think of nonviolent campaigns as being either strikes or protest marches. Sharp pinpoints 198 specific methods of nonviolent protest, including mock funerals, skywriting, and the withdrawal of bank deposits. Throughout, he stresses the need for preparation and planning, moving from low-risk, confidence-building actions that achieve limited objectives to bolder initiatives. It is fair to say that for many activists, *From Dictatorship to Democracy* is close to scripture. In the course of my reporting, I met Venezuelans, Iranians, Tibetans, and Egyptians who could quote it chapter and verse.

On a dreary winter morning in February 2010, I visited Sharp at his home in East Boston. He lives in a simple town house that doubles as the offices of the Albert Einstein Institution, an organization Sharp founded in 1983 to help promote his work. The organization is no more than two small adjoining rooms on the town house's first floor. Its staff is Sharp and one assistant. Sharp has lived at this address since 1968, when he found the building abandoned and bought it for $150. Although the place remains in modest disrepair, he says it is nothing like the condition in which he found it. "The house was in ruins," Sharp tells me. "When it rained, the water went through the back wall's bricks and made a lake on the third floor. There was no heating. No toilets." Today, he lives on the second floor, rents the third floor to tenants, and keeps the fourth floor as an indoor greenhouse to "help clear my head."

The first-floor office is dimly lit. The only light comes from two desk lamps that shine small spotlights on his immediate work space. The room itself is almost impossible to navigate, covered as it is with towering stacks of books, boxes, and what appears to be an old aquarium no longer in use. Besides a few oriental wall hangings, there is a single framed picture of Gandhi. Occasionally, while we talk, a small tan dog—"she is named Sally, but I call her good girl"—emerges to be petted and then disappears behind a stack of books. He recently adopted her from an animal rescue north of Boston after his Great Dane, Caesar, passed away.

It is hard to imagine Sharp as a dangerous man. At eighty-two, he is stooped, speaks in a whisper, and walks with the help of a cane. But for many of the world's dictators, he is the closest thing to public enemy No. 1, a threat worthy of diatribes and denunciations. Burma's generals call him an "American spy" who engages in "dirty and wicked psychological warfare." Hugo Chávez has alleged that the octogenarian is in league with the CIA and is attempting to overthrow his government. The Iranian government took Sharp seriously enough that it requested his books. ("We sent them," he says.) The Iranians have allegedly set up a unit devoted to spotting and countering the techniques of strategic nonviolence. He has been denounced or had his books banned in Belarus, China, Russia, and Vietnam, to name a few places. Sharp sees all the attacks, charges, and government-backed conspiracy theories as a positive. "It's a good sign," he says. "It means that the knowledge that this kind of struggle can be powerful has gotten through to them. It's a compliment."

The strange truth is that Sharp is probably better known in the world's least free places than anywhere else. On the day that I visit, his assistant, Jamila Raqib, tells me she had just received a new request from Venezuela. Someone there was interested in doing a local printing of Sharp's work. Most people get their hands on his writing by downloading it from the organization's Web site. Typically, she says, they have no idea of the identity of those who contact them seeking books or reprints. "If people do contact us directly, they often do so anonymously. It is one thing to pick up a book and read in your own space. It's another to be in touch with a U.S.-based organization that has this high profile, has been denounced by your government and linked to the White House and all these other crazy things," she says. "People are very intelligent. They know the risks they should be taking and what they shouldn't do."

Raqib knows, for example, that Sharp's work is popular in her native Afghanistan. (She fled the country with her parents when she was five years old in the wake of the Soviet invasion.) "[Afghans] find very attractive the idea that we actually can be responsible for our own future. We can be self-reliant," she says. "We don't have to wait for outsiders, because outsiders have only caused harm. We are on our own here, and violence has not worked."

Although the demand may come from all over, there is one refrain they hear time and again. "'This book was written for us.' We have heard that a number of times," Raqib says. "It's an indication of the quality of the analysis."

For his part, Sharp is optimistic. He thinks it is becoming harder to be a dictator today and, more important, the people who are challenging regimes are getting smarter. "We are learning more about the means of struggle and how to wage them skillfully, as well as what not to do." Nonetheless, he is struck by the number of people who take up such dangerous work and still fail to think strategically. "The advocates of political freedom aren't using their heads as much as they need to," says Sharp. "This is tremendous power, and people can grasp it. But they must do their homework."

Sometimes, they also need teachers.

War Stories

It is pouring rain in South Charleston, West Virginia. I am sitting on Bob Helvey's back porch, which sits high up in a dense neighborhood overlooking the Kanawha River. We are drinking our second cup of coffee as he tells me the basics of training democratic activists in nonviolent conflict. His coffee cup says a little about his past. It reads, "Burma Democracy Leader," and shows a picture of Aung San Suu Kyi, the Nobel Peace Prize winner and head of the country's democratic movement. After Burma, Helvey went on to train activists in Belarus, Venezuela, Nigeria, Iraq, Palestine, and Zimbabwe, among others. He says he thinks one of the reasons he ended up training so many groups is that people were intrigued to hear a military man discuss nonviolent strategy. "I think it has opened doors," says Helvey, referring to his military experience. "People think, 'What's this infantry officer doing teaching this shit? We better listen to him. He may be crazy, but we better listen to him.'"

What they hear is an expert tactician take three decades of military service and apply it to principles of defeating a dictator nonviolently. He teaches them the rudiments of thinking strategically, down to the way they see their streets and neighborhoods. "Life is nothing more than pattern analysis. Planning involves the habit of pattern analysis, and every living thing lives by a pattern," says Helvey. "We need to know what that pattern is so that when it changes, the first question we ask is, 'Why?'

"When the young policeman walks away from the pretty girls to the ugly old woman, I want to know why. Maybe she is an informant? Maybe she is a drug pusher? I want to know why," Helvey continues. "And that's one of the things you want to teach the people you are training. That you are always looking for an opportunity. Then you start to develop a menu of opportunities you can pull from because you have done this pattern analysis."

He teaches them how to make a strategic estimate that establishes the movement's objective or mission. While quoting Clausewitz and the British strategist Liddell Hart, he teaches them how to break down the regime's sources of power and understand the difference between its capabilities and its intentions. He offers small pieces of wisdom from past conflicts. (For example, there is tremendous value in recruiting the children of generals and police officers to your movement. "Generals don't like to attack crowds with their children in the front ranks.")

But if you take a course from Bob Helvey, the thing you may understand best is the power of propaganda. In a contest where you are unarmed, your message is critical. "How do we want them to see our movement?" asks Helvey. "We want to convert these people into believing that this movement for democratic change is nonthreatening to different groups, especially military people." An opposition group's propaganda is often its first assault on a regime's legitimacy, and you must ultimately destroy its legitimacy. "My personal view is that the greatest weapon is propaganda," says Helvey. "People don't like to use that word, because it sounds cheap. They like to say 'media relations' or 'PR.' But it is all propaganda."

Helvey takes the example of Hugo Chávez's Venezuela. On its face, the Venezuelan case is a difficult one. Chávez's government is able to claim more legitimacy than most authoritarian regimes because of its success at the ballot box, even if that success is highly engineered. Still, Helvey believes a propagandist has many openings to exploit. First would be Chávez's reliance on foreign governments, especially Fidel Castro's Cuba. "Who are these fucking foreigners? Are you telling me we can't train our own people to become medical doctors? We are buying fucking Russian jets, Russian missiles, Russian planes, instead of training our own doctors. Are you telling me that we can't train our own people to be security officers for our own country? Why are we depending on the only Communist state in the Western Hemisphere to staff our government? Oh, boy, we got a good one here," says Helvey, rubbing his hands together. "Tell your propagandist, 'Get on this jerk! Never let go of it. Every time something happens, blame it on those fuckheads. If there is a flood somewhere, that isn't an act of God; that is an act of incompetence on the part of the government.'"

Helvey trains his students to be exceptionally disciplined, especially when it comes to their message. "No spokesman or representative of the movement should ever say anything hateful about anybody. Don't hate the policeman, don't hate the intelligence officer, because, as a democratic movement, we want to pull those people into our camp, and we can't do that spewing hate," he says. "We have to have a majority to win. Strategic nonviolent movements are not minority movements. If hate has to come, you focus it as narrowly as possible. One man: Mugabe. If you want to hate somebody, don't hate everybody in the regime. Hate Mugabe."

And there is another point on which Helvey counsels his students: the need for patience. "The thing about strategic nonviolent conflict is that I like to use the word 'yet'—we haven't won yet," says Helvey. "Using the word 'yet' means the struggle is continuing. Like any long war, you have good days and you have bad days. The thing about insurgents, which basically is what opposition movements are, is you don't lose until *you* say you have lost. We determine when we lose, the government doesn't. That is our decision to make, not yours. And that is a powerful message if you can get the people to understand what that means. We decide when it's over."

Three hours later the rain wasn't letting up. Gullies were overflowing on one side of his property as water raced down the hillside. Still sitting on Helvey's back porch, I asked him if any of the groups he ever trained stood out. Was one outfit the most impressive? "The Serbs," he replied. "They looked intelligent before they even said a word. They were focused. They kept their eye on me and what I was saying, and every now and then would mumble something to each other."

In the spring of 2000, Helvey traveled to Budapest to meet with some of the members of Otpor, the democratic Serbian youth group. They had already had remarkable success challenging Slobodan Milošević's regime, but they feared they had reached a plateau and would not be able to maintain their momentum. Before the seminar began, Helvey asked to meet with a few of the Serbs, just to get a sense of them and where they stood as a movement. "I asked them to give me an idea of how they were structured," Helvey recalls.

"We don't have a structure," one replied.

"Who is your leader?"

"We don't have a leader," answered another.

"Wait just a fucking minute," said Helvey. "I didn't fall off the turnip truck yesterday. You have a countrywide movement, the pillars of support around the Milošević regime are collapsing, things are happening, demonstrations occur all over the country and they are synchronized, and you are telling me you don't have an organization and you don't have anyone running it."

The young Serbs just smiled. "That's what we tell everybody."

Helvey knew right away he did not need to instruct them in tactics or how to establish a nonviolent movement; they had already come up with innovative methods, and they approached the task with the discipline and rigor of a military operation. The Serbs, he said, had all the pieces. They simply hadn't figured out how to put them together, as well as how to plan for the final days of the regime. But he was certain when the seminar was finished that they would succeed. "Their minds were like sponges. Nobody should be surprised that they won. They are risk takers," says Helvey. "I thought these guys have what it takes. They never rested. I would not want to be in opposition to those guys."

One person in particular stood out. A twenty-seven-year-old named Srdja Popovic. "As soon as I saw him, I knew this guy is one of their leaders," says Helvey. "He was so intense." A creative and clever tactician, Srdja was in fact one of the original eleven leaders of Otpor (Resistance). Tall, lanky, and with a sly, mischievous smile, Popovic was the self-styled political commissar of the movement. His charisma and energy made him a natural for heading up the recruitment and training of new members, especially Serbian youth. Srdja, like other former members of Otpor I met, exuded confidence and the savvy street smarts of a veteran activist.

Helvey was right to believe Srdja and his colleagues would win out. Months later, on October 5, 2000, the small band of youth activists helped lead a national movement that toppled Serbia's brutal twentieth-century dictator. When in the final hours Milošević called on his shock troops to open fire and disperse the crowds by any means necessary, the police put down their guns and let the Serbian people seize the parliament. What Milošević hadn't realized was that Popovic and his compatriots had spent more than a year winning the regime's police and security services over to their side. Few had predicted that Milošević would fall, let alone that he would do so in a bloodless democratic coup.

As if on cue, a large gray tabby trots from the house onto the back porch and jumps on the table. He walks toward Helvey and lowers his head, looking for a scratch on the scruff of his neck. "In fact, my cat is named Srdja," says Helvey, smiling. "And Srdja the cat will kill anything his size or smaller."

More Than Just Another Dictator

Bob Helvey didn't need to describe Srdja Popovic to me. I had met him a year earlier, in June 2009. The occasion was a five-day seminar on nonviolent strategy hosted by the International Center on Nonviolent Conflict. The center, founded and funded by the former investment banker Peter Ackerman, held an annual meeting in Boston that brought together democratic activists from around the world. More than forty activists from thirty-five different countries, including Egypt, Malawi, Nigeria, Syria, Tibet, and Tunisia, came to hear experts, scholars, and veterans of nonviolent campaigns. But for many of these foot soldiers of democratic struggles, Popovic's talk was the highlight. As one Nigerian explained, he and others had come because they wanted to hear "how [Popovic] had done it and whether we could do it in our own countries, too."

The night before he was to speak, Srdja and I met in a bar in Davis Square, near the Tufts University campus. For several days, the world had turned its attention to the streets of Tehran, where thousands of people, especially young Iranians, had come out to denounce the apparent theft of the presidential election. He had co-founded CANVAS six years earlier and now spent roughly a hundred days a year on the road, either conducting workshops or speaking to groups. CANVAS had trained seven opposition groups in Iran. In a preview of his lecture for the next day, I asked him what he made of the Iranian uprising, which people were now calling the Green Movement.

Popovic shook his head. "It is going to be bloody," he replied. It was too early to tell, but he was already worried that the Iranian opposition was on the verge of making serious strategic mistakes. After unsettling the regime with their massive groundswell of support, the protesters should have "retreated from Tehran's public squares and dispersed to Iran's twenty largest cities," engaging in "high-visibility, low-risk tactics" like graffiti, vigils, and boycotts. They had shown their size as a movement, but now they needed to prove that they were not only centered on Tehran. More important, they needed to keep the regime guessing. Popovic believes there is nothing more dangerous for a movement than to become predictable. Once a movement has put a regime on its heels, it is crucial to keep the initiative and not allow the government to settle in to plan its response. If the movement is going to sway the loyalties of key parts of the regime, it needs to continue to stay one step ahead, infecting the government's backers with self-doubt while raising the confidence of the protesters and the public alike. He feared that some of the young Iranians CANVAS trained knew what to do but couldn't implement it because too many of the country's opposition groups were still being led by "graybeards." Popovic, who majored in biology at the University of Belgrade, is fond of making analogies to the animal kingdom. "Movements are like sharks," he explains. "They need to constantly move to stay alive. If the shark stops, the shark dies. Sharks can only swim in one direction—forward. Our movement [in Serbia] was successful by maintaining the offensive, constantly moving, and staying one step ahead of the regime."

The next morning Popovic walked to the podium to address the assembled activists. The charisma and humor that made him an effective leader to thousands of Serbian youth—30 percent of Otpor's members were teenagers, the movement's average age was twenty-one—immediately showed. With members of the audience hanging on his every word, he began by telling them, "My organization sees [these struggles] as a form of warfare." As such, he stressed the need for unity, planning, and nonviolent discipline. He talked about recruitment and the need to be on the level with new members. "You should be clear with them. There will be casualties. It is very fair to tell this to your people at the beginning," he said. "People will be beat up. They will be arrested. They will have their friends and family hurt. They may be intentionally infected with HIV. In the Maldives, people were intentionally made drug addicts."

But nothing the regime does is an excuse to break a movement's commitment to nonviolence. Otpor stressed its nonviolent focus during a person's recruitment. During the initiation—something it created to help establish discipline—the final thing a person heard was "Violence is the last sanctuary of the weak." The danger that members could resort to violence, thereby giving the regime an excuse to crack down violently, was something always to guard against. Further, the moment a movement turns violent, it alienates the very members of the regime it hoped to make sympathetic to its cause. "You need to see what individuals or groups within your movement can turn violent," Popovic cautioned. "You need to identify them, isolate them, talk to them, and either have them explain or kick them out."

For the next day and a half that Srdja remained at the seminar, activists peppered him with questions inspired by their own fights. They would corner him in the hallways, share a smoke outside, or stay up late over drinks trying to glean whatever additional bit of experience and insight they could. They wanted to know how decentralized the group's leadership should be. ("The top eleven activists never met in the same place.") How effective was the regime's intelligence on Otpor? ("When we saw our dossiers after the revolution, we had like two hundred pages each. They knew our movements. But there was no analysis. So, so what?") What do you do when the regime brings hardened shock troops from a different part of the country to lead the crackdown? ("You need to create stronger bonds with the local police. We developed ties with the local police so they would warn us what streets to avoid. Every regime has a limited number of special units.")

For the next two years, Popovic and I kept in touch. Every few months we would exchange an e-mail or talk on the phone to discuss events unfolding in one authoritarian country or another. Not long after Ben Ali and Mubarak had fallen, during the height of the Arab Spring, we met for breakfast in Washington, D.C. The events in Tunisia and Egypt had been good for CANVAS. Media outlets in the United States and Europe had run a slew of stories on his organization and the role it played helping activists promote democratic revolutions, especially in Egypt. The higher profile has, in turn, led to more requests for workshops.

The Arab Spring, however, has done more than crowd CANVAS's calendar with future workshops. Popovic believes it has destroyed more myths about nonviolent conflict than any of the revolutions before it. For starters, it proved, once and for all, that Arabs could do it. The idea that the Middle East could only be the home to dictators, that for some reason the people there were destined to be left behind as democracy advanced elsewhere, was proven wrong. And the fact that Tunisia and Egypt fell first—two of the United States' staunchest allies in the Middle East—destroys the idea that nonviolent revolutions were spreading with the help of the CIA or the American government. CANVAS may have tried to help where it could, but the revolutions were successful, says Popovic, because they were homegrown. "These young Egyptians overstated what we taught them. I think it's 100 percent their achievement," he says. "There is no way that a million Egyptians would follow what a Serb told them, no matter how fancy a suitcase or laptop he has."

But Popovic wouldn't be a very good strategic thinker if he didn't know an opportunity when he sees it. "We have this historical phenomenon which is shaping the world in front of our eyes. Now it's the Middle East, before it was eastern Europe, tomorrow it may be in Africa or Asia," says Popovic. He sees this moment as a possible pivot point, a chance when greater gains could be made. "This is not about toppling one more dictator," he continues. "It is about transforming knowledge on a wide scale. There is a chance to leverage this knowledge."

Popovic is positioning CANVAS to be a part of this effort to shape the future. He is building a curriculum in the strategy of nonviolent conflict and partnering with universities in the United States and Europe to teach it. As an obvious first step, he has already recruited Egyptian activists to serve as new trainers. "These guys are really bright," he says, smiling. "They are ideal trainers for the Arab world."

Training Camp

The beginning of a workshop can always be a little rocky. As anxious as activists may be to learn new ideas on how to counter a regime, they are reluctant to believe that they have been approaching the job the wrong way. That is the mood on the second floor of the hotel overlooking the Mediterranean.

The twenty Middle Eastern activists are asked to break up into small groups to draw up what the CANVAS trainers call their "vision for tomorrow"—their vision for the change they want their movement to create. It's a simple enough idea: lay out your movement's ostensible mission. But the Serbian instructors have put a twist on it. They have asked the activists to outline it in terms that five very different segments of society will find appealing. They need to express their goals for the future of their country in a way that will resonate with businessmen, religious scholars, teachers, students, and members of the media. "When Otpor became an organization credible in the eyes of the public, then our numbers grew," says Aleksandar,* one of the trainers, a heavyset Serb with an expertise in political organization. "And numbers are what we are always seeking."

It proves a tough assignment for everyone. When they report back to the main group, most haven't been able to find common denominators across five different strata of society. Instead, they want to explain why making common cause among so many disparate people in their country is next to impossible. One of the older activists says, "Well, it's complicated. We are unique." Another chimes in, "We are a bit different." A chorus of the activists start explaining how there are many competing interests, divided opinions, different groups, and so on. The trainers look on and listen, as if they're expecting these excuses. Finally, one of the female activists, clearly frustrated by the whole exercise, blurts out, "It's impossible."

Dragana, the other trainer, a striking blonde with a wry smile, says flatly, "You cannot change anything if you remain a minority. It's as simple as that."

"I don't think you understand," says one of the activists, a young man with tattoos up and down his forearms. "How willing should we be to degrade our politics to widen our struggle?"

"Why do you see it as degradation?" replies Aleksandar. "It's a beginning. They cannot rule the country without the people. But you need the people."

The activists' reaction to the exercise is a common one. The trainers anticipated it. Popovic had told me once before that almost every

---

*The names of the trainers have been changed.

movement thinks that its situation is wholly unique. People attending the workshop are always quick to point out why the Serbian example wouldn't translate to their own political environment, or why the regime they are up against is unusually brutal, clever, or insidious. The Ukrainians said they had to worry about Russian interference, since Moscow was backing the regime. In Egypt, activists pointed to the fact that Mubarak could count on American support. They are usually quick to mention how large the regime's domestic security budget has become or how many police or informants walk the streets. Popovic is the first to admit that no two situations are identical. If they were precisely the same, then the Serbs would have no problem telling people what to do. But he insists, much as Gene Sharp argues in *From Dictatorship to Democracy*, that the fundamentals are the same. Understand those building blocks, and you can build your own plan of attack.

It takes time for it to sink in. The activists admitted at the beginning of the workshop that one of their biggest problems is that the majority in their country does not view them sympathetically. They know they have a message problem. The Serbs acknowledge that it can be difficult to craft a vision that encompasses enough key groups. In the case of Otpor, they sent members out to various parts of the country to interview people about what they wanted. They spent time identifying who some of the most respected people in the country were. In some rural areas, it was the doctors. In other places, it was the teachers. Either way, the thinking was that if these people could be won over, it would add even more numbers to their movement. Eventually, one of the Middle Eastern activists, one of the youngest in the room, says what is painfully obvious: "Well, we probably haven't thought enough about how we could build supporters."

"Finally," whispers Dragana. It's a start.

The Serbs now turn the discussion to what the activists are up against. They ask the group to identify the regime's pillars of support—for example, the military, police, bureaucracy, educational system, organized religion—the main institutions from which it draws its strength. The next step is for the activists to make what they call a "power graph." It's an analytical tool developed by Slobodan Djinovic, one of CANVAS's founders. "This makes us focus on who is with us and who is against us, and how we can influence them," says Aleksandar.

Again in small groups, the activists chart each institution's reaction—along a spectrum of varying degrees of positive, neutral, and negative—to significant political events, protests, actions, or moments in a chronology going back roughly ten years. Popovic told me that producing the power graph was always a key moment in the workshop. And so it was for this group of activists. What they found when they isolated the different pillars of the state was that their loyalty or attitude toward the regime had fluctuated over time. For example, parts of the educational establishment had been somewhat sympathetic to some of their actions, if only because students had participated. In other instances, the media had taken a slightly critical opinion of the government, if only slightly. By looking at the regime this way, the activists immediately understand two things: the regime is not a monolith, and its loyalties are malleable. "Loyalty is not carved in stone. It can be changed," says Dragana. "Loyalties can be shifted."

The Serbs stress that if you attack a part of the regime, the natural reaction is for the rest of the regime to rally around that portion that has been targeted. They perceive their own interests to be more aligned with the regime under attack than with your movement. "The goal will be to pull the pillars of the regime with persuasion, not to push them through attacks," says Aleksandar.

Some pillars are obviously more susceptible to persuasion than others. The military and the police are usually the last to come around. But then again, movements do not require the support of security services; they just require their ambivalence. And, as the Serbs explained, even the most thuggish cops can be neutralized.

During their struggle, the Serbs encountered one particularly brutal police chief. He operated with the impunity of a king in the small city where he was stationed. "He enjoyed beating people up, torturing them," says Dragana, pursing her lips in disgust. "He got off on it." So they figured they could not sway him, at least not directly.

Instead, they took photographs of him beating up young members of the movement. They had those photographs made into posters and put his name and cell phone number on them. Then they plastered them everywhere his wife shopped. They put the posters up on her route to the kindergarten where his child went to school. The posters urged people to call and ask him why he was torturing our children. His wife was appalled. The family would quickly become pariahs. "We didn't attack him in uniform," says Dragana. "We attacked him in his home through his wife. We weren't going to let this bastard hide behind the system or the badge."

The example resonated with the group. "There are these monstrous people, and they hide behind the seal of the regime," one activist responded. "This gives the regime a face." People nodded in agreement.

After each day's session, the activists would meet in their own groups to digest that day's lessons and analysis, debating the meanings for them. Clearly, the discussion was raising fundamental questions for some members of the group, very much the types of questions that the movement's leadership wanted discussed. "It's a shock for some of them," one of the leaders says to me. "Like, whoa, you mean we weren't doing everything right?" But the majority of the activists are engaged and eager to learn more.

One of the key sources of power for any regime is authority. The perception of authority alone—and the fear of defying it—are the causes of most people's obedience. So if a movement wants to encourage people to withdraw their consent, to interrupt their obedience to the regime, then undermining the regime's authority is a key objective. For Otpor, the answer was laughter. "Humor undermines the authority of the opponent. Humor is also the best cure against fear. Use it as much as you can," says Aleksandar. "Try to surprise the enemy. Use as many combinations of actions as possible. That is our strong recommendation."

Humor may, in fact, have been Otpor's signature weapon. Members of Otpor came up with countless ways to reduce the authority of the regime through humor and ridicule. One example involved turkeys. Milošević's wife, Mirjana, often liked to wear a white flower in her hair. Members of Otpor saw it as an opportunity. They got their hands on several turkeys and put white carnations on their heads. Then they released them in downtown. The turkeys walked down the city streets. Anyone who saw a turkey with a white carnation would immediately know it was a reference to Milošević's wife. (As Dragana points out, laughing, "In Serbia, calling a woman a turkey is one of the worst things you can do.") Police were dispatched to apprehend the turkeys. Members of Otpor were at the ready to snap photographs of police officers desperately trying to corral the birds. When they eventually did, the turkeys were taken down to a local police station. Anticipating this, Otpor immediately issued a call for the turkeys' release, saying that they had been unlawfully arrested and they had reason to fear for the birds' safety.

CANVAS's trainers call this and similar stunts dilemma actions. When done correctly, they are low risk and put the focus on what your opponent will or will not do. "The purpose of these actions is to create a dilemma for the adversary," Aleksandar explains to the group. "The actions create a dilemma for the police, who are forced to choose between two unfavorable choices. They can't let a turkey mocking the president's wife walk around. But they know they look like fools chasing a turkey." Anyone who is asked to chase turkeys in a city's downtown is going to lose respect for the regime. And the regime itself hardly looks intimidating when its police are left herding birds. "At that point, we didn't have a way to listen to their communications," says Aleksandar, still laughing, "but I would have loved to have heard them call this one in to headquarters."

The Middle Eastern activists left the room to try to design some of their own dilemma actions. Meanwhile, I talked with Dragana about her time as a CANVAS trainer. Of the forty workshops she had helped lead, she said a group of Bolivians was one of the most impressive. They learned fast, maybe too fast. "On the fourth day, we came into the room, and they had put newspapers on all the chairs. The newspaper was reporting on the front page an action they had done that night, after the workshop! I came in and they said, 'Look what we did!'" she recalled. "A lot of times [after the workshops], I find out later what they have done, and I say, 'Oh my God, they were planning that all along.'"

Sometimes plans backfire, too. Dragana told me about one group of Iranians who failed to think through everything. There were shortages of gasoline in Iran at the time, and the group thought this was an issue they could exploit. "These guys planned to hold a silent protest at gas stations. The plan was to line up at gas stations holding empty containers," she recalled. "What they failed to predict was how fast [bystanders] would join in. There were two hundred people at one gas station in an hour. The number kept growing, and riots started. They burned sixty gas stations." The problem is that the action quickly grew to include people who were not part of the movement, so there was no way for members to maintain nonviolent discipline. Later, Dragana heard from members of the Iranian diaspora who were happy with the whole episode. She was appalled. "No, no," she said. "This is not what I taught them. Burning gas stations will not help their cause."

Of course, there are some groups that CANVAS simply refuses to work alongside. In one instance, while in Johannesburg, CAN-VAS was contacted by a member of the British consulate. The official wanted to contract with CANVAS to work in the Kingdom of Swaziland, which has been ruled by the same corrupt family for decades. The problem was CANVAS wouldn't have been working with a home-grown movement; it would have been nonviolent struggle by proxy. "He said money is no object," recalls Dragana, laughing. "Well, that's nice, but that is not how we operate. We are not mercenaries."

As the seminar continued, the focus shifted to evaluating some of the movement's own actions. The activists had achieved a number of successes. Through sheer persistence, they had won the ability to operate in certain areas and neighborhoods that would have been unthinkable eighteen months earlier. They had also earned the support of several well-known and respected academics, who had lent their names and reputations to the cause. They had a strong brand, and the movement's numbers had grown. But after listening to the trainers, the activists realized another mistake they had made. They had operated with a siege mentality for so long they had forgotten to declare their victories. It is not just a matter of morale boosting. Declaring victory is an important opportunity to communicate with the public and build credibility. "When we were accommodated, we never publicized it as a victory," one of the activists said. "We never marked it with a big V. That was a mistake."

The Serbs referred to it as "doing postproduction." "Everything you do should be capitalized," says Aleksandar. "First of all, proclaim the victory. Second, be sure that potential members and supporters know about it. You need a victory every week, even small victories. If you are on the defensive, you lose.

"You always need to be a step ahead. You need to answer the what-if," Aleksandar continued, reinforcing the need for advance planning, something that had become a mantra over the course of the week. "Do your homework, choose a target, and build a winning record."

At the end of the seminar, the Serbs stayed for an extra couple of days for some sun and sand. They wanted to spend time relaxing on the nicer beaches, a world away on the other side of the island.

The activists had to get home. They took the short cab ride to the airport and caught one of the last flights out. A few weeks later their country had waves of marches and demonstrations. They were the largest protests in a generation.

CHAPTER 8 THE TECHNOCRATS

||

Peeople had been asked to assemble at 2:00 p.m. No one knew who had issued the call. A group, identifying itself only as the "organizers of China Jasmine Rallies," had posted a message on Boxun, a Chinese-language news Web site based in the United States. It read, "We call upon each Chinese person who has a dream for China to bravely come out to take an afternoon stroll at two o'clock on Sundays to look around. Each person who joins will make clear to the Chinese ruling party that if it does not fight corruption, if the government does not accept their supervision, the Chinese people will not have the patience to wait any longer." The calls for a "Jasmine Revolution"—borrowing the name from the revolution in Tunisia a month earlier—quickly spread to other Web sites and on the Chinese equivalent of Twitter. The group behind the message identified specific locations in Beijing, Shanghai, Tianjin, and more than a dozen other major cities around the country where people were to come out for a "stroll."

The designated spot in Beijing was a two-story McDonald's in Wangfujing, an upscale shopping area not far from the Forbidden City and Tiananmen Square. On the second Sunday of protests, a friend and I arrived at the McDonald's more than an hour before the appointed time. If you did not already know that the revolutions in the Middle East had frayed the nerves of the country's leadership, visiting Wangfujing that afternoon made it abundantly clear. Police and security officers were everywhere. Hundreds of blue-uniformed police officers had been deployed to just one block. Some were patrolling up and down the street; others stood on the sidewalk or in doorways, staring at each and every person walking past. Security volunteers, wearing red armbands, supplemented their numbers. And, adding to the show of force, plainclothes officers mixed among the people; the number of undercover police was overwhelming. At moments, in the crowds, almost every third person seemed to have an earpiece and wire coming out from under his shirt.

We ducked into the McDonald's. As on any day, the fast-food restaurant was busy and filled with customers. Ten or twenty years ago, as a foreigner traveling in China, you grew accustomed to having Chinese gawk at you for no other reason than you were foreign. That is seldom the case today, especially in cosmopolitan places like Beijing. But on this particular day, as soon as we walked inside, most of the patrons stared at us across their trays of food. A fair number of them had crew cuts and earpieces, too.

We took our burgers and fries to the second floor to kill some time. After we had been sitting for a few minutes, two bulky, stern-looking men sat at the table next to us. They weren't wearing uniforms or earpieces, but they were clearly with the Public Security Bureau, as it is called in China. Their boots were military issue, and they ate their burgers in silence.

We remained as long as we could, but after we finished our meals, it became awkward to sit next to the security officers. Plus, it was getting close to 2:00 p.m., so we decided to return to the street. As we approached the stairs, I noticed five thuggish-looking guys at a table at the top of the landing, staring out across the restaurant, expression-less. Halfway down the stairs, I stopped and looked back up. One of the men had pulled out a small video camera and was taping us exiting the restaurant. He saw me catch him filming and smiled.

Back outside, the number of people milling about was growing. It was impossible to say whether the people walking up and down the street had come for the protest or were simply Sunday shoppers. That was the brilliance of the tactic the organizers had chosen. In places as politically restrictive as China, people going to the streets with banners or bullhorns to challenge the ruling regime do not last long. A frontal attack on the Chinese Communist Party is almost never tolerated; such protesters are hauled away to be imprisoned, "reeducated," or never heard from again. In contrast, the call for people to "take an afternoon stroll" struck the balance of putting the regime on edge without asking people to take an unnecessary risk. Indeed, it is a tactic with some history. In 1980, members of Poland's Solidarity movement learned that the Communist regime intended to fire on them when they went on a planned strike in the Gdańsk shipyards. So rather than begin with a ploy that might provoke the police and snuff out the burgeoning movement, they took the less confrontational approach of strolling in large numbers in public places. As in Poland, Chinese authorities were being put in the awkward position of trying to prevent a demonstration that wasn't even happening.

The afternoon took on a surreal quality as more and more people turned up, walking slowly in a loop on the block or two near the McDonald's. It is hard to characterize the crowd as a whole. The people were neither predominantly young nor predominantly old; no one stood out. Some were stylishly dressed; others looked like everyday Beijingers. By far, the regime's police officers and security personnel were the largest group there. The second-largest contingent was probably the throng of foreign journalists who had shown up, curious to see if anything would happen. But the sidewalks began to clog as the crowds of Chinese steadily grew. Many, even most, of these people may have been unaware of the call for a Middle East–inspired protest. Just as likely, they were curious about why so many police officers had been deployed to this high-end shopping district, and as people stopped to stare, it had the effect of making more people do the same.

By 2:30 p.m., the Chinese authorities had begun to demonstrate their expertise in crowd-control techniques. Ahead of the day's event, the authorities had narrowed the public space in front of the McDonald's by erecting wooden barricades that read, "Street Repair." (Of course, there was no construction evident.) No one was allowed to stop and gape for long. Police kept people moving, channeling the crowd in one direction and then redirecting it in another. A large sanitation vehicle began to spray the street with high-pressure jets of water; it circled back and forth, cleaning the same street corner again and again, preventing anyone from lingering. Police officers with German shepherds and Rottweilers ensured that people stayed on the sidewalks. Roads leading to the intersection were roped off, preventing more crowds from joining us. An exit from a mall near the McDonald's was closed. I kept making loops up and down the block: down one side, then across the street, and up the other. I would see the same people again and again as the security officers moved us as if in some elaborate, choreographed ballet. Similar scenes reportedly occurred in Shanghai and other cities, where the police presence was equally impressive. In Urumqi, the capital of restive Xinjiang Province, almost no citizens were allowed near the protest site.

The regime's heavy-handed response revealed its own worries that the protests ripping through authoritarian regimes in North Africa and the Middle East could somehow find their way to China. There was no hint of revolution in the air in February 2011, but China's leaders intended to take no chances. Even before the first Sunday stroll, dozens of dissidents and human rights lawyers were rounded up and preemptively detained. Some were held under house arrest; others simply disappeared for weeks. China's president, Hu Jintao, called together provincial, ministerial, and top military leaders for a special study session at the Central Party School in Beijing on how the regime should tailor its tools for "social management." All the members of the Politburo Standing Committee—the nine most powerful men in China—attended Hu's speech at the meeting, which underlined the importance of tightening the regime's control of information. The Chinese characters for "jasmine" had already been blocked from the Internet. People's ability to send text messages to multiple recipients was suspended. Boxun, the Chinese-language Web site, came under attack and was temporarily shut down. In a more conciliatory gesture, Premier Wen Jiabao held a Sunday morning Internet chat in which he pledged to sideline corrupt officials, rein in mounting inflation, and ensure that the fruit of China's economic growth was more evenly distributed.

But when an authoritarian regime is rattled and insecure, it has a tendency to extend its ordinary prohibitions even further. In early 2011, China was no different. The organizers behind the anonymous protests had been shrewd to latch onto the "Jasmine Revolution" label. The name obviously linked their effort to the revolution in Tunisia, where the rebellions against Arab autocrats had begun. But the jasmine flower has deep resonance and symbolism in Chinese culture as well. The white flower appears frequently in Chinese paintings dating back hundreds of years. Almost immediately, renditions of "Mo Li Hua," a popular ode to the jasmine flower from the eighteenth century, were deleted from Web sites. These included videos of Hu and his predecessor, Jiang Zemin, belting out the tune. (The folk song is so popular it was played during the medal ceremonies at the 2008 Beijing Olympics and at the opening ceremony of the 2010 Shanghai Expo.) Authorities followed by imposing a ban on jasmines in Beijing florists and the city's flower markets. Vendors were told to report people showing interest in buying the now-controversial flower. In such a politically charged environment, the mere mention of "jasmines" became something to be avoided. In my meetings with party officials, no one would even say the word, preferring to refer to "that flower."

Outside China, the People's Republic is perceived as an economic powerhouse. And rightly so: the Chinese government's economic performance since beginning reforms in 1978 is nothing short of spectacular. For thirty years, China has averaged more than 9 percent growth. At that pace, the Chinese economy has doubled in size every eight years. In 2010, it surpassed Japan as the world's second-largest economy, a position Japan had held for much of the last four decades. Most economists expect China to surpass the United States as the world's largest economy in the next fifteen to twenty years. When Deng Xiaoping first launched the country's reform era, China's economy was less than 8 percent the size of the U.S. economy.

The significance of this extraordinary growth has been greatest for the people of China themselves. More than 300 million Chinese citizens—essentially the population of the United States—have risen from absolute poverty in this time. Today, China has a vibrant middle class that makes its home in new urban boomtowns. The country can also boast a burgeoning class of wealthy and superrich elites. In 2010, the value of IPOs on Chinese stock markets was more than three times greater than that of those in New York. China has more than 800,000 millionaires and 65 billionaires, second only to the United States. In the summer of 2011, as the Standard & Poor's rating agency was downgrading the creditworthiness of the U.S. government, the Communist country's leaders—after a fair amount of gloating—

expressed their faith in American capitalism. After all, as the largest foreign lender to the United States, China wants to protect its investment. (At the time, the U.S. government owed each Chinese citizen roughly $900—and rising.) To be sure, the Chinese economy has no shortage of risks and frailties, including rising inflation, a housing bubble, and institutionalized corruption. Nevertheless, for a country of 1.3 billion people, the Chinese Communist Party has led the most astonishing economic achievement of not just our generation but any generation.

Yet for all the superlatives and accomplishments, China hardly behaves like a confident power. Its image as a modern economic colossus obscures an equally true picture of an insecure regime constantly tamping down the forces it believes could lead to its destruction. Indeed, it is fair to say that no regime thinks more about its own demise than the Chinese Communist Party. China's leaders, judging by their actions, policies, and statements, are fixated on the weaknesses that run through their political system. It is an insecurity that manifests itself in ways that can in one instance be trivial and in another terrifying. Internationally, a representative of China is now one of the most important people in the room, whether the setting is the G20, the World Bank, or Davos. But domestically, it is a regime that mobilizes thousands of police because someone writes on a foreign Web site that Chinese citizens should "go for a stroll."

Thus, today, two statements are true. The Chinese Communist Party is the largest, wealthiest, and most powerful political organization in the world. And it is also afraid of a flower.

"If Today Is Better Than Yesterday . . ."

Mikhail Gorbachev's plane landed in Beijing on May 15, 1989. The occasion was a long-planned summit between the Soviet leader and Deng Xiaoping to heal the enmities that had roiled the relationship between these two Communist neighbors for decades. Both leaders sought a well-choreographed diplomatic triumph. The timing could not have been worse. Gorbachev was arriving as Deng and the Chinese leadership were facing the greatest popular rebellion since the regime's founding in 1949. Tiananmen Square, the heart of the

People's Republic, had been overrun by peaceful demonstrators. A movement that began with calls for reform, lower inflation, and an end to corruption had quickly intensified; students, workers, pensioners, monks, taxicab drivers, businesspeople, even schoolchildren, now shouted slogans and held banners demanding Deng's resignation. In a clever play on Deng's name, Xiaoping, which in Chinese sounds like the words for "little bottle," people smashed glass bottles on the pavement. In a makeshift tent city built in the square, three thousand students began hunger strikes demanding democratic reform.

The uprising threw the three-day summit into disarray. The welcoming ceremony was hastily moved from Tiananmen Square to the airport. Chinese authorities were so distracted they failed to roll out the red carpet for Gorbachev. His tour of the Forbidden City and the imperial palace had to be scrapped. He was smuggled through a service entrance into the Great Hall of the People in order to attend his meeting with President Yang Shangkun. Gorbachev's presence only seemed to feed the protests, in part because his introduction of new political and intellectual freedoms in the Soviet Union had marked him as a reformer. Some protesters held signs that read, "In the Soviet Union, They Have Gorbachev. What Do We Have?" By the last day of the summit, more than a million Chinese citizens had occupied the square.

What followed is well known. Around 9:00 p.m. on June 3, tanks and armored personnel carriers began to rumble forward. On Deng's order, heavily armed troops from the Twenty-Seventh Army and hardened soldiers loyal to China's paramount leader attacked their own people. As they carved a path through Beijing, breaking through barricades of buses, debris, and overturned cabs set out by the protesters, the troops lashed out indiscriminately. Infantry armed with AK-47s fired on civilians at close range; some civilians were even bayoneted. Soldiers gunned down crowds and shot randomly at people who were visible in apartment buildings as they passed. Beijing's hospitals were soon overwhelmed by the dead and the wounded. By early in the morning of June 4, the morgues were, too, as bodies, mainly of young men, piled up. At 2:30 a.m., troops had sealed off three sides of Tiananmen Square, and the students who remained fled as riot police moved in to crush the final remnants of the protest. The soldiers tore down the tent city that had been the students' home for weeks, destroying with it the thirty-seven-foot foam-and-plaster sculpture that had become known as the Goddess of Democracy. Before dawn, the People's Liberation Army had reoccupied the square. The Avenue of Eternal Peace, one of the routes the tanks took to Tiananmen, was stained in blood.

It was a horrendous and appalling act. The party and its leadership had been shaken to the core by the uprising. In the aftermath, the regime conducted a purge of those who had been sympathetic to the demonstrators, which included Deng's own protégé. And the protests in Tiananmen Square were not the only shock the party would experience in 1989. That same summer, the Soviet Empire began to crumble. Indeed, on the day that Deng unleashed his military on China's citizenry, Poles went to the ballot box to vote the Polish Communist Party out of power. Five months later the Berlin Wall came down. On Christmas Day 1991, Gorbachev signed his resignation, becoming the last general secretary of the Soviet Communist Party.

These twin shocks—the Tiananmen Square protests and the collapse of the Soviet Union—served as a wake-up call for the Chinese regime. It was a near-death experience that would remake the social compact between China's rulers and its people. In the years that followed, Beijing did not respond by turning inward, becoming a police state, or cutting itself off from the world. Instead, the party launched a meticulous study of communism's failings and altered its own formula for maintaining power. Teams of researchers were dispatched to Russia, eastern Europe, and central Asia to study the former regimes and conduct a postmortem on the errors that led to their extinction. The party understood after Tiananmen that Gorbachev's failure could also become its own.

The catalog of the Soviet Union's mistakes was thick. Its economy was hidebound. Living conditions had fallen hopelessly behind the West—a secret that was long in plain view. When faced with its own vulnerabilities, Moscow became more doctrinaire and imperious in its ideology. The lack of nuance and innovation likewise infected the Soviet bureaucracy and its party organs, which became ossified, top-heavy, and remote from the lives of the people. In sum, the Soviet Union's cancer had grown from the inefficiency and rigidity of totalitarianism. In such a weakened state, Gorbachev's early experiments in political reform opened a process that he could not control, accelerating the regime's demise. In retrospect, China's neighbor to the north had offered a case study in how not to run a Communist dictatorship.

China was already more than a decade into its economic reforms when the Soviet Union collapsed, and the event only cemented Deng's decision to pursue economic liberalization—not political reform—as a first step. But the reforms and adjustments the party embarked on went beyond economics. China's ruling party struck a broad new bargain with its people.

The fact is that most Chinese have a far freer life today than ever before. Chinese citizens increasingly live where they want and with whom they want. Limits on one's personal lifestyle have all but disappeared. In the past two decades, more than 200 million people have opted to move from the countryside to one of China's new metropolises. They can own property, maybe even a car, and choose their own career or line of work. A generation ago, few if any Chinese tour groups would have been spotted in Europe or Hawaii. In 2010, over fifty-five million Chinese tourists traveled abroad, more than twice the number from five years earlier.

Even if they are not part of the growing middle class, Chinese citizens have access to more and better information than ever before. The commercialization of Chinese media has led to a lively news and entertainment environment, with newspapers, magazines, and television stations pushing the boundaries to compete for audiences. As long as journalists tread carefully, government censors remain silent. Likewise, more personal communication tools—from smart phones to a Chinese version of Twitter—have become a part of everyday life. On the Internet, Chinese surf their favorite Web sites, go shopping, or play video games. And, perhaps most welcome of all, the Chinese Communist Party shows almost no interest in controlling people's private lives. The party, unlike a couple of decades ago, no longer hounds citizens about their "socialist purity."

To be sure, freer does not mean free. Freedom of assembly and association remains within tightly drawn red lines, and breaching them can trigger a frighteningly harsh response. Censors keep a firm handle on media accounts that could embarrass the regime. The party's control of political decision making is opaque and nearly total. Organized political opposition and independent labor unions are banned. Minorities, especially Tibetans and Muslims in Xinjiang Province, are routinely repressed. Oddly, given the regime's Communist roots, overall, individual freedoms have grown for most Chinese, while wider political freedoms remain constrained. But in general the same rule applies across all areas of modern Chinese life: as long as you do not threaten the party's monopoly on power, you can go about your business and maybe even prosper.

For an autocratic regime set on maintaining its power, the party is remarkably open to where it finds the tools to sustain itself. Indeed, beyond learning from communism's failings, it also studies and borrows ideas from democracy's success. China has implemented a wide array of reforms—including term limits, local elections, public hearings, and participatory budgeting—in an attempt to win greater acceptance of its rule. Of course, the party rarely adopts anything wholesale, preferring to take the slice that best suits its needs without jeopardizing its legitimacy. "We don't waste our time with what is capitalism or what is socialism," one adviser to the party's leadership told me. "If today is better than yesterday, then I like the policy."

Having shed its Communist ideological straitjacket, the party understands that its legitimacy stems from its ability to perform—especially when it comes to keeping the country's economy humming. Rather than viewing private entrepreneurs as a threat, the party has welcomed the country's professionals and leading businesspeople into the fold. A party that was founded as a platform for workers and peasants is now largely a coalition of government, economic, and social elites. As a result, many of the groups most likely to be at odds with the regime—intellectuals, students, and middle-class professionals—have become allies. As one Chinese scholar in Beijing recently told me, "People are more conservative than in 1989. There would be no 'Goddess to Democracy' statue today."

The party's approach has never been a strategy of liberalization for liberalization's sake. If there was one other lesson that China's rulers took from Gorbachev and the Soviet Union's collapse, it is the danger of flirting with democratic reform. After the Tiananmen Square protests, Jiang Zemin, the Shanghai party secretary, was elevated to be Deng's new successor. His promotion was based in part on how effectively he had combated large-scale protests in Shanghai. The following year, in a meeting with Henry Kissinger, Jiang warned, "Efforts to find a Chinese Gorbachev will be of no avail." Indeed, anyone with those leanings had been rooted out. In April 1992, even as Deng committed China to greater economic reforms, he made it clear that this path should not be misinterpreted as a political opening. The *People's Daily* quoted him saying that "liberalism and turmoil destroy stability" and that "as soon as elements of turmoil appear, we will not hesitate to use any means whatsoever to eliminate them as quickly as possible." The party has hewed closely to this pledge ever since.

A few months after the calls for a Jasmine Revolution, some of the lawyers and activists who had been detained or kidnapped in February began to be released. As a group, these legal advocates are not easily cowed. They have already braved years of illegal detentions, beatings, and sometimes torture. These abuses hadn't dissuaded them from speaking out in the past, often about the very indignities their captors had inflicted on them. But this time it appeared to be different. There was an ominous silence from most of these typically vocal regime critics. The fact that many seemed so reluctant to speak out left many wondering just what type of pressure or abuse they had endured while imprisoned. After being detained and released after only two days, one well-known lawyer, Li Xiongbing, tweeted, "I'm really afraid right now; please don't try to reach me, okay?" China's repression since Tiananmen is no less real or brutal; it is simply more calculated and discreet.

Talking About a Revolution

In the evening, long after all the crowds had left Wangfujing, I took a cab to the Jasmine Restaurant & Lounge. The modern, fusion-style restaurant is on the east side of the Workers' Stadium, in the Chaoyang District of Beijing. A friend who had passed by earlier in the day tipped me off. He had seen that people had left flowers in front of the restaurant and scribbled messages supportive of the protests in chalk. Someone had told the authorities, too. By the time I arrived, the flowers were gone and the messages scrubbed away. Nevertheless, I went inside to speak to the frazzled manager, who probably could not believe his misfortune in having a business with a name that was now associated with democratic revolution. He denied that anyone had left flowers or notes in front of his establishment. But he had heard from the police, who told him to contact them if anyone tried anything. He was clearly anxious about my questions and relieved to see me go.

In February 2011, it was immediately obvious that some party members had not yet wrapped their minds around the significance of the revolutions moving through the Middle East. I met with one well-known Chinese academic ten days after Hosni Mubarak had been ousted. Because of the sensitivity of the moment, he asked that we speak off the record. Indeed, he did not even want to meet at his university office. Instead, he chose a coffee shop in a Beijing shopping center.

He began by reciting the ways in which the events in Egypt bore no resemblance to the conditions in China. Mubarak's government had been completely unprepared for a popular uprising. The protests in Egypt had been propelled by the economy, but the economy in China was performing better than anywhere. "And, third, it is cultural. You have to understand that Chinese culture is an ancient culture, and—"

I cut him off. "I'm sorry. What about Egypt? I mean, wouldn't you say Egyptian culture is an ancient one?"

He blushed even before I spoke. It dawned on him the moment the words came out of his mouth that he was walking into a blind alley. This old talking point—that an ancient culture like China's would somehow be inured to democratic forces—seemed out of place as the land of the pharaohs clamored for representative government. It had been a reflexive response. He closed his eyes for a moment, as if to make a mental note not to repeat this line of reasoning when discussing Egypt.

I brought up the obvious point that the Chinese regime appeared to be nervous, even on edge. The wave of preemptive arrests of lawyers and human rights advocates suggested as much. When the Chinese media did cover the events unfolding in North Africa or the Middle East, they played up the dangers of chaos and unrest, not the underlying democratic demands that had given rise to the wave of popular rebellions. If it wasn't something they found alarming, why censor it? He was not interested in speculating about the regime's disposition, replying with a terse acknowledgment: "Yes."

His own fears were focused not on the threat of unrest but on the government's ability to respond. "This generation of leaders have never faced a crisis," he replied. "They are more reformist than Brezhnev or Mubarak, but they are technocrats, so they think in terms of procedure and they make small fixes."

He was offering a take I had heard often from everyday citizens who had a romantic nostalgia for the epic, if deeply flawed, leaders from China's past. In his view, China's leaders might be precisely the types of political figures to fight rising inflation or take the air out of a housing bubble, but no one could say how they would respond to a crisis that struck at the regime's legitimacy. They were untested. "They have much more economic resources and money to deal with a crisis than Deng," he continued. "But they are less tough, more selfish, and lack the strategic vision. What is decisive is what you do in the moment."

No matter what one thinks of China's leaders past or present, there is no question the current crop are a bland, colorless version of their predecessors. Only two men in modern China's history—Mao Zedong and Deng Xiaoping—have had the revolutionary credentials and force of personality to sit astride all of China. Chairman Mao, for all the suffering and torment he caused the Chinese people, was the founder. He was one of the most charismatic figures of the twentieth century, and only his own death could put an end to his reign as China's modern-day emperor. Like Mao, Deng had fought the Japanese, survived the Long March, and commanded Communist troops in the civil war that expelled Chiang Kai-shek's Nationalists to Taiwan. A feisty and independent native of Sichuan, Deng was known for expectorating into a spittoon, sometimes while meeting other world leaders. Deng's greatest feat may have been not surviving China's civil war but Mao himself. The Great Helmsman's mass campaigns and calls for "permanent revolution" had a way of culling the party's senior leaders. Twice Mao purged Deng from power. And twice Deng was rehabilitated. Within a year of Mao's death in September 1976, Deng had been reappointed to all of his former positions. Two years later, he launched the economic reforms that put China back on the world stage.

No Chinese leader today can offer a similar pedigree. They are apparatchiks and bureaucrats, not revolutionaries and guerrilla fighters. Even a figure as senior as President Hu Jintao must lead by building careful consensus. As a result, no man is bigger than the party he serves. China is led by a collective leadership, not a strongman. For most Chinese, the shift looks like progress. Having witnessed the price China paid during the Cultural Revolution, people find a more institutionalized system appealing, inasmuch as it is less likely to be hostage to the whims of a single man. After Deng's death in 1997, the party implemented new norms for leadership succession. China's top two leaders—the president and the premier—now serve for two five-year terms before passing their posts to the next generation of leaders who rise to the positions after intense internal jockeying, all of it behind closed doors. Thus, in 2012, Hu Jintao and Wen Jiabao are expected to pass the baton to Xi Jinping and Li Keqiang, two men that few Chinese know much about.

The danger, in the view of this Chinese academic, who is a foreign policy expert, is that the system is not producing the senior leaders the regime most requires. The men who are likely to rise in such a political machine are cautious, risk-averse, bureaucratic survivors notable less for their brilliance than for their ability not to offend or threaten any powerful faction that could stymie their rise. Buttoned-up technocrats with red ties and dyed black hair might make for good finance ministers, but how would they respond to the party's next existential crisis? "We have had many great dynasties. For the first fifty to eighty years, they are led by great people. But then, gradually, they . . ." The professor stopped himself, his voice trailing off.

Another party member I sat down with was more sanguine. He is a leading expert on the Middle East for the party and has traveled there for the last twenty-five years. He was following the events in Egypt closely and could even recite the day, time, and order in which Egyptian generals had gone to Tahrir Square to attempt to mollify the protesters. When I walked into the InterContinental Hotel for our appointment, he had already claimed a table in the hotel's restaurant. Chain-smoking from a pack of Double Happiness cigarettes, he confessed he was tired because he had been in wall-to-wall meetings for weeks. Everyone in the senior reaches of the party wanted a briefing on what was behind the revolutions in the Arab world. "We've been surprised, totally surprised, in terms of the size and scale," he told me right away. "We have a problem even divining what to call it. Some say it is a movement of democracy. Some say it is a movement of youth. Some say it is a demand for a better life. We are very concerned and watching very closely."

Since he was the expert, I asked him what he thought: Why now? Why did these revolutions erupt when they did? "Any population with 60 percent of its people under thirty is like something floating," he replied, "and you don't know which way it will go.

"My personal belief is that there are so many causes: thirty years of autocratic rule, demographics, unemployment, the economy. But a very important factor was the computer, Facebook, and Twitter," he continued. "It's the twenty-first century! People are very conscious of democracy and freedom. The combination of all these factors made everything go out of control. All of a sudden everything that was impossible seemed possible."

In his view, the regime had established the right mix of controls to keep a lid on instability. Unlike Egypt and other Arab autocracies, the party understood the importance of changing the set of faces that sat atop the regime. (At one point, the analyst laughed, just thinking about Mubarak's method. "I mean, thirty years with one guy in charge? Who does that anymore?") China's tight control of the Internet had clearly been a wise policy given the role it had played in helping young Arab protesters organize. The party was working to improve people's lives and respond to social demands as quickly as possible, he said. And the calls for a Jasmine Revolution did not worry him much. "We have seen some effects. Some people have thought they could use the same means [in China]," he said. "But we don't have Facebook, and that is our advantage."

Did he think the government was up to the challenge of maintaining stability? "It requires the highest skill," he said. "I always tell [the leadership] that development itself does not mean stability. At this moment, the Chinese way is the best. It's not perfect, but it's the best. It doesn't mean the system doesn't need to improve."

———

Democracy Is a Good Thing

Not long before I visited him in his office in Beijing, Yu Keping had published an article arguing that Communist Party leaders should make clear that the constitution and its laws, not the party, are supreme. His biggest claim to fame is a 2006 essay, "Democracy Is a Good Thing," that argued that "even if people have the best food, clothing, housing, and transport but no democratic rights they still do not have complete human dignity."

Yu is not some dissident intellectual, however. Far from it. He is a Communist Party member and deputy director of the Central Compilation and Translation Bureau and is said to have a line to President Hu Jintao. In the past, the bureau's main task has been translating works by Chinese leaders or classic Marxist texts like *Das Kapital* and *The Communist Manifesto*. Today, despite its drab setting and uninspiring name, it has also become a hothouse of innovation for the ruling party. Sitting in his office framed by a wall of books, Yu makes clear right away that his definition of democracy should not be confused with Western-style democracy. Most Westerners he meets think very little of the political reforms in China because they equate democracy with a multiparty system and the direct election of a president. They are wrong, he says. "There is an enormous divide in our opinions and Western opinions," Yu tells me. "China's change is huge not only economically but politically as well."

Yu believes the shift to a collective leadership and the introduction of term limits are important signs of progress, but those are not the political changes he has in mind. He is thinking about change at the grassroots level, in villages and townships across the country. "The changes in my eyes are as follows," he says. "In terms of elections, we have had massive change. For the first time in thousands of years, we have village elections in China. It is not a direct election, but they can recommend people, and they can be elected. We have a hearing system. For the first time, the rule of law has been written into China's constitution. In a lot of places, the local people can sue the government, and this too is unprecedented in thousands of years of Chinese history. In recent years, you see China has established an administrative law. These are all milestones."

All the democratic mechanisms Yu cited—elections, public hearings, the right to sue the government, and so on—have in fact been instituted, but in measured doses, or else they have not been permitted to advance beyond the most local levels, where they can be prevented from posing a threat to the party's political monopoly. But Yu thinks this is as it should be. "In the information age, the top task for the government is to better their political system," he says. "If you change from one-party rule to a multiparty system and there is chaos, then that is no good." He believes the party is on the cusp of a new phase of its rule, moving from a period when "to serve the people" was "only a slogan" to something more substantive. "The first thirty years [of the People's Republic] was political struggle. The second thirty years was economic development. The next thirty years, I predict, is gradually transforming from economic reforms to political and social reforms. I think our objective is good governance."

Yu is actually attempting to help foster this change from the bottom up. He runs an institute housed within the bureau that rewards innovations in local democracy across the country. Since the program began in 2000, more than fifteen hundred local government initiatives have competed for recognition. Ten winners are picked every two years. In 2010, Yu's institute recognized a program in Qingdao that developed an innovative public opinion polling system to measure government performance. Another winner was the Open Decision-Making Program in Hangzhou, which began broadcasting government meetings and public hearings on the Internet to encourage public participation. Hangzhou saw nearly a 12 percent drop in citizen grievances against the local government after the first year. Other programs involved improved health-care systems in Fujian and new day-care centers for the children of migrants in Shaanxi Province. By bringing these local efforts national recognition, Yu aims to encourage other local governments to develop their own creative programs and reforms to improve the delivery of basic services.

Part of Yu's motivation may come from the fact that he begins from a premise that many others do not share. "The people have the right to take power from the party if they do not take care of the people," he tells me. "Our ruling power is not forever." The revolutions that were toppling Arab autocrats, in his opinion, revealed the necessity of the work he is doing. "The lesson we can learn from the chaos in Middle Eastern countries is the need for better public service and people's participation—transparency, accountability, and social justice."

Lai Hairong, the deputy director of another institute within the Central Compilation and Translation Bureau, agrees with the need for more democratic forms of governance at the local level. With a Ph.D. from the Central European University in Budapest, he is intimately familiar with the mistakes made in the old Soviet Empire. Lai, an expert on China's local election experiments, is clear-eyed and not hesitant to contradict the official line on some recent political events. (For example, when discussing the "color revolutions," Lai tells me, "Well, to me, it very obviously was an indigenous [revolution], not the result of outside influence.") Whereas the party has done an exceptionally good job implementing economic reforms, he believes its implementation of reform within the party is far from complete. It is still "too top-down in structure and hierarchical." People want to be more involved in the process of governing, he believes. They have more information at their disposal, and they want to participate. Therefore, the local government innovations like the ones that Yu Keping and his colleagues are publicizing are vital. "[These programs] are the mechanism of getting more people involved in the political process so that the work is based on consensus rather than on power," says Lai. "It's not a question of whether these mechanisms will be introduced or not; it is only a question of when and in which way. Is it very gradual, peaceful, and progressive? Or is this process accompanied with messy events? But you have to do it."

One of the most striking aspects of these "reforms," "innovations," or "mechanisms" is that they are all democratic. In nearly every instance, the method or procedure being imported, tailored, and implemented is a regular feature of democracies around the world. As Yu and Lai both explained, the purpose is by no means to bring about a full-scale Chinese democracy; rather, the aim is to make the government more responsive, improve the delivery of social services, and win the public's trust to enhance the durability of the Chinese Communist Party's rule. The notion that these reforms would result in a true competition for power is not a consideration; indeed, it is a risk to be managed in exchange for the benefits that flow to the regime for ruling through greater consensus. It is democratic innovation in the service of Chinese authoritarianism.

The idea of trying to save the Chinese political system by introducing elements fundamentally at odds with it is not a new one. In the late nineteenth century, with the Qing dynasty in decline, reform-minded officials known as "self-strengtheners" developed a unique framework for instilling new life into the flagging dynasty. The concept, known by the shorthand *ti-yong*, referred to a dichotomy between "essence" *(ti)* and "practical use" *(yong)*. These officials lobbied the Qing emperor to adopt foreign know-how and practical expertise to preserve the spirit of the Confucian state. Foreign knowledge of technical fields—such as steelmaking, shipbuilding, and the assembly of military munitions—could be imported in order to prop up the dynasty, all the while cabining off Western influences from contaminating those unique elements that made the Chinese system Chinese. It was a strategy that permitted the adoption of the new to preserve the old. And it may have worked for some time. Although Karl Marx famously predicted in the late 1850s that the Qing dynasty would soon collapse, it sputtered forward until 1911.

Near the end of our meeting, I suggested this analogy to Yu Keping. Admittedly, the Qing dynasty—unlike modern China—was far weaker than the Western powers and facing financial ruin. But in terms of politics and governance, wasn't China again looking abroad to import foreign innovations to prop up its own political system? He shook his head. China was doing something far more ambitious than those Qing officials of old.

"I don't agree with you," Yu replied. "The *ti* was part of the problem. China is going its own way. It is different from the Soviet Union, the United States, Singapore, or other Asian countries. We are changing the *ti*."

Back to School

If Yu is right, and the goal is to change the Chinese "essence" of governance, it also requires changing how some Chinese officials think. The party has embarked on an ambitious effort to give its public officials the training, skills, and expertise they need to administer and

govern the increasingly complex situations that test the regime's resil-
ience. Part of this schooling involves sending some of the regime's rising stars abroad to study in specially designed programs at the world's
finest universities. More than a decade ago, the first crop of promising
young officials were sent to Harvard. Today, the Chinese government
has expanded the program to include Stanford, Oxford, Cambridge,
the University of Tokyo, and many more. "This was a big decision,"
says Lu Mai, the head of the China Development Research Foundation, who oversees the program. "We have already sent more than
four thousand [officials]. I don't know any other country that sends on
this scale."

The sixty-four-year-old Lu is perhaps a natural to steer a study-
abroad program for Chinese officials. He was in his last year of high
school when the Cultural Revolution began. Mao's revolutionary campaign forced Lu to leave Beijing and spend six years in the countryside doing manual labor. Afterward, he spent four years working in
a factory in Beijing, not very far from the foundation's modern office
building where we met. In 1977, he was among the first class of
young students to pass the college entrance examinations and return
to school, where he studied economics. In the 1980s, he worked on
rural development issues with a group of reformers with ties to Zhao
Ziyang, Deng Xiaoping's intended successor. In late May 1989, as
the crowds in Tiananmen Square grew, Lu left China to come to the
United States, where he spent one year at the University of Colorado
and several more at Harvard, earning a degree from the Kennedy
School of Government. Zhao had been immediately sacked because
of his sympathies for the protesters in Tiananmen Square. I asked
Lu if the political turmoil in 1989 had played a part in his decision
to leave when he did. He demurred, saying his plans to leave for the
United States had preceded the protests by several months. Even if
his departure was simply coincidental, scholars and officials with a
reformist bent, especially those with even a loose connection to Zhao
Ziyang, had reason to be concerned in the immediate aftermath of the
Tiananmen crackdown. After six years abroad, Lu returned to China
and took up the role he plays today.

The Harvard curriculum, specially designed for this program,
resembles a mid-career executive course. Harvard faculty teach Chi-

nese officials in broad areas of leadership, strategy, and public management. Relying on case studies and real-world examples, the course work zeroes in on specific topics such as U.S. policy and institutions, how the U.S. media thinks and operates, negotiation strategy, and even social media. The classroom work is supplemented by site visits to the Boston Redevelopment Authority, the Massachusetts State House, State Street Bank, and larger institutions like the World Bank, the International Monetary Fund, and the United Nations. Besides its main leadership program, Harvard runs more tailored courses for Chinese officials. One is focused on crisis management. Another is entirely devoted to the Shanghai municipal government. "The goal is to help the Chinese government work in this environment of globalization," says Lu. "To catch up."

The party handpicks the officials who will be sent abroad. The program is exceptionally competitive, with the party's Central Organization Department—the highly secretive institution in charge of party appointments across the country—heavily vetting those who get the opportunity to participate. The range of officials selected can vary; they may be municipal officers, mayors, provincial governors, all the way up to the central government's vice-ministers. In a country as populous as China, it is important to remember that even junior officials can have a portfolio that affects the lives of millions of Chinese. What they all have in common is that they have distinguished themselves as rising stars in the government. Lu told me that more than half of the officials sent to Harvard received a promotion not long after they returned. "We don't know if it's because of the training or because they already were so good," he says. "But we try to claim it is because of the training."

Indeed, the program at Harvard has been in place long enough to build up an impressive list of alumni. Li Jiange is now the chairman of the China International Capital Corporation, something akin to China's first investment bank. Zhao Zhengyong is the governor of Shaanxi Province, and Chen Deming is the minister of commerce. No alumnus has risen higher than Li Yuanchao. Li is the first Harvard-trained member of the Politburo. Specifically, he heads the Organization Department, a post that was previously held by Deng Xiaoping, Deng's protégé Hu Yaobang, and Zeng Qinghong, a master political operator who served Jiang Zemin. During the upcoming leadership shuffle in 2012, Li is expected to rise to the Politburo Standing Committee, making him one of the nine most powerful men in China.

Providing some additional polish for elite officials is hardly sufficient to meet China's vast administrative needs, however. If China is to ward off the ills that infected the Soviet Union and its satellite states, it must continually root out the rot in its own ranks. At the highest reaches of power—the Central Committee, the Politburo, and the Politburo Standing Committee—the party appears to have been largely successful. Despite concerns about their strategic vision, by objective standards, the senior leaders are impressive. They are the most educated lot to rule China since the regime's founding. Unlike their predecessors, who were grounded in engineering, agriculture, or Marxism, the new generation of leaders is more likely to have experience in finance, economics, and law. Nearly 20 percent of the government's ministers and vice-ministers have spent a year or more at a foreign university. And unlike most authoritarian regimes, the leaders at the top of the pyramid have not been permitted to make their positions anything close to permanent. In the last two party congresses, in 2002 and 2007, the party's senior leadership had an incredible degree of turnover. More than half of the Central Committee, Politburo, and Standing Committee rotated out of office. As the China scholar David Shambaugh has noted, with the exception of Stalin-era purges, no Communist Party leadership has had so many senior leaders stand down and retire. Indeed, there is less turnover of political elites in most democracies than there is in the upper echelons of the Chinese Communist Party.

Of course, most Chinese have no contact with the upper reaches of the party. What matters in everyday life is the professionalism and competence of local officials, the rung of the government that most people interact with and recognize. While it is impossible to generalize about a country the size of China, the party knows the signs are not good. The vast majority of the protests, demonstrations, and riots that occur in China are sparked by the corruption and abuses meted out by local officials. One ten-year survey found that Chinese citizens' satisfaction with government officials drops significantly the lower the level of government they are evaluating. In other words, the closer you get to the actual governance in the daily lives of Chinese, the poorer the performance. This finding is also the direct opposite of what one finds in the United States, where most people's complaints are directed at the national, not local, government. All of the regime's efforts to modernize could be for naught if its officials are not considered more professional, disciplined, and worthy of respect.

With the party's membership at more than eighty million people—roughly the population of Egypt—raising standards while ferreting out the unqualified is no small enterprise. Here the party's Organization Department plays a vital role. Some of its methods for screening officials and identifying talent are as old as imperial China. Officials, for example, are regularly rotated through a diverse set of assignments in very different pockets of the country to test their skills and competency. Far from being based solely on familial connections, as in so many other authoritarian regimes, advancement is largely competitive. In recent years, the party has instituted a wide range of requirements to raise the quality of the general pool of officials. All party officials now have an annual performance review. The Organization Department evaluates officials using a host of methods, including interviews, surveys, spot inspections, and examinations. During one eighteen-month campaign launched in 2005, all party members (at the time, more than seventy million people) were examined for their commitment and effectiveness. Nearly forty-five thousand people were expelled from the party. If your performance was deemed questionable or borderline, you soon had the opportunity to prove yourself in one of the party's mid-career training programs. Indeed, according to a relatively new directive, all party officials must have at least three months of training every five years. Many, however, receive more than that.

That instruction takes place at any of the party's twenty-eight hundred schools. The party's national network of schools is a crucial piece of its ability to keep tabs on its cadres, impart its priorities, and develop necessary skills. In addition to ideological training, the schools offer more practical training, such as how to handle press conferences, monitor social media sites, or respond in the first hours of a natural disaster. Some of the more lavishly funded schools have taken on particular roles. For example, the Central Party School in Beijing is considered an incubator for innovative reforms, policies, and initiatives. The most stunning party school—at least in its physical appearance—is the newly established China Pudong Cadre Academy. (English-speaking visitors know it as the China Executive Leadership Academy Pudong, which officials thought would sound more pleasing to the foreign ear.) Nestled in a yuppie neighborhood of eateries, coffee shops, and pricey lofts, the Pudong Academy fits neatly into Shanghai's modern, futuristic landscape. The school is set on more than forty acres, and its main building has an enormous, extended red roof that is meant to resemble a Ming dynasty scholar's desk. The curriculum appears to be more likely to churn out M.B.A.'s than Communist Party members. While Marx is still on some reading lists, foreigners teach a good percentage of the courses, and a parade of executives from companies like Goldman Sachs, Citibank, and Procter & Gamble visit to give guest lectures. The school is literally right off Future Expectations Street.

Small Earthquakes

Not everyone agrees that China's future lies in borrowing ideas from the West. A conservative scholar at Beijing University, Pan Wei takes a dim view of the supposed advantages of democratic innovation and political pluralism—and he will not hesitate to tell you so. In the first five minutes, Pan says that those who favor the spread of democracy at local levels in China are mainly interested in legitimizing the wealth they have already stolen, that the majority principle is an illegitimate principle, and that electoral politics has very little to do with the success of Western democracies. In Russia, he points out, the introduction of democracy did little more than "help the rulers cheat and mislead the common people." And even the most basic arguments in favor of democracy—for example, that it offers feedback on the public's priorities and helps to hold officials accountable—do not apply to China, he says. Election cycles of two or four years are just too slow. Says Pan: "China moves faster than that."

Pan is one of the more outspoken Chinese voices on democracy's shortcomings. Typically, Chinese critics of Western democracy have rested their arguments on cultural grounds, suggesting that too much political pluralism was somehow ill suited to Chinese society. Now people like Pan increasingly make their case by simply pointing to the state of the world's democracies. They cite the high levels of voter apathy, or the intense political partisanship that freezes the gears of democratic governments in the United States, Europe, India, and Japan. The fact that a populist movement like the Tea Party can single-handedly tie up the U.S. political agenda, they say, is equal parts absurd and alarming. The political deadlock that led to the Standard & Poor's rating agency downgrading U.S. creditworthiness was utterly mind-boggling to Beijing. One of the strengths of a Leninist system is its ability to direct massive amounts of resources at a specific target. It doesn't matter if the target is economic growth, disaster relief, a dissident political movement, or even environmental policy. For good or ill, the system can mobilize around a goal, marshal its manpower, and move swiftly. Even the financier and philanthropist George Soros, who has spent a large portion of his wealth trying to open authoritarian societies, admits that China has a "better functioning government than the United States." Pan agrees. In his view, the advantages of a more free and open system are hardly obvious when it consistently produces such poor results.

The day I met with him in his office at Beijing University, most people were focused on the budding revolution in Libya. But Pan was looking at another uprising—in Wisconsin. There, Democratic legislators had fled across state lines in order to deny Republicans the necessary quorum to pass budget legislation they opposed. It was week one of a standoff that would continue for nearly a month. "Every system has its shortcomings," says Pan, as a sly smile spreads across his face. "And stresses. I can see right now that Wisconsin is like that. It seems like it's just a malfunctioning of the system."

The critic becomes an unabashed advocate when the topic turns to the modern Chinese system of governance. "The major difference between Western and Chinese political civilization is that the Western governments emphasize accountability and the Chinese government emphasizes responsibility," says Pan, in fluent English he probably mastered while getting his Ph.D. at Berkeley in the early 1990s. "So what is responsibility? It means balancing three groups of interests. Number one is partial interest versus the interest of the whole. Number two is to balance the interest of the present versus the interest of the future, for example, the environment versus people's demand for wealth today. And thirdly, it is to balance the interest for change and the interest for order. A government needs to balance these three groups of interest and this is called responsibility. And I think the politics of responsibility is much more sophisticated than the politics of accountability."

Pan's formulation is a very Chinese notion of meritocracy where the state is administered by intelligent, capable, and virtuous public servants. Today, modern examples of such a system would be Singapore and Hong Kong, successful, smooth, and effectively administered governments in which the state's attachment to the rule of law is intended to nullify the need for boisterous electoral politics. While China's size and complexity pose far greater challenges than a city-state like Singapore, Pan believes the rising standards for Chinese officials—the examinations, appraisals, rotations, schooling, and so on—have set the country on the right path. "The Chinese governing body is the youngest in the world," says Pan, referring to the strict term limits and age-mandated retirement that keep turnover high. "How could you get to the top before you are too old? That's competition."

But if China has another archetype as old as the virtuous Confucian scholar who administers wisely, it is probably the tyrannical local official who terrorizes the people, safe in the knowledge that the emperor and his court are too far removed to do anything about it. Indeed, stories of the corruption and venality of local officials have provided grist for some of China's greatest works of poetry, music, and literature. (Three of China's four classic novels—*Journey to the West, Outlaws of the Marsh,* and *A Dream of Red Mansions*—offer rich descriptions of official corruption through the ages.) The party knows that corruption is the one weakness that has beset all authoritarian regimes, past and present. Tunisia, Egypt, and Libya are just new entries in a ledger with a long list of names.

Pan Wei makes light of the problem, though. "If we say Chinese government officials are wildly abusing their power, no, it's not true," he says. "None of the South American or Central American governments—except maybe Puerto Rico and Chile—are cleaner than the Chinese government. On the entire continent of Africa, not a single government is better than China in terms of corruption. And in central Asia nothing is comparable. And in Europe, I think China is better than some and worse than others. Maybe around the level of France, but certainly better than Italy!"

He glosses over the fact that in many of these countries, especially the democratic ones, when corruption is revealed, people have a means of holding officials accountable. In China, the party polices itself. It has made an effort to do so because it realizes corruption is a surefire way for its legitimacy to erode quickly. Between 1997 and 2002, the top body charged with holding party members accountable—the Central Discipline Inspection Commission—punished nearly 850,000 members and expelled more than 137,000 from the party. In recent years, the commission has established "accusation centers" where people can file anonymous complaints, and it has set up a confidential hotline to report abuses. In 2005, more than 115,000 party members were reportedly punished across the country. In 2010, the number stood at roughly 146,000 officials.

The numbers are less impressive when you realize that the vast majority get off with nothing more than a warning. Furthermore, these investigations represent a small percentage of the number of cases reported to the commission. Minxin Pei, a leading China scholar, has calculated that the odds of a corrupt official getting jail time are at most three in one hundred. All of which suggests that those who do face serious consequences either are the losers from political turf battles or committed abuses so egregious that even the party could no longer ignore them. Either way, corruption remains endemic. When the National Bureau of Corruption Prevention set up a Web site in 2007 for citizens to report abuses, it crashed within hours. It could not handle the traffic.

Being so bullish on China's political system, Pan was not worried about the wave of revolutions in the Middle East reaching China's shores. "[The government] fears this flower movement, so they have spent money monitoring it," he told me. But after all, the mistakes that these Arab regimes made are "common sense here," so he believed the popular uprisings would probably do more to complicate U.S. foreign policy in the years ahead than to negatively affect China. That may be true, but it was also true that the United States did not need to spend time, energy, and money censoring the news coming out of the Middle East. While losing Arab allies might force U.S. foreign policy to adjust, the demise of dictators thousands of miles away did not threaten the legitimacy of the American form of government. Pan conceded there could be some "disturbances" in China, but there were advantages to this as well. "Many smaller earthquakes are better than a big one," he replied.

At the end of our meeting, as I was preparing to leave, Pan had one more thought. "I think the Communist Party is just a new dynasty," he said.

Given that Chinese dynasties rise and fall, I asked, "Do you think it's early in its life? Do you think it's middle-aged?"

"I think it's early," he replied. "The average life span is 270 years or so in China, for the major dynasties."

So, by his reckoning, the regime has a little more than 200 years left. For some, though, that may be too long to wait.

Stability Maintenance

The shortest route to the government office building was through a dense warren of *hutongs,* a network of narrow alleys and traditional courtyard homes. It had snowed overnight, and in the early morning patches of ice and snow remained in the shadows of these low, sprawling structures. As I made my way through the maze of streets, I came across a crowd of forty or fifty farmers huddled closely together in the cold. You could tell instantly that they were farmers, most of them middle-aged or older, their faces drawn and weathered, their clothes dark and ragged. I did not understand why they were all gathered there, until I noticed where they were standing: in front of the petitioning office of the Ministry of Land and Resources.

This clutch of farmers, all from the same village in Shandong Province, was engaged in a time-honored practice: petitioning the central government with their grievances. They told me that local officials had taken their land and that they were collectively owed more than a million dollars. A middle-aged woman in a padded wool jacket pushed her way forward. She explained that they started petitioning the government three years ago, but they have been sent from one bureau to the next. The official inside the Ministry of Land and Resources office told them that they should go back to Shandong and deal with the local government. That was a week ago, but they decided to return each morning to press their case. An older man, in a snug cap and leather coat, scoffs and says, "Our local government is no better than a legalized mafia." A week later I passed by the same spot. The farmers from Shandong were still there.

Unfortunately, they are hardly alone. The Chinese government's petitioning system is swamped by letters, calls, and people who make the trip to Beijing seeking redress. By some estimates, more than ten million petitions are ongoing at any time. The system itself is a hold-over from imperial China, when people would seek justice from a noble official or the emperor himself. If the practice is ancient, the motivation remains the same. With little faith in China's courts and a fear that local officials will punish them for their complaints, millions take up the vain pursuit of circumventing the system by going directly to the source.

The cause is relatively hopeless; as one recent Chinese study esti-mated, roughly two in one thousand petitions delivered in person are ever resolved. And worse, petitioners can face dark consequences when they return home. It is not uncommon for villagers to be beaten or jailed for taking their grievances to the national level. No mayor or governor wants to attract unwanted attention from the central govern-ment by having a string of his constituents come to Beijing to air their complaints. Not surprisingly, a market has sprung up to prevent peti-tioners from ever successfully making the journey. Local governments send their own officials to Beijing to intercept petitioners when they arrive, putting them back on the next train home before they see any-one. Others have contracted out such work to security companies. The Anyuanding Security Technology Service reportedly had "petitioner-interception contracts" with nineteen different provincial govern-ments. The company would be paid for each petitioner detained and transported home.

The national government has made repeated attempts to reform the system—and even protect petitioners from abuse—but to little effect. In January 2011, in a symbolic gesture, Premier Wen Jiabao became the first Communist leader to ever visit the national petition office, urging the personnel there to handle the cases with speed and care. Calls by experts to abolish the system have been ignored, probably because the government knows its legal system could not absorb the added weight. Worse, the end of petitioning might trigger the very wave of angry protests it was meant to prevent.

If there is a silver lining for the regime in having so many citizens line up to petition its offices, it is that it suggests some lingering faith in the system. When people lose faith in nearly everything—local government, the courts, petitions, and their leaders—they are more likely to take to the streets. And that is precisely what the party has witnessed in recent years. In 1993, the Ministry of Public Security reported that nationwide there were roughly 8,700 "mass incidents," a category that includes strikes, demonstrations, marches, and sit-ins. In 2005, the number had skyrocketed to 87,000, a tenfold increase. Five years later, in 2010, the number of protests had more than doubled to 180,000—or nearly 500 each day. The list of causes is long: corruption, land seizures, forced evictions, police brutality, layoffs, ethnic discrimination, failing infrastructure, health risks, and environmental pollution. The triggers are so varied it is hard to imagine easy solutions for tamping down the anger and resentment that gave rise to them.

In this atmosphere, the singular worry of the Chinese bureaucracy is what it calls "stability maintenance." In recent years, the party has redoubled its effort to clamp down on social unrest by investing heavily at all levels in the tools to keep its own population in check. In the wake of the "color revolutions" and in anticipation of the 2008 Olympics, the budgets for China's security barons surged. Ethnic unrest in Tibet and Xinjiang in 2009, as well as the spike of "mass incidents" nationwide, likely fed these bottom lines. In 2010, China spent more on its internal security than it did on its national defense. In 2011, that remained the case, as the published budget for police and domestic surveillance leaped nearly 14 percent to $95 billion, compared with $91.5 billion for the Chinese military. (Many suspect the actual figures are even larger.) Sizable hikes in spending have occurred at lower levels of government, too. In 2010, after the worst ethnic clashes in decades, the provincial government in Xinjiang raised its spending on public security by 88 percent. In Liaoning, 15 percent of the province's overall budget is eaten up by "stability maintenance."

The money has bought a substantially beefed-up security architecture. Large sums have been spent controlling information, whether tightening the government's grip on the flow coming in via the Internet or broadcasting its own message out. Propaganda authorities monitor news coverage carefully, sending out detailed instructions on how sensitive stories should be covered, often by text message. (In the aftermath of a high-speed train crash in July 2011, the central government forwarded a number of bullet points to Chinese media: "Do not report on a frequent basis"; "More touching stories are to be reported instead, i.e., blood donation, free taxi services"; "Do not reflect or comment.") A substantial expansion of the security budget appears to have come at the local level, where protests or demonstrations begin. Thousands of stability maintenance offices have opened across the country, with more than 300,000 government personnel. They in turn have hired networks of neighborhood informants to report unrest before it builds. The authorities offer cash to the local cadres who are most effective in defusing angry citizens. If there are no mass incidents for a whole year, the bonuses get bigger.

Chinese often refer to the cyclical pattern of political seasons, where a period of opening *(fang)* is followed by a period of closing *(shou)*. By anyone's measure, China had already experienced an extended season of *shou* when the Arab uprisings of 2011 began. Some dated it to the lead-up to the 2008 Olympics, when the government wanted to ensure the games went off without a hitch. Others say it may have been rooted in the "color revolutions" a few years earlier. Either way, the regime had tightened its grip on Chinese civil society. A large number of NGOs, especially those that received foreign funding, came under pressure from tax authorities and other bureaucratic agencies. Groups whose work had never been targeted before, such as the Women's Law Studies and Legal Aid Center, an NGO that fights against domestic violence and employment discrimination, lost sponsorships and economic support. "You don't win points within the party in the past two decades for being a liberal," one Western expert with longtime experience working with Chinese NGOs told me. "But I have never seen the party so suspicious and so repressive. Harassment would be too polite a word."

In February 2011, after Mubarak fell from power and the calls for a Jasmine Revolution appeared online, the regime ratcheted the pressure up to what was the strongest national response since Tiananmen

Square. The crackdown was far more selective and targeted, but it was no less real. The last time the regime acted as swiftly was in 1999 when it began a campaign to eradicate the Falun Gong, the banned spiritual movement. The religious group had stunned authorities in April of that year when ten thousand of its followers held a silent protest around Zhongnanhai, the senior leadership's compound. Within months, the regime had broken the movement's back, rounding up members in raids and subjecting thousands to prison and torture. The difference in 2011 was that the party acted preemptively, moving against a disparate group of people who belonged to no single organization or group. The regime's dragnet targeted the people who speak out for others, the lawyers, advocates, and public figures who sometimes represented those at odds with the party. The government may have calculated that silencing these voices was the most effective way of quashing a movement before it began and, in so doing, redrawing the red lines of what is deemed permissible. Whatever the thinking, the party has begun to increasingly rely on secret arrests, detentions, and kidnappings to make its critics literally disappear. What's more, it does not seem to be a tactic the party will soon abandon. The government recently proposed rewriting the national criminal procedure to make such abductions legal.

The party no doubt takes heart from its successes. It is true, for example, that the regime's domestic security apparatus has prevented any nationwide protest or movement from gaining steam. The Falun Gong had been so threatening because it had grown, right under the regime's nose, creating a movement with an allegiance higher than the party that connected people of different walks of life across great distances. Today, even as protests and demonstrations have become more frequent, they remain local events. The party requires an atomized society, and for now that is what it has. But there is no question the system is straining. For all its effort and investment, the party has not been able to reverse the trends. The Chinese economy may continue to grow, but so too does the number of people unhappy with their lot in the new China. "The ideology and legitimacy of the Chinese Communist Party has already disappeared," says Pu Zhiqiang, one of the country's leading rights lawyers. "It's naked interests. The slogans, they don't work anymore. They need to buy people."

It can be done for now. But the costs of "stability maintenance" are rising. And another question lurks in the distance: What happens when a technocratic fix is not enough? What happens when it matters more to be legitimate than correct?

A Second Tiananmen

As I traveled from one authoritarian country to the next, the only place everyone talked to me about was China. Its passage from a struggling economic backwater to the top echelon of nations is an object of fascination, envy, and awe. In Venezuela, Chavistas spoke of the Chinese Communist Party in hushed tones, with something approaching reverence. A few blocks from the Kremlin, members of Putin's ruling party brought up China's success almost defensively, arguing why it was an unfair yardstick to measure them against. In Cairo, officials with close ties to Gamal Mubarak—who they thought would soon sit on his father's throne—explained that Egypt needed to follow China's example of pursuing economic reform first, then political reform. Human rights activists everywhere considered themselves fortunate that they were not up against a regime as sophisticated and brutal as the one in Beijing. But whatever one's perspective or disposition, China was on everyone's lips. It is the topic that always came up.

For authoritarian regimes, China is a tantalizing example. In 1989, no one could have expected that the Chinese Communist Party would be vastly stronger twenty years later. It had been pushed to the brink by revolt, faced divisions within its ranks, and lost most of its natural allies with the collapse of the Soviet Empire, then rebounded to enjoy what has been its most powerful chapter yet. The party defied the experts who said that economic liberalization would lead inexorably to political freedom, in part because no one anticipated its unique blend of state capitalism, political repression, and open markets. Far from falling victim to a dictatorship's most common ailments, it is succeeding beyond expectation. It is an intoxicating brew for one-party states concerned with their own preservation. The People's Republic offers a non-Western, undemocratic beacon for authoritarians everywhere to follow. To them, China looks like the future.

But for all their success, the task before China's leaders is becoming infinitely more difficult with time. The trouble for the party is that it may be entering a period when technocratic fixes are not equal to the problems it faces. Take, for example, an incident from November 13, 2005. On that day, an explosion at a chemical plant in the northeast province of Jilin dumped a hundred tons of benzene into the Songhua River. The river is one of the main sources of drinking water for millions of Chinese, including the residents of Harbin, a city of ten million people in the neighboring province Heilongjiang. At first, the authorities in Jilin stonewalled. They announced that the accident posed no risk of air pollution and denied that any toxins had been released into the river. For days, as the fifty-mile slick of poison made its way down the Songhua, the officials kept their secret. Nearly a week after the explosion, Jilin's authorities informed their counterparts in Heilongjiang of the danger headed their way. It is unclear when China's central government leaders first learned of the environmental disaster. But even with news of the spill, the officials in Harbin did not level with residents about the risks. Instead, they announced that the water supply to the city was being temporarily shut off for maintenance. Such a bizarre and unprecedented announcement set off a wave of panic, as many residents suspected that an earthquake or other disaster was imminent. Only then, on November 21, did Chinese authorities tell their citizens that their water had "perhaps" been poisoned. Environmental crews scrambled to catch up to a spill that was already a week old. China then offered an apology to the Russian government; the toxic belt of water would soon be arriving in Siberian cities downstream.

The disaster and the subsequent cover-up reveal the limits to the party's political dexterity. For all the effort to alter the regime's Leninist machinery, to make it more responsive and attuned to the needs of the people, the party has not reinvented its fundamental Leninist character. It remains, at heart, a top-down system of government that gives officials very little incentive to send bad news up the chain of command. Local officials who govern at the will of the central authorities and lack any independent source of legitimacy have every reason to conceal, hide, and bury their mistakes. Of course, China's leaders know those lies could be costly. But the natural solutions—more openness, greater accountability, deeper democratic reform—would risk the party's own grip on power. For all the sophistication, expertise, and training of its officials, this weakness is hardwired into the regime. The party has had the wisdom to engage in reform, but because of the contradictions over which it presides, it must also undermine those very reforms before they advance too far. This tension was captured in something Lai Hairong, the official at the Central Compilation and Translation Bureau, said to me. "In China, it is not about yes or no. It's about where the balance should be," he said. "It's about the extent. It's wrong to say that China is a democratic regime or a dictatorship. It's the extent of authoritarianism or the extent of democracy."

The ability to find the proper "extent" grows more difficult as the ground shifts under the party's feet. Middle-class Chinese citizens—the very people who are supposed to be co-opted, conservative, and content—are increasingly demanding a greater say in the decisions that affect their daily lives. People's awareness of their rights and willingness to step forward are rising. In late 2011, an unprecedented number of Chinese citizens launched independent campaigns to run for seats in local people's congresses, often building support for their candidacies through a Chinese version of Twitter. In August 2011, roughly twelve thousand Chinese in the prosperous coastal city of Dalian filled the public square to protest a chemical factory that they believed was vulnerable to typhoons and natural disasters. It once would have been easier for authorities to stop such a demonstration, but the call to protest moved too quickly across Chinese social media. Beijing's tools for keeping its society atomized are slowly eroding. One of the biggest outbreaks of ethnic unrest occurred in Xinjiang in 2009. It is believed that nearly two hundred people died in the clashes between Uighurs and Han Chinese. Rioting began in Urumqi after rumors that Muslims from Xinjiang working thousands of miles away in Guangdong Province had been murdered; the rumors had spread on the Internet. Today, a misstep by a local official in one part of the country is a potential fuse for unrest or instability in another. As much as the party learned from the events of Tiananmen Square, those lessons become less relevant the further it moves from 1989.

Mao famously remarked, "A single spark can light a prairie fire." Today, the sparks the party must douse come from every direction. An environmental disaster, a train crash, a public health scare, a lie that is told for too long—any of these can start a chain reaction that may be too difficult to contain. When a regime's legitimacy is derived from its performance, any crisis—and how the party responds to it—can raise existential questions about the regime's right to rule. In such a moment, the party's expertise, even if well applied, may be meaningless. It will no longer be a matter of making adjustments or turning the knob in one direction or another. People will not be looking for the right answer; they will question whether the regime has the legitimacy to try again.

And, as the Arab Spring reminded everyone, it is not enough for China's leaders to worry solely about turmoil within their borders. The fortunes of authoritarian regimes everywhere are a cause for concern, lest their own citizens draw inspiration from the battle. Surely, someone in the party saw the signs in Tahrir Square that read, "Down with Mubarak!"—in Chinese. Shortly after Mubarak resigned, one Chinese posted, "Even though the people we are watching are Egyptian, even though the voices we are hearing are those of Egyptians, our ears are ringing with the echoes of history. This is the sound of the German people tearing down the Berlin Wall, of the Indonesian students taking to the streets, of Gandhi leading the people down the road of justice."

I asked one party member if there was any one thing that the party saw in Tunis, Cairo, or Benghazi that might strike a chord or be a cause for alarm? Yes, he replied. The party had survived its Tiananmen moment, but few think it can survive another. What Chinese leader would have the authority to fire on the people today? "If they let that many people go to a public square again," he said, "they will have already lost."

EPILOGUE

||||||||||||||||||||||||||||||||||||||||||||||||||||||||||||||||||||||||||||||||||||||||||||||||||||||||||||||||||||||||||||||||||||||||||||||||||||

In July 2011, Srdja Popovic and I sat down in a restaurant in Washington, D.C., to talk about the revolutions and uprisings that were crisscrossing the globe. The year had been like no other, as people living in a string of repressive countries rose up to challenge tyrants and the regimes they led. "It's been a bad year for bad guys," Srdja said, smiling. Six months before no one would have predicted that "Ben Ali and Mubarak would be out, Gaddafi and Saleh would be on their knees, and Assad would be seriously challenged. If you would have seen that in your crystal ball and then told people on TV, men in white coats would have come to take you away."

But it was no hallucination. A few weeks later Libya's Muammar Gaddafi, who had been forced to flee Tripoli, was hunted down in the streets of his native home of Sirte. Rebels found the former dictator cowering in a drainage pipe. Gaddafi was the third Arab strongman to fall in nine months. Although the Arab world had been at the center of the revolutionary storm, the tumult was not limited to the Middle East or North Africa. By the year's end, authoritarian leaders in a long list of countries—places as far-flung as Belarus, China, Malaysia, Russia, even the Kingdom of Swaziland—faced a more assertive public clamoring for a say in their futures. The phenomenon was so great *Time* magazine declared "the protester" to be the 2011 Person of the Year.

And what had these millions of people making demands revealed about the dictators? That strongmen are less interested in sophisticated strategies when they feel cornered. For example, in early December 2011, Russia's ruling party suspected it might not perform well in the upcoming parliamentary elections. Polling ahead of the vote had shown its candidates faring badly. So, in Chechnya, perhaps the most repressive corner of the country, Putin's United Russia brazenly claimed to have won 99 percent of the vote—much like the Soviet Union of old. Putin's first response to protests denouncing the stolen election was to blame the United States for trying to destabilize the country—the same desperate conspiratorial claim that had been made by Ben Ali, Mubarak, and Gaddafi.

The sophisticated artifice of the modern authoritarian had been intended to prevent the people from ever coming out to rally in the square. Fundamentally, the dictator on his learning curve seeks ways of renewing dictatorship, to keep it resilient, agile, and in some way effective. A basic goal is to keep the people apathetic and uninvolved. But when the system fails, when the people do assemble, dictators typically jettison these political maneuvers for a starker set of choices. They show themselves for what they truly are. In March 2011, a month after Mubarak was ousted, one Egyptian ruling party official privately expressed his regrets to a friend of mine. Looking at how other Arab regimes were responding to their own uprisings by resorting to force, the Egyptian official said, "We were stupid. Yemen was smarter than us. They are managing it. Bahrain was smarter than us. They are managing it. Libya was smarter than us. Leaving aside the morality, they are *managing* it."

"Managing it" was, of course, a euphemism for violence. Indeed, early on, Gaddafi invoked China's 1989 massacre in Tiananmen Square to stress the violent ends he was willing to pursue to remain in power. In Yemen, Ali Abdullah Saleh's military loyalists repeatedly opened fire on street protesters. Bahrain's monarchy hired Pakistani soldiers to attack its own people. Violence did not save Gaddafi, however, and any regimes that massacred their citizens risked losing whatever thin claims to legitimacy they still had. They may persevere for the moment, much like how Iran's hard-liners clung on after the 2009 Green Revolution, but they cannot expect their rule to be easier with a simmering population more alienated, angry, and embittered than before.

Syria's Bashar Assad was another who had opted for a bloodbath. Each day, for months, the body count grew. By the end of the year, the United Nations estimated that more than five thousand Syrians had perished while protesting—men, women, and children shot in the street. As the uprising widened, elements of the military defected and joined the rebellion. Cities were torn apart and left in pitched battles as the country appeared on the cusp of civil war. The savagery of Assad's regime drew denunciations from the Arab League, long a diplomatic safe haven for the region's authoritarian rulers. In November, the league suspended Damascus's membership and enacted a slate of tough sanctions, the first indication that it might be preparing for a post-Assad future. Increasingly isolated and with no legitimacy left, the Syrian government appeared less tenable by the day. In the face of a twenty-first-century revolution, Assad had opted for a slow-burning twentieth-century crackdown.

Of course, even in the tumultuous atmosphere of 2011, authoritarian regimes did not face a narrow choice between caving in to demands for democracy and simple repression. After stumbling, some quickly regained their footing and looked to pursue a familiar middle path. In Saudi Arabia, this meant massive handouts: in March 2011, King Abdullah unveiled sixty thousand new public-sector jobs, raises for state employees, and greater stipends for the unemployed. Altogether the measures amounted to more than $93 billion in public spending. But the Saudi kingdom is clearly a unique case. No other regime can compete with its oil-rich coffers. Others must rely more on their wits than their wallets to restore stability.

A chief example was Jordan. It too had taken immediate steps to raise public-sector salaries and pensions and increase food and energy subsidies. But Jordan's King Abdullah II understood these economic measures would not suffice. After sacking unpopular government leaders and appointing a new prime minister, he proposed rewriting the constitution. Six months later he put his stamp on forty-two proposed amendments; they included the creation of a constitutional court, limiting the power of the regime's domestic security courts, and adding independent monitors for future elections. Naturally, none of these reforms would curb the king's own broad powers. They were instead, as he said, intended to prove that Jordan could "revitalize itself."

Shortly before I visited Malaysia in February 2011, Prime Minister Najib Razak had reacted defensively to the early uprisings of the Arab Spring. He warned those who would seek change in his own country that Malaysia was not Egypt. "Don't think that what is happening there must also happen in Malaysia," Najib fumed. "We will not allow it to happen here." In July, inspired in part by the protests in the Middle East, tens of thousands of Malaysians took to the streets to demand clean elections. Afterward, though, Najib kept his cool. After months of promising greater reforms, the ruling party did the opposite, passing a law in November banning future street demonstrations. When later asked about the wave of summer protests, Najib referred to them as a "sign of a mature democracy." It was the perfectly tailored reply of the modern authoritarian.

Perhaps the most surprising case was Burma. By the end of 2011, it appeared that this pariah state wanted to come in from the cold. After nearly five decades of harsh rule since the military seized power in 1962, the Burmese government unexpectedly began to embark on a series of wide-ranging reforms. The authorities lifted curbs on the Internet, unblocking foreign news sites. Domestic press freedoms expanded. The image of the leading dissident and Nobel laureate Aung San Suu Kyi was splashed across the front page of Burmese newspapers. Hundreds of political prisoners were released. The regime promised these moves would be followed by others. What had changed? Was the regime's desire to have international sanctions lifted so great that it was willing to experiment with gradual political and economic liberalization? Had Yangon been spooked by the wave of revolutions whipping across the globe and calculated that it was best to confront these forces on its own terms? It seemed unlikely that Burma's rulers had simply awoken to the desirability of democracy. The regime was more likely wagering that preemptive reforms would best ensure its survival, becoming the newest dictatorship to attempt to move up the learning curve.

The gamble will test Burma's regime as nothing else has. Even if its rulers are able to liberalize the country without losing their political perch, they, like others before them, will soon find that they are boxed in. If they move too quickly, they could become another Soviet Union. If they move too slowly, they risk being the next Mubarak. And time and experience will not make the task easier. History—indeed, a dictatorship's own longevity—can itself become a vulnerability for a regime bent on nothing beyond its own survival.

As a modern dictatorship with a long history, China is perhaps the best example of this peril. The longer the Chinese Communist Party stays in power, the more politically sensitive anniversaries the regime accumulates. The calendar has become littered with dates that remind people of the regime's crimes or serve as potential flash points. A quick rundown of the Chinese political calendar would include March 10 (the anniversary of the 1959 Tibetan Uprising), May 4 (anniversary of the 1919 May 4 Movement), June 4 (the 1989 Tiananmen Square massacre), July 5 (the 2009 suppression of Muslims in Xinjiang), July 22 (the 1999 crackdown on the Falun Gong movement), and October 1 (the 1949 founding of the People's Republic). Any of these dates are times when the regime must be on the lookout for those who might try to rally people against the Communist Party. Indeed, the fear was great enough in 2009—when many of these dates had important anniversaries—that the party reportedly established a special high-level task force called the 6521 Group. (The numbers 6521 referred to the 60th anniversary of the People's Republic, the 50th anniversary of the Tibetan Uprising, the 20th anniversary of the Tiananmen massacre, and the 10th anniversary of the Falun Gong crackdown.)

I ran up against the regime's sensitivity in the reporting of this book. I wanted to travel to China when the political climate would be relatively relaxed. Originally, I had planned to go there in December 2010. But when it became clear that the Chinese scholar and dissident Liu Xiaobo would receive the Nobel Peace Prize in early December, I scrapped my trip, choosing instead to travel to China in February 2011. Besides the Chinese New Year celebrations, nothing happens in February. Of course, that was before the uprisings in the Middle East and the calls for a Chinese Jasmine Revolution. A new date was added to the Chinese calendar, another potentially sensitive moment for an insecure regime to anxiously monitor its streets and Web sites.

It would be a mistake, however, to believe that the advance of democracy over dictatorship is just a matter of time. History has not moved in some inexorable path of progress. The totalitarianism of the twentieth century—a tyranny that claimed more than 100 million lives—was worse than anything mankind had seen before it.

Each age is not necessarily more liberal and tolerant than the one that preceded it.

Nor is political freedom somehow inevitable. It is true that the wave of democratic transitions that Samuel Huntington identified, beginning with Portugal's in 1974, led to an impressive expansion of political and economic freedom in corners of the globe that had known little of either. But it is also true that the past forty years gave rise to skillful new forms of authoritarianism that blurred our definitions of democracy and dictatorship. As much as we may welcome the fall of tyrants in 2011, our enthusiasm must be tempered by the challenges that lie ahead for each of these societies. The Russian people's first experiment in democracy was short-lived and led to the authoritarianism of Putin. Venezuela had been a functioning democracy for decades before the rise of Chávez. Long after Mubarak, the Egyptian people will still be in the thick of their revolutionary struggle. 2011 was a year of political rupture. Whether it becomes a turning point for the advance of democracy over dictatorship will be determined by the months and years that follow.

Personally, I grew more optimistic about the prospects for democratic change over the course of my travels. That optimism did not stem from the rightness of the cause or even the fundamental flaws of any of the authoritarian countries I visited. Flawed regimes had long been capable of squashing the most just and inspirational ideas of political pluralism. Rather, my optimism grew as I sat down to meet with the people who had committed themselves to fight for these freedoms. These were not blind idealists. In place after place, the people I met were hardened, battle-scarred activists who approached their work with intelligence, care, and skill. They were accomplished strategists, propagandists, and political analysts. Although almost none had had careers that might have fostered these skills, they had learned quickly through trial and error—and sometimes by copying others who went before them.

What I never expected is that they would accomplish so much so soon. At the end of 2011, many of the people who had been relatively unknown figures when I first met them had risen to national prominence. In Russia, Yevgenia Chirikova, the environmentalist and mother of two, addressed the tens of thousands of people who poured out into Moscow's streets to protest the stolen parliamentary elections. She was now regularly referred to as one of the faces of a new generation of Russian opposition leaders. In Egypt, Samira Ibrahim, the young victim of the military's "virginity tests," continued to speak out against the military's crimes. She brought a suit against the Supreme Council of the Armed Forces, and in December an Egyptian court unexpectedly ruled in her favor, ordering that the military end this humiliating abuse of female protesters. In Malaysia, the regime's trumped-up trial of Anwar Ibrahim ended in January 2012 with an acquittal. Within minutes of the verdict, Anwar turned to Twitter, writing "this corrupt government will be toppled from its pedestals of power." In China, the party continued to struggle with growing incidents of citizen unrest. Indeed, in late December, an entire city in southern China went into open revolt, chasing all of the police and local officials out of town. In Venezuela, the political opposition was the most organized and disciplined it had been since Chávez came to power. Henrique Capriles, Leopoldo López, and María Corina Machado were among a slate of leading contenders in the opposition's political primaries. They all participated in the first presidential debate in decades, one that had been organized at the insistence of the Venezuelan student movement. In February 2012, Capriles won those primaries, making him the man who would challenge Chávez in the fall.

In every recent battle between a dictator and his people, the tyrant's first response has been the same: to deny that the protests are genuine. In Tunisia, Ben Ali claimed that the youth in the streets were "masked gangs" engaging in "terrorist acts." In Bahrain, the monarchy blamed the unrest on Iranian agents. Like Mubarak, Egypt's military rulers pinned the continued protests in Tahrir Square on "foreign influences." Gaddafi famously referred to Libyan rebels as "drug addicts." Assad, like many before him, blamed the West for attempting to foment revolution. These were the most desperate lies of dictators. The truth is that the protests of 2011 were so potent because they came from the people. In the end, the people actually mattered. For a dictator, there is nothing more terrifying.

ACKNOWLEDGMENTS

ltogether it came to 93,268 miles. That is my best estimate of the distance I traveled over two years for the writing and reporting of this book. If the next destination never seemed that far away, it was because I was never alone. Over the life of this project, a countless array of people came forward to help me find my way, offering advice, wisdom, and sometimes a place to sleep. My deepest respect and admiration go to the activists in each of these countries who risk so much for an idea that many of us take for granted. They did not need to take the time—and sometimes added risk—to meet with a journalist with a notebook full of questions. But they opened their homes, told me their stories, and introduced me to their families, friends, and neighbors. Some, because of the risks they continue to take, must remain nameless here. For me, they are nothing short of heroes and the best hope for freedom's future.

The journey would have never begun without my champions back in New York, in the offices of Doubleday. Chief among them is my editor, Kristine Puopolo, who from Day One understood what this book could be and offered her wholehearted support for it. She never asked me to cut corners, and she patiently awaited every dispatch and installment. I am also grateful for the support of her colleague William Thomas and for the efforts of Stephanie Bowen, who saw to it that the trains ran on time and that the author remained on track.

I did not know it at the time, but one of the most important moments for this book came when I met my agent, Will Lippincott.

An advocate, counselor, and friend, Will played an integral role every step of the way. His enthusiasm and optimism kept my spirits high when they might have otherwise flagged. Quite simply, I cannot imagine this book existing without him.

In the last several years, I was fortunate to have the support of several fine institutions. The Carnegie Endowment for International Peace provided me with an intellectual home for the first twelve months of the book. I am especially grateful to Jessica Mathews and Paul Balaran, whose support was instrumental in getting this project off the ground. A media fellowship to Stanford University's Hoover Institution offered me a timely opportunity to conduct additional research, and I am grateful to David Brady and Mandy MacCalla for helping to arrange a productive week of meetings and workshops while on campus. During the height of the Arab Spring, Fred Hiatt, the editorial page editor of the *Washington Post,* offered me an incredible opportunity to provide daily analysis of those dramatic events for the paper's *PostPartisan* blog. Likewise, Carlos Lozada, editor of the *Post*'s Outlook section, commissioned pieces from me at almost every significant milestone for dictators in 2011. I am exceptionally grateful to Fred and Carlos for those assignments that forced me to clarify my thinking at a time when clarity seemed in short supply.

Long before I launched my study of authoritarianism's strengths and frailties, I had the privilege of working alongside some of the best editors and journalists in the business. Most of them have no idea how much they shaped the way I approach my work, but I am much richer for having had the chance to learn from them over the years. First and foremost was Fareed Zakaria. Working for Fareed—first at *Foreign Affairs,* later at *Newsweek International*—was an opportunity to learn at warp speed, and I will always be grateful for his friendship and wise counsel. At *Newsweek International,* I was surrounded by sharp, gifted editors who worked minor miracles almost every week, among them Nisid Hajari, Jeffrey Bartholet, Michael Meyer, Fred Guterl, and Marcus Mabry. At *Foreign Policy,* I was privileged to work with a team whose creativity, intelligence, and passion inspired me every day: Travis Daub, Kate Palmer, Carolyn O'Hara, Jeffrey Marn, Blake Hounshell, Jai Singh, James Forsyth, David Bosco, Mike Boyer, Christine Chen, Josh Keating, Prerna Mankad, Preeti Aroon, Sarah Schumacher, and Beth Glassanos.

For this book, I spent a lot of time working in foreign countries. On all these trips, I was assisted by a remarkable group of interpreters and fixers; their work went far beyond translation and logistics. In Russia, I traveled with Ludmila Mekertycheva, a consummate professional who never took *nyet* for an answer. Over glasses of vodka, I had great fun hearing tales of the foxes she raised at her dacha. There was almost no one in Egypt whom Nagwa Hassan hadn't already met. With a grin and a cigarette, she navigated the snarl of Cairo's traffic better than any cabbie ever could. Ahmed Salah introduced me to everyone in Tahrir Square. In China, David Yang, an emerging Chinese journalist in his own right, kept up an indefatigable pace, always one step ahead of me. In Venezuela, I was deeply fortunate to have Francisco Márquez at my side. A veteran of Venezuela's student movement, Francisco is completing his graduate studies at Harvard's Kennedy School and plans to return to Caracas after graduation. It is people like him who make me so hopeful for Venezuela's future.

As I traveled, trusted friends also served as invaluable guides. Vinod Sekhar long ago convinced me that Kuala Lumpur could be my second home, and the friendship and hospitality of Vinod and his wonderful wife, Winy, have made it just that. Edward Cunningham has many gifts. In China, two stand out: he knows the best dish on the menu, and he knows how to open doors. I am incredibly fortunate to have him in my corner. And no one could ask for a better guide to Egyptian politics than my longtime friend Tarek Masoud. He picked me up at Cairo International Airport for my first interview in 2006 and has been furthering my education in all things Egyptian ever since. My understanding and appreciation for this magnificent country owe more to him than to anyone, and I will always be grateful.

In Venezuela, it was the kindness of not merely individuals but entire families. First, I owe a tremendous debt to Maruja Tarre, Isabel Lara, and their family. My first trip to Caracas was as warm as a homecoming because of their generosity. I also owe special thanks to Karla Velazquez and Alvaro Partidas for advising me on every detail. Alejandro Tarre, a Venezuelan journalist and shrewd analyst of the country's politics, offered excellent suggestions and has become a true friend. On each trip to Venezuela, Ricardo Márquez and María Lara Márquez made me feel like a member of the family. I hope that I will one day have the opportunity to return the favor.

This book would never have been possible if so many people had not been willing to sit for lengthy interviews, sometimes on several occasions. This collection of people included professors, lawyers, politicians, businessmen, writers, students, intellectuals, bloggers, military men, and activists. Although the list is too long to thank everyone individually, there are some who must be singled out: Anwar Ibrahim, Nurul Izzah, Peter Ackerman, Gene Sharp, Jamila Raqib, Robert Helvey, Srdja Popovic, the entire CANVAS team, Patrick Meier, Karim Sadjadpour, Omid Memarian, Hazem Hallak, Mohsen Sazegara, Saba Vasefi, Emily Jacobi, Mark Belinsky, and Tendor Dorjee. In Venezuela, Alfredo Croes, Douglas Barrios, Carlos Vecchio, Henrique Capriles, Leopoldo López, María Corina Machado, Magalli Meda, Ismael García, Andrés Cañizález, Luis Vicente León, Eugenio Martínez, Teodoro Petkoff, Virginia Rivero, Judge María Afiuni, Raúl Baduel, Antonio Ledezma, Milos Alcalay, Carlos Ocariz, Roberto Patiño, Nizar El Fakih, Yon Goicoechea, Geraldine Alvarez, David Smolansky, Phil Gunson, Robert Serra, Calixto Ortega, and Iris Varela.

In Egypt, I learned from Hossam Bahgat, Gasser Abdel-Razek, Mostafa el-Naggar, Saad Eddin Ibrahim, Dina Guirguis, Gamal Eid, Ahmed Maher, Mohamed Adel, Essam el-Erian, Ahmed Kamal Aboul Magd, Ahmed Salah, Ahmed Amer, Ibrahim Mohamed, Ahmed Mamdoh, Kamel Arafa, Samira Ibrahim, Sherif el Robi, Sherif Mickawi, Hafez Abu Saeda, Sherif Osman, Omar Afifi, Esraa Rashid, Aida Seif al Dawla, Ghada Shahbender, Hossam el-Hamalawy, Hisham Kassem, Mohamed Waked, Shady Talaat, Ayman Nour, Wael Nawara, Dalia Ziada, Ali Eddin Hilal, Mohamed Kamal, Gehad Auda, Alia el Mahdi, the retired major general Mohamed Kadry Said, Michele Dunne, and Moheb Zaki.

In Russia, I am grateful to Arseny Roginsky, Alexander Verkhovsky, Boris Nemtsov, Ilya Yashin, Vladimir Milov, Sergei Mitrokhin, Olga Radayeva, Dmitri Makarov, Ivan Ninenko, Karinna Moskalenko, Ludmilla Alexeeva, Tanya Lokshina, Yevgenia Chirikova, Mikhail Khotyakov, Yaroslav Nikitenko, Ivan Smirnov, Evgeny Gontmakher, Grigory Shvedov, Gleb Pavlovsky, Igor Mintusov, Maria Lipman, Nikolay Petrov, Sergei Markov, Sergei Popov, Alexander Brod, and Elena Zelinskaya. Eve Conant, Jeffrey Tayler, and Sarah Mendelson also helped to make valuable introductions in Moscow. In China, there are many people whom I hope to thank one day. For now, I offer my appreciation to

Pu Zhiqiang, Zhang Jingjing, Fang Ning, Feng Yue, Zhou Shuguang, Yu Keping, Lai Hairong, Lu Mai, Du Zhixin, Pan Wei, Yang Jisheng, Wang Weizhi, Mao Xianglin, Wang Xuedong, and Yang Jianli. Demetri Sevastopulo, a true comrade, made vital introductions in Beijing. I also have great gratitude for Minxin Pei and David Shambaugh, both for their scholarship and for their willingness to discuss it with me.

I am immensely lucky to be able to call on a deep bench of friends and colleagues who have been sustaining me for years. Allison Stanger, my professor and friend, has been teaching me ever since I walked into PS 311 in the fall of 1992. Mark Jordan, Robert Trager, Rodney Rothman, John Oberdiek, and Alexander Okuliar are the lifelong friends who keep me grounded. I am particularly indebted to a small circle who volunteered their time to read early drafts of selected chapters and offered me their critiques and corrections. They include Kate Palmer, Carolyn O'Hara, Stacey Abrams, Tarek Masoud, Edward Cunningham, Maria Lipman, Alejandro Tarre, Francisco Márquez, and the incomparable Janine Zacharia.

For nearly two decades, Stacey Abrams has been my consigliere and the truest friend a person can have. Her contribution to this project cannot be measured in the hours she spent reading drafts and helping me see what mattered most.

Through conversations on the phone and at kitchen tables coast-to-coast, my family has been extraordinarily supportive. My uncle William Joyce and aunt Gay Bush were there from the beginning, indulging me with questions late into the night. Frances Cole, Tracy Cole, and Richard, Allison, and Megan Barker are a constant source of support and provided vital help on the home front when I was away. The West Coast Coles—all world travelers in their own right—followed my progress and chimed in with words of encouragement. Neither my father, W. Joel Dobson, nor my father-in-law, Barry G. Cole, lived to see this book completed. I like to think they both would have enjoyed it.

The best teacher I ever had was also my first. My mother, Barbara Joyce Dobson, raised me and made me the person I am today. It was just my good fortune that she happened to be an inspirational English teacher, too. At an early age, she sat with me at my desk and taught me how to write (and rewrite) essay after essay. She was endlessly patient, loving, and quick to praise. She wanted nothing more than to provide me with the best opportunities available, and my life has taken remarkable turns because of her strength and perseverance. I am grateful for her every day.

When you begin a journey like this one, your family comes along, sometimes whether they like it or not. My deepest appreciation goes to my wife, Kelly Cole. She lived every page of this book, and at times suffered both my absences and a husband who was lost in thought. At key moments, as always, it was Kelly who clarified my thinking and showed me the way. For me, she is equal parts love and humor, strength and resolve. What's more, she managed all of this during the very years our family began to grow, first with the arrival of our daughter, Kate, and then two years later with our son, Liam. The only thing better than our life together are the days still to come. Because, although our house is a noisy place, there is no place better to be.

NOTES

||||||||||||||||||||||||||||||||||||||||||||||||||||||||||||||||||||||||||||||||||||||||||||||||||||||||||||||||||||||||||||||||||||||||||||||||||||||||||||||||||||

INTRODUCTION

1   *talking to me about "risk returns"*: Peter Ackerman, interview with author, Washington, D.C., August 2011.

1   *Ackerman earned $165 million*: Kurt Eichenwald, "S.E.C. Report Attacks Big Drexel Bonuses," *New York Times*, October 4, 1991.

1   *When an insider-trading scandal broke*: Franklin Foer, "Regime Change Inc.," *New Republic*, April 25, 2005. Foer offers a thoughtful profile of Ackerman and his work.

2   *"The game is the most subversive thing"*: Ackerman, interview.

3   *it literally pulled the plug on CNN's broadcast*: Orville Schell, *Mandate of Heaven: The Legacy of Tiananmen Square and the Next Generation of China's Leaders* (New York: Touchstone, 1994), p. 126.

3   *an expedition of European mountain climbers*: Joseph Kahn, "Video Disputes China's Claim Shooting Was in Self-Defense," *New York Times*, October 16, 2006.

3   *To be precise, they began at 12:25*: Robert Harvey, *Portugal: Birth of a Democracy* (London: Macmillan, 1978), p. 14.

3   *that day marked the beginning*: To be more precise, Huntington termed it the Third Wave. He had also identified two previous democratic waves (as well as corresponding reverse waves). The first ran from the expansion of voting rights in the United States in 1828 to the rise of Italian fascism in the early 1920s. The second wave began with the Allied victory in World War II and ended in 1962, with a wide spate of military coups in South America, Asia, and Africa. His writing on the subject is absolutely required reading, in particular *The Third Wave: Democratization in the Late Twentieth Century* (Norman: University of Oklahoma Press, 1991).

3   *After Portugal, a string of right-wing dictatorships*: One of our leading thinkers on democracy and authoritarianism, Larry Diamond, offers an even grander overview of these years of democratic advance in *The Spirit of Democracy: The Struggle to Build Free Societies Throughout the World* (New York: Henry Holt, 2008).

4   *Political freedom around the world declined*: All data on the number of democracies and dictatorships comes from Freedom House's annual

survey, *Freedom in the World*. For an overview of these declines in political freedom, see Arch Puddington, *Freedom in the World 2011: The Authoritarian Challenge to Democracy* (Washington, D.C.: Freedom House, 2011).

5   "*For my friends, everything*": Author interview with Venezuelan activist, Caracas, November 2009. The phrase originates with the Brazilian president Getúlio Vargas, who led the country first as a dictator from 1930 to 1945 and then as a democratically elected leader from 1951 until his suicide in 1954.

5   *Chinese Communist Party leaders regularly invoke democracy:* Richard McGregor, *The Party: The Secret World of China's Communist Rulers* (New York: HarperCollins, 2010), p. 4.

6   "*My father used to say*": Alvaro Partidas, interview with author, Washington, D.C., September 2009.

6   *he never did violence to the Russian constitution:* Daniel Treisman, *The Return: Russia's Journey from Gorbachev to Medvedev* (New York: Free Press, 2011).

7   "*Human rights defenders are in demand*": Ludmilla Alexeeva, interview with author, Moscow, April 2010.

7   *the dictatorship of the Soviet system required closed borders:* Ludmilla Alexeeva made this point to me when we first met. Later, Ivan Krastev, the editor in chief of the Bulgarian edition of *Foreign Policy* magazine and a brilliant observer of authoritarian regimes, expounded on this idea in the seventh annual Seymour Martin Lipset Lecture on Democracy in the World on October 19, 2010. His remarks appear in his essay "Paradoxes of the New Authoritarianism," *Journal of Democracy* 22, no. 2 (April 2011).

10   "*There isn't an expert*": Ackerman, interview.

CHAPTER I: THE CZAR

13   *Putin was stationed in Dresden:* David Hoffman, "Putin's Career Rooted in Russia's KGB," *Washington Post*, January 30, 2000.

13   *It kept secret files:* Michael Meyer, *The Year That Changed the World: The Untold Story Behind the Fall of the Berlin Wall* (New York: Scribner, 2009), p. 25.

13   *stretch almost seven miles:* Hoffman, "Putin's Career."

13   *According to the regime's own records:* Meyer, *Year That Changed the World*, p. 25.

13   *Putin was shocked at how "totally invasive":* Quotations from Putin reflecting on his life in Dresden and the collapse of the Soviet Empire come from Vladimir Putin, *First Person: An Astonishingly Frank Self-Portrait by Russia's President* (New York: Public Affairs, 2000), p. 77. This book is a unique volume. It is the only work I know in which Putin speaks candidly about himself and his past. Put together by three experienced Russian journalists—Nataliya Gevorkyan, Natalya Timakova, and Andrei Kolesnikov—the book is purely a transcript of their interviews with Putin on the eve of his first term in office. Putin sat for the interviews on six occasions for four hours each time. He was still a political novice at the time and had not yet learned not to speak to journalists.

14   *These reports documented the rising demands:* Charles S. Maier, *Dissolution: The Crisis of Communism and the End of East Germany* (Princeton, N.J.: Princeton University Press, 1997), p. 106.

14   *There was a run on Dresden banks:* Meyer, *Year That Changed the World,* p. 165.

14   *crowds tried to fight their way onto trains:* Ibid., p. 124. For more on the mounting protests in Dresden, see Maier, *Dissolution,* p. 145.

15   *"He who does not regret":* Pierre Hassner, "Russia's Transition to Autocracy," *Journal of Democracy* 19, no. 2 (April 2008), p. 11.

16   *"stability, certainty, and the possibility of planning":* Clifford G. Gaddy and Andrew C. Kuchins, "Putin's Plan," *Washington Quarterly* (Spring 2008), p. 121.

16   *Putin began with the oligarchs:* For an authoritative account of Russia's leading oligarchs, see David Hoffman, *The Oligarchs: Wealth and Power in the New Russia* (New York: Public Affairs, 2002).

17   *Putin brought the media to heel:* For an excellent overview of how the media has become a tool of the Kremlin, see Maria Lipman, "Media Manipulation and Political Control," Chatham House paper, January 2009.

17   *roughly 93 percent of all media outlets:* Fraser Cameron, "Dead-End Russia," *New York Times,* February 11, 2010. It is not, however, easy to reduce the Kremlin's control of the media to neat percentages. For example, Ekho Moskvy, a Moscow radio station that offers a critical view of political and social issues, is owned by Gazprom Media, a subsidiary of the state-run gas firm.

17   *the directors of the three major TV channels every Friday:* Mikhail Fishman and Konstantin Gaaze, *Russian Newsweek,* August 4, 2008.

18   *they engineered space for a small handful of opposition parties:* For more on the Kremlin's creation of opposition parties, see Luke March, "Managing Opposition in a Hybrid Regime: Just Russia and Parastatal Opposition," *Slavic Review* 68, no. 3 (Fall 2009).

18   *"the most different strata":* Gaddy and Kuchins, "Putin's Plan," p. 121.

19   *According to the Russian journal* Ekspert: Nikolay Petrov, Maria Lipman, and Henry E. Hale, "Overmanaged Democracy in Russia: Governance Implications of Hybrid Regimes," Carnegie Paper, no. 106, February 2010, p. 26.

19   *"What's the difference between communism and Putinism?":* Boris Nemtsov, interview with author, Moscow, April 2010.

20   *"Putin has created a kind of dream":* Ilya Yashin, interview with author, Moscow, April 2010.

20   *"They don't want to lose control":* Alexander Verkhovsky, interview with author, Moscow, April 2010.

21   *"90 percent of the civil laws":* Sergei Popov, interview with author, Moscow, April 2010.

21   *an onerous 2006 law:* C. J. Chivers, "Kremlin Puts Foreign NGO's on Notice," *New York Times,* October 20, 2006. For a more detailed analysis, see Graeme B. Robertson, "Managing Society: Protest, Civil Society, and Regime in Putin's Russia," *Slavic Review* 68, no. 3 (Fall 2009), p. 540.

22   *the Ministry of Justice led 13,381 NGO inspections:* Human Rights Watch, *An Uncivil Approach to Civil Society: Continuing State Curbs on Independent*

NGOs and Activists in Russia (New York: Human Rights Watch, 2009), p. 32.

22 *A slew of foreign human rights organizations:* Chivers, "Kremlin Puts Foreign NGO's on Notice." At the time, I was employed by the Carnegie Endowment for International Peace, which had long had an office in Moscow. Although the Carnegie Endowment came under considerable scrutiny by authorities, it was not suspended.

22 *Putin followed this law with a 2008 decree:* Human Rights Watch, *Uncivil Approach*, p. 16.

22 *it takes roughly two months to register an NGO:* Ibid., p. 27.

23 *the authorities intend to have two thousand of these offices:* Popov, interview.

23 *this body is a consultative forum:* Robertson, "Managing Society," p. 541.

24 *"The Public Chamber is allowed to be critical":* Tanya Lokshina, interview with author, Moscow, April 2010.

24 *United Russia announced a new center:* Paul Goble, "United Russia Revives Another CPSU Tradition—Watching Officials in the Regions for Moscow," *Window on Eurasia* (blog), July 31, 2010.

27 *"There are a lot of instruments of control":* Author interview with Moscow activist, Moscow, April 2010.

27 *The European University in St. Petersburg learned this lesson:* Author interview with Moscow activist, Moscow, April 2010. See also Human Rights Watch, *Uncivil Approach*, p. 56.

27 *"interference by a foreign quasi-government":* Human Rights Watch, *Uncivil Approach*, p. 56.

28 *"The term 'Gongolization' was invented":* Author interview with State Department official, Washington, D.C., January 2010.

28 *"The only message from his press conference":* Lokshina, interview.

29 *"The activity of an NGO is not really possible":* Alexander Brod, interview with author, Moscow, April 2010.

29 *According to the Committee to Protect Journalists:* Committee to Protect Journalists, *Getting Away with Murder: 2011 Impunity Index* (New York: Committee to Protect Journalists, 2011).

30 *"We sat at my kitchen table talking":* Tanya Lokshina, "Another Voice Silenced in Russia," *Washington Post*, July 17, 2009.

31 *he unexpectedly told a crowd of Washington policy wonks:* Robert Coalson, "Behind the Estonia Cyberattacks," Radio Free Europe/Radio Liberty, March 6, 2009.

32 *"We have no competition inside the party":* Sergei Markov, interview with author, Moscow, April 2010.

33 *autocracies and democracies have developed at the same rate:* Joseph T. Siegle, Michael M. Weinstein, and Morton H. Halperin, "Why Democracies Excel," *Foreign Affairs*, September/October 2004, p. 59.

33 *when South Korea was a developing authoritarian state:* Yun-Hwan Kim, "The Role of Government in Export Expansion in the Republic of Korea: A Revisit," Asian Development Bank, EDRC Series, February 1994, www .adb.org/Documents/EDRC/Reports/rs61.pdf.

33 *oil and gas accounted for 70 percent:* Russian Federation Federal State Statistics Service, Commodity Structure of Exports of the Russian Federation, www.gks.ru/bgd/regl/b09_12/IssWWW.exe/stg/d02/26-08 .htm.

33 *it kept state employment at a relatively lean 12.5 percent:* Tianlun Jian,
    "Priority of Privatization in Economic Reforms: China and Taiwan
    Compared with Russia" (paper at the Harvard Institute for International
    Development), www.cid.harvard.edu/hiid/566.pdf.

33 *state-owned enterprises employ nearly 40 percent of workers:* Carsten
    Sprenger, "State-Owned Enterprises in Russia" (presentation at the
    OECD Roundtable on Corporate Governance of SOEs, October 27, 2008),
    www.oecd.org/dataoecd/23/31/42576825.pdf.

33 *Russia's annual spending per high school student: Education at a Glance
    2007,* OECD report, September 18, 2007, p. 173, www.oecd.org/document
    /30/0,3343,en_2649_39263238_39251550_1_1_1_1,00.html#data.

34 *Graft erases roughly one-third:* Ira Iosebashvili and William Mauldin,
    "Russia's Economic Czar Tackles Deficit, Bureaucracy," *Wall Street
    Journal,* June 23, 2010.

34 *the number of billionaires in Russia:* "Forbes List Sees Russian Billionaire
    Numbers Double," BBC, April 16, 2010.

34 *The national economy contracted almost 8 percent:* Paul Abelsky, "Russian
    GDP May Grow 4.5% in Bumpy Recovery, World Bank Says," *Bloomberg
    Businessweek,* June 16, 2010.

35 *"Practically, we can say":* Gleb Pavlovsky, interview with author, Moscow,
    April 2010.

36 *learning about Western democracy promotion:* For more on Pavlovsky, see
    Andrew Wilson, *Virtual Politics: Faking Democracy in the Post-Soviet World*
    (New Haven, Conn.: Yale University Press, 2005).

37 *"You should understand the mechanism":* Markov, interview.

38 *Lunch with Mintusov can reportedly cost:* Wilson, *Virtual Politics,* p. 50.

38 *"He pointed to the budget for research":* Igor Mintusov, interview with
    author, Washington, D.C., April 2010.

40 *"The electoral district where I voted showed":* Sergei Mitrokhin, interview
    with author, Moscow, April 2010.

41 *Medvedev went before television cameras:* Clifford J. Levy, "President Pick
    Would Name Putin Premier," *New York Times,* December 12, 2007.

41 *"What is Putin's main dream?":* Nemtsov, interview.

41 *it wasn't as if he had any vision:* Author interview with Medvedev adviser,
    Moscow, April 2010.

41 *"we will be able to maintain the course":* Clifford J. Levy, "Putin Protégé
    Secures Election Victory," *New York Times,* March 3, 2008.

42 *"As a rule, the skeptics":* Arseny Roginsky, interview with author, Moscow,
    April 2010.

42 *peppered with criticism for the political system:* Vidya Ram, "Medvedev's Mea
    Culpa," *Forbes,* September 11, 2009.

42 *"Our state is the biggest employer":* Daniel Treisman, *The Return: Russia's
    Journey from Gorbachev to Medvedev* (New York: Free Press, 2011), p. 141.

42 *66 percent did not believe his reforms:* "Most Russians Expect No Results
    from Medvedev's Reforms," *Ria Novosti,* May 2, 2010.

42 *38 percent of his presidential orders:* Michael Bohm, "Dmitry Gets No
    Respect," *Moscow Times,* March 26, 2010.

42 *it wasn't as if he had many centers of support:* Treisman, *Return,* p. 144.

43 *"You can see the whole tactics":* Grigory Shvedov, interview with author,
    Moscow, April 2010.

43 *the Kremlin didn't need "brown-nosers":* Anna Nemtsova, "Beset by a Million Bureaucrats," *Newsweek*, February 21, 2010.

43 *the institute released a report:* Ellen Barry, "Research Group's Report Urges Radical Changes in Russia," *New York Times*, February 4, 2010.

43 *"Our main goal is as a provocation":* Evgeny Gontmakher, interview with author, Moscow, April 2010.

45 *he reminded those assembled that Franklin Roosevelt:* "Vladimir Putin's Valdai Vision," *Economist*, September 7, 2010.

45 *Putin's thirteen-hundred-mile drive across Siberia:* Amy Knight, "The Concealed Battle to Run Russia," *New York Review of Books*, January 13, 2011.

45 *"Any leader who occupies a post":* Neil Buckley, Charles Clover, and John Thornhill, "Medvedev Rules Out Poll Tussle with Putin," *Financial Times*, June 19, 2011.

45 *"I think the chance for Medvedev":* Nemtsov, interview.

46 *"I think it would be correct":* "Russia's Putin Set to Return as President in 2012," BBC, September 24, 2011.

46 *"Nothing can stop us":* A video clip of Putin's remarks is available at www .youtube.com/watch?v=3ynB2CjtXhQ.

46 *75 percent of Russians still did not plan:* "Time to Shove Off," *Economist*, September 10, 2011.

48 *In his first televised response:* Putin also could not resist the opportunity to insult the protesters, comparing the white ribbons they had pinned to their clothes to limp condoms.

CHAPTER 2: ENEMIES OF THE STATE

49 *"Some leader will tell the secret police":* All quotations from Pu Zhiqiang come from an interview with the author, Beijing, February 2011.

50 *In a special meeting the day after:* Perry Link, "The Secret Politburo Meeting Behind China's New Democracy Crackdown," *NYR* (blog), *New York Review of Books*, February 20, 2011, www.nybooks.com/blogs/nyrblog/2011/feb/20 /secret-politburo-meeting-behind-chinas-crackdown/.

52 *"The Communist Party always talks about law":* Zhang Jingjing, interview with author, Beijing, February 2011.

53 *"Sometimes the losses produce":* Yevgenia Chirikova, interview with author, Moscow, April 2010.

56 *the case of Chen Guidi and Wu Chuntao:* Philip P. Pan, "In China, Turning the Law into the People's Protector," *Washington Post*, December 28, 2004, p. 1. For more on this case and Pu Zhiqiang, I highly recommend Philip P. Pan's *Out of Mao's Shadow: The Struggle for the Soul of a New China* (New York: Simon & Schuster, 2008).

56 *"It could ignore the evidence":* Pan, "In China, Turning the Law."

59 *"When we lived in Moscow":* All quotations from Yevgenia Chirikova come from interviews with the author in Moscow and Khimki in April 2010, unless otherwise noted.

61 *new roads in Russia cost roughly $237 million a kilometer:* Anne Garrels, "Anti-graft Crusade a Dangerous Business in Russia," National Public Radio, October 13, 2009, www.npr.org/templates/story/story .php?storyId=113763047.

61 *its roadway infrastructure is ranked 111th:* World Economic Forum, *The Global Enabling Trade Report 2010* (Geneva: World Economic Forum, 2010), p. 233.

61 *Levitin is the head of several commercial enterprises:* Aeroflot later dismissed Levitin as the company's chairman in June 2011. The move came shortly after President Dmitri Medvedev said that deputy prime ministers and ministers should not simultaneously serve on the boards of major state-owned companies. See Henry Meyer, "Medvedev Bid to Oust Officials Is 'Small Revolution,'" *Bloomberg Businessweek*, April 3, 2011.

64 *Even in his Khimki hospital bed:* Clifford J. Levy, "Russian Journalists, Fighting Graft, Pay in Blood," *New York Times*, May 17, 2010, p. 1.

64 *Russia was until recently the third-deadliest country:* Committee to Protect Journalists, *Anatomy of Injustice: The Unsolved Killings of Journalists in Russia* (New York: Committee to Protect Journalists, 2009).

64 *18 journalists were murdered with no one held accountable:* Committee to Protect Journalists, *Getting Away with Murder: 2011 Impunity Index* (New York: Committee to Protect Journalists, 2011).

64 *The governor, Gromov, led the Fortieth Army:* For more on Gromov's experience in Afghanistan, see Michael Dobbs's brilliant book *Down with Big Brother: The Fall of the Soviet Empire* (New York: Alfred A. Knopf, 1997).

68 *The attack she long expected:* Claire Bigg, "Fate of Russia's Khimki Forest Uncertain After Ecologists Attacked, Detained," Radio Free Europe/Radio Liberty, July 23, 2011.

68 *"These were big guys":* Yevgenia Chirikova, interview with author, Moscow, January 2011.

69 *"He had always been my idol":* Ibid.

70 *According to a poll conducted by the Levada Center:* Yevgenia Chirikova, interview with author, Moscow, January 2011. See also Ashley Cleek and Aleksandra Saenko, "Russian Government OKs Controversial Highway Through Khimki Forest," Radio Free Europe/Radio Liberty, December 14, 2010.

70 *In an unexpected move:* Michael Schwirtz, "Kremlin Relents, for Now, to Foes of Russia Highway," *New York Times*, August 26, 2010, p. 4.

70 *But the powerful interests behind the highway:* Yevgenia's phone call to the real estate development company, posing as a buyer, is available at www .youtube.com/watch?v=oygFt-xgg34&feature=player_embedded.

71 *"The main idea of Putin":* Boris Nemtsov, interview with author, Moscow, April 2010.

72 *"The tailor has his tools":* All quotations from Omar Afifi come from an interview with the author in Washington, D.C., in July 2009, unless otherwise noted.

79 *"I am not here":* Omar Afifi, interview with author, Falls Church, Va., July 2011.

CHAPTER 3: EL COMANDANTE

80 *"Yes, sir. I will follow them":* Reported by the author, Los Teques, July 2010.

84 *"We paraphrased the oath":* Raúl Baduel, interview with author, Los Teques, July 2010.

85 *Baduel sent an elite team:* For a riveting account of the April 11, 2002,

coup and Baduel's dramatic rescue of Chávez from Orchila Island, I recommend Brian A. Nelson's *The Silence and the Scorpion: The Coup Against Chávez and the Making of Modern Venezuela* (New York: Nation Books, 2009).

85 *Baduel felt compelled to resign:* Raúl Baduel, "Why I Parted with Chávez," *New York Times,* December 1, 2007.

86 *Military intelligence officers forcibly detained:* Juan Forero, "Chávez Ally-Turned-Critic Is Detained by Venezuelan Military," *Washington Post,* October 4, 2008; and Simon Romero, "Chávez Seeks Tighter Grip on Military," *New York Times,* May 30, 2009.

87 *it was the wealthiest country in South America:* Ricardo Hausmann and Francisco Rodríguez, eds., *Venezuela: Anatomy of a Collapse* (University Park: Penn State University Press, forthcoming).

87 *Colombians, envious of their neighbor's success:* Nelson, *The Silence and the Scorpion,* p. 3.

87 *the highest per capita debt in Latin America:* Ibid.

87 *Real per capita income dropped 15 percent:* Benn Eifert, Alan Gelb, and Nils Borje Tallroth, "Managing Oil Wealth," *Finance and Development* 40, no. 1 (March 2003).

87 *poverty rose 150 percent:* Gustavo Márquez Mosconi and Carola Alvarez, "Poverty and the Labor Market in Venezuela, 1982–1995," Inter-American Development Bank paper, December 1996, p. 1, idbdocs.iadb .org/wsdocs/getdocument.aspx?docnum=815518.

87 *By 1998, Venezuela's per capita GDP:* Stephen Haber, "Latin America's Quiet Revolution," *Wall Street Journal,* January 31, 2009.

87 *Two-thirds of the country's banks had collapsed:* Nelson, *The Silence and the Scorpion,* p. 4.

87 *More than 50 percent of the population:* Javier Corrales and Michael Penfold, *Dragon in the Tropics* (Washington, D.C.: Brookings Institution, 2011), p. 17. Corrales and Penfold are two of the most authoritative Venezuela watchers. For a primer on Chávez's takeover of the Venezuelan state, I also highly recommend Javier Corrales's "Hugo Boss," *Foreign Policy,* no. 152 (January/February 2006), p. 32.

87 *In one survey:* Kenneth Roberts, "Social Polarization and the Populist Resurgence in Venezuela," in *Venezuelan Politics in the Chávez Era: Class, Polarization, and Conflict,* ed. Daniel Hellinger and Steve Ellner (Boulder, Colo.: Lynne Rienner, 2004), p. 65.

88 *you need to understand A, B, C, D, and E:* I am indebted to Luis Vicente León, one of Venezuela's leading pollsters and the president of Datanálisis, for his thorough overview of the country's socioeconomic divisions and the voting behavior of each group (Caracas, November 2009).

88 *"For the first twenty years":* Alfredo Croes, interview with author, Caracas, November 2009.

89 *his approach is the inverse of Russia's Vladimir Putin:* To my knowledge, the first person to make this point was Ivan Krastev; see his "Democracy's Doubles," *Journal of Democracy* 17, no. 2 (April 2006), p. 52.

89 *"This is not Cuba":* Teodoro Petkoff, interview with author, Caracas, November 2009.

90 *"What happens to a society":* Virginia Rivero, interview with author, Caracas, November 2009.

90 *"I was very embarrassed"*: Maruja Tarre, interview with author, Washington, D.C., June 2011.

91 *his supporters carefully drew up electoral rules*: Corrales and Penfold, *Dragon in the Tropics*, p. 19.

92 *"If the majority of people think democracy"*: Luis Vicente León, interview with author, Caracas, November 2009.

92 *"Elections are not a threat"*: Eugenio Martínez, interview with author, Caracas, November 2009.

93 *"Election Day is not a problem"*: Author interview with former National Electoral Council member, Caracas, November 2009.

93 *as much as 30 percent*: Martínez, interview.

94 *a bump of nearly three million*: I am grateful to Eugenio Martínez for these figures.

94 *it took only 42,000 votes*: I am indebted to María Corina Machado for this election data.

95 *a so-called mixed electoral system*: The election rules guiding voting in Venezuela are very complex. For a more detailed explanation, I recommend Alejandro Tarre, "Venezuela's Legislative Elections: Arm Wrestling with Hugo Chávez," *Fletcher Forum of World Affairs* 35, no. 1 (Winter 2011), p. 139.

95 *Martínez showed me how*: Martínez, interview.

96 *Chávez's party and the opposition captured roughly*: For an excellent analysis of the September 2010 National Assembly elections, see Tarre, "Venezuela's Legislative Elections," pp. 137–44.

96 *Chávez has enacted more decrees*: Carlos Vecchio, interview with author, Caracas, November 2009.

96 *Chávez had shocked Venezuelans*: For a full account of Chávez's exhumation of Bolívar's body, see Thor Halvorssen, "Behind Exhumation of Simón Bolívar Is Hugo Chávez's Warped Obsession," *Washington Post*, July 25, 2010.

97 *"I believe we will have very good results"*: Robert Serra, interview with author, Caracas, July 2010.

98 *"If the oligarchy is allowed to return"*: Javier Corrales, "For Chávez, Still More Discontent," *Current History*, February 2009, p. 81.

98 *One of the most notorious examples*: For a full account of the Tascón List and the Maisanta, see Human Rights Watch, *A Decade Under Chávez: Political Intolerance and Lost Opportunities for Advancing Human Rights in Venezuela* (New York: Human Rights Watch, 2008), pp. 15–25.

100 *Statistical analysis supports the anecdotal evidence*: Chang-Tai Hsieh, Edward Miguel, Daniel Ortega, and Francisco Rodríguez, "The Price of Political Opposition: Evidence from Venezuela's *Maisanta*," *American Economic Journal: Applied Economics* 3, no. 2 (April 2011), pp. 196–214.

100 *The government brought charges*: Human Rights Watch, *Decade Under Chávez*, p. 218.

101 *"They choose people in every sector"*: María Corina Machado, interview with author, Caracas, July 2010.

101 *Machado stepped up her opposition*: Machado would later win her seat in the National Assembly and raise her level of opposition again by becoming a candidate in the opposition's presidential primaries.

101 *"Our communication strategy"*: Magalli Meda, interview with author, Caracas, July 2010.

103 *"They record everything we say"*: Tarre, interview.

104 *"Who do you want to see?"*: Reported by the author, Los Teques, July 2010.

104 *Judge Afiuni had been presiding*: Simon Romero, "Criticism of Chávez Stifled by Arrests," *New York Times*, April 3, 2010.

104 *"The intelligence officers"*: María Afiuni, interview with author, Los Teques, July 2010.

105 *"more serious than an assassination"*: Juan Forero, "Venezuelan Judge Is Jailed After Ruling Angers President Hugo Chávez," *Washington Post*, April 25, 2010, p. A16.

105 *"That judge must pay"*: Chávez's statement condemning Judge María Afiuni on national television on December 11, 2009, can be seen at www .youtube.com/watch?v=WXtibicptRA.

106 *"public attitude . . . undermines the majesty"*: Human Rights Watch, *Decade Under Chávez*, p. 48.

107 *Caracas is the most dangerous capital*: I first came across these estimates from a presentation by Marcos Tarre Briceño, the director of the nongovernmental organization Secure Venezuela (Caracas, November 2009). When official figures were leaked in August 2010, the blogger Francisco Toro made a similar comparison at *Caracas Chronicles*, one of the most original and intelligent blogs on Venezuelan politics. His post "And All That Without Suicide Bombings" appeared on August 21, 2010, and is available at www.caracaschronicles.com/2010/08/21/and-all-that -without-the-suicide-bombings/. See also Simon Romero, "Venezuela, More Deadly Than Iraq, Wonders Why," *New York Times*, August 22, 2010.

107 *there were 19,133 murders*: "Shooting Gallery," *Economist*, August 19, 2010.

107 *91 percent of murders go unprosecuted*: The security expert Marcos Tarre Briceño calculated the percentage as 93 percent (interview with author, Caracas, November 2009). Another security expert calculated it as 91 percent. See Pedro Pablo Peñaloza, "Experts Complain That 91 Percent of Murders Go Unpunished in Venezuela," *El Universal*, September 2, 2010. The government refuses to share the information publicly. Given the small difference in these independent estimates, I have chosen to reproduce the more conservative one, which remains astonishingly high.

108 *One afternoon I attended a lunch*: Reported by the author, Caracas, November 2009.

108 *it is also the only country in South America*: According to the International Monetary Fund's World Economic Outlook Database, in Central and South America and the Caribbean, only Venezuela and a handful of Caribbean countries saw their economies contract in 2010. It was accessed on November 16, 2011, at www.imf.org/external/pubs/ft /weo/2011/02/weodata/index.aspx.

108 *Its levels of inflation have exceeded even Africa's*: Kejal Vyas, "Venezuela Inflation Highest Among Top Emerging Economies," *Wall Street Journal*, December 29, 2010; and Daniel Cancel and Charlie Devereux, "Venezuela's Inflation Rate Rises at Fastest Pace in 7 Months," *Bloomberg Businessweek*, November 4, 2011.

108 *a negative balance sheet for foreign investment*: Victor Salmerón, "Foreign Direct Investment Plunges $1.4 Billion in Venezuela," *El Universal*, May 5, 2011.

108 *"The problem is the price [controls]":* Author interview with local butcher, Caracas, July 2010.

109 *he delivered nearly two thousand cadenas:* Committee to Protect Journalists, "Attacks on the Press 2010," February 2011, www.cpj.org/attacks/.

109 *"The cadenas are a huge form of control":* Andrés Cañizález, interview with author, Caracas, November 2009.

110 *The centerpiece of Chávez's media universe:* Juan Forero, " 'Aló Presidente,' Are You Still Talking?" *Washington Post,* May 30, 2009.

110 *If Chávez's antics are unrehearsed:* I am indebted to Andrés Cañizález, a professor at the Andrés Bello Catholic University and one of the foremost experts on Chávez's media strategies, for this background.

111 *Chávez shuttered 34 radio stations:* Francisco Toro, "Welcome to Censorship in the 21st Century," *New Republic,* August 5, 2010.

112 *he appointed a former head of the intelligence police:* Cañizález, interview.

112 *the National Assembly passed laws forbidding:* Richard Allen Greene, "Critics of Venezuela's New Media Laws Fear 'Dangerous' Crackdown," CNN, December 22, 2010.

113 *"This is not a totalitarian society":* Teodoro Petkoff, interview with author, Caracas, November 2009.

115 *"The rejection of Chávez":* Alfredo Croes, interview with author, Caracas, November 2009.

116 *"Chávez is weaker":* Luis Vicente León, interview with author, Caracas, November 2009.

116 *Chávez effectively hollowed out:* Rachel Jones, "Hugo Chávez Gives Himself a Big Christmas Gift," *Time,* December 29, 2010.

117 *he unilaterally revised the tax on oil revenues:* William J. Dobson, "Chávez's Easter Gift—to Himself," *PostPartisan* (blog), *Washington Post,* April 26, 2011, www.washingtonpost.com/blogs/post-partisan/post/chavezs-easter -gift—to-himself/2011/04/26/AFVs4gqE_blog.html.

117 *What matters is the way in which a democracy's leaders:* Samuel P. Huntington, *The Third Wave: Democratization in the Late Twentieth Century* (Norman: University of Oklahoma Press, 1991), p. 259.

CHAPTER 4: THE OPPOSITION

120 *"It's not going to be a fair fight":* Henrique Capriles, interview with author, Pedro Gual, November 2009.

121 *"They are extremely sophisticated":* Vladimir Milov, interview with author, Moscow, April 2010.

122 *Capriles was arrested for inciting:* Jackson Diehl, "In Venezuela, Locking Up the Vote," *Washington Post,* April 10, 2006.

124 *little more than "robberies, stripping cars, and rape":* Yovanny, interview with author, Caracas, July 2010.

126 *"There were forty days of campaigning":* Carlos Ocariz, interview with author, Caracas, November 2009.

127 *One of his more innovative educational initiatives:* Author interview, Caracas, November 2009. Also, the blogger Juan Cristóbal Nagel offers an excellent analysis of Ocariz's program at *Caracas Chronicles.* His post "Red with Envy" appeared on January 13, 2011, and is available at http://caracaschronicles.com/2011/01/13/red-with-envy/.

128 *the opposition lost seventy-six elections:* Leopoldo López, interview with author, Caracas, November 2009.

128 *The head of the Venezuelan military:* Ezequiel Minaya, "If Chavez Loses Venezuelan Election, Transition May Be Rocky," *Wall Street Journal,* September 12, 2011.

129 *Chávez unveiled a new instrument:* Christopher Toothaker, "Chávez Opponents Say Charges Trumped Up to Bar Them from Running," Associated Press, May 24, 2008. Russián's list of 400 politically banned candidates was later reduced to 270.

129 *One of the candidates banned:* Girish Gupta, "Venezuela's Exclusion of Anti-Chávez Candidates Faces a Challenge," *Time,* March 13, 2011.

130 *"I want to express my support":* The clip of Chávez's speech appears in the documentary *Banned! Political Discrimination in Venezuela* (Ciudadania Activa, 2009) and is available at www.youtube.com /view_play_list?p=46572AE8BBE93290.

131 *"You have the historic responsibility":* López's remarks to the court appear in ibid.

131 *More than eight hundred candidates:* Gupta, "Venezuela's Exclusion."

131 *The mayoral post was stripped:* Juan Forero, "Venezuela's Chávez Sets Up Obstacles for Opponents Who Won in Fall Elections," *Washington Post,* February 12, 2009.

132 *the Inter-American Human Rights Court sided:* Simon Romero and María Eugenia Díaz, "A Bolívar Ready to Fight Against the Bolivarian State," *New York Times,* October 21, 2011.

134 *"I am not disappointed":* Rifaat El-Said, interview with author, Cairo, January 2006.

134 *His parents had been good friends:* Author interview, Cairo, March 2010.

137 *"I went back to prison":* Ayman Nour, interview with author, Cairo, March 2010.

137 *Life had not been easy:* Ibid.

138 *"They are draining my resources":* Saad Eddin Ibrahim, interview with author, Washington, D.C., March 2010.

140 *an Egyptian court upheld Nour's forgery conviction:* Matt Bradley, "Egypt Court Bars Opposition Hopeful," *Wall Street Journal,* October 17, 2011.

140 *"We ousted a military ruler":* Stephanie Rice, "Ayman Nour Speaks About Disqualification from Egyptian Presidential Election," *Global Post,* October 17, 2011.

141 *"I have three more events":* Anwar Ibrahim, interview with author, Penang, February 2011.

143 *one figure looms above all others:* For a look at Mahathir Mohamad's twenty-two-year rule, I recommend Barry Wain's *Malaysian Maverick: Mahathir Mohamad in Turbulent Times* (New York: Palgrave Macmillan, 2010).

144 *"It is the ruling party that is worried":* Anwar Ibrahim, interview with author, Kuala Lumpur, April 2008.

145 *"Only one Malaysian has ever":* Author interview with Malaysian businessman, Kuala Lumpur, February 2011.

145 *"We are going to Taiwan":* Thomas Fuller, "Malaysians Go to Taiwan Amid Strife," *New York Times,* September 8, 2008, p. 10.

145 *"I knew the moment":* Anwar Ibrahim, interview with author, Kuala Lumpur, February 2011.

146 *"Here, among the Malays":* Ibid.
147 *"Mahathir probably underestimated me":* Anwar, interview, April 2008.
148 *"Your passion for democracy":* Ibid.

CHAPTER 5: THE YOUTH

149 *Up ahead, a checkpoint stretched:* This account of the events of February
16, 2010, comes from Ahmed Maher, interview with author, Cairo, March
2010.
151 *Venezuelan students had higher approval ratings:* Roberto Patiño (student
leader), interview with author, Caracas, November 2009.
152 *"Our power is that we are not a political party":* Maher, interview.
152 *"It allows us to effectively":* Douglas Barrios, interview with author, Caracas,
December 2010.
153 *Polls showed that 65 to 80 percent:* Juan Forero, "Protests in Venezuela
Reinvigorate Opposition," *Washington Post,* June 2, 2007.
154 *he does remember sitting:* Barrios, interview.
154 *"It was the first time I felt":* Geraldine Alvarez, interview with author,
Caracas, December 2010.
154 *But a small group of students:* My account of events from May 28, 2008,
comes from my interviews with student leaders, including Geraldine
Alvarez, Douglas Barrios, Yon Goicoechea, Francisco Márquez, and David
Smolansky.
156 *"We did not achieve a concrete objective":* Yon Goicoechea, interview with
author, Caracas, December 2010.
156 *It was an incredibly bold proposal:* Simon Romero, "Students Emerge as
a Leading Force Against Chávez," *New York Times,* November 10, 2007;
Simon Romero, "Venezuela Vote Sets Roadblocks on Chávez Path," *New
York Times,* December 4, 2007; and Tim Padgett, "Chávez Tastes Defeat
over Reforms," *Time,* December 3, 2007.
159 *Sometimes when they blocked roads:* Alvarez, interview.
160 *One day the Venezuelan vice president:* Goicoechea, interview.
161 *By most estimates, more than 150,000 Venezuelans:* Author interviews
with student leaders Douglas Barrios, Yon Goicoechea, and Francisco
Márquez.
163 *He had no idea:* Goicoechea, interview.
165 *And if you looked closely:* Adrian Karatnycky, "Ukraine's Orange
Revolution," *Foreign Affairs,* March/April 2005.
166 *"We see what's happening":* Alexander Bratersky, "Nashi Celebrates Fifth
Year with Kremlin Support," *Moscow Times,* April 16, 2010.
166 *"The Nashi movement is the movement":* Ibid.
166 *"After the Orange Revolution, all the opposition":* Author interview with
Kremlin official, Moscow, April 2010.
167 *In 2008, Nashi was awarded:* Human Rights Watch, *An Uncivil Approach to
Civil Society: Continuing State Curbs on Independent NGOs and Activists in
Russia* (New York: Human Rights Watch, 2009), p. 21.
167 *It receives an even greater share:* Steven Lee Myers, "Youth Groups Created
by Kremlin Serve Putin's Cause," *New York Times,* July 8, 2007.
167 *the organizers made headlines:* Neil Buckley, "Cadre's Campfire Song to
Russia," *Financial Times,* July 18, 2007.

167 *During the 2010 summer retreat:* Anna Arutunyan, "Nashi Seen Behind Pamfilova's Ouster," *Moscow News,* August 2, 2010.

167 *"Have you heard of Komsomol?":* Ilya Yashin, interview with author, Moscow, April 2010.

168 *A similar youth group, tied to United Russia:* Owen Mathews and Anna Nemtsova, "Young Russia Rises," *Newsweek,* May 27, 2007.

169 *When such a force is created:* Ellen Barry, "Russian Journalist Beaten in Moscow," *New York Times,* November 6, 2010.

169 *When he arrived home:* A security camera outside Kashin's apartment captured his brutal beating by two attackers. The video can be seen at www.youtube.com/watch?v=ow-YhStbTkc.

169 *the focus of Kashin's reporting:* Oleg Kashin speculates about who was behind his attack. Oleg Kashin, "A Beating on My Beat," *New York Times,* December 12, 2010.

169 *one poll conducted in 2007:* Sarah E. Mendelson and Theodore P. Gerber, "The Putin Generation: The Political Views of Russian Youth" (presentation, CSIS, July 25, 2007), http://csis.org/images/stories /mendelson carnegie moscow corrected.pdf.

169 *A comparison between Ukrainian and Russian youth:* Taras Kuzio, "Ukraine Is Not Russia: Comparing Youth Political Activism," *SAIS Review* 26, no. 2 (2006), p. 74.

170 *The same 2007 poll indicated:* Sarah E. Mendelson and Theodore P. Gerber, "Soviet Nostalgia: An Impediment to Russian Democratization," *Washington Quarterly* 29, no. 1 (Winter 2005–6), p. 85.

170 *"You really have to admit":* Dmitri Makarov, interview with author, Washington, D.C., February 2010.

170 *"If you would directly ask":* Ivan Ninenko, interview with author, Moscow, April 2010.

170 *A rare instance when authorities:* Ibid.; Cathy Young, "Kenny Will Live," *Reason,* October 10, 2008.

172 *his most recent arrest:* Mostafa el-Naggar, interview with author, Cairo, March 2010.

173 *Sixty percent of the population:* Pew Forum on Religion & Public Life, *The Future of the Global Muslim Population* (Washington, D.C.: Pew Forum on Religion & Public Life, 2011).

173 *the youth population in the Middle East:* Jack A. Goldstone, "Understanding the Revolutions of 2011," *Foreign Affairs,* May/June 2011, p. 12.

173 *college graduates were ten times more likely:* Ibid.

173 *"I have fallen in love":* Khalid, interview with author, Cairo, March 2010.

173 *No one would have predicted:* Marc Fisher, "In Tunisia, Act of One Fruit Vendor Unleashes Wave of Revolution Through Arab World," *Washington Post,* March 26, 2011, p. 1.

175 *"It started when I was at university":* Ahmed Maher, interview with author, Cairo, March 2010.

176 *the UN World Food Programme reported:* "Soaring Food Prices Anger Egyptians," *Al Jazeera,* March 18, 2008.

176 *there were fewer than a hundred labor protests:* I am indebted to Khaled Ali of the Egyptian Center for Economic and Social Rights, for these figures. He very patiently spent hours going over these numbers on recent labor activity with me (Cairo, March 2010).

178 *the Facebook group exceeded:* Esraa Rashid, interview with author,

Washington, D.C., March 2010. See also Samantha M. Shapiro, "Revolution, Facebook-Style," *New York Times Magazine*, January 22, 2009, p. 37.

178 *"The [regime's] security had fallen"*: Ahmed Salah, interview with author, Cairo, March 2010.

179 *The streets, however, were*: "Egypt Police Clash with Protesters After Foiled Strike," Agence France-Presse, April 6, 2008; and Nasser Nouri, "Clashes in Nile Delta After Strike Aborted," Reuters, April 7, 2008.

180 *"We had talked about"*: "Egypt to Raise Wages After Unrest," *New York Times*, May 1, 2008.

182 *Among all the youth movements*: Mohamed Adel, interview with author, Cairo, March 2011.

184 *"The idea was to try"*: Salah, interview.

185 *"The Tunisian revolution gave faith"*: Kamel Arafa, interview with author, Cairo, March 2011.

185 *It was Afifi who*: Salah, interview; and Omar Afifi, interview with author, Falls Church, Va., July 2011.

185 *It instructed demonstrators to wear*: Adel, interview; and Afifi, interview.

CHAPTER 6: THE PHARAOH

187 *Samira was still there*: Samira Ibrahim, interview with author, Cairo, March 2011.

188 *"We started sending SOS messages"*: Ahmed Amer, interview with author, Cairo, March 2011.

189 *Egyptians love their military*: Robert Springborg, a professor at the Naval Postgraduate School, is one of the foremost experts on the Egyptian military. For an excellent analysis of the relationship between the Egyptian military and the regime, see Robert Springborg and Clement M. Henry, "Army Guys," *American Interest* 6, no. 5 (May/June 2011). See also Ellis Goldberg, "Mubarakism Without Mubarak: Why Egypt's Military Will Not Embrace Democracy," *Foreign Affairs*, February 2, 2011.

190 *"People worship the army"*: Author interview with human rights activist, Cairo, March 2011.

191 *the empire that today's Egyptian military*: David Kilpatrick, "Egypt's Military Discourages Economic Change," *New York Times*, February 17, 2011; Thanassis Cambanis, "Succession Gives Army a Stiff Test in Egypt," *New York Times*, September 11, 2010.

192 *Indeed, far from relaxing*: William J. Dobson, "Worse Than Our Worst Nightmare During Mubarak," *PostPartisan* (blog), *Washington Post*, March 17, 2011. See also Human Rights Watch, "Egypt: Retry or Free 12,000 After Unfair Military Trials," September 10, 2011.

192 *"We have found the regime"*: Hayam Ahmed, interview with author, Cairo, March 2011.

193 *Mubarak, an unremarkable, colorless vice president*: As vice president, Mubarak was always in Sadat's shadow. During a meeting with Sadat, Henry Kissinger had mistakenly assumed that Vice President Mubarak was a junior aide to Sadat. See Mary Anne Weaver, *A Portrait of Egypt* (New York: Farrar, Straus and Giroux, 1999), p. 36.

193 *Mubarak is said to have*: For the assassination of President Anwar Sadat, I relied on ibid., p. 61.

193 *Roughly 44 percent of Egyptians:* Joel Beinin, "Egyptian Workers Demand a Living Wage," *Foreign Policy*, May 12, 2010.

193 *Fewer than half the homes:* Max Rodenbeck, "No Paradise," *Economist*, July 15, 2010.

193 *Roughly 30 percent of the adult:* Ibid.

194 *The Ministry of Interior . . . employed more than 1.5 million people:* Jason Brownlee, "Egypt's Incomplete Revolution: The Challenge of Post-Mubarak Authoritarianism," *Jadaliyya*, July 5, 2011, www.jadaliyya.com /pages/index/2059/egypts-incomplete-revolution_the-challenge-of -post. Brownlee is a leading scholar of both Egypt and authoritarianism. I thoroughly recommend his book *Authoritarianism in an Age of Democratization* (Cambridge, U.K.: Cambridge University Press, 2007).

194 *The message was center stage:* Author interview with NDP official, Cairo, March 2010. See also Heba Saleh and Roula Khalaf, "Regime Faces an Uncertain Future," *Financial Times*, December 16, 2009.

194 *"Mubarak recognized that it isn't":* Ali Eddin Hilal, interview with author, Cairo, March 2010.

195 *The previous ten years had been:* I am grateful to the blogger Hossam el-Hamalawy for his full account of these years and the role that bloggers began to play (Cairo, March 2010).

197 *Take, for example, a basic element:* I am indebted to Gasser Abdel-Razek for this observation (Cairo, March 2010).

197 *"So the red lines are not the red lines":* Gasser Abdel-Razek, interview with author, Cairo, March 2010.

198 *"In 2000, if there was a UN event":* Hossam Bahgat, interview with author, Cairo, March 2010.

199 *"the brain of the party":* Author interview with NDP official, Cairo, March 2010.

199 *Egypt's economy grew:* Youssef Boutros-Ghali, "Egypt: Trendsetter in the Mideast," *Washington Post*, November 5, 2010.

200 *"The same as you, I suspect":* Mohamed Kamal, interview with author, Cairo, January 2006.

200 *"The NDP can reinvent itself":* Mohamed Kamal, interview with author, Cairo, March 2010.

201 *"play the game forever":* Author interview with NDP official, Cairo, March 2010.

203 *Ezz's holdings were estimated:* Richard Leiby, "The Rise and Fall of Egypt's Most Despised Billionaire, Ahmed Ezz," *Washington Post*, April 9, 2011.

203 *"We needed a plan":* Author interview with NDP official, Cairo, March 2010.

204 *The weakness of the party's brand:* I am indebted to Tarek Masoud for this point. For more on the ruling party's election strategy and performance, see Masoud, "Why Islam Wins: Electoral Ecologies and Economies of Political Islam in Contemporary Egypt" (Ph.D. diss., Yale University, 2009).

204 *Several officials told me:* Mohamed Kamal, Gehad Auda, and Ali Eddin Hilal, interviews with author, Cairo, March 2010.

204 *"What I do is more organizational":* I am indebted to Janine Zacharia, the former Jerusalem bureau chief for the *Washington Post*, for sharing the transcript of her unpublished April 2010 interview with Ahmed Ezz.

204 *The NDP captured more than 90 percent:* Amr Hamzawy, "Egypt Faces a Legitimacy Crisis Following Flawed Elections," *Daily Star,* December 14, 2010; and Robert F. Worth and Mona El-Naggar, "Egyptian Election Shuts Out Islamists," *New York Times,* November 30, 2010.

205 *"Let them entertain themselves":* Mohamed Abdel-Baky, "Shadow Play," *Al-Ahram Weekly,* December 23–29, 2010.

206 *Boutros-Ghali's vanity:* Author interview, Washington, D.C., December 2005.

206 *I interviewed several members of the council:* Author interviews with current and former members of the council included Hafez Abu Saeda, Ahmed Kamal Aboul Magd, and Bahey el-din Hassan, Cairo, March 2010.

206 *"Why did they decide to get rid of me?":* Ahmed Kamal Aboul Magd, interview with author, Giza, March 2010.

207 *"These two curves had to collide":* Wael Nawara, interview with author, Cairo, March 2011.

208 *The people had been warned:* For an account of the June 28 clashes, see Sharif Abdel Kouddous, "Five Months of Waiting," *Foreign Policy,* July 15, 2011.

209 *"I don't believe in the credibility":* Kamel Arafa, interview with author, Cairo, March 2011.

209 *No one knows how powerful:* Cambanis, "Stiff Test," September 11, 2010. For a deeper look at the Egyptian military, I recommend Steven Cook, *Ruling but Not Governing: The Military and Political Developments in Egypt, Algeria, and Turkey* (Baltimore: Johns Hopkins University Press, 2007).

210 *"The one thing we cannot discuss":* Bahgat, interview.

210 *The twenty-year-old blogger was:* I am grateful to Gamal Eid, the executive director of the Arabic Network for Human Rights Information, for discussing this case with me at great length (Cairo, March 2010).

210 *"It happened because this is a red line":* Bahgat, interview.

211 *One famous Egyptian television host:* Zeinab El Gundy, "Famous Egyptian TV Host Sacked After Challenging Ex-army Officer on Air," *Ahram Online,* July 25, 2011.

211 *Maikel Nabil was highly critical:* Frederick Kunkle, "Egyptian Tribunal Sentences Blogger to Three Years for Criticizing Military," *Washington Post,* April 11, 2011.

211 *Military courts quickly became:* Hossam Bahgat and Gasser Abdel-Razek, interviews with author, Cairo, March 2011. See also Human Rights Watch, "Egypt: Retry or Free 12,000 After Unfair Military Trials."

212 *"In the old system, with all its violence":* Abdel-Razek, interview, March 2011.

213 *the government's military-appointed cabinet:* David D. Kilpatrick, "Egypt Military Aims to Cement a Muscular Role in Government," *New York Times,* July 16, 2011; David D. Kilpatrick, "Egypt's Military Expands Power, Raising Alarms," *New York Times,* October 14, 2011; and Matt Bradley, "Egyptians Bristle at Military's Plan," *Wall Street Journal,* November 3, 2011. In the months that followed, representatives of the Supreme Council of the Armed Forces issued contradictory statements about the role the incoming parliament would have drafting a new constitution, continuing to raise suspicion that the military did not intend to cede some controls and protections for itself.

213 *"They understand the game now"*: Sherif Mickawi, interview with author, Cairo, March 2011.

213 *"I had a really magnificent network"*: All quotations from Sherif Osman come from three separate interviews conducted in July 2011.

221 *"These days everyone is a constitutional expert"*: Author interview with activist, Cairo, March 2011.

222 *"The creation of the dictatorship"*: Abdel-Razek, interview, March 2010.

223 *"Please trust that we are not an extension"*: I am grateful to Tarek Masoud for the transcript from a meeting with a visiting delegation of Egyptian generals in Washington, D.C., on July 25, 2011.

CHAPTER 7: THE PROFESSIONALS

226 *"We always feel in a state of emergency"*: Reported by the author, summer 2011.

226 *"We are not thinking through what we gain"*: Author interview, summer 2011.

227 *"the critical distance"*: All quotations with Serbian trainers took place at the CANVAS workshop in the summer of 2011.

227 *Zaire's strongman . . . is said to have been horrified:* Samuel P. Huntington, *The Third Wave: Democratization in the Late Twentieth Century* (Norman: University of Oklahoma Press, 1991), p. 288.

227 *the Chinese leadership beefed up security:* David Shambaugh, *China's Communist Party: Atrophy and Adaptation* (Berkeley: University of California Press, 2009), p. 47.

227 *Vladimir Putin and Hu Jintao are said:* Ibid., p. 91.

227 *Arab interior ministers . . . met annually to compare notes:* Gamal Eid (executive director of the Arabic Network for Human Rights Information), interview with author, Cairo, March 2010.

228 *Saudi Arabia sent its own troops:* Neil MacFarquhar, "Saudi Arabia Scrambles to Limit Region's Upheaval," *New York Times,* May 27, 2011.

228 *Take, for example, Girifna:* William J. Dobson, "Learning How to Topple a Tyrant," *PostPartisan* (blog), *Washington Post,* March 31, 2011, www .washingtonpost.com/blogs/post-partisan/post/learning-how-to-topple-a -tyrant/2011/03/31/AFw76pBC_blog.html.

228 *the Sudanese movement produced a parody:* Both soap commercials are available online. The Sudanese commercial is at www.youtube.com /watch?v=lE4FbdhLpUo; the original Serbian commercial is at www.youtube.com/watch?v=hEZYdGDkkV4&feature=related.

229 *"We had no idea"*: Srdja Popovic, interview with author, Washington, D.C., March 2011.

229 *"For me, it was an eye-opener"*: All quotations from Srdja Popovic are from a July 2011 interview with the author unless otherwise noted.

230 *"There is no such thing"*: Srdja Popovic, interview with author, Boston, June 2009.

230 *between 1900 and 2006 more than 50 percent:* Erica Chenoweth, "Give Peaceful Resistance a Chance," *New York Times,* March 10, 2011. For exceptional analysis of the historical efficacy of nonviolent struggle, I recommend Erica Chenoweth and Maria J. Stephan, *Why Civil Resistance Works* (New York: Columbia University Press, 2011).

231 *"I had never had experience with [the program]"*: All quotations from

Robert Helvey are from a July 2010 interview with the author in South Charleston, W.V.

231 *His leadership and courage:* Charles A. Krohn, *The Lost Battalion of TET: The Breakout of 2/12th Cavalry at Hue* (Annapolis, Md.: Naval Institute Press, 2008), p. 18.

231 *One of the officers:* Ibid., p. 12.

231 *His citation describes his bravery:* Helvey's citation for the Distinguished Service Cross can be found at www.1stcavmedic.com/DSCs-CAV/Helvey .htm.

234 *It has been published:* Gene Sharp's *From Dictatorship to Democracy* can be downloaded in twenty-six different languages, including Amharic, Azeri, Tigrigna, and four ethnic languages of Burma, at www.aeinstein.org.

234 *"Whatever the merits of the violent option":* Gene Sharp, *From Dictatorship to Democracy* (Boston: Albert Einstein Institution, 1993), p. 4.

234 *"Dictators require the assistance":* Ibid., p. 16.

235 *Sharp has lived at this address:* Gene Sharp, interview with author, Boston, February 2010.

235 *"The house was in ruins":* Ibid.

235 *Burma's generals call him:* Gene Sharp, "Burmese Dictatorship Attacks Nonviolent Struggle and Its Advocates, February–July 1995," unpublished report of the Albert Einstein Institution, p. 2.

235 *Hugo Chávez has alleged:* Simon Romero, "Students Emerge as a Leading Force Against Chávez," *New York Times,* November 10, 2007. See also Sharp's open-letter response to accusations made by Chávez on June 3, 2007, at www.aeinstein.org/Chavez.pdf.

236 *"If people do contact us":* Jamila Raqib, interview with author, Boston, February 2010.

240 *Srdja, like other former members of Otpor I met:* For an excellent look at Otpor's campaign in Serbia and a profile of some of its leaders, see Tina Rosenberg, *Join the Club: How Peer Pressure Can Transform the World* (New York: W. W. Norton, 2011).

241 *"how [Popovic] had done it":* Author interview with Nigerian activist, Boston, June 2009.

241 *"It is going to be bloody":* Popovic, interview, June 2009.

249 *issued a call for the turkeys' release:* Otpor perfomed this particular dilemma action in Kragujevac, Serbia's fourth-largest city. It is believed that none of the turkeys were harmed.

CHAPTER 8: THE TECHNOCRATS

252 *"We call upon each Chinese person":* This open letter is reproduced and available at www.hrichina.org/content/4895.

254 *In 1980, members of Poland's Solidarity movement:* For a gripping and insightful look at the roots of Poland's Solidarity movement, I recommend Timothy Garten Ash's *Polish Revolution: Solidarity* (New Haven, Conn.: Yale University Press, 2002).

255 *Even before the first Sunday stroll:* Andrew Jacobs, "Chinese Government Responds to Call for Protests," *New York Times,* February 20, 2011; and Ian Johnson, "Calls for a 'Jasmine Revolution' in China Persist," *New York Times,* February 23, 2011.

255 *China's president, Hu Jintao, called together:* Minnie Chan, "Hu Lecture on

Harmony as Protests Roil Mideast," *South China Morning Post,* February 20, 2011.

256 *Almost immediately, renditions of "Mo Li Hua":* Andrew Jacobs and Jonathan Ansfield, "A Revolution's Namesake Is Contraband in China," *New York Times,* May 10, 2011.

256 *the Chinese government's economic performance:* For a comprehensive look at the Chinese economy, I recommend Barry Naughton's *Chinese Economy: Transitions and Growth* (Cambridge, Mass.: MIT Press, 2006).

256 *it surpassed Japan:* David Barboza, "China Passes Japan as Second-Largest Economy," *New York Times,* August 15, 2010.

256 *the value of IPOs on Chinese stock markets:* Niall Ferguson, "Gloating China, Hidden Problems," *Daily Beast,* August 14, 2011.

257 *At the time, the U.S. government owed:* Fareed Zakaria, "China's Not Doing Us a Favor," *Global Public Square* (blog), CNN, August 14, 2011.

257 *Mikhail Gorbachev's plane landed:* My account of the events leading up to the killings in Tiananmen Square relied on Orville Schell's superb *Mandate of Heaven: The Legacy of Tiananmen Square and the Next Generation of China's Leaders* (New York: Touchstone, 1994).

259 *the party launched a meticulous study:* I am indebted to David Shambaugh's exhaustive research into the Chinese Communist Party's response to the collapse of the Soviet Union. For those who would seek more on this crucial turn in the party's evolution, his book *China's Communist Party: Atrophy and Adaptation* (Berkeley: University of California Press, 2008) is required reading. In early 2011, over lunch, Professor Shambaugh also kindly shared his views on more recent trends within the party.

261 *For an autocratic regime set on maintaining:* For a look at China's adoption of some deliberative elements of governance, see John L. Thornton, "Long Time Coming," *Foreign Affairs* 87, no. 1 (January/February 2008).

261 *"We don't waste our time":* Author interview with party adviser, Beijing, February 2011.

261 *"People are more conservative":* Author interview with Chinese academic, Beijing, February 2011.

262 *"Efforts to find a Chinese Gorbachev":* Henry Kissinger, *On China* (New York: Penguin Press, 2011), p. 457.

262 *The* People's Daily *quoted him:* Schell, *Mandate of Heaven,* p. 415.

262 *But this time it appeared to be different:* Paul Mooney, "Silence of the Dissidents," *South China Morning Post,* July 4, 2011.

263 *"And, third, it is cultural":* Author interview with Chinese academic, Beijing, February 2011.

264 *No Chinese leader today:* For expertise on Mao Zedong, Deng Xiaoping, and Chinese elite politics, I highly recommend the work of Professor Roderick MacFarquhar. Although his scholarship on China's Cultural Revolution is unsurpassed, a more general reader may wish to begin with his edited volume *The Politics of China: The Eras of Mao and Deng* (Cambridge, U.K.: Cambridge University Press, 1997).

265 *"We've been surprised":* Author interview with Chinese Middle East expert, Beijing, February 2011.

267 *Yu is not some dissident:* For an excellent profile of Yu Keping's ideas, I recommend Mark Leonard's recent history of contemporary Chinese thinkers, *What Does China Think?* (New York: Public Affairs, 2008).

267 *"There is an enormous divide":* Yu Keping, interview with author, Beijing, February 2011.

269 *"Well, to me, it very obviously":* Lai Hairong, interview with author, Beijing, February 2011.

270 *The concept, known by the shorthand* ti-yong: For a fuller explanation of this formulation and its adherents, I recommend Jonathan Spence, *The Search for Modern China* (New York: Norton, 1990).

271 *"This was a big decision":* Lu Mai, interview with author, Beijing, February 2011.

271 *Harvard faculty teach Chinese officials:* Anthony Saich, telephone interview with author, October 2011.

273 *Nearly 20 percent of the government's ministers:* Edward S. Steinfeld, "China's Other Revolution," *Boston Review,* July/August 2011.

273 *More than half of the Central Committee:* Shambaugh, *China's Communist Party,* p. 36.

273 *One ten-year survey found:* I am indebted to Edward Cunningham for drawing my attention to this survey conducted by Anthony Saich and Edward Cunningham, "Satisfaction with Government Performance: Public Opinion in Rural and Urban China," unpublished manuscript. See also Anthony Saich, "Citizens' Perception on Governance in Rural and Urban China," *Journal of Chinese Political Science* 12, no. 1 (Spring 2007).

274 *Here the party's Organization Department:* These figures come from Shambaugh's *China's Communist Party.* For the single best look at the party's Organization Department, I recommend Richard McGregor's *Party: The Secret World of China's Communist Rulers* (New York: HarperCollins, 2010).

275 *"help the rulers cheat":* Pan Wei, interview with author, Beijing, February 2011.

276 *George Soros, who has spent a large portion:* Tamsin McMahon, "Billionaire Soros Wins CIC Globalist of the Year Award," *National Post,* November 16, 2010.

278 *the top body charged with holding:* Shambaugh, *China's Communist Party,* p. 133.

278 *the odds of a corrupt official:* I am indebted to Minxin Pei for emphasizing the limits of many of the party's reforms to me while we were colleagues at the Carnegie Endowment for International Peace. This particular calculation comes from Minxin Pei, "Corruption Threatens China's Future," Carnegie Endowment Policy Brief, no. 55, October 2007.

280 *"Our local government is no better":* Author interview with Chinese farmer, Beijing, February 2011.

280 *more than ten million petitions:* Minxin Pei, *China's Trapped Transition: The Limits of Developmental Autocracy* (Cambridge, Mass.: Harvard University Press, 2006), p. 202.

280 *The cause is relatively hopeless:* Ibid.

280 *The Anyuanding Security Technology Service reportedly:* Xu Kai and Li Weiao, "The Machinery of Stability Preservation," *Caijing,* June 6, 2011. An English translation of this article is available from the *Dui Hua Human Rights Journal,* www.duihuahrjournal.org/2011/06/translation-machinery-of-stability.html.

281 *In 1993, the Ministry of Public Security reported:* Leonard, *What Does China Think?*, p. 72.

281 *the number of protests had more than doubled:* Michael Forsyth, "180,000 Protests in 2010," *Bloomberg News,* March 6, 2011.

281 *China spent more on its internal security:* Ibid.

281 *the published budget for police and domestic surveillance:* Chris Buckley, "China Internal Security Spending Jumps Past Army Budget," Reuters, March 5, 2011.

281 *the provincial government in Xinjiang:* Edward Wong, "China Nearly Doubles Security Budget for Western Region," *New York Times,* January 13, 2010.

281 *In Liaoning, 15 percent:* Andrew Jacobs and Jonathan Ansfield, "Well-Oiled Security Apparatus in China Stifles Calls for Change," *New York Times,* February 28, 2011.

282 *Thousands of stability maintenance offices:* Ibid.

282 *"You don't win points":* Author interview with Western NGO expert, Beijing, February 2011.

283 *The last time the regime acted as swiftly:* I was living in China in 1999 when the brutal crackdown against the Falun Gong was launched. In 2011, many Chinese I met were aware of the regime's arrests of lawyers and activists. In 1999, however, I had no idea that the campaign had begun until I read about it outside China.

283 *The government recently proposed rewriting:* Michael Wines, "More Chinese Dissidents Appear to Disappear," *New York Times,* September 2, 2011.

283 *"The ideology and legitimacy":* Pu Zhiqiang, interview with author, Beijing, February 2011.

286 *"In China, it is not about yes or no":* Lai, interview.

286 *an unprecedented number of Chinese citizens:* Keith B. Richburg, "China Sees Surge of Independent Candidates," *Washington Post,* September 9, 2011.

286 *a misstep by a local official:* To my knowledge, Hugo Restall first made this point in his article "The Urumqi Effect," *Asian Wall Street Journal,* July 10, 2009.

287 *"Even though the people we are watching":* This post is available at the China Elections and Governance blog at chinaelectionsblog.net/?p=12468.

287 *"If they let that many people go":* Author interview with party member, Beijing, February 2011.

EPILOGUE

288 *"It's been a bad year":* Srdja Popovic, interview with author, Washington, D.C., July 2011. Popovic later used the phrase "a bad year for bad guys" as the title of a TEDx talk he gave in Krakow, Poland, in November 2011, available at www.youtube.com/watch?v=Z3Cd-0EvEog.

289 *Putin's United Russia brazenly claimed:* Thomas Grove, "Analysis: Chechnya: How Did Putin's Party Win 99 Percent?," Reuters, December 21, 2011.

289 *"We were stupid":* Author interview, Cairo, March 2011.

289 *Gaddafi invoked China's 1989 massacre:* On February 22, 2011, Gaddafi said, "When Tiananmen Square happened, tanks were sent in to deal

with them. It's not a joke. I will do whatever it takes to make sure part of the country isn't taken away." The quotation can be found in Fang Lizhi's "The Real Deng," *New York Review of Books*, November 10, 2011.

290 *the United Nations estimated:* Wright Bryan, "Death Toll Rises in Syria, Adding to U.N. Estimate of 5,000 Killed So Far," National Public Radio, December 13, 2011.

290 *this meant massive handouts:* Angus McDowall and Summer Said, "Saudis Raise Pay and Plan Polls, but Woes Linger," *Wall Street Journal*, March 24, 2011.

290 *Six months later he put his stamp:* Tobias Buck, "Jordan: Rifts in the Valley," *Financial Times*, August 15, 2011.

291 *"Don't think that what is happening":* John Lee, "Egypt's Fate Could Yet Be Malaysia's Future," *Australian*, February 25, 2011.

292 *a special high-level task force:* Michael Wines, "China Sees a Calendar Full of Trouble," *New York Times*, March 10, 2009.

INDEX